KANSU MORTUARY URNS OF THE PAN SHAN AND MA CHANG GROUPS

半山及马厂随葬陶器

(影印)

〔瑞典〕巴尔姆格伦 著

BY

NILS PALMGREN

·1934·

甘肃人民出版社

甘肃·兰州

图书在版编目（CIP）数据

半山及马厂随葬陶器 /（瑞典）巴尔姆格伦著 .
影印本 . -- 兰州：甘肃人民出版社，2024.9. -- ISBN
978-7-226-06167-1

Ⅰ . K876.34

中国国家版本馆 CIP 数据核字第 2024JA2422 号

责任编辑：袁尚
封面设计：孔庆明珠

半山及马厂随葬陶器（影印）
BANSHAN JI MACHANG SUIZANG TAOQI（YINGYIN）
甘肃人民出版社出版发行
（730030 兰州市读者大道568号）
甘肃宏翔文化传媒有限责任公司印刷
开本889毫米×1194毫米 1/16 印张24.25 插页4 字数80千
2024年9月第1版 2024年9月第1次印刷
印数：1~1000
ISBN 978-7-226-06167-1 定价：198.00元

出版说明

1923—1924年，中国北洋政府农商部矿政顾问、瑞典学者安特生在中国西北地区开展一系列考古工作，获取了一批石器时代和青铜时代的考古资料。1925年，根据中、瑞双方的合作协议，安特生将这批资料运回瑞典，他的助手巴尔姆格伦对其中半山、马厂期陶器进行了系统的整理和研究，于1934年在中国出版了《半山及马厂随葬陶器》一书（《中国古生物志》丁种第三号第一册）。该书对安特生所获的半山、马厂期陶器进行了详细介绍、分析和研究，是研究西北地区史前文化、彩陶艺术的重要文献，在学界影响深远。

因时代久远、印数有限，原书现在难以见到。有鉴于此，在马家窑文化发现100周年之际，经中国社会科学院考古研究所提议并联络，中国历史研究院图书档案馆提供原版图书，甘肃临洮马家窑文化研究院组织影印出版《半山及马厂随葬陶器》一书，以飨学界。本次影印出版，保留了原版图书的原貌，未作任何改动，特此说明。

THE GEOLOGICAL SURVEY OF CHINA

Palaeontologia Sinica

BOARD OF EDITORS:

V. K. TING, T. C. CHOW, A. W. GRABAU, J. S. LEE,
Y. C. SUN, C. C. YOUNG, T. H. YIN

Series D, Volume III,
Fascicle 1

KANSU MORTUARY URNS OF THE PAN SHAN AND MA CHANG GROUPS

BY

NILS PALMGREN

PLATES I—XLI AND 228 TEXT FIGURES

PEIPING (PEKING) 1934

FOR SALE AT THE FOLLOWING OFFICES: PEIPING: GEOL. SURV. LIBRARY, 9 PING MA SZE, WEST CITY; FRENCH BOOKSTORE, GRAND HOTEL DE PÉKIN; SHANGHAI: KELLY & WALSH, LTD., 12 NANKING ROAD; LONDON: EDWARD GOLDSTON, 25 MUSEUM ST., W. C. 1; NEW YORK: A. G. SEILER & CO., 1224 AMSTERDAM AVE; G. E. STECHERT & CO., 31—33 EAST 10TH STREET; LEIPZIG: MAX. WEG, KÖNIGSTRASSE 3; BUCHHANDLUNG GUSTAV FOCK, POSTSCHLIESSFACH 100; STOCKHOLM: ÖSTASIATISKA SAMLINGARNA, SVEAVÄGEN 65; TOKYO: MARUZEN COMPANY.

Series D.   Vol. III. Fasc. 1.

PALÆONTOLOGIA SINICA

Board of Editors:
V. K. Ting, T. C. Chow, A. W. Grabau, J. S. Lee,
Y. C. Sun, C. C. Young, T. H. Yin

Kansu mortuary urns of the Pan Shan and Ma Chang groups

BY

NILS PALMGREN

Plates I—XLI and 228 text figures

Published by the Geological Survey of China.

Peiping (Peking) 1934

STOCKHOLM 1934
A.-B. HASSE W. TULLBERGS BOKTRYCKERI

CONTENTS.

	Page
Preface by J. G. Andersson	V
Introduction	VII
How the painted Pan Shan funeral urns were made	1
The forms of the painted Pan Shan sepulchral vessels	8
The production, form and ornamentation of the unpainted Pan Shan sepulchral vessels	36
The painting and ornamentation of the Pan Shan funeral urns	46
How the Ma Chang pottery was made	88
The forms of the Ma Chang vessels	92
The painting and décor of the Ma Chang pottery	108
The different ceramic forms summarized	156
Summary review of the décor on the Pan Shan and Ma Chang pottery	165
Marks on the painted Pan Shan and Ma Chang pottery	174
Examples of Pan Shan and Ma Chang pottery in literature or in private collections	180
Bibliography	199
Catalogue of the Pan Shan and Ma Chang vessels not reproduced in the plates	203
Plates	

PREHISTORIC STAGES OF KANSU [1])

Early Iron Age   Sha Ching stage

Bronze Age   { Ssu Wa stage
              Hsin Tien stage

Late Neolithic or   { Ma Chang stage
Chalcolithic Ages   Yang Shao stage [2]) (Pan Shan)
                   Ch'i Chia stage

---

[1]) See: J. G. Andersson: Archaeological Research in Kansu, p. 23. Bibl. 6 and later publications of the same author.
[2]) The Pan Shan sepulchral pottery is to be placed here.

PREFACE.

THE MORTUARY URNS FROM THE PAN SHAN HILLS AND THE SLIGHTLY more recent but closely related urns that have been named the Ma Chang group form a voluminous and at the same time spectacular part of the prehistoric material collected by me in Kansu.

The delicate task of cleaning these beautiful urns was most diligently carried out by my assistant Mr. Nils Palmgren, and consequently the scientific study and description of this splendid material has been entrusted to him.

The greenstone axes, jade rings, stone pendants etc. will be described by me in another volume of the Palaeontologia Sinica, "*Stone objects from the Pan Shan hills*".

The question of the age of these ceramics, as well as the significance of the painted designs, will be discussed by me in a comparative review intended to form the final volume relating to the prehistoric material from Kansu. In the meantime it should be noted that a popular account of our present state of knowledge in regard to these problems has been given in my book "*Children of the Yellow Earth*", Routledge & Sons, London 1934.

A detailed account of the localities referred to in this paper will be given in my report: *Prehistoric Sites of Northern China*, Palaeontologia Sinica, Ser. D, Vol. II, Fasc. 1, now in course of preparation.

In the meantime some brief notes will serve as an orientation for the reader.

The Pan Shan grave-field is situated near the T'ao Ho, a tributary of the Yellow River, which it joins from the south about 60 km. above Lanchow, the capital of Kansu. The Pan Shan grave-field lies west of the T'ao river, 70 km. due south of Lanchow.

In this part of its course the T'ao river has cut down a broad open valley, about 400 metres deep, in easily eroded Tertiary sediments. The site of the Pan Shan gravefields is not in the valley itself but close to the side of it upon the remnants of the old plateau, about 400 metres above the bottom of the present river valley.

The Pan Shan area comprises 4 or 5 grave-fields situated some few kilometres apart and occupying the highest hill-tops in the area. Pan Shan forms the centre of the group. About 1 600 m. to the south-west is Wa Kuan Tsui, by far the richest archaeological site. 1 400 m. due east from Pan Shan lies Pien Chia Kou, which yielded the only undisturbed grave, which was excavated by me personally. A full kilometre north from Pan Shan is Wang Chia Kou, a locality which I was not able to visit owing to my hurried departure.

With the exception of the well-recorded Pien Chia Kou grave and some few other specimens, we are forced to rely for information regarding the vast majority of the funeral urns upon the statements of the local Mohammedans, who had plundered the graves and excavated nearly all the mortuary urns weeks before my arrival. But most of the urns were bought on the spot by me or my own assistants, and there is hardly any doubt that every urn recorded in this paper as having come from Wa Kuan Tsui, Pan Shan, Pien Chia Kou or Wang Chia Kou, actually came from the Pan Shan area, and it is quite likely that even the detailed statements are correct. However, there always remains a possibility that in some instances the seller thought it to his advantage to mention a hill other than Wa Kuan Tsui, where undoubtedly a large majority of the urns had been found, to judge from the extensive diggings and the innumerable potsherds spread all over the ground.

Mortuary urns of the Pan Shan type have also been found in some other places in Kansu. For instance, I personally excavated some few broken specimens at P'ai Tzŭ P'ing down in the T'ao Ho valley, just below the Pan Shan area. In other instances n which pots are reported from Kao Lan Hsien, Nien Po Hsien etc. I cannot assume any personal responsibility for the correctness of such statements. It is very likely that they are correct, but there is always some uncertainty in regard to any locality that was not checked up by me personally.

When in the spring of 1924 hundreds of pots were taken to Lanchow and offered to me, long before I had succeeded in locating the sites, I bought the best of these urns and labelled them simply: Bought in Lanchow. It is probable, though far from proved, that most of these urns came from the Pan Shan area, particularly from Wa Kuan Tsui.

The one half of the Pan Shan material, belonging to the National Geological Survey of China, was at an early date returned to that Institution. Consequently the plates reproduced in this paper have been based principally upon the material remaining in Stockholm, and this is altogether the case with the coloured plates, which were prepared, immediately before the completion of this work, direct from the painted urns.

Stockholm, The Museum of Far Eastern Antiquities. December 1933.

J. G. Andersson.

INTRODUCTION.

When Professor J. G. Andersson returned from China in 1925, the author was appointed his assistant. The tasks that had to be tackled were of many and various kinds and included the work of preserving the pottery discovered by Professor Andersson.

Consequently, the author's first acquaintance with the material dealt with in this work was in connection with the task of cleaning the vessels. This involved removing various foreign substances that covered the pots and which consisted mainly of loess earth and lime sinter. These substances usually covered only certain portions of the pot or occurred in patches, the rest of the ware being left quite exposed. In other cases a coating of lime of varying thickness was found to be spread over the greater part or — quite exceptionally — over the whole of the pot. By bathing the vessels in a very weak solution of hydrochloric acid — the proportion of HCl and H_2O being about 1:3000 — it was possible after three or four days' treatment to remove all extraneous matter without damaging the painted décor. The residue from the acid was subsequently removed by thoroughly rinsing the vessels in running water. The work, which had at first to proceed with the utmost caution and along more or less experimental lines, was subsequently carried on by almost industrial methods, and so great was the number of vessels that had to be treated that the work took something like six months to accomplish. Looking back on it, I now realize how arduous the task was; at the same time it was extremely interesting.

The material consisted of earthenware pots possessing a somewhat divergent character and a rich variety of patterns. Gradually, in the course of the work of preservation, I came to be, so to speak, more and more intimately acquainted with the pots. I learnt to distinguish vessels of the various periods from one another, and their individual differences came frequently under discussion. Without fully realizing whither the work was leading me, I gradually added detail to fresh detail, until there evolved quite naturally out of these observations and discussions the scheme for a system of classification — comparative down to the smallest particular — that was destined to form the basis of this work.

When therefore, some time later, Professor Andersson gave me the task of measuring and describing the Pan Shan and the Ma Chang materials, I accepted the commission with pleasure, in spite of its voluminous scope and its somewhat one-sided nature. Originally the idea had been simply to give a description of the pots, but later I received Professor Andersson's permission to embody my observations in a paper, which I eventually submitted to the Professor of Art History at the University of Stockholm, Doctor Andreas Lindblom, for my licentiate. It is out of that paper, after thorough revision, that the present treatise has emerged.

Conforming to my agreement with Professor Andersson, I have concentrated upon making a technical investigation of the material and a detailed analysis of its forms and decorative designs. Accordingly, I have almost completely disregarded all material other than that available to me here in Stockholm, my efforts being rather directed towards gaining some insight into the manner in which forms and patterns arose and evolved out of their own peculiar attributes. Obviously, a method of investigation of this kind has its limitations, indeed, even its palpable weaknesses, but it must of course be supplemented later on by an exhaustive comparison between the Kansu material and other ceramic material. An investigation conducted along the present lines brings us no further than to a relative chronology, though even such a result may not be without some significance. By way of a comparative investigation we shall naturally arrive at the problem of the absolute chronology — which has been entirely disregarded in this work.

It goes without saying that I have primarily to thank Professor J. G. Andersson, the discoverer of the Kansu pottery, for the bringing into being and the final accomplishment of this treatise. I therefore place on record here my feelings of the deepest gratitude to him, firstly for having placed this eminently rich and beautiful material at my disposal, secondly for the indefatigable support and advice he has given me all these years in deciding the best way of dealing with the material and the final form the treatise was to take, and thirdly for his having enabled me through his connections with China to have this work printed.

To the Director of the Geological Survey of China, Doctor Wong Wen Hao, I beg to extend my respectful thanks for his generosity in undertaking to defray the cost of printing the book. To Messrs. A. Börtzells Tryckeri Aktiebolag, Stockholm, I offer my thanks for their careful and painstaking work in preparing the plates. I am deeply indebted to Monsieur C. T. Loo, of Paris, and to Madame Wannieck, also of Paris, for their great kindness in placing their collections of Kansu pottery and photographs at my disposal. I have also to thank the Ethnographical Department of the Riksmuseum, Stockholm, its Director, Professor Gerhard Lindblom, and his assistant, Doctor Gösta Montell, for the readiness and kindness they have shown in permitting me to examine and make drawings of the Kansu pottery in that Museum. In compiling the bibliography and the arrangement of the statistical tables I have received invaluable assistance from Doctor Ivar Schnell, to whom I extend my best thanks. My patient and excellent translator, Mr. Leonard B. Eyre, and my exceptionally reliable adviser in all textual questions, Doctor Carl Ernolv, I cannot thank enough. The figures and illustrations in the text have been executed by the very able artist Mr. Sven Ekblom. The photographs reproduced in this work have been taken partly by Mr. Sten Sundberg, of Råsunda, partly by the painstaking staff photographer attached to the Museum of Far Eastern Antiquities, Stockholm, Mr. Nils Lagergren, and partly by myself. To these my collaborators I proffer my hearty thanks. The Museum commissionaire, Mr. C. H. Gustafson, has been my constant assistant and adviser throughout all these years, and I am much indebted to him. Finally, I cannot fail to include among those to whom I owe deep thanks the name of my wife, Gertrud Palmgren, who during all these years, whenever it was necessary, sometimes for days and nights, has worked indefatigably for me at her typewriter.

To indicate the form and pattern systems described in this treatise I have for the sake of clearness introduced a number of abbreviations. Thus, for the form types are used the initials P. S. = Pan Shan, and M. C. = Ma Chang, also P. S:r = Pan Shan decorated in relief. The Pan Shan décor families are denoted by the letter P, and the Ma Chang décor families by the letter M. The abbreviation Bibl., followed by a number, refers to the Bibliography at the end of the book.

In the figures inserted in the text the naked ware is denoted by entirely white surfaces, the red décor by a dotted area, while the black décor is reproduced all in black.

Stockholm, February 1934.   *Nils Palmgren.*

HOW THE PAINTED PAN SHAN FUNERAL URNS WERE MADE.

The painted funeral urns of the Pan Shan culture are made of clay, which, after being shaped, dried, polished and painted, has been fired. The ware has a smooth surface, and generally in the fracture no appreciable granulation is visible to the naked eye. The clay, at any rate that from the central Pan Shan district, has been of excellent quality, or else all coarser grains have been removed from it by washing. Moreover, its nature was such that it could be used direct without any admixture of sand, ash or other material. In a few exceptional cases the granulation is slightly more pronounced, as for instance in the pot K. 5610 (Pl. XVII, fig. 3) from Kao Ying, Kao Lan Hsien, but this happens to be a product made outside the central district.

No potter's wheel has been used in making these vessels, as is seen from their invariably slightly irregular shapes and from the absence of any concentric striation, which is characteristic of "throwing", on the surface of the vessels. Only in the case of necks and collars is there any sign of striation. We shall have more to say on this point later.

The technique employed in constructing the Pan Shan painted vessels, or at least the vast majority of them, is the "ring" method. This method, which is common amongst primitive peoples, consists in the potter's shaping bands of clay, which he bends into rings or fairly broad belts, arranging them one over the other until the pot has acquired the desired form. In other cases a long strip is shaped bit by bit as required and then coiled in a gradually rising spiral until the vessel is completed. The strips used for building up the pots may be either broad and round or narrow and flat in section. In the former case the wall of the vessel becomes fairly thick, and in the latter case thinner in construction. Generally speaking, broad, flattened bands fashioned into thin ware have been most commonly employed in the Pan Shan culture.

There exists absolutely reliable evidence that the ring method was used. The rings on the neck of a small vessel such as K. 5496 (Pl. XXXI. fig. 1) are easily observable. The neck is built up of three rings, the lowest inserted into the body and the upper ones consecutively into the subjacent rings.

One also occasionally finds this method of construction clearly indicated on the insides of the larger vessels. For instance, the collar on the vessel K. 5021 (Pl. XXXI, fig. 2) consists of six or seven rings, which are insufficiently baked together on the inside. Vessel K. 5151 has a neck consisting of seven or eight rings, which are likewise fairly distinct on the inside. Many examples of this could be quoted (K. 5031, K. 5069, K. 5150).

If we carefully examine the inside of vessels K. 5025 (Pl.XXXI, fig. 3), K. 5149 and K. 5184, we can perceive more or less distinctly the rings of which the bodies are composed. After a little practice the eye can distinguish in most vessels traces of this building-up method.

The head K. 5472 (Pl. XIX, fig. 7) clearly shows the process of building up the crown. As the inside testifies, the whole is built up of rings, of which the two uppermost are easily discernible. A slab of clay has then been placed from above like a lid over the round hole formed by the innermost ring. Generally, however, every effort has been made to remove from both the inside and the outside all traces of the method of construction.

On the inside this has generally been done by means of the fingers or with a spatula or some similar implement, presumably of wood. The fingers of the right hand were pressed firmly against the clay, the hand moving from the bottom upwards, while the left hand rotated the jar in a clockwise direction[1]) (see detailed photograph of the lower part of the inside of pot K. 5797, Pl. XXXI, fig. 4). In this process the cracks between the bands were smeared over by the hand, and the bands were thus baked together as one piece. The spaces between the fingers are clearly visible owing to the more or less high ridges left on the inner walls of the vessels (see detailed photograph of the pot K. 5962, Pl. XXXI, fig. 5). Thus the insides often exhibit two systems of ridges: 1. Indistinct broad ridges, running in a horizontal direction (see detailed photograph of pot K. 5962, Pl. XXXI, fig. 6), which represent the marks made by the bands. 2. Narrower ridges ending indistinctly at top and bottom, but otherwise well defined, running anti-clockwise obliquely from the bottom upwards, particularly towards the bottom, sometimes radially from the bottom upwards, particularly towards the top (see detailed photograph of jar K. 5797, Pl. XXXI, fig. 7) — traces of a finishing process. Both systems of ridges may thus be accounted for as indicating the use of the ring-method in the manufacture of these vessels.

On the outside of the vessels the finishing process has been carried considerably further. Only the upper half or the upper two thirds of the bodies of the vessels (this portion we shall hereinafter call the "mantle") are painted. The lower half or

---

[1]) The result would be quite the same if the right hand rotated the jar in a clockwise direction, the left hand being pressed against the clay.

third part, the base, is unpainted. The pots, with their attractive "mantle" ornamentation, were intended to be seen mainly from above. The treatment of the two kinds of surface is different. The unpainted surface is certainly far smoother than the inside of the vessel, but the finishing process has not been quite thoroughly carried out. Traces of the flat spatulae used for smoothing the surfaces are clearly visible as an irregular striation, running generally from the bottom upwards from left to right. Likewise, in the treatment of the outside, as the striation shows, the left hand rotated the pot in a clockwise direction, while the right hand performed the work of smoothing out the uneven places.

Only in very exceptional cases is it possible to discern quite clearly on the outside the rings that form the mantle (e. g. on pot K. 5041, Pl. XXXII, fig. 1). They are more commonly seen on the bases, e. g. K. 5053 (Pl. XXXII, fig. 2), K. 5155 (Pl. X, fig. 4, and Pl. XXXVII, fig. 1), K. 5287 (Pl. XII, fig. 7). With a little practice, however, one can observe also on the outside of a great many of the other pots traces of rings in the form of alternately shaded and unshaded bands. This band formation is particularly clearly seen when the light is allowed to fall upon the pot in a direction parallel to the base, the contrast between light and shade then being sharper.

The upper exterior part of the body of the vessel, the mantle, is, as already pointed out, entirely smoothed over and polished. For this purpose the hand has not proved a sufficiently delicate tool. The vessel that is composed of rings and is subsequently smoothed over has first been allowed to dry in the open air, after which the surface of the mantle has been polished with special implements of a hard and smooth quality, probably with stones, or with polishers made of burnt clay, or with smooth seeds[1]).

The only part of the pots that sometimes shows concentric striation is the neck. This striation is often so distinct, on both the inside and the outside, that, if one had not made a close study of the pots in other respects, one would be inclined to say that they had been fashioned on a potter's wheel (see e. g. the pot K. 5284, Pl. XVIII, fig. 6, to which reference has already been made). The necks have been formed with the aid of modelling discs (templets) of wood or similar material, the structure of which, uneven in fine detail, has left a striation in the moulded clay. The templets served a twofold purpose: to round off the upper edge and to give the profile of the neck the desired regular curvature. In the low-necked pots the striation is very conspicuous on both the inside and the outside of the upper half of the neck. The templet was

---

[1]) A polishing process, doubtless fairly similar to that undergone by the Pan Shan vessels, is described by Fr. W. v. Bissing (See Bibl. No. 19).

about half as long as the height of the neck. Occasionally the striation continues along the entire length of the neck (e. g. K. 5610) and in this case the templet must have been as long as the height of the neck. In the high-necked vessels the striation appears only on the uppermost part of the neck, so that here the templet has been considerably shorter than the neck. On a number of the pots there is visible on the inside, a couple of centimetres below the edge, a very distinct horizontal furrow, which represents the inner and lower end of the templet. This horizontal furrow is still more clearly seen in the more highly developed types of vessel, the necks of which are more curved at the top (e. g. in the vessel K. 5169).

As is clearly seen from the pot K. 5213 (Pl. XXXII, fig. 3), the bottom hole in the lowest zone was not filled up until after the base had been made. It is extremely rare, however, for the bottom to be left in this incomplete state. Moreover, the surface of the bottom is generally smooth and finished, and the traces of the manufacturing process are very faint. The pot K. 5781 (Pl. XXXII, fig. 4), however, shows clearly how this was done. The bottom hole having been filled in, a thin bottom-plate was prepared, of a size to cover both the central filling and the lowest ring or zone surrounding it. This plate was then pressed firmly on to the bottom of the vessel and its edge cut round obliquely so as to coincide with the base. The suture between the bottom-plate and the lowest zone was then closed so firmly that the join is hardly visible in most pots.

Handles and ears and other projecting details are affixed on the outside of the pots, that is to say, without holes' being drilled in the walls of the vessels. Evidence of this is found in the head K. 5472 (Pl. XXXII, fig. 5), in which the horns and one ear are missing, and also in the pot K. 5492 (Pl. XXXII, fig. 6), in which the method of affixing the handle is clearly demonstrated. This comparatively primitive and somewhat insecure method of affixing projections is reinforced in the case of the handles of larger vessels by making recesses in the body of the vessel, into which the handles are then fitted (K. 5165, Pl. XXXII, fig. 7).

As a result of the firing, the surface of the ware acquired a light brownish-red colour, which is usually very uniform and gives the painted pottery an extremely warm and pleasant tone. The colour of the ware is slightly different in each vessel. Sometimes it is of a warm reddish hue, occasionally a pure brown, and sometimes — though very rarely — it is grey with a tinge of brown or red. A cold, grey, dead tone, like that of the unglazed ware dating from the Han dynasty, is never found in the Pan Shan pottery. The latter is of a particularly hard and firm quality and not very porous.

To judge from its colour and hardness, it is probable that, generally speaking, the Pan Shan ware was subjected in firing to a temperature of between 900 and 1 000° C. One comes across isolated cases of over-firing, as e. g. in the vessel K. 5163 (Pl. X, fig. 6), in which large parts of the surface have melted into a blistery, glaze-like mass of grey-green colour, so that the painting has been either wholly or partially destroyed. This over-firing appears to have occurred at about 1 100—1 200° C.[1]).

The pots found in the cemeteries of the Pan Shan culture give evidence, on the whole, of extraordinarily uniform firing. Nevertheless the colour on different parts of the surface of the ware may vary considerably in individual pots. Reddish patches alternate with less red or greyish patches, as e. g. on pot K. 5085 (Pl. XXXVI, fig. 2), and in several vessels reddish spots appear on a more coldly coloured ground. These flame-like patches found in the ware are attributable to the firing's being occasionally not quite uniform, one part of the vessel being burned at a higher temperature than the other.

In certain rare instances the surfaces of vessels of a more highly developed type are covered with a thin and even layer of clay of finer quality than the interior ware. When fired, this layer becomes lighter-coloured than the rest of the ware, and its object has evidently been to render the surface smoother and lighter as a ground for painting on. The pot K. 5030 (Pl. VII, fig. 6, and Pl. XXXVI, fig. 3) affords a good example of this kind of primitive slip. Here the entire pot was dipped into a thin clay sludge, so that both the outer and the inner surfaces became covered with the slip. In this specimen chipped parts of the surface in several places reveal the inner ware. The pot K. 5167 has likewise been completely dipped in a clay sludge, but in this instance the slip did not stick very well to the ground-surface of the ware, especially on the inside of the neck, and dislodged flakes afford good evidence that such a coating of clay was actually applied.

The ware varies somewhat in the fracture. In many cases it is, to the naked eye at least, quite homogeneous both in colour and material. Usually, however, one can clearly distinguish three layers, a superficial layer on the exterior of the pot, a second superficial layer on the inside of the pot, and a core or middle layer between the two surface layers. These latter are generally of a warmer red colour. Occasionally, however, the contrary is the case, the middle layer being of a warmer colour and the superficial layers of a greyer hue. The structure of the middle layer is often remark-

---

[1]) In literature dealing with the question of the temperature employed in firing (see Bibl. 15, 28, 29, 31, 40—42, 71), the temperature in the case of Neolithic vessels that have become red in the burning is sometimes estimated at a lower figure (see Bibl. 71). Seeing however that the material relating to the Pan Shan culture is of such an excellent and homogeneous quality, and as over-firing resulting in a glaze-like substance on isolated vessels shows that the temperature must in some cases have been at least 1 100° C., the temperature of 900—1 000° C. mentioned here is more likely to be correct.

ably porous, evidently a result of the firing process. There is not always a sharp line of demarcation between the different layers. The most conspicuous is usually the interior surface layer, whereas in places the exterior surface layer is not infrequently merged or passes imperceptibly into the core. This shows that the interior surface has been subjected to more equable conditions of heat and air than the exterior. Where there is a finishing slip a further very thin, lighter-coloured superficial layer arises.

The method of firing was as follows: a number of vessels, having already been dried in the open air, were piled together in the kiln. The excellent results of the firing is a fairly clear indication that a kiln was used. The fact that several vessels were fired at the same time is evident from the brand-marks found on a large number of pots. These marks occur either on the basal surfaces or on the mantle surfaces. On the basal surfaces they consist of flat or slightly concave, sometimes reddish spots with greyish or often somewhat darker centres (see K. 5781, Pl. XXXII, fig. 4). There are often discernible on these spots impressions of a pattern of e. g. dentated, black bands and plain, red bands, or else of delicate black trellis-work, etc. On the mantle surfaces the brand-marks are frequently found in conjunction with more or less concave depressions in the otherwise convex surfaces (K. 5155, Pl. XXXII, fig. 8). Here too the ware has sometimes changed colour where the marks occur, being flame-coloured and red in the peripheral parts and greyer in the centre. Moreover, one not infrequently finds in these spots fragmentary impressions of other patterns all mixed up anyhow with the true pattern on the mantle (Pl. XXXII, fig. 8). But a still more common occurrence is for the pot's own mantle pattern to lose its clearness and colour-tone where the spots are and to leave its colouring matter as an impression on another pot (Pl. XXXVII, fig. 4).

The brand-marks show firstly that several pots were fired together, and secondly that the painting was done on the un-fired pots, which when first placed in the kiln had not yet quite lost their plasticity. Seeing that sometimes two or more brand-marks occur on the mantle and two or more on the basal surface, as e. g. the four brand-marks on the pot K. 5155 (Pl. XXXVII, fig. 1), and five on the pot K. 5831 (Pl. XXXVI, fig. 4), of which three are on the mantle and two on the base, it is clear that at least three tiers of pots could be piled on top of one another. Occasionally this has proved too much for one or two of the pots in the lowest tier and they have collapsed. This has happened, for instance, with pot K. 5080 (Pl. XIII, fig. 4). In this case, indeed, the mantle was buckled so severely that the neck likewise got out of shape. The pot must have been at the time in a state of semi-plasticity, which at first made it buckle considerably, but eventually the wall gave way to the pressure, and a fracture and crack resulted. In spite of its being misshapen, however, the pot has been used as a funeral gift, which proves how highly the people valued their pottery.

Further clear evidence of the high value placed upon the local pottery is found in the pot K. 5078 (Pl. XXXII, fig. 9), a typical Pan Shan funeral urn bought in Lanchow. The neck of the vessel, which was fairly short, was broken off at the top but was mended before the pot was placed in the grave. A couple of holes, drilled after the pot was fired, were used for fixing in place the piece of pottery, which has now disappeared (evidence of riveting). A round piece has been knocked out of the bottom of the same vessel and is now lost. Around half of the periphery of the hole there is a group of five drill-holes. Half of a sixth drill-hole is visible at the edge of the opening just below the outermost drill-hole on the left. Originally the damage to the bottom was not so considerable as it is now, being confined to only about half the extent of the present hole. In this case too the damage was repaired by riveting. In the mantle of pot K. 5962 there are two drill-holes placed on either side of a crack.

In spite of some funeral urns' having been broken prior to their being placed in graves, they were nevertheless deemed serviceable as funeral gifts. They were repaired by riveting, the vessel and the sherd having been drilled and bound together with sinews or strings. No traces of any further stopping can be observed. These painted vessels have obviously been used for preserving dry necessaries and not liquids. The manner of repairing the vessel K. 5078 is so complicated that it was undoubtedly done at home in the village. The vessel was evidently smashed during the preliminary ceremonies or actually at the potter's works, and was then mended. It was carried in the funeral procession in its repaired form.

THE FORMS OF THE PAINTED PAN SHAN SEPULCHRAL VESSELS.

The Pan Shan pottery is remarkable for the great wealth of form displayed by its various types of vessels. Moreover, the vessels vary greatly in size. The largest pots can hold as much as 35 litres (Pl. XII, fig. 7). Very small pots with a capacity of a decilitre or less also occur (Pl. IV, figs. 2 and 7, Pl. XVII, fig. 8, Pl. XIX, figs. 10 and 11).

In spite of this considerable variation both in form and in size, there is at least one characteristic feature common to all these sepulchral vessels, namely, their flat, circular bottom surface. Among the sepulchral vessels not one has so far been found with a clearly defined foot.

The vessels may be divided into two natural main groups: vessels with a neck or brim (Pl. I, figs. 5 and 9, Pl. IX, fig. 3), and vessels without these details, which are often characteristic features of the different types (Pl. I, figs. 1—3).

Both groups are fairly large. Vessels without neck or brim appear to be more primitive than those provided with neck or brim.

One or two other points may perhaps serve as bases of classification. The vessels either possess (Pl. I, fig. 1) or do not possess (Pl. XIX, fig. 6) handles. Those without handles are on the whole of a more primitive type than those with handles. Further, there is a group of vessels that may possibly have been intended to be fitted with thongs or cords by which they could be suspended (Pl. I, fig. 14). They can also be placed on their flat bottoms on a level surface. The other forms of vessels are only intended to stand. However, these two latter bases of classification seem to me to be of less importance compared with the first one I have mentioned.

The neckless and brimless forms consist of plates, bowls, hanging-bowls and cups.

The forms with neck or brim consist of bowls, spouted bowls, hanging-bowls, basins, cups, jugs, pots, beakers, double-spouted vessels and covered vessels provided with a spout.

The dishes are never quite flat, and they have broad sides and small bottoms. The neckless and brimless bowls vary widely in shape but their walls are usually quite high. The neckless cups generally have a bulbous body, as also have some of the types of bowls.

The necked group comprises perhaps the most characteristic forms of all the Pan Shan sepulchral vessels. The neck may be high or low. Sometimes it is nothing but a low collar or a narrow brim round the mouth of the vessel. The true neck is in some cases — this applies to earlier forms — quite vertical, but otherwise it widens out more or less sharply upwards. In the advanced forms the side elevation is concave.

In the vessels with necks the shapes of the bodies vary according to the types of vessels. An inverted-pear-shaped body, truncated at the top and the base by neck and bottom, more hemispherical in its upper part, more like an inverted cone towards the lower part, is however undoubtedly the predominant form, at any rate among the larger sepulchral vessels (Pl. III, fig. 1). This type of body may sometimes assume a more spherical form, sometimes a more lenticular form. It varies from vessel to vessel, and two identically similar vessels are hardly ever to be found. The impression this type of body gives is that of an original ceramic basic form. It is primitive — here in the sense of being natural in relation to the material — and easily fashioned, i. e. it hardly requires any very high degree of skill in the potter, but it is nevertheless extremely useful both for sacred and profane purposes, and is consequently a highly functional form. Finally, it is beautifully proportioned and its silhouette is harmonious and restful. The shape of body that is most common among the Pan Shan bowls next after that described above is markedly bulbous (e. g. Pl. I, figs. 2 and 3), broad and rotund in the upper part, narrowing down sharply and rapidly to a small bottom surface. This shape is likewise conceivable as a basic ceramic form, at any rate in the Far East. Both of these shapes have been preserved throughout the ages in a number of variations right up to modern epochs.

The majority of the various types of vessels have handles that are curved or annular, usually fairly flat though not particularly broad. Some possess two vertical, more or less strong, diametrically opposed handles, affixed somewhat below the widest part of the belly (examples in Pl. II). In one type of vessel horizontal handles take the place of these vertical handles; they too are diametrically opposed, being placed just below the widest part of the belly (Pl. I, fig. 2). In another group, again, there are two vertical handles fastened diametrically opposite to one another at the mouth of the vessel (e. g. Pl. I, fig. 13). In such cases they usually cover the edge of the neck or brim with their upper parts and are fastened below to the uppermost part of the body. Two types of vessels show a pair of handles that are in silhouette non-symmetrically placed (Pl. VI, fig. 2, and Pl. XV, fig. 9). Several different types of vessels possess only one handle, which may be placed on the uppermost part of the body (in the neckless types, Pl. I, fig. 3), or embrace the neck (Pl. XV, fig. 8) or else start at the lower part of the neck and be fastened below to the upper part of the body (Pl. I, fig. 5). The vessels of the Far East dating from the Late Neolithic period possess well-fashioned and functionally admirable types of handles, the designs of which had obviously evolved very rapidly — to a certain extent in contrast to, for instance, the primitive types of vessels found in Egypt.

Instead of curved or annular handles, certain types of vessels have massive handles in the shape of a ridge or knob (e. g. Pl. I, fig. 9). Sometimes they have a scalloped or notched edge and may exhibit transitional forms, subsequently becoming the ears of which mention is made below. These ridge- and knob-handles occur in fairly different designs and in widely differing types of vessels. Whether they are rudimentary forms of true handles it is difficult to decide; probably they are in certain forms, while in others it is hardly likely that they are so. These handles are found to occur in more or less advanced designs as well as in a manifestly rudimentary form. It can hardly be said, on the other hand, as in the case of certain Western forms, that they have acquired an in any way naturalistic character serving the purpose of an anthropomorphic representation. In our material they have scarcely been employed to represent nipples or phallic symbols.

Besides handles, one finds in the Pan Shan pottery a kind of ears (see e. g. Pl. X, figs. 1 and 6—8). They occur in different types of vessels and on the figurines belonging to this kind of pottery, being used on the latter as true ears, though they may also be applied as beards and eyebrows (Pl. XIX, fig. 9). These ears consist of semicircular discs with a hole in the middle and a scalloped edge. Horizontally imposed, scalloped ears with holes in them occur in the two forms of covered vessels with spouts. Vertically imposed, scalloped ears with holes in them are found in greater numbers in two of the types of hanging vessels (Pl. I, fig. 14). The high-necked pots usually have at the openings of the necks two diametrically opposed, vertically placed ears attached in the plane of the handles. These ears likewise consist of semicircular discs, either large or small in size; they possess scalloped or smooth edges and are often provided with a hole in the centre. In some cases they are more or less rudimentary, and they then have neither scalloped edge nor hole. In fact, they are sometimes so rudimentary that they merely consist of exceedingly small ridges.

Double pairs of ears placed crosswise on the necks occur in one isolated pot (Pl. X, fig. 4). Of the short-necked pots there are one or two specimens (Pl. III, fig. 6) having pairs of vertically imposed ears at the mouth of the vessel or on the neck where it meets the body. Rudimentary ears are also found in the double-necked type of vessel, each neck having a vertical pair attached to its upper part.

The formation of the upper edges of the mouths varies very greatly in different vessels. Sometimes they are truncated straight in a horizontal plane, sometimes obliquely but sharply (Pl. I, fig. 9), in other cases they are folded back to form an astragal (Pl. II, fig. 5), which may be thick or thin; sometimes the mouths are bent outwards into a narrow-brimmed opening with a sharp or rounded edge (Pl. IX, figs. 3 a—b).

In certain exceptional cases there is beneath the rim on the outside a plastic ornamentation in the form of a narrow horizontal band either scalloped (Pl. I, fig. 8) or else provided with a lower wavy edge (Pl. III, fig. 4).

These forms of Pan Shan pottery include a number of frequently occurring vessels representing more primitive types than the others. They apparently belong, if not to the earliest, at any rate to the earlier, types of pottery in use in the human economy. They had already come into existence in the very childhood of the potter's art to supply everyday, simple and essential needs, emanating out of the general constitution of Man, and they have lasted more or less unchanged throughout the ages. It is therefore easily explainable, apart from any theories of migrations, that they are found both in the West and in the East, and likewise here amongst our Pan Shan ceramic finds from Kansu. Among these primitive forms I count, for instance, the dish of the type P. S: I, the bowl of the type P. S: II, the basins of the types P. S: III and P. S: IV, the cups of the types P. S: XI and P. S: XII, the jug of the type P. S: XVIII, the bowl of the type P. S: XX, and the most primitive vessels of the predominant types P. S: XXIII and P. S: XXIV (the A and B types).

Far more elegant shapes, requiring greater skill and a surer eye, and which have manifestly arisen out of more complex and more cultivated needs, are seen in the medium-sized jug of the type P. S: XV, in the small bottle- or vase-form of the type P. S: XVII, in the small jug of the type P. S: XIX and in the beaker types P. S: XXXI — P. S: XXXIII (the X-Y-Z group).

Finally, there is a third class of vessels of this kind. They differ from the other vessels in having original and often complicated shapes. They do not occur so frequently as the types dealt with above; indeed, in many cases our collections contain unique specimens. Their manufacture has often required great skill, their invention has been the result of very careful designing and no doubt also of a great deal of experimenting, and they testify to a fairly advanced cultural stage. I venture to call the two jugs of the types P. S: XXIX and P. S: XXX, with their two non-symmetrically placed handles, intermediate forms between this and the previous group. Typical representatives of this third group are the spouted drinking-bowls of types P. S: XXXIV and P. S: XXXV, the peculiar pot of the type P. S: XXXVI, the two covered, spouted vessels of types P. S: XXXVII and P. S: XXXVIII, and the double-necked vessel of the type P. S: XXXIX.

On the whole, then, it may be said that the Pan Shan pottery shows a majority of primitive basic forms, a substantial number of elegant and refined types and a not inconsiderable group of complicated and carefully studied forms. The material as a whole thus points to the proximity of a primitive culture, though it is one that has already been succeeded by and intermingled with typical refined and complex products of industrial art.

In order to give a somewhat clearer idea of the variation in form, the vessels are classified in a series of types, within which the variation from vessel to vessel may be quite considerable. But certain common features characterize each type and divide the vessels into natural groups.

The form types P. S: I—P. S: VI represent different types of dishes and bowls. The first two types represent the primitive, original types without brim and without handles or other projecting details of any kind (bosses, knobs, ridges etc.). Type P. S: III is a form of bowl with a brim but without any projecting details. Types P. S: IV—P. S: VI are basins and bowls varying greatly in size but all provided with both a brim and a pair of knobs, bosses or ridges for handles.

Form type P. S: I.

A small, fairly deep dish with small bottom and more or less straight profile. (The type is reproduced on the annexed page of diagrams as fig. 1.) The dish widens out towards the top. The edge has no brim, nor is there a handle of any kind. The shape is very primitive. The dish is unpainted on the outside, but on the inside it is decorated both on the bottom and on the sides.

Form type P. S: II.

Deep bowls (Pl. XIX, figs. 1, 2, 5 and 6) with wide mouth and a comparatively small, flat bottom. The bowl widens out towards the top, the profile being more or less straight towards the bottom and usually fairly convex towards the top. No brim or handles. The bowl is painted on the inside only. The shape is very primitive.

Form type P. S: III.

Bowl with small, flat bottom, high sides and wide mouth provided with a narrow brim (Pl. IX, figs. 3 a and b). The bowl widens out rapidly from its small bottom, the

P. S. I. K. 5789.
Fig. 1.

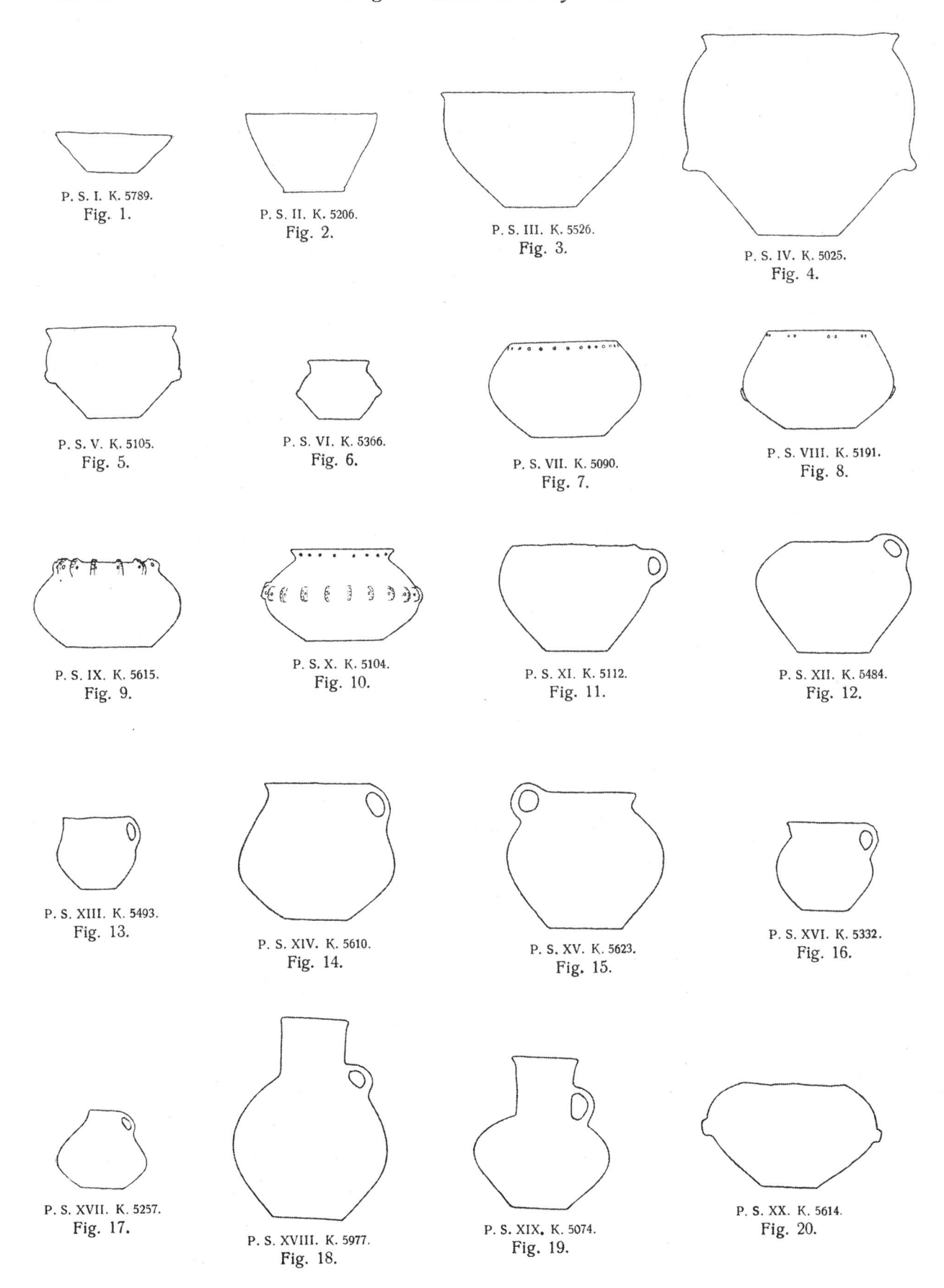

P. S. II. K. 5206.
Fig. 2.

P. S. III. K. 5526.
Fig. 3.

P. S. IV. K. 5025.
Fig. 4.

P. S. V. K. 5105.
Fig. 5.

P. S. VI. K. 5366.
Fig. 6.

P. S. VII. K. 5090.
Fig. 7.

P. S. VIII. K. 5191.
Fig. 8.

P. S. IX. K. 5615.
Fig. 9.

P. S. X. K. 5104.
Fig. 10.

P. S. XI. K. 5112.
Fig. 11.

P. S. XII. K. 5484.
Fig. 12.

P. S. XIII. K. 5493.
Fig. 13.

P. S. XIV. K. 5610.
Fig. 14.

P. S. XV. K. 5623.
Fig. 15.

P. S. XVI. K. 5332.
Fig. 16.

P. S. XVII. K. 5257.
Fig. 17.

P. S. XVIII. K. 5977.
Fig. 18.

P. S. XIX. K. 5074.
Fig. 19.

P. S. XX. K. 5614.
Fig. 20.

profile being straight towards the bottom and convex towards the top. No handles. The bowl is painted on the inside, but not on the outside. It is an obvious development from type P. S: II.

Form type P. S: IV.

A fairly large bowl-shaped vessel with small flat bottom, high sides and a profile convex towards the top, wide mouth and a large brim widening out upwards, or rather a very short neck gradually widening out towards the top (Pl. I, fig. 9). The body is like an inverted pear, truncated at the lower end by the small bottom and at the top by the brim of the mouth. The vessel has a pair of diametrically opposed handles in the shape of a knob or ridge affixed somewhat below the centre-line of the body and slanting downwards. The rim of the mouth is sharply truncated. The bowl is painted on the outside only. The shape is fairly primitive.

Form type P. S: V.

A small bowl (Pl. I, figs. 10 and 11) with flat bottom, the sides relatively lower than in the previous form type P. S: IV, a wide mouth and a high or low brim. The body is bulbous in shape. The bowl is provided with a pair of diametrically opposed ridge- or knob-like projections affixed to the centre of the sides, often with somewhat scalloped edges. There is ornamentation on the outside of the vessel and on the inner surface of the brim, while there is no decoration on the interior sides or bottom. Bowls of this type represent a manifest development from type P. S: II. The variation within the type is fairly considerable, particularly as regards the relative size of the bottom, the vertical section of the sides and the size and slope of the brim of the mouth, as well as the shape of the paired projections. It is however not possible to discover any definite evolution within the type.

Form type P. S: VI.

A very small vessel with a small bottom, relatively low sides, neck of medium height, and a fairly wide opening. (This type is illustrated in the annexed page of diagrams as fig. 6). The vessel widens rapidly from the bottom towards the equatorial line and then narrows down, likewise fairly rapidly, towards the neck. The vertical section is convex. In the equatorial line there are two diametrically opposed boss-like or nipple-shaped projections. The neck is vertical and straight. Round the mouth runs a slightly defined brim. The vessel is painted on the outside and on the inner surfaces of the brim and neck; otherwise the inside is not ornamented. The shape of this type can hardly be directly associated with form type P. S: II, but it might possibly be a further development of type P. S: V.

Form types P. S: VII—P. S: X represent a second series of strongly related forms. Round the mouth or the equatorial line of the body they are provided either with holes pierced in the walls of the vessel or else with vertical, semicircular projections, ears, with holes in the centre. It is evident that cords or sinews have been drawn through these holes and ears, probably for carrying purposes. Another possible explanation of the use to which these holes and ears were put is that sinews were attached to them and then passed through lids of perishable material. I am inclined, however, to accept the first assumption as being more reasonable, and I therefore call them hanging-bowls or swinging-lamps. It is not at all certain, however, that they were used for lighting purposes, for nothing in the structure of the vessels nor any soot marks or suchlike indicate any such use. Three of the typical shapes, viz. P. S: VII—P. S: IX are without any brim, but P. S: X has one. The most primitive is P. S: VII, with its simple profile, which occurs also in P. S: IX. This type, P. S: VII, is evidently the prototype of the other types in this series as well: P. S: VIII, with its more elegant profile and pair of knoblike projections just above the basal surface, P. S: X, with its brim and its large number of ears on the equatorial line and P. S: IX, which also has a large number of ears, but in this case they are placed round the mouth.

Form type P. S: VII.

A hanging-bowl (Pl. I, fig. 12) with small flat bottom, bulbous body, wide mouth, and around it a large number of holes drilled in one or two (K. 5807) rows through the walls of the vessel. The holes were made prior to firing. There is no brim to the mouth. In regard to shape the vessel is one of the most primitive forms belonging to the Pan Shan group and the prototype of the three following hanging-bowls. The vessel is decorated on the outside only.

Form type P. S: VIII.

A hanging-bowl (Pl. XVII, fig. 11) with very small bottom, strongly curved sides, pairs of holes round the mouth and a pair of bosslike, diametrically opposed projections on the border-line between base and mantle. There is no brim to the mouth. The bowl widens out rapidly from the flat surface of the bottom, is widest at a height of about $1/3$ from the bottom, then narrows gradually towards the mouth. The profile is quite graceful. The holes were drilled prior to firing. The surface of the mantle on the outside is decorated, as is also an inner band round the mouth. The design of this type is far more graceful and refined than that of the previous type. Apart from the painted ornamentation, this type acquires a plastic, though somewhat rough, decorative effect through the pair of bosses, which can scarcely have served any practical purpose.

Form type P. S: IX.

A hanging-bowl (Pl. I, fig. 14) with a fairly large flat bottom, a convex profile and, round the mouth, which has no brim, a number of vertical ears scalloped round the edges and provided with holes in the centre. The body itself is shaped as in type P. S: VII and is thus of very primitive design. There is painted decoration on the outside only.

Form type P. S: X.

A hanging-bowl (Pl. XIV, fig. 10) of a more or less composite type with a fairly large bottom, the profile of the body being strongly convex and the brim of the mouth curved outwards[1]). The mouth is of medium size. The brim is pierced by a series of holes. On the equatorial line is a large number of vertical ears with scalloped edge and a hole in the centre. The shape of the body is a development from that of type P. S: VII. In this kind of vessel strings or sinews could be fastened either to the brim or else to the ears. There is no definite correspondence between the holes in the brim and those through the ears, seeing that the number of holes actually drilled in the brim is 24 and the number of ears is 22. It should be noted however that, while the holes in the ears were made in the wet clay, those in the brim were drilled subsequently, from the top downwards, after the vessel was fired. It is also to be observed that these holes in the brim are of larger diameter and seem to have actually been in use, whereas the ear-holes are generally extremely small and can hardly have served any purpose. It looks to me, therefore, as if the ears may perhaps have originally been intended as a means of suspending the vessel, but that after it had been fired the potter abandoned the idea and let them remain more as a decoration; he then pierced holes in the brim for the vessel to be suspended by instead. It may be that before he did this there were small holes in the brim, made prior to firing, but that their number was insufficient. There is painted decoration on the outside of the vessel and also on the inside of the brim.

A third series of inter-related form types consists of jugs, cups and vases, all of which are characterized by the fact that they have a handle attached to the mouth,

---
[1]) Only one example known.

neck or uppermost part of the body. The series includes forms that are more primitive and others that are more advanced. The vessels are medium-sized, and smaller. It is in some cases difficult to determine the boundary-line between the different types, as they vary quite considerably. The group is divisible into neckless and brimless forms, forms with a brim to the mouth or a low neck and forms with a high neck. The series embraces P. S: XI—P. S: XIX, of which the most primitive forms are represented by the types P. S: XI and P. S: XII, both of them entirely without brim and neck and in the shape of the body strongly related to the likewise extremely primitive types P. S: II and P. S: VII. The suggestion of a brim is seen in type P. S: XIII and in the vase P. S: XVII, which, as a matter of fact, has in silhouette a graceful and quite refined shape. Type P. S: XIV — likewise a not very primitive design in silhouette — has a low collar or brim round the mouth. Low but clearly defined necks are observed in the jug type P. S: XV and in the cup type P. S: XVI. In these last four vessels the handle is affixed partly to the edge of the collar or brim and partly to the top of the body. A unique type is the small jug P. S: XIX, which differs from the former in size and in its proportionately larger and higher neck. This last characteristic, however, is also found in certain transitional forms which I have referred to form type P. S: XVIII, and which will be dealt with more fully later on.

Form type P. S: XI.

A fairly large cup or mug (Pl. I, fig. 1) with small bottom, high sides having on the whole a convex profile, wide brimless mouth and a handle affixed just below the rim of the mouth and to the upper part of the body. It widens out fairly rapidly from the bottom, the greatest width being at a height of $^2/_3$ from the bottom, afterwards gradually narrowing down towards the mouth. The profile is almost straight towards the bottom and strongly curved towards the top. The handle is of fairly strong design. The vessel's shape, which is very primitive, has evolved from type P. S: II, to which a handle has been affixed. The vessel is painted only on the outer surface of the mantle.

Form type P. S: XII.

A fairly large cup or mug (Pl. I, fig. 3) with a small bottom, high, rotund sides, medium-sized mouth and a handle affixed to the rim of the mouth and the upper part of the body. The vessel widens out rapidly from the bottom, acquiring its greatest width just above the centre part, and then narrowing down again rapidly towards the mouth. The vessel is bulbous in shape and to a certain extent evolved out of the previous type. The handle extends slightly above the plane of the mouth and is comparatively strong. Only the outside of the vessel is painted.

Form type P. S: XIII.

A cup with a small bottom, high sides and a vaguely defined, almost vertical neck or brim, a wide mouth and a handle attached to the rim of the mouth and the upper part of the body. (The type is illustrated among the diagrams as fig. 13). The body's profile is more or less straight towards the bottom, convex in the middle and towards the upper part, passing finally into the neck or brim, which widens out slightly towards the top. The body is widest in the middle. The shape of the vessel is obviously primitive. The vessel is painted on the outside and also on the inner surface of the brim.

Form type P. S: XIV.

A medium-sized mug (Pl. XVII, fig. 3) with very small bottom, very high sides, a clearly defined brim and a strong handle attached partly to the rim of the mouth and partly to the upper part of the body at a fairly considerable distance from the brim. The profile of the vessel is quite graceful. The vessel widens out rapidly from the bottom, describes a very pronounced curve, acquiring its greatest width about $1/3$ of the way up, and then gradually narrows down in a practically straight line up to the brim, which again rapidly widens out towards the mouth. There is no clear line of demarcation between brim and body, both of which resemble in form type P. S: XXXIII, the only difference being that in the latter there are two handles attached to the neck. I regard the shape of this mug as a distinct advance. The vessel is painted on the outside and also on the inside of the brim.

Form type P. S: XV.

A medium-sized jug (Pl. XIX fig. 12, Pl. XV, fig. 8) with a spherical body, low neck with a more or less concave profile and a strong annular handle attached to the rim of the mouth and the top of the body. The bottom may vary somewhat in size but is usually fairly broad. The mouth is of medium size. The handle projects slightly above the plane of the mouth. The profile of the neck passes without any clear line of demarcation into the profile of the body. The vessel is painted on the outside and also on the inside of the neck.

Form type P. S: XVI.

A small cup with spherical body and clearly differentiated, low neck, medium-sized mouth and a handle fixed to the rim of the mouth and the uppermost part of the body. (This type is illustrated as fig. 16.) The bottom surface is of medium size. The neck widens out gradually towards the top and has a straight profile. The handle is fairly strong. The design of the vessel is similar to that of the foregoing type, but the cup is much smaller and has doubtless been used as a drinking-vessel, not for the preservation of its contents. The vessel is painted on the outside and on the inside of the neck.

Form type P. S: XVII.

A small bottle (Pl. XVII, fig. 8) of elegant shape, with relatively small bottom, high sides, a very low and vaguely defined neck, a very narrow mouth and a handle affixed to the neck and the uppermost part of the body. The vessel widens out rapidly from the bottom, is widest at a point about $1/4$ of the way up from the bottom, and then narrows rapidly towards the neck, which passes into the body without any clear line of demarcation. The vessel may perhaps have been used for toilet purposes. By reason of its handle it may well be incorporated in this series, but it must be regarded as a product of a fairly refined sense of form and in this series is a patently isolated phenomenon. The vessel is painted on the outside and around the mouth.

Form type P. S: XVIII.

A large or medium-sized jug (Pl. I, fig. 5, Pl. IV, fig. 2, Pl. VI, fig. 6, Pl. IX, figs. 4 and 7, etc.), the body of which is more or less spherical or resembles an inverted pear (truncated by the bottom), high neck and a handle starting from the middle of the neck, or slightly lower down, and ending on the uppermost part of the body. A very large number of pieces come within this category and the variation within the type is very wide. A distinct progressive development is observable within the type. The neck is sometimes straight and rigid (in the more primitive vessels within the type, e. g. Pl. I, figs. 5 and 6), gradually widening out towards the top with a straight profile (Pl. VI, fig. 4), or else it has a somewhat concave profile (Pl. XIV, fig. 5), or again it may be straight in its lower part and widen out slightly towards the top (Pl. IX, fig. 7). Both the latter forms of neck are probably advanced. For the rest, the neck may be of a very predominant size and its height as much as $2/3$ of that of the body. The vessels with this predominant neck are to a certain extent transitional forms leading to the next form type. The vessels are painted on the exterior only.

Form type P. S: XIX.

A small jug (Pl. XXXVIII, fig. 5) with a bulbous body, which is truncated by the bottom, a high straight neck, widening out at the top into a narrow brim, and with a handle attached to the middle of the neck and the upper part of the body. This jug differs from the foregoing type in its small size and very large neck, and may indeed be regarded as an advanced variation of the previous type. It has probably been used as some kind of toilet article (oil-vessel or suchlike). The vessel has a painted ornamentation on the outside and on the narrow brim round the mouth.

In a fourth series of forms I have incorporated three types of bowl. They possess certain common features. The bodies of all three bowls are bulbous, and two handles (or rudimentary handles) are placed at diametrically opposite points on or close to the equatorial lines of the bodies. In all three the bottoms are very small and the mouths wide or fairly wide. Here the resemblance ceases. The first of these types of bowls, P. S: XX, is the most primitive of the three and is closely akin to the primitive vessels in the foregoing series. Like the latter, this type has no brim round the mouth and no neck. The handles here are placed in the horizontal plane. In type P. S: XXI the neck is less clearly differentiated on the outside but very distinctly so on the inside, and there is also a horizontal brim. Two vertical handles are a characteristic feature of this type of bowl. The third type in the series has a low neck and two very rudimentary horizontal, ridge-like handles. The horizontal handles found in this type and in P. S: XX form rare exceptions in Pan Shan pottery. Otherwise the rule is that the handles lie in the vertical plane. There is certainly no close evolutional connection between the different vessels in the series.

Form type P. S: XX.

A medium-sized bowl (Pl. I, fig. 2) with small bottom, bulbous body, fairly wide mouth and two diametrically opposed, horizontal ring-shaped handles affixed to the equatorial line of the body. From the bottom to the handles this type of vessel widens out somewhat rapidly into a curved profile, narrowing down again still more rapidly from the handle to the mouth, likewise forming a curved profile, which has a smaller radius than the former curve. There is neither brim nor neck. This vessel's shape is obviously very primitive. Only one broad painted band runs round the mouth on the outside of the vessel.

Form type P. S: XXI.

A medium-sized bowl with a fairly small bottom, convex profile, low neck, wide mouth with brim and, on the widest part of the body, two diametrically opposed, ring-shaped vertical handles. (This type will be found illustrated as fig. 21). The bowl widens out rapidly from bottom to handles, giving a fairly straight profile, which then follows the line of a convex curve, passing gradually into the somewhat concave exterior profile of the neck. The inside of the neck is more clearly defined than the outside. The mouth is given a narrow brim with a horizontal extension. The handles are proportionally fairly broad and the holes in them are almond- or bean-shaped. The shape of the bowl is of a highly advanced and peculiar design. The interior profile in particular is very uncommon. The vessel is painted only on the inside and on the upper side of the brim.

Form type P. S: XXII.

A medium-sized bowl (Pl. XIV, fig. 7) with small bottom, convex sides and low, gradually widening neck with straight profile. The mouth is wide, and two more or less ear-shaped handles are placed diametrically opposite to one another at a distance from the bottom about $1/3$ of the height of the body. They lie in the horizontal plane. The belly is very rotund in profile, its widest part being about the middle. Vessels of this type are painted on the outside and on the inside of the neck.

The most typical forms of Pan Shan vessels consist of large and medium-sized pots or urns holding 10—35 litres, while a few are smaller. The bodies of the vessels vary quite considerably, but in most cases the base is like an inverted cone truncated by the bottom, and the upper part is more or less hemispherical. Sometimes they are more spherical in form, sometimes they have the shape of an inverted pear, in which case the lower part is likewise truncated by the bottom. They all have a centrally placed, short or long neck, and two diametrically opposed, fairly sturdy, vertical handles, fixed at or somewhat below the equatorial line, the widest part of the belly. The vessels are bilaterally symmetrical in two planes. Viewed directly from above they are circular with that slight variation which the skilled hand-made product necessarily exhibits. The necks, too, when viewed from above, are circular, the marginal silhouette being in the horizontal plane. These pots have undoubtedly served as storage pots to hold dry necessaries for the use of the dead. We may distinguish two forms among these urns: the types P. S: XXIII and P. S: XXIV. The former has a low neck, the latter a high one. I regard them as fairly primitive types. In both a distinct progression can be traced

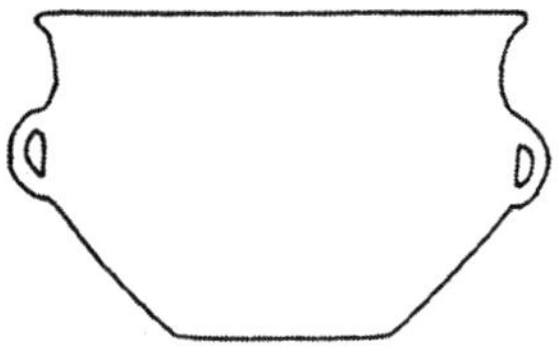

(I) 22   *Palæontologia Sinica*   Ser. D.

P. S. XXI. K. 5221.
Fig. 21.

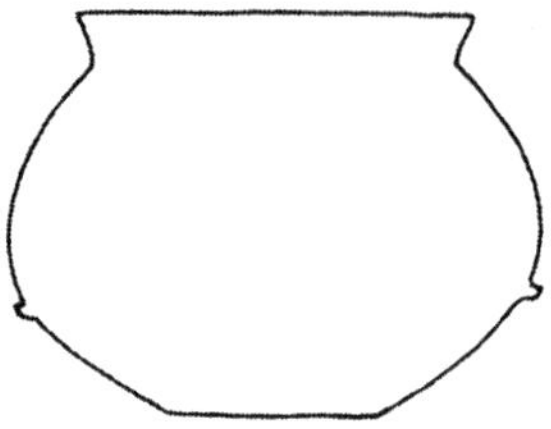

P. S. XXII. K. 5485.
Fig. 22.

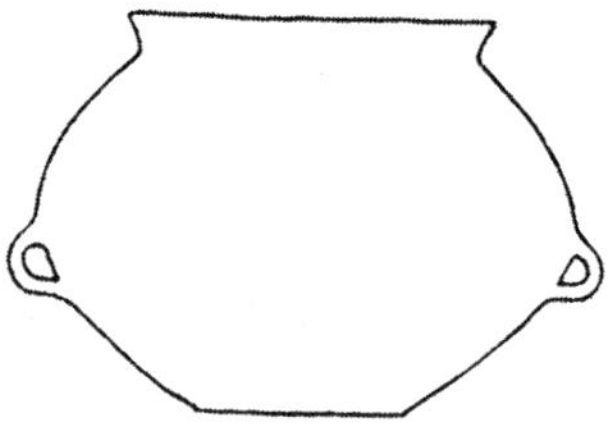

P. S. XXV. K. 5111.
Fig. 23.

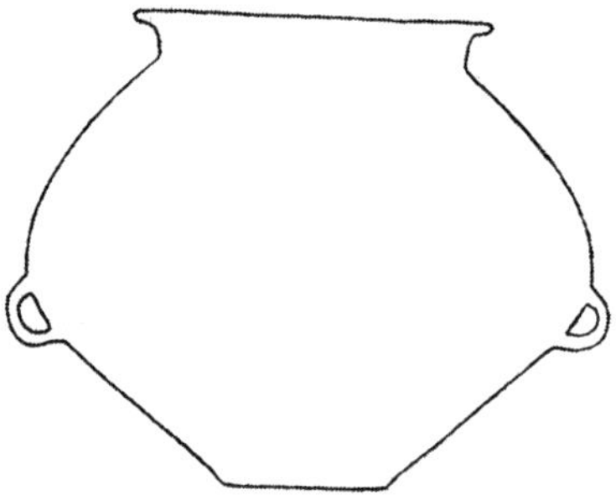

P. S. XXVI. K. 5064.
Fig. 24.

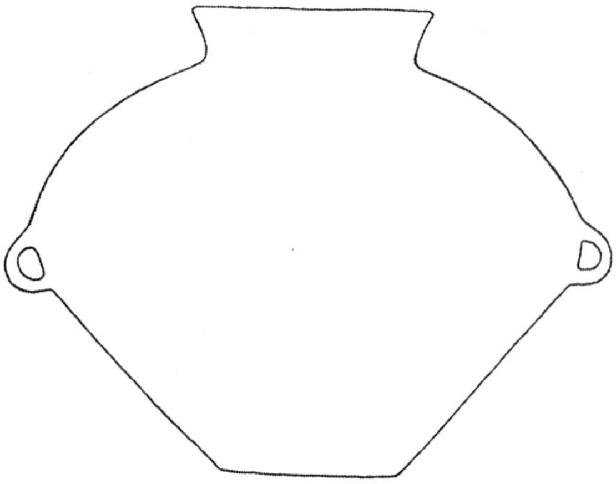

P. S. XXIII. K. 5035.
Fig. 25.

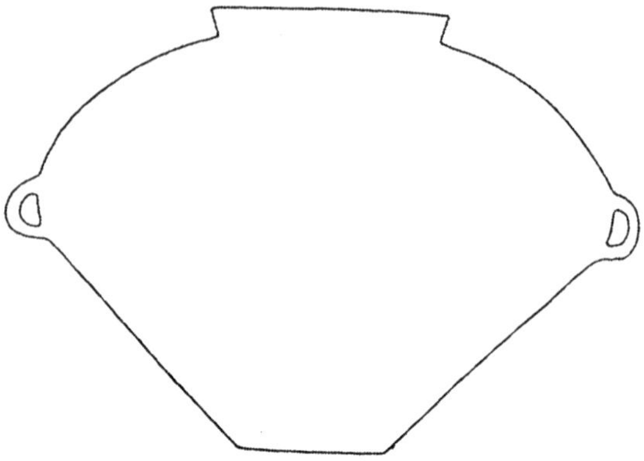

P. S. XXIII. K. 5057.
Fig. 26.

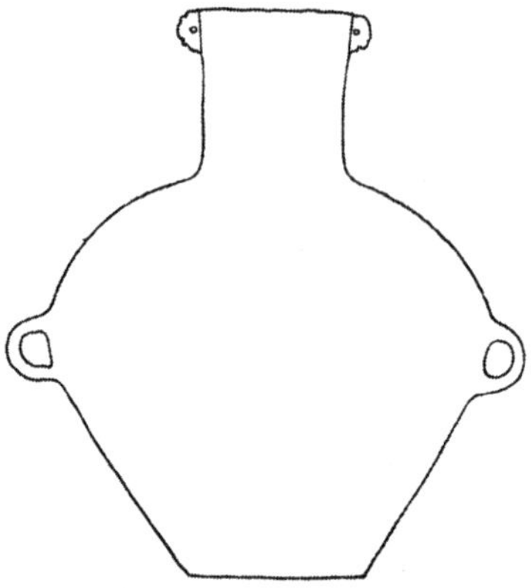

P. S. XXIV. K. 5150.
Fig. 27.

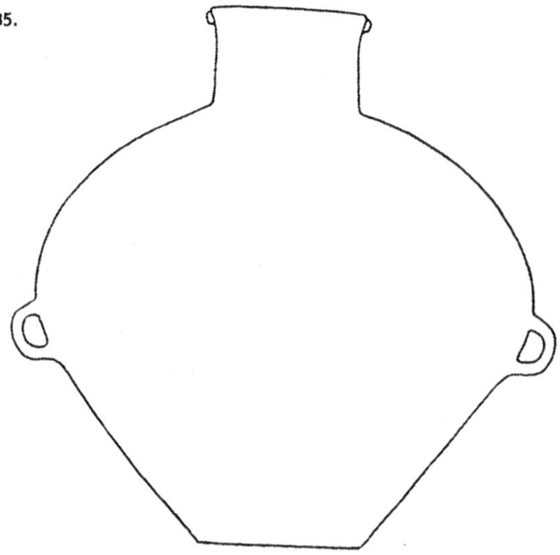

P. S. XXIV. K. 5050.
Fig. 28.

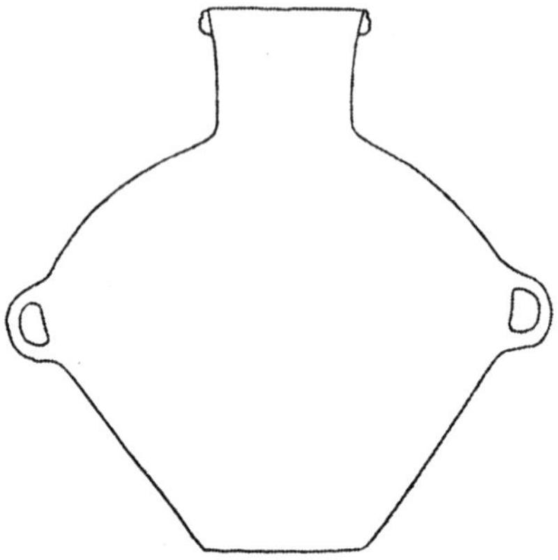

P. S. XXIV. K. 5062.
Fig. 29.

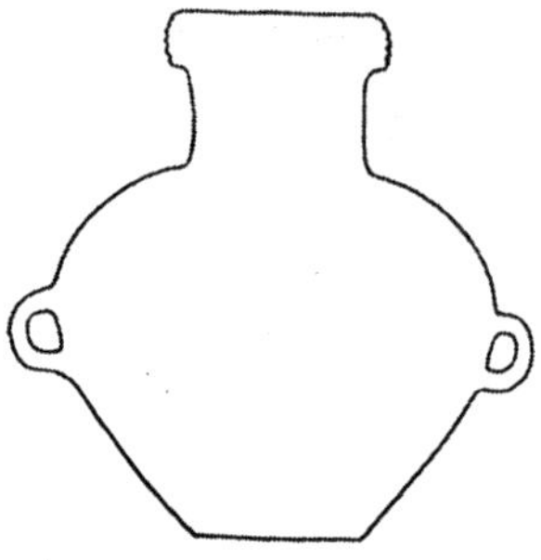

P. S. XXVII. K. 5069.
Fig. 30.

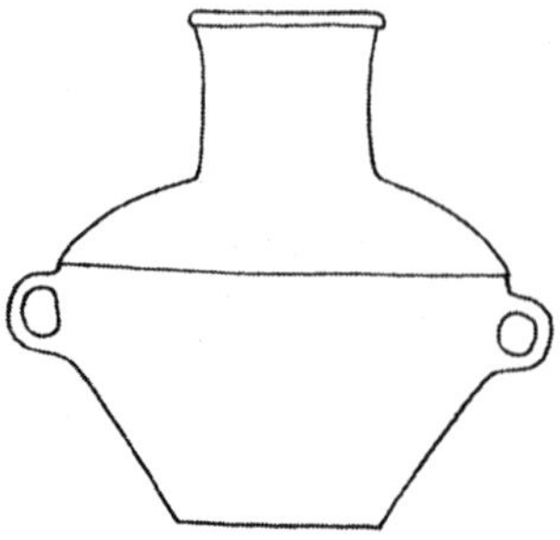

P. S. XXVIII. K. 5274.
Fig. 31.

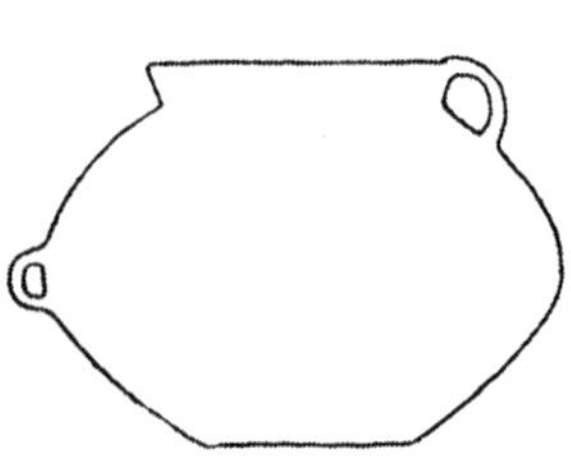

P. S. XXIX. K. 5110.
Fig. 32.

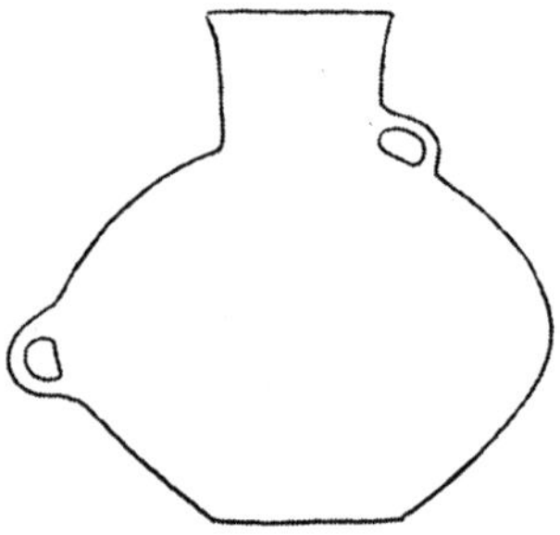

P. S. XXX. K. 5970.
Fig. 33.

up to an ever richer silhouette effect. As these pots are quantitatively predominant in Pan Shan pottery, I have ventured for the purpose of easier recognition, apart from their numerical references P. S: XXIII and P. S: XXIV, to designate them as respectively A and B vessels, and the group as the A—B group.

Form type P. S: XXIII (type A).

The body of this type is more spherical at the top, the base more like an inverted cone truncated by the bottom; the A vessel has, further, two diametrically opposed, vertical handles on or slightly below the equatorial line, a low, clearly differentiated neck, which usually widens out rapidly, and a wide, brimless mouth. The handles are generally fairly stout. It is only in very exceptional cases that the low necks possess ears. The breadth of the bodies is in general considerably greater than their height. The most common proportions are:

$\frac{\text{breadth of body}}{\text{height of body}} = \frac{47}{36}$ (Pl. V, fig. 5). The following proportions are also fairly common:

$\frac{\text{breadth of body}}{\text{height of body}} = \frac{46}{36}$ Pl. III, fig. 2) and $\frac{\text{breadth of body}}{\text{height of body}} = \frac{45}{36}$ (Pl. II, fig. 7).

In rare cases the breadth is still greater:

$\frac{\text{breadth of body}}{\text{height of body}} = \frac{52}{36}$ (Pl. II, fig. 2) and $\frac{\text{breadth of body}}{\text{height of body}} = \frac{50}{36}$ (Pl. III, fig. 6).

Pots of smaller breadth occur, though not very frequently, as e. g.

$\frac{\text{breadth of body}}{\text{height of body}} = \frac{41}{36}$ (Pl. II, fig. 6).

The profiles of the necks are often straight but widening towards the top (Pl. II, figs. 1, 2, 6 and 7), though more or less concave neck-profiles also occur (Pl. II, fig. 3, Pl. V, fig. 3). The height of the necks varies considerably. They are sometimes very low (Pl. III, fig. 3): the proportion between height of neck and height of body = 1:15 and in other cases considerably greater (Pl. III, figs. 4 and 5): the proportion between height of neck and height of body in fig. 4 = about 1:5 and in fig. 5 = about 1:8. The size of the mouths likewise varies a good deal. On the whole they are far wider in this type than in the following high-necked type. The diameter of the mouths of these vessels varies between somewhat more than one-hal (Pl. II, fig. 7) and somewhat less than one-third (Pl. III, fig. 3) of the vessel's maximum diameter.

Where there are ears they are placed vertically and are attached to the outside of the neck close to the edge (Pl. III, fig. 4) or on the border-line between neck and belly (Pl. III, fig. 6). In the former case they are set in the plane of the handles diametrically opposite to one another, in the latter case they are likewise diametrically opposite to one another but in a plane at right angles to that of the handles. The vessels belonging to type P. S: XXIII are painted on the outer surface of the mantle and on the inside of the neck.

Form type P. S: XXIV (type B).

This type generally has a somewhat higher body than the foregoing type. Here too the handles are in pairs and are set diametrically opposite to one another in or slightly below the equatorial plane. The necks are higher and the mouths narrower than in type P. S: XXIII. The necks have a pair of diametrically opposed ears on the outside below the rim of the mouth. In this type also the breadth of the bodies varies considerably in proportion to the height.

Type P. S: XXIV has on the whole somewhat more slender bodies than the foregoing type. The greatest breadth is found in pots such as those shown in Pl. XI, fig. 7, and Pl. XII, fig. 6, of which the $\frac{\text{breadth of body}}{\text{height of body}} = \frac{45}{36}$. There are variants however, in which the $\frac{\text{breadth of body}}{\text{height of body}} = \frac{40}{36}$. The average for this type of pottery would appear to be about $\frac{42}{36}$. The early representatives of the type are on an average $\frac{40}{36}$, i. e., the breadth is slightly greater than the height (Pl. II, figs 4 and 5). In the representatives of the middle and late period of this pottery the breadth is somewhat increased; the average works out at: $\frac{\text{breadth of body}}{\text{height of body}} = \frac{41}{36} - \frac{45}{36}$ (Pl. XII). In the very late representatives of Pan Shan pottery, however, the height is increased at the expense of the breadth, i. e., breadth and height become practically equal. The average for these very late representatives is: $\frac{\text{breadth of body}}{\text{height of body}} = \frac{38}{36}$ (Pl. XVIII, figs 5, 6 and 7). In a few isolated representatives of these very late vessels the proportion is: $\frac{\text{breadth of body}}{\text{height of body}} = \frac{36}{36}$, i. e., the breadth is equal to the height (Pl. XVIII, fig. 4).

The width and height of the necks vary considerably within the type. Certain early vessels of this type have a very high and narrow neck (Pl. X, fig. 7), the proportion being: $\frac{\text{height of neck}}{\text{height of body}} = \frac{2}{7}$ and $\frac{\text{breadth of neck}}{\text{breadth of body}} = \frac{1}{4}$. Other vessels representing the type's middle period have necks of medium height with a mouth of medium width, while others again have relatively low necks and wide mouths (Pl. V, fig. 7); the proportion being: $\frac{\text{height of neck}}{\text{height of body}} = \frac{2}{9}$ and $\frac{\text{breadth of neck}}{\text{breadth of body}} = \frac{1}{3}$. The late vessels within the group have relatively low and fairly broad necks (Pl. XII, figs. 2, 3, 5 and 6): $\frac{\text{height of neck}}{\text{height of body}} = \frac{1}{5}$ and $\frac{\text{breadth of neck}}{\text{breadth of body}} = \frac{1}{3}$. The necks of the earlier vessels are either straight or else widen out just slightly towards the top (Pl. II, figs. 4 and 5, Pl. VII, fig. 5, Pl. VIII, fig. 5, Pl. X, figs. 1 and 7). Later on the necks widen out towards the top and the silhouette becomes more or less concave (Pl. XII, Pl. XVIII). We might possibly refer to transitional forms between types P. S: XXIII and P. S: XXIV a small and otherwise clearly differentiated family of pots with string patterns. They have been included above amongst the most advanced group within the type P. S: XXIV. Here the shape of the bodies is distinctly that of an inverted pear. It is in this group of vessels that the height is greatest in proportion to the breadth, the maximum ratio being $\frac{\text{breadth of body}}{\text{height of body}} = \frac{36}{36}$. It is also in this group that the necks are lowest of all vessels in type P. S: XXIV, the ratio being: $\frac{\text{height of neck}}{\text{height of body}} = \frac{1}{5}$. The profile of the neck is concave, and there is a suggestion of a brim to the mouth. The necks have no ears. For the rest, the vessels have thin walls and are of extremely skilled workmanship. The vessels belonging to this group (Pl. XVIII) were all bought at Lanchow.

Type P. S: XXIV contains all gradations between ears that are of practical use, large, provided with holes and with scalloped edges, and ears that are absolutely rudimentary. The above-mentioned transitional group and the advanced pot K. 5287 (Pl. XII, fig. 7) have no ears at all. We should perhaps mention already at this point that these ears are systematically important. For we find a certain contrast arising between vessels that have well developed ears and such vessels as have only rudimentary ears. The latter cannot be supposed to have been made at a period prior to the former. The vessels of type P. S: XXIV are painted on the outer surface of the mantle and very occasionally on a narrow band on the inside of the mouth.

Closely allied to the group just dealt with containing types P.S:XXIII and P.S:XXIV are a number of medium-sized and smaller vessels. Each one possesses characteristic features, but they have all manifestly been evolved out of the foregoing types. They might perhaps be included in them, but in that case the variation within those types would be far too wide.

Associated with type P. S: XXIII are two low-necked types P. S: XXV and P. S. XXVI. The former is characterized by a very broad belly and two handles, which are set more or less below the equatorial plane. Moreover, it has a very wide mouth. Type P. S: XXVI likewise has a body broader than the ordinary examples of type P. S: XXIII, though not so broad as in type P. S: XXV. Type P. S: XXVI also has a pair of handles set fairly low beneath the equatorial plane. It has a somewhat narrower mouth than the foregoing type and round the mouth is a clearly defined brim.

Associated with type P. S: XXIV are two other types of, on the whole, similar forms. These are small vessels. Both types have necks of preponderant size. Type P. S: XXVII has a bulbous body with a finely rounded outline, whereas the body of type P. S: XXVIII shows a silhouette line that is broken towards the top.

Form type P. S: XXV.

A medium-sized type of pot with small bottom, very broad body, rotund profile, low neck with a wide mouth, and two handles set more or less below the equatorial line, often even very low. The shape of the pot is very closely akin to that of type P. S: XXIII, but the pot is lower and broader. The proportions of the pot shown in Pl. VI, fig. 3 are: $\frac{\text{breadth of body}}{\text{height of body}} = \frac{56}{36}$, so that in this case the pot is particularly broad. Pl. XIV, fig. 8 shows a pot whose proportions are: $\frac{\text{breadth of body}}{\text{height of body}} = \frac{55}{36}$. In all these vessels the relative breadth is considerably greater than the greatest breadths in type P. S: XXIII. Type P. S: XXV is painted on the outside of the vessel and on the inside of the neck.

Form type P. S: XXVI.

A medium-sized type of pot (Pl. XIV, fig. 1) with small bottom, rotund profile, two stout, diametrically opposed handles set considerably below the equatorial line, low neck, wide mouth and the brim of the mouth in the horizontal plane. The proportions are: $\frac{\text{breadth of body}}{\text{height of body}} = \frac{47}{36}$, that is to say, the breadth is fairly great in proportion to the height. The handles are set obliquely in a downward direction. This type of vessel is painted on the outside, and also on the inside of the brim and the neck.

Form type P. S: XXVII.

A smallish or small pot, the body of which is bulbous (Pl. XV, figs. 4—7) or in the shape of an inverted pear (Pl. IV, fig. 3), and is truncated by the small surface of the bottom. It has two diametrically opposed handles at the widest part of the belly and a high, straight neck with a relatively small mouth. In very exceptional cases the bottom may be fairly large (Pl. XV, fig. 1). The body's profile usually describes a fine curve. The profile line of the neck is generally absolutely vertical or very slightly concave. $\frac{\text{Height of neck}}{\text{Height of body}} = \text{about } \frac{1}{2}$, i. e., the neck is very high, being about $1/3$ of the entire height of the vessel. The mouth is almost without exception turned down to form an astragal. Towards the top of the neck there are two large, diametrically opposed ears set in the plane of the handles and having a scalloped edge and one or two holes. In a few exceptional cases there are no ears. This type of vessel is painted on the outside and on the astragal round the mouth. The mantle is fairly large, while the basal surface is very low. The above type of vessel is frequently combined with décor group 15 P.

Form type P. S: XXVIII.

A medium-sized or small pot (Pl. IV, fig. 7) with small bottom, the side being constructed in two planes, two diametrically opposed handles set in the uppermost part of the lower plane, broken profile and a very high neck with a medium-sized mouth, and the rim of the mouth turned down to form an astragal. On the upper part of the neck there are in most cases fairly large ears pierced with single or double holes and having a scalloped edge. The lower part of the belly has a straight or slightly curved profile and narrows down rapidly from the handles to the small bottom. The upper part of the belly is in the shape of a skull-cap and narrows rapidly up towards the neck. The handles are fairly stout, each containing a circular hole. $\frac{\text{Height of neck}}{\text{Height of body}} = \frac{1}{2}$. The neck thus comprises $1/3$ of the height of the pot as in the foregoing type. The pot is painted on the outside (neck, upper part of the mantle and the upper portion of the base).

Still another group of vessels is manifestly derived from the immediately preceding group (P. S: XXIII and P. S: XXIV). A characteristic feature of this new group is that the one handle is placed on the vessel's equatorial line while the other has been moved up to or in the neighbourhood of the neck. This converts the vessel into a kind of jug, provided with double, non-symmetrically placed handles. Thus these vessels assume in a way an intermediary position between the group of jugs discussed above, particularly vessels P. S: XIV and P. S: XVIII, and the immediately preceding group of vessels P. S: XXIII and P. S: XXIV. This group contains two different types, one with a low neck, P. S: XXIX, and one with a high neck, P. S: XXX.

Form type P. S: XXIX.

A medium-sized jug (Pl. XV, fig. 9) or mug with small bottom, the body towards the lower part like an inverted cone, towards the upper more spherical, and a low neck with wide mouth. The vessel has two handles, the one fixed on or slightly below the equatorial line, the other fixed just below the neck on the uppermost part of the body, or else partly at the rim of the neck and partly on the uppermost part of the body. The lower handle may be either an ordinary one (Pl. XV, fig. 9) or else a ridge handle in the shape of an ear (Pl. IV, fig. 5). These two different types of lower handle might perhaps justify the division of this form type into two different types, but I have preferred to combine them into one, as there are important points of resemblance between the vessels. I regard this type as a variation of type P. S: XXIII or type P. S: XXV. It should be pointed out, however, that there are at the same time great similarities between it and the mug of the type P. S: XIV. The vessel is painted on the outside, and on the inside of the neck.

Form type P. S: XXX.

A large (Pl. XIV, fig. 9) or medium-sized (Pl. VI, fig. 5) jug with small bottom, the body spherical or having the shape of an inverted pear truncated by the bottom surface, high neck with a relatively narrow mouth with or without a brim, and two handles, the one fixed on or slightly below the equatorial plane of the body, the other on the lower part of the neck and, at the lower end, on the uppermost portion of the body. The neck may be high (Pl. VI, fig. 2) or low (Pl. IX, fig. 5), it may be more or less straight or else have a concave profile. The handles are fairly strong. The vessel is closely akin to type P. S: XXIV, but it is also related to the jug P. S: XVIII, assuming an intermediate position between the two. It is painted on the outside only.

Another series of vessels is represented by bowls or beakers with double, diametrically opposed handles embracing the neck and affixed to its rim and to the upper part of the mantle. I have in this series distinguished three different types, P. S: XXXI —

P. S: XXXIII, though I am aware that there exist transitional forms between these three types, and a larger number of basic types might possibly be determined. As the vessels belonging to this group are extremely numerous, and seeing that the types of vessels still exist in various stages of development in Ma Chang and Hsin Tien pottery, with a view to their being more readily recognized I have called them, besides types XXXI, XXXII and XXXIII, the X, Y and Z vessels, denoting the whole group as the X-Y-Z group, on the analogy of the group P. S: XXIII and P. S: XXIV (the A-and-B group).

Form type P. S: XXXI (type X).

A small bowl (Pl. I, fig. 13, Pl. XIV, fig. 3) with a fairly low, broad body, low neck, with its profile widening out towards the top, and a very wide mouth. The vessel has two diametrically opposed, stout handles, fixed at the top to the rim of the mouth or slightly lower and at the bottom to the surface of the mantle at some distance from he boundary-line of the neck. The body is sometimes lenticular in shape (Pl. I, fig. 13) or like an inverted skull-cap (Pl. XIV, fig. 3), and the breadth is always very considerable in proportion to the height: $\frac{\text{breadth of body}}{\text{height of body}} = \frac{79}{36}$ in the pot shown in Pl. I, fig. 13, and $\frac{\text{breadth of body}}{\text{height of body}} = \frac{72}{36}$ in the pot in Pl. XIV, fig. 3. The handles may be of large or small size, and the profile of the neck straight or concave. The pot shown in Pl. XIV, fig. 11 represents a transitional form between this type and type P. S: XXXIII. The type here described is painted on the outside, and on the inside of the neck.

Form type P. S: XXXII (type Y).

A small bowl or beaker with a low, broad body, which is lenticular or bulbous in form, proportionally high neck having on the whole a vertical profile, and a mouth of medium width or perhaps even narrow, also two proportionally very large handles fixed to the rim of the mouth and to the upper part of the body at a varying distance from the boundary line of the neck. The profile of the neck is either quite vertical (Pl. IX, fig. 9) or slightly concave (Pl. XIX, figs. 10 and 11). In proportion to its height, the breadth of the body is not quite so great as in the foregoing type, as e. g. Pl. XIX, fig. 10: $\frac{\text{breadth of body}}{\text{height of body}} = \frac{59}{36}$. The height of the neck comprises over $1/3$ of the entire height of the vessel. The vessel is painted on the outside, and on the inside of the neck.

Form type P. S: XXXIII (type Z).

A smallish beaker with small bottom, high sides and low, often indistinctly differentiated neck, medium-sized mouth and two diametrically opposed handles fixed partly to the rim of the mouth and partly a little way down on the uppermost portion of the mantle. The beaker is often considerably larger than the foregoing type of vessel. A characteristic feature of this type is its graceful silhouette. The widest part of the strongly rotund side is fairly low, usually below and sometimes considerably below the centre of the body. Variations in this respect are found in Pl. IX, fig. 8, Pl. IX, fig. 1, Pl. XII, fig. 9, Pl. XVII, fig. 5, and Pl. XVII, fig. 9. This makes the profile more convex towards the bottom and straighter towards the top. The neck, which widens out into a straight line or a gentle curve as it rises, frequently passes imperceptibly into the part that forms the mantle. Sometimes it is fairly low (Pl. XII fig. 9), sometimes it is fairly high (Pl. XVII, fig. 10). The handles are fairly large and generally quite thin. At the upper point of attachment they generally project somewhat above the plane of the vessel's rim. The beakers are painted on the outside, and also on the inside of the neck.

As a special group, standing to a certain extent in contrast to all the other groups of form types, I have collected a number of vessels of a more or less complicated nature. In one respect or other they possess peculiar details and are not so primitive in structure as the majority of the foregoing. They may be likened to the "fancy forms" which Flinders Petrie distinguished in the prehistoric Egyptian pottery. Some of them are derived from types of vessels I have dealt with above, and which have in some way or other assumed a complicated character by the addition of more or less conspicuous details. Others of these forms are obviously new creations in Pan Shan pottery. Compared with the majority of the foregoing types they are of later origin. Examples of types belonging to the foregoing category are the forms P. S: XXXIV—P. S: XXXVI, and to the latter category P. S: XXXVII—P. S: XL. The bowls P. S: XXXIV and P. S: XXXV have their prototypes in types P. S: II and P. S: III respectively, to whose simple bodies have been attached a spout immediately below the rim of the vessel, and also different forms of handles. The pot P. S: XXXVI is a development of type P. S: XXIII (type A), to which have been added one or two characteristic features. Types P. S: XXXVII and P. S: XXXVIII are to a certain extent, in spite of the considerable difference in size, kindred forms. Both vessels are covered and both have a spout set in the side. Type P. S: XXXIX has two high necks

P. S. XXXI. K. 5010.
Fig. 34.

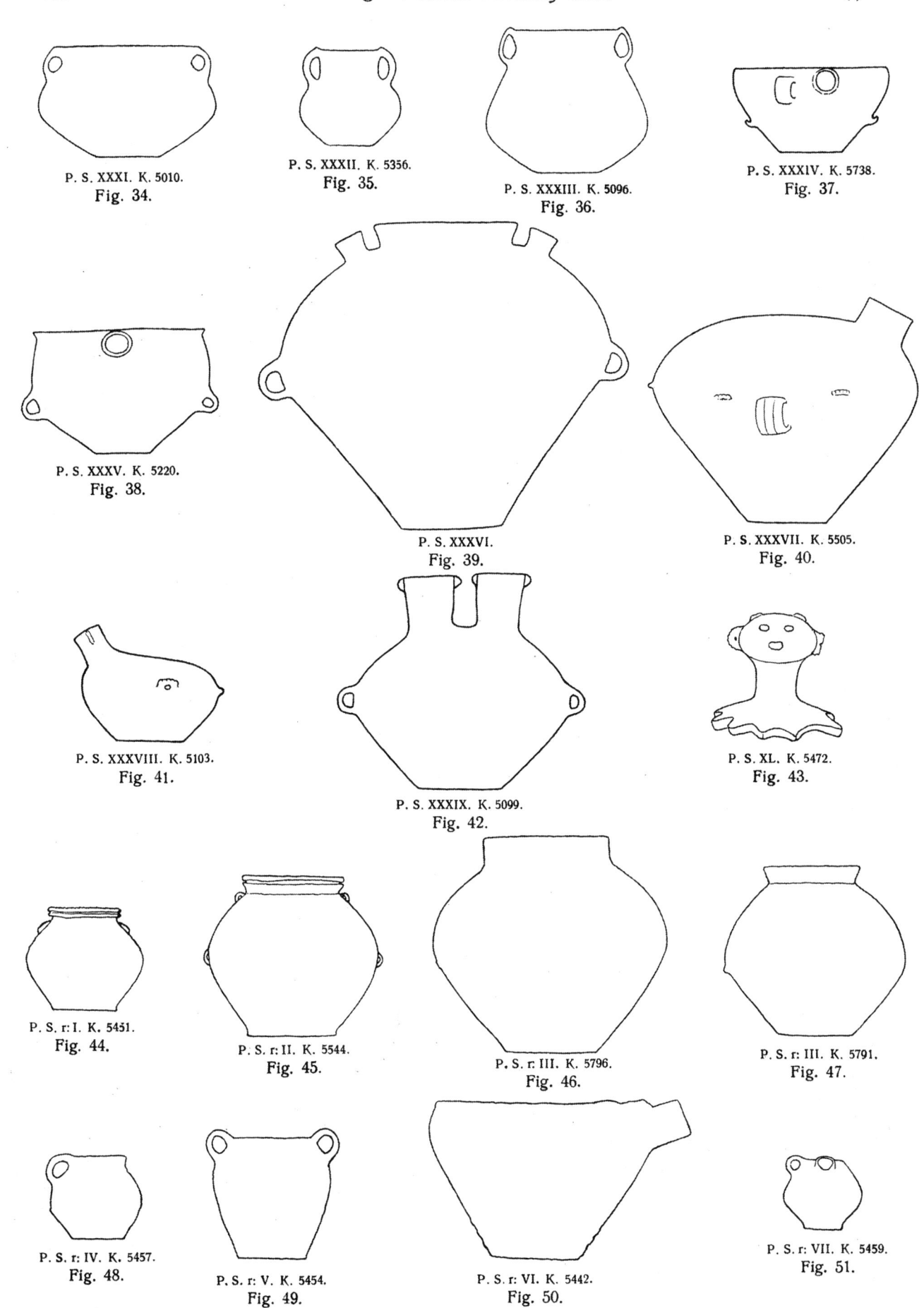

P. S. XXXII. K. 5356.
Fig. 35.

P. S. XXXIII. K. 5096.
Fig. 36.

P. S. XXXIV. K. 5738.
Fig. 37.

P. S. XXXV. K. 5220.
Fig. 38.

P. S. XXXVI.
Fig. 39.

P. S. XXXVII. K. 5505.
Fig. 40.

P. S. XXXVIII. K. 5103.
Fig. 41.

P. S. XXXIX. K. 5099.
Fig. 42.

P. S. XL. K. 5472.
Fig. 43.

P. S. r: I. K. 5451.
Fig. 44.

P. S. r: II. K. 5544.
Fig. 45.

P. S. r: III. K. 5796.
Fig. 46.

P. S. r: III. K. 5791.
Fig. 47.

P. S. r: IV. K. 5457.
Fig. 48.

P. S. r: V. K. 5454.
Fig. 49.

P. S. r: VI. K. 5442.
Fig. 50.

P. S. r: VII. K. 5459.
Fig. 51.

and is thus in a special class by itself. Finally, type P. S: XL possibly represents a form of lid and is fashioned as a human bust with head, neck and breast.

Form type P. S: XXXIV.

A medium-sized or smallish bowl (Pl. XIX, figs. 3 and 4), the body of which is of the form described under type P. S: II with small flat bottom, the sides widening out towards the top, and a somewhat convex profile, the mouth wide and without any brim. Just below the centre of the body are set two diametrically opposed ridge-handles pointing slightly upwards. Not quite in the centre between the two handles there is a short spout just below the rim of the mouth. The spout is circular in section and points upwards and outwards. Its longitudinal axle is not quite parallel to the plane of the mouth. If the spout is facing the observer, there is seen to the left of it a vertical handle of fairly considerable breadth with an almond-shaped loop. The angular distance between spout and handle is about 40°. The handle with its loop, which is about large enough for an index finger, can only be held by the left hand. All indications go to show that the bowl has been used for drinking purposes. The index-finger of the left hand has been put into the loop of the handle, the bowl has been supported from behind and below and lifted with the right hand, the spout has been raised to the mouth, and then the bowl has been tilted and emptied of its contents. The right hand, as it grasps the vessel below and behind, is able to obtain a firm grip by means of the scalloped edges of the handles. The bowl is thus a drinking vessel. It is a fairly complicated form derived from form type P.S: II and has undoubtedly been achieved only after much experimenting. It is not inconceivable that it is a type imported from the West. To discover whether this is so or not would however require a special study of the subject, which considerations of space forbid my undertaking here. The vessel is painted on the inside, on an external ring round the mouth, on the lip of the spout, and on the outer side of the annular handle.

Form type P. S: XXXV.

A medium-sized bowl (Pl. XIV, fig. 2) with small bottom, a more or less hemispherical body, wide mouth with brim, two diametrically opposed handles sloping obliquely downwards and placed slightly below the widest portion of the vessel, and a short slightly upturned spout set just below the brim of the mouth and exactly between the handles. The vessel may be regarded as a direct complication of type P. S: III, with which it fully agrees both in size and in the type of body. It is probably a drinking-vessel intended to be grasped by the handles with both hands and to be raised with the spout towards the mouth. It is painted on the outer border round the mouth and also on the inside.

Form type P. S: XXXVI.

A vessel (Pl. XX, figs. 2 and 3) resembling type P. S: XXIII (type A) in shape. Its bottom is small, its body formed like an inverted pear truncated by the bottom, the neck low with a wide brimless mouth. The vessel has two sturdy ring-handles fixed just below its widest part, and two diametrically opposed, eggcup-shaped protuberances set at the side of the mouth in the plane of the handles. These cup-shaped tubes on the upper surface of the vessel are its most characteristic feature. In profile they resemble two spouts, but their lower ends have no passage leading to the interior of the vessel — blind alleys in fact. At the top each of them has two small holes just below the mouths. These holes are diametrically opposite to one another and form a line at right angles to the plane of the handles. The tubes can hardly be merely decorative forms but undoubtedly had some special function, as is evidenced for instance by the holes, which are far too inconspicuous to have a purely decorative purpose. I presume that these tubes have been used for the purpose of fastening ornaments to the vessel (feathers etc.), or else for attaching a lid of some perishable material. The vessel is painted on the mantle portion of the outside and on the inside of the neck.

Form type P. S: XXXVII.

A largish vessel (Pl. XX, fig. 1), having a body shaped like an inverted cone truncated by the small bottom, the upper part a vaulted surface in which is set laterally a fairly thick, short spout pointing obliquely upwards and outwards. Slightly below the vessel's widest part are two diametrically opposed handles divided into three vertical lobes and placed laterally in relation to the spout. In a circle around the widest part of the vessel there are five horizontally placed ears, of which two pairs are set close to the handles. The fifth ear is placed right at the back in relation to the spout. The ears have scalloped edges and are provided with holes. The ears in this type may possibly have been used for suspending the vessel. The vessel is painted only on the vaulted part of the outside and on the spout.

Form type P. S: XXXVIII.

A small vessel (Pl. XX, figs. 4 and 5) with a bulb-shaped body closed at the top and provided on one side with a thick spout pointing obliquely upwards and outwards. The vessel has three ears, of which two are laterally placed in relation to the spout and one is set right at the back. The spout also has two ears running alongside. The ears are pierced with holes and have a scalloped edge; they are certainly stout enough to permit of the vessel's being hung up with strings passing through them. The vessel is painted only on the upper side and on the spout. Both this and the foregoing type resemble a form in use in China at the present day as a chamber-pot for men.

Form type P. S: XXXIX.

A medium-sized pot (Pl. XIV, fig. 6) with fairly small bottom, the body in the shape of a bulb or an inverted pear, truncated below by the bottom surface, two stout, diametrically opposed ring-handles affixed to the widest part of the body, and two high necks set on the upper surface of the vessel in the plane of the handles. These necks form the most characteristic feature of the vessel. They widen out slightly towards the top, have narrow brimless mouths and are each provided with a pair of diametrically opposed, fairly rudimentary ears without holes or scalloped edge and set in the plane of the handles. The double necks doubtless represent a form arrived at only after much experimenting, and which is an exceedingly suitable one if the vessel holds a liquid that is to be rapidly poured out. The air then enters through the one neck and the liquid runs out through the other. The shape of the vessel is as complicated as it is beautiful, and the type is one of the most interesting forms found in Pan Shan pottery. The vessel is painted only on the exterior mantle and on the outside of the necks.

Form type P. S: XL.

Bust-like figurines with broad breast, high neck and human head. The breast part has on the outside a regular or irregular spiniform border (done prior to firing and painting) and is slightly arched. Mouth and eyes are represented by holes made in the wall. There are ears, which are pierced with holes and are scalloped along the edges. The eyebrows marked on the head that was purchased in Paris (Pl. XIX, fig. 9) are turned outwards like ears and have a slightly scalloped edge. On the chin of this figurine there is also an ear with a hole in the centre and a scalloped edge (beard?). The noses of these figurines are either with or without holes. On the forehead there are or have been two horn-like excrescences with holes in the top to receive ornaments long since destroyed (Pl. XIX, fig. 9). The backs of the heads of the figurines are invariably highly arched. On the one bought in Paris a plastically fashioned snake coils round the throat and neck. The snake's head rests above the brow of the figurine between the horns (Pl. XIX, fig. 9[1]). The mouth is open. The head shown in Pl. XIX, fig. 7, may possibly indicate stronger, masculine forms, whereas the head shown in Pl. XIX, fig. 8, has more graceful, womanly features. The figurine purchased in Paris likewise has obviously masculine features.

This form type may possibly have served as a lid to vessesl used rarely in funeral practice. Some of the low-necked sepulchral urns may possibly have been covered with an inverted bowl, on the bottom of which these bust-like lids were placed[2]). In that case the large pot formed the body of the set of pottery, the inverted bowl with the brim of the figurine its breast, and the figurine itself its neck and head. This however is merely a hypothesis[3]). In Pan Shan pottery these figurines represents a very peculiar feature. In their use they manifestly resemble the "canopic vases" (see Bibl. 27) known to European and Egyptian archæology, though I hardly think that these Chinese clay heads exhibit any direct connection with Europe's similar sepulchral practice. The same practice has arisen out of similar conditions. The whole of the exterior upper surface of the figurines is painted, whereas the under-surface of the brim of the breast is unpainted.

[1]) In this case I find the connection with the snake worship of India and Persia, and thence with that of Crete and the Mediterranean seaboard, to be admissible, though not very certain. The most obvious resemblance is with the snake-ornamented pottery of Susa, though here too a parallelism is conceivable. It is indeed over this very zone of Eurasia that the very poisonous snakes are mainly distributed, and this fact may have caused the same reaction in people in different areas — a reaction strong enough to inspire them to introduce snake motifs into their art. See Toscanne: »Ètudes sur le serpent» (Bibl. 89) and A. Salmony: »Eine neolitische Menschendarstellung in China», (Bibl. 74). In the last-mentioned work the influence that is only demonstrable in the Pan Shan pottery as regards this isolated vessel is certainly exaggerated.

[2]) In the material at my disposal there is a bowl (K. 5613) with a very irregular excision at the bottom, deeply lobate along the edge. It was found in the course of excavations at Ssu Wa Shan in Ti Tao Hsien, Kansu, though it probably does not belong to the true Ssu Wa Shan pottery but has no doubt come from a dwelling-site of the Yang Shao period existing in Ssu Wa Shan. Whether it has any connection with figurines of a kind similar to those described above cannot be determined with any certainty.

[3]) A short paper on American and Eastern Asiatic calabash vessels with lids fashioned in the shape of a star is published in »Comparative Ethnographical Studies» (Bibl. 54). Whether in the lids described above we are dealing with copies of such calabashes is extremely uncertain, seeing that otherwise the Pan Shan pottery can show nothing whatsoever in the way of imitations of calabash vessels.

THE PRODUCTION, FORM AND ORNAMENTATION OF THE UNPAINTED PAN SHAN SEPULCHRAL VESSELS.

The Pan Shan pottery is divided into two entirely different groups. In the one group, the production of which has just been discussed, there is a rich ornamentation painted on the vessels prior to firing; in the other group there is no painting, but usually instead a plastic ornamentation. This may take the form of a positive decoration raised in relief above the rest of the surface of the vessel, or else — in rare cases — of a negative decoration incised in the surface. In one or two cases the vessel is entirely without ornamentation (Pl. XX, fig. 6).

The plastically decorated, unpainted vessels are in a considerable minority among the Pan Shan sepulchral ware. Out of twelve vessels in the large grave in Pien Chia Kou only four are unpainted and plastically decorated. In the grave containing skeleton No. 3 found at P'ai Tzu P'ing only one out of four pots is unpainted. The grave with skeleton No. 2 from the same place contains only one vessel, which however is of the unpainted type. Among the purchased pottery from the same period and culture there are proportionately very few unpainted vessels.

The unpainted vessels are made of a clay that is of inferior quality and contains a strong admixture of sand. Even after firing there are often grains of quartz, felspar and mica still clearly visible on the surfaces of the vessels, making them rough and uneven. Grains of lime are also frequently found mixed in the clay.

The method of building up the vessels has been the same as that applied to the painted pottery: the walls are fashioned of rings. Definite evidence of this is provided by the inner surface of vessel K. 5808, in which the joints are still visible. Slighter traces of this method of construction are found in vessels K. 5442 and K. 5454.

The bottoms, too, are fashioned in the same way as those of the painted Pan Shan sepulchral vessels. Vessel K. 5455 has no outer bottom-slab, so that one can see how the hole in the nethermost ring has been filled by a lump of clay being pressed into it. In the other pots this primary bottom is covered with an outer slab of clay. This slab and its method of attachment can be studied in vessel K. 5808, in which it has become loose round the edges and partially fallen off.

In pots K. 5457 and K. 5442 (Pl. XXXIII, figs. 1 and 2) there are visible on the underside of the bottoms impressions made by aid of plaited mats. In pot K. 5457 the structure of the plaited mat is particularly clear and the details very distinct. The details on the bottom of the larger vessel K. 5442 are not so distinct. These impressions show that — after the outer bottom-slab had been affixed — the vessel was pressed against a plaited mat. The object of this has apparently been to decorate the bottom or possibly to increase its superficial area. In the latter case the vessels might be judged to be cooking utensils. Similar matting impressions on the bottom of vessels have also been found in other Neolithic cultures. They have sometimes been assumed to be the marks of matting used in fashioning the vessels in order to enable them to be more easily rotated[1]). The mats would thus have represented the most primitive form of potter's wheel. In our present case this interpretation can probably be rejected, seeing that, as shown above, the bottom slabs were manifestly the last details in the process of manufacturing the vessels, with the possible exception of the plastic decoration.

The outer surfaces of the vessels are very rough (Pl. XXXIII, fig. 3), owing partly to the granulation of the ware and partly to the fact that the surfaces have not been polished in any way. It looks rather as if the surfaces were purposely made as rough as possible. Sometimes they have actually been roughened up [K. 5448[2])], and in certain cases (K. 5457, Pl. XXI, fig. 8) the surfaces of the mantle show distinct impressions of rough textile material. Superficially, vessels of this kind have points of contact with that form of Eastern European pottery that Pelsi and others have called "textile pottery". But in that case the textile impression is the result of the vessels' having been fashioned in a mould covered inside with textile material. As pointed out above, in the Pan Shan pottery the ring method has been employed in constructing the vessels, so that textile material is unnecessary for their manufacture. We must look for other means of explaining the textile impression. In a vessel such as K. 5457 (Pl. XXI, fig. 8) they undoubtedly lend a decorative touch to the mug, and, as a matter of fact, they are only applied between bands that form true horizontal borders. It is perhaps best to interpret them here as purely ornamental. But this vessel, and also a number of others of these unpainted and plastically decorated vessels belonging to the Pan Shan pottery, show more or less distinct sootmarks on their surfaces, marks that could hardly be the result of the primary firing.

---

[1]) See Ebert: Reallexikon: vol. 13, p. 330. (Bibl. 42).
[2]) Textile material has been used at least partially for roughing up this vessel.

They have presumably been used as cooking-vessels[1]). The roughing up of the surfaces may then perhaps be interpreted as a technical manoeuvre to increase the amount of area in contact with the fire.

The methods of attaching handles and ears have been the same as in the case of the painted vessels.

The unpainted vessels have not been given the same careful firing as the painted vessels. The ware is usually of a dirty grey colour, occasionally greyish red or covered with red spots. In the fracture it is granulated and flakey, but generally of a fairly homogeneous colour. The temperature of the firing kiln probably ranged around 800° C.

The vessels are as a rule of small size. One or two of those at my disposal are about as large as the medium-sized painted vessels (K. 5796, Pl. XX, fig. 12). The rest are among the smallest found in the sepulchral pottery from Pan Shan. Only some few form types occur amongst the vessels so far discovered. They conform to the painted Pan Shan forms in their flat bottoms and in their lack of a foot, but their necks are less pronounced and shorter than the latter's. Their bodies are as a rule of very primitive shape. Two form types have no neck at all[2]).

The most common *first form type*, P. S. r: I, consists of a small pot or vase with a more or less bulb-shaped body, low neck and wide mouth, and a flat bottom (Pl. XX, fig. 7). Its neck has two horizontal collars or brims set close together or else separated from one another by a small space. These brims are scalloped along the edges, as also are the ornamental bands. The ring formed between the lower brim and the upper rim of the body is sometimes slightly "godrooned" (Pl. XXI, fig. 1), a decorative invention which thus has very old traditions in China. Vessels of this first type usually have scalloped ears with or without holes. The ears are set in pairs, one ear on each side of the neck, either tangentially (Pl. XXI, fig. 2) or radially (Pl. XXI, fig. 1). In both cases they enrich the vessels' vertical silhouettes, but, in the latter case in particular, thanks to the way of placing these ears, the rhythmical scalloping that forms the decoration has been effected with extraordinary consistency and taste.

In a *second form type*, P. S. r: II, the ears have been replaced by miniature handles (Pl. XX, fig. 9), four in number. The silhouette is the same as in the foregoing type, the neck is similar with a godrooned ring and the mouth is of the same relative breadth. Of the handles, one is placed on either side of the neck and two diametrically opposite to one another at the widest part of the vessel. They are

---
[1]) These vessels would in that case have been used in the home, or else in the course of the funeral ceremonies, before being deposited in the grave.
[2]) These form types are illustrated on page 31.

very small and consist of semicircles with halfmoon-shaped eyelets. They are all set in the same sectional plane. It is hardly likely that either ears or miniature handles had any true function; here they are rather to be considered as relics of functional details that have gradually come to serve a purely decorative purpose.

A closely related *third form type*, P. S. r: III (Pl. XX, fig. 12), consists of simpler vessels than those described above. The body is bulb-shaped or somewhat more spherical (Pl. XX. fig. 11). The neck is low and has a straight, simple silhouette; it either has parallel sides or else widens out towards the top. Sometimes there are horizontal ridge-handles at the widest part of the body, sometimes there are none. The bottom is flat. This type of vessel is related to types P. S: XXIII, P. S: XXV and P. S: XXVI, though it is still more primitive.

A cup or mug occurring fairly frequently among this kind of pottery constitutes a *fourth form type*, P. S. r: IV (Pl. XXI, figs. 8 and 11). Its body is bulb-shaped or more or less spherical. Its neck is low, the mouth is wide and the bottom flat. It thus agrees in many features with the type first described. Its most characteristic feature is a stout grip, fixed partly to the upper rim of the neck and partly to the upper portion of the body. The uppermost part of the handle usually projects somewhat above the plane of the neck. The cup is very closely related to the painted types of pottery P. S: XIV and P. S: XVI.

A *fifth form type*, P. S. r: V (Pl. XX, fig. 10), possesses a higher body and very low neck, wide mouth and, on either side of the latter, a strong ring-handle placed radially in relation to the mouth. These handles project considerably above the plane of the mouth. The vessel has a body shaped like an inverted pear, truncated through neck and bottom. This type of vessel is most closely allied to the form group P. S: XXXI — P. S: XXXIII (the X-Y-Z group) and is most closely akin to its type P. S: XXXIII (the Z vessel), though it is more primitive in shape and has not the latter's graceful silhouette.

A *sixth form type*, P. S. r: VI (Pl. XXXVIII, fig. 6), consists of a high, fairly large bowl, which widens out considerably upwards from the comparatively small, flat bottom. There are no handles. There is no suggestion of a neck at the very wide mouth. Below the edge of the bowl there is on one side a fairly strong, short spout pointing obliquely upwards. The vessel has to some extent its counterpart among the painted forms (related to the painted vessels of type P. S: XXXIV) but is more primitive.

A *seventh form type*, P. S. r: VII (Pl. XX, fig. 6), has a small body of a distinctly bulbous shape, is without a neck, has a medium-sized mouth and beneath the rim a short spout pointing obliquely upwards, and about a quarter turn to the left of it a ring-shaped handle attached partly to the rim and partly to the upper portion of the body. This form type is the most complicated of the whole group. It is related even more closely than the sixth form type to the type of painted vessels P. S: XXXIV. Features common to both this form of vessel and the painted vessels of the type P. S: XXXIV are the spout and the handle. Here too we probably have a drinking-vessel, which with the left hand grasping the handle and the right hand supporting it from underneath was raised with the spout towards the mouth.

It is fairly clearly seen from the above summary of the forms that they represent a uniform group. Compared with the painted types of vessels they are on the whole more primitive. The seventh type is however an exception, as it is closely akin to the complicated type P. S: XXXIV belonging to the painted series.

The positive plastic decoration consists of applied bands of clay (Pl. XXXIII, fig. 3), usually scalloped or godrooned (Pl. XX, fig. 12). Occasionally these bands are accompanied or replaced by impressions or striae on the surface of the vessel. The bands may be narrow or broad, quite thick or thin. Very thick and broad bands occur as a decoration on the mantle of one vessel (Pl. XXI, fig. 11) found in the large grave at Pien Chia Kou. The commonest forms of decorative bands are narrow, graceful and thin.

The decorative effect of the bands raised in relief is twofold. Firstly, they liven up the surface of the vessel by reason of the rhythm applied to them, and secondly they are decorative as being true pattern-forming features, so that the flat, broad surfaces between them form part of the ornamentation by the effect of contrast.

By means of impressions made in the moist clay with nails, fingers or implements specially made for the purpose, presumably of bone or wood, the bands have been provided with incised and raised portions, valleys and ridges, which as a rule are placed at right angles to the band's longitudinal direction, giving a rhythmical effect. This rhythm sometimes moves in slow waves, sometimes it is extremely rapid, in which case it describes a closely scalloped line. In this latter case, which is the most common, the raised scalloped band, owing to the shadow effect, forms a dark line, which shows up against the lighter background of the vessel's surface. The light does not so easily reach the deepened, scalloped parts of the band. This fact does not however eliminate the rhythmical effect of the band; rather it strengthens the decorative impression and often lends it the character of a dark, limiting contour-line on the lighter intermediate basal surfaces. I shall revert to this point when I discuss the painted pottery.

The scallop-pattern — as pointed out above — is continued also on the rings surrounding the neck and on the ears. In the latter the scalloped edge is thus an expression of the general style of the vessel. Scalloped ears also occur however in the painted pottery. In the latter they do not represent an element in the general style but are undoubtedly transferred from the unpainted pottery with its scalloped decorative element representing a more primitive ceramic form, which was no doubt cultivated even prior to the invention or importation of the technique of painting.

The plastic decoration is further extended to the handles, which in some vessels are divided into lobes (Pl. XXI, fig. 9) and in others consist of three bands joined together and twisted into spirals (Pl. XXI, figs. 10—11). Other vessels, again, have bands laid in relief on the handles, these bands having a wavy or scalloped surface. The plastic ornamentation on the handles has also been applied in rare cases to the painted types of pottery, though this is very exceptional. Lobed handles are found in some painted vessels (e. g. Pl. XX, fig. 1). Handles decorated with wavy bands occur, for instance, in the painted vessels shown in Pl. IX, fig. 9 and Pl. XIX, fig. 11.

The ornamentation on the unpainted pottery appears mostly on the upper half of the surface of the body. It is however quite common for the basal surface to be decorated with one or more — in the latter case sparsely applied — horizontal bands (Pl. XX, figs. 7 and 9).

The ornamentation is of a primitive geometrical character, as is necessitated by the material, the applied clay bands. The following elements occur: 1. Single horizontal bands (Pl. XX, fig. 12). 2. Zigzag bands, either one or two or several under one another and accompanied at top and bottom by triangular elements filling up the spaces (Pl. XX, fig. 7). 3. Straight bands running obliquely from bottom to top. (Pl. XXI, fig. 9). 4. Semicircles and arcs (Pl. XXI, figs. 3 and 5).

As I have already pointed out, in isolated cases there are no decorative elements at all. A vessel such as K. 5608 (Pl. XX, fig. 6), bought in Kao Lan Hsien, Kao Ying, although quite undecorated, must nevertheless be referred to this group. Its ware is of just the same quality as that in the other vessels belonging to the group. Its peculiar form is fully identical with the sixth form type described above. As a matter of fact, another vessel of the same form type and with scalloped ornamentation was purchased at the same place (K. 5607, Pl. XXI, fig. 3).

The decorative elements are combined on the vessels to form more or less complicated patterns. Several vessels often have the same pattern and their ornamentation is then said to belong to the same pattern-scheme.

The simplest pattern-scheme consists of merely horizontal elements, which in a primitive manner divide up the vessel and delimit parts that possess a different function in the vessel's tectonics. In a vessel such as K. 5796 (Pl. XX, fig. 12) the ornamentation consists of horizontal bands, an upper band representing the border-line between neck and body, and a lower band slightly below the widest part of the body. If we compare these bands with the horizontal elements of the painted pottery, the upper band takes the place of the painted pottery's stereotyped, red marginal band between neck and body, and the lower band takes the place of the nether border. The godrooned element in the lower band is replaced by the frequently occurring undulating pattern on the lower painted border. The portion between the upper and the lower horizontal bands, although undecorated, has the same position as the decorated mantle surface in painted pottery. This portion becomes a truly decorated mantle surface in vessel K. 5457 (Pl. XXI, fig. 8), in which it is decorated between the two horizontal elements with textile impressions. In this case the part beneath the lower horizontal band has no textile impressions and represents an undecorated basal surface. Vessels of the third and fourth form types belong to this group.

In a second group of vessels a pattern scheme emerges as a result of these upper and lower, so to speak constructive, horizontal bands' being connected with one another by vertical or slanting straight bands. In vessel K. 5455 (Pl. XXI, fig. 9) we find both the marginal band between neck and body and the marginal band between mantle and basal surface. They are here joined together by a series of bands running, approximately equidistant from one another, from the upper band in a slightly slanting direction until they reach the lower band. Vessel K. 5442 (Pl. XXXVIII, fig. 6) is without a neck. In this case therefore the upper horizontal band forms a natural finishing-off fillet round the mouth. The zone beneath the band that represents the lower border is here decorated with two additional horizontal bands. The band round the mouth and the band that forms the border are in this case connected by four groups of double bands running at an angle of 45° between the horizontal bands. Vessel K. 5454 (Pl. XX, fig. 10) shows a close affinity to the vessels just discussed, but here the ornamentation is reduced in one or two respects. The very short neck has no marginal band, and only in exceptional cases do the vertical bands, which occur in this vessel also, reach down to the lower horizontal band. A very degenerate style of decoration, which is clearly derived from the same form-scheme, is seen in vessel K. 5788 (Pl. XXI, fig. 11). The ornamentation within the group looks as if it had been copied from a string suspension arrangement. It is possible, however, that this is only an apparent resemblance. In disproof of such an imitation there is the fact that the connecting bands do not run vertically but obliquely between the horizontal bands. In reality, of course, the strings are bound to follow the supporting, vertical lines of force. On the other hand, this change may be a later artistic development of an imitational style. Considering the paucity of the vessels at our disposal here we can hardly arrive at any definite conclusion on this question of style and imitation. Vessels of the fourth, fifth and sixth form types belong to this group.

The third and largest decorative group among these unpainted vessels has the surface of the mantle ornamented with horizontal zigzag bands and angular bands to fill out the spaces. In a vessel such as K. 5460 (Pl. XXI, fig. 1) the upper horizontal marginal band occurs as a fillet round the neck, while the mantle and the basal surface are separated by a lower, narrow border. Between these horizontal elements extends the rich characteristic pattern, the zigzag pattern, which entirely fills up the surface of the mantle with a motif in double rhythms (the more expansive rhythm of the zigzag band and the band's own scalloped rhythm). This pattern lends the group its richest and most consistent design, particularly in the case of those vessels that have scalloped fillets round the neck and scalloped, radially placed ears (Pl. XXI, fig. 1). In most of the vessels belonging to the group the basal surfaces are also decorated. In this case the decoration consists of one or two narrow horizontal bands (Pl. XX, fig. 9). The ornamentation in vessel K. 5790 (Pl. XXI, fig. 10) may be regarded as a reduced decoration of this decorative type. There the lower border is absent, while the upper horizontal marginal band has been shifted a little lower down and doubled. Here we find only one single zigzag line, which hangs down from the lower horizontal band. By the fact of these two changes in the pattern the logic in this style is entirely eliminated. A similar change and reduction in pattern occur in vessel K. 5448 (Pl. XXI, fig. 7), but here the logic is saved by a fresh device. At the lower points of the zigzag band the vessel is decorated with elevated nipples. Here the zigzag band thus runs between the upper horizontal band and its nipple-like attachments to the vessel. In this case too one cannot fail to imagine a resemblance to a device for suspending the vessel. The most pronounced case of reduced pattern is that of vessel K. 5791 (Pl. XX, fig. 11), in which all horizontal bands are eliminated and there remains of the pattern only a couple of zigzag bands round the vessel just below the neck. The majority of this group's vessels belong to the first form type. An occasional vessel belongs to the second and third, and one or two to the fourth, form type. The most consistent and the richest pattern is found in vessels of the first form type, the pattern being reduced in vessels belonging to the other form types.

We find a fourth pattern-scheme in a couple of vessels of the seventh form type

(Pl. XXI, figs. 3 and 5). These vessels have no necks and no upper horizontal band. On the other hand, there is a marginal band between mantle and basal surface. To this band are attached four or five series of "arc bands" pointing upwards. Each series consists of two or three more or less concentric arcs. In this case also we can hardly resist the impression that we have here an imitation of a suspension arrangement.

Incised lines that have no connection whatsoever with the imposed bands have been found so far in the case of only one vessel of this unpainted ceramic group — K. 5442 (Pl. XXXVIII, fig. 6). On the inside of the somewhat straight under-part of the wall of the vessel there are five groups of lines incised in the surface. Each group consists of five or six vertical lines. The ornamentation and technique here seem to be extremely primitive.

Summary: The decoration in this ceramic group is manifestly derived from the technique which is here consistently applied. The ornamentation has been done with the aid of the simplest implements, the fingers and a pointed stick being the principal agents. There are no traces whatever of any comb-like instrument, dies of any kind, or strings used in ornamenting the vessel or intended for making impressions. On the other hand, textile impressions have been used for decorative, and possibly other, purposes (see above). Further, the pottery lacks all trace of coloured decoration. Nor is there a single vessel showing traces of chalk or other filling substance pressed in between the scallops. As a consequence of this simple technique the pattern-scheme has acquired an extremely unelaborated geometrical character, in which the tectonics of the vessel is frequently emphasized by simple means. It is possible that string suspension devices have to a certain extent been prototypal of some of these geometrical pattern-schemes, though it is not at all certain. In view of the facts just mentioned one has the impression that this group of pottery is a ceramic survival. Its origin must date back to the technique existing prior to the invention of colouring, and during the Pan Shan period it was to all appearances undergoing a process of degeneration. The vessels of this ceramic type found in the large sepulchre at Pien Chia Kou (Pl. XX, figs. 11 and 12, Pl. XXI, figs. 10 and 11), belonging to a fairly wide range of pattern-schemes, all show manifest symptoms of degeneration, and this harmonizes well with the fact that the painted pottery found in the grave is of a very advanced type with rudimentary ears, black colour predominating in the pattern, and large spiral nuclei. On the other hand, as we have shown in another part of this work, the style appropriated in connection with this pottery was copied during the early Pan Shan period on the painted vessels.

A plastic decoration of a similar character to that described above occurs in another unpainted ceramic group found in Kansu, which Professor Andersson refers to the Ch'i Chia period, dating it prior to the Pan Shan pottery.

This decorated pottery is made of similar ware and was presumably fired at the same temperature as the unpainted pottery described above. It employs, on the one hand, positive relief, and, on the other, incised negative patterns. The incised patterns are far more common and predominant than in the unpainted Pan Shan sepulchral pottery. Basket impressions are common, true string impressions apparently occur, and combs of various kinds have been constantly used in decorating these vessels. As only potsherds have been found, the elements are more conspicuous than the pattern as a whole. These elements give indications, inter alia, of simple horizontal bands, zigzag lines, undulating lines, horizontal zones with oblique lines, that is to say, primitive elements, which recur in the Pan Shan sepulchral pottery, both painted and unpainted. The pattern scheme however contains other elements that do not recur in these latter kinds of pottery, and which, from a decorative point of view, are often of a fairly carefully thought-out design. The plastic technique is far more advanced and variable than that in the unpainted group of the Pan Shan pottery. Here we find plastic decoration on the neck, the patterns being more complicated than in the unpainted Pan Shan vessels. Plastically decorated "annular handles" with a rich ornamentation are common. The semicircular ears pierced with holes and scalloped along the edges, which we find in the Pan Shan sepulchral pottery, do not occur on the necks of plastically decorated Ch'i Chia vessels, their place being taken by fairly long ridgelike protuberances with deeply scalloped edges and slightly wavy contours. These decorative protuberances have no holes. In this pottery they manifestly have a tendency to become more and more extended[1]).

A certain connection between the plastically decorated group of Ch'i Chia pottery and the unpainted sepulchral pottery of the Pan Shan period exists primarily in the spirit that is common to them both. But there are hardly any direct points of contact between the two ceramic groups.

---

[1]) This tendency for the ears to be converted into long decorative horizontal bands with scalloped or wavy edges is known also in Egyptian pottery and is dealt with by Petrie.

THE PAINTING AND ORNAMENTATION OF THE PAN SHAN FUNERAL URNS.

As a rule two colours were used in the decoration of the painted funeral urns of the Pan Shan area in Kansu. These colours show up against the naked ware, which serves as a light background. Of these colours the one is black and the other red.

The red colour, however, comprises an entire group of chromatic tones, the variegations of which are due to differences in the quality of the pottery clays used, to the thickness of the pigment, the duration of the firing and possibly also to the purity and quality of the colouring matter. Crude or sharp red tones do not occur. Notwithstanding the subdued scale, however, the red colour may sometimes acquire a deep tone. It readily tends towards brown, turns to a subdued blood- or liver-red, and very occasionally to dark orange. Purple, violet and blue tones are more common than yellow and brown ones. The quality of the red in a whole group of vessels has been so poor that the contrast between the red and the black after firing is scarcely discernible, or only discernible upon comparison with other vessels. The fact that a pattern scheme occurs also in other vessels enables one to realize that the contrast was actually aimed at but was not successfully achieved.

The black colour seems also to have been sometimes of poor quality, thin, greyish, brownish, and even to have had an almost reddish tone. Generally, however, it is an extremely good deep black, which is further enhanced by the lustre afforded by the glossy nature of the underlying surface. It is not often that a vessel is found to possess a colour of poor quality as well as at the same time other primitive characteristics. The quality of the colour has hardly anything to do with the age of the vessels, that is to say with the position they take in relative chronology. The colour of early vessels may be of good quality, while late graves may contain vessels with colours of inferior quality and with highly undifferentiated colouring (for instance, the large grave found at Pien Chia Kou).

In the ornamentation of the painted vessels from the Pan Shan area there has been evolved a distinct scheme of décor, the principles of which have usually been faithfully followed in different localities and by different potters. Cases occur in which the potter has worked on freer lines, but such individualism is extremely rare. The individual readily subordinates himself to the tribe, and if ever he has been tempted to show some independence in his creative art, manifestly he has soon mended his ways, so to speak. On the other hand, a slow but sure change in differences of detail, making up an evolutionary chain, is distinctly discernible. In the Pan Shan pottery, however, this evolution takes place on a broad front and is due, in my opinion, to a common change of conception and taste and not to personal inventions of a revolutionizing nature.

First a few words on the various parts of the vessels. They generally consist of two separate parts, the body and the neck or collar. Vessels belonging to the form types P. S: I—III, VII—IX, XI, XII, XX, XXXIV and XXXV have no neck or collar, as is indicated in the chapter dealing with the form types. The majority of the Pan Shan vessels have an unpainted base. This unpainted lower portion usually comprises about one-third of the surface of the body. In rare cases the unpainted lower part may comprise as much as one-half or more of the body's height. In the bowl- or dish-like types P. S: I, II, III, XXXIV and XXXV, the greater part or the whole of the exterior, usually more or less convex, surface is unpainted, but in that case their interior, often somewhat concave, surfaces are painted instead (see e. g. K. 5206, K. 5205, K. 5738, K. 5218, K. 5495, Pl. XIX, figs. 1—6, K. 5526, Pl. IX, fig. 3 and K. 5220, Pl. XIV, fig. 2). In a number of mugs and vases of types P. S: XV and P. S: XVII, the painting is generally continued right down to the bottom, or else only a narrow band above it is left unpainted (K. 5623, Pl. XIX, fig. 12 and K. 5257, Pl. XVII, fig. 8).

The surface in which the ornamentation is given freest play in these vessels is the broad band between the base and the neck — that part which is called the mantle.

Towards the bottom the décor starts with a single, delimiting, black band, or as frequently with a combination of two or three elements, they too usually executed in black. These lower delimiting elements may conveniently be termed *"the lower border"*, irrespective of whether it is composed of one or more elements. The most commonly employed elements in these borders are straight, horizontal bands and wavy bands. In a few cases primitive spiral bands serve as a border. Wavy bands with short, closely recurrent, waves, lightly, though at the same time somewhat nonchalantly, drawn, are one of the most typical features of the Pan Shan style and moreover differentiate it fairly distinctly from the Ma Chang style. In the Ma Chang borders the waves move at a slower rhythm and in curves that are longer and not so deep, and moreover the bands are more precisely, though more stiffly, drawn.

Towards the top the décor of the body ends in a band painted on the light-coloured original ground, and which at the same time marks the lower boundary of the decoration on the neck. In the funeral vessels the border-line between the décor of the neck and that of the body consists, with but a very few exceptions, of a red band. These exceptions belong partly to family 16 with a bottle or vase pattern (notably a number of smaller vessels) and partly to some other sporadic vessels (K. 5029, Pl. IV, fig. 8, K. 5116, Pl. XXXIV, fig. 6 and K. 5623, Pl. XIX, fig. 12). The red band may be shifted slightly up towards the neck or down towards the body, it may be narrow or broad, in the latter case extending partly on to the surface of the body and partly on to the neck; nevertheless, it remains a regular, conventional element.

Below the red border-band on the body itself there usually runs a black horizontal band, which has fine or coarse dentations and with these verges upon the red border-band. Exceptions occur in cases where the broad black band is resolved into several black lines without dentations. Sometimes the dentated band is duplicated, while occasionally two black dentated bands surround an entire red band. Whether one or several, these bands serve as *the upper border of the body.*

These two elements, the red demarcating band between neck and body and the upper border, together represent one of the most peculiar features of the Pan Shan sepulchral pottery.

A very rich and variegated external neck ornamentation is found on the high-necked Pan Shan vessels, which of course lend themselves particularly well to that purpose. The decoration covers the entire surface from the border-line on the body to the upper edge of the neck.

Vessels with a low collar either possess or do not possess decorations on the outside of the neck. In the former case the décor is of a somewhat modest and sparse character. Obviously the more or less strongly excurvated and low collar widening towards the top offers a poor external surface, though an interior surface that is all the more suitable, for decorative purposes.

On the inside of the low collars and occasionally also on the higher necks, which are less suited to the purpose, there is a décor, the most common element of which is what we might conveniently call a garland decoration. On the low-collared vessels it extends as a rule over the whole of the visible interior surface. In the high-necked vessels it consists merely of an inner wreath around the mouth.

As the external and internal decoration of the neck will be dealt with in discussing the separate décor families, we shall not enter into details here. However, in the Pan Shan style the neck ornamentation represents a very important decorative complex. Moreover, this decoration renders it possible to date the vessels relatively to one another.

In his writings on Chinese Late Neolithic pottery[1]) Professor J. G. Andersson has pointed out and strongly emphasized the significance of one characteristic feature of the Pan Shan style in Kansu, viz. *the fact that the black-and-red figured vessels, all of which are apparently funeral vessels, have a constantly recurring element in their ornamentation: Red bands or loops are surrounded by black bands or surfaces provided with a serrated or dentated edge, which together with the uncovered ground visible between the dentations verge upon the red bands. Professor Andersson calls this the "death pattern", because it occurs only on funeral vessels.* It is not a pattern in the ordinary sense of the word but a decorative system, used in quite orthodox fashion in a great many different patterns. Even in a body of material comprising several hundred pots the exceptions from this system are extremely few (K. 5109, Pl. VII, fig. 3, K. 5225, K. 5023 and K. 5029, Pl. IV, figs. 3, 4 and 8; see also figs. 208 and 210). In one or two of these cases the structure of the ornamentation proper forms an obstacle in the way of the use of the death pattern (K. 5225 and K. 5029). In another case it is a question of a surprisingly primitive product, executed apparently by a child or by a person quite inexperienced in the potter's art (K 5023). A small group of bowls painted on their inner surface is without dentated ornamentation.

The system being based on two colours, it is obviously impossible for it to be transferred to the household vessels from the same culture, which are ornamented in black only. But even in these vessels there is occasionally found a symmetrically arranged dentated border on black surfaces, and this is undoubtedly traceable to the death pattern.

The question, then, arises: where do the dentated edges originate? Their decorative function is undoubtedly to render important contour-lines in the ornamentation more distinct and vivid. This is illustrated if we compare the uninteresting and inartistic manner in which red and black bands often merge into or border upon one

---

[1]) (See Bibl. 5—10).

another in the Ma Chang pottery and the facile and elegant way in which they run side by side with one another in the Pan Shan style. In the latter the effect is achieved by the very rapid rhythm arising out of the alternation of the black-painted dentations and the light, unpainted fields between them. A similar rhythmical effect is however observable also on the unpainted ware. As already described above, geometrical fields are here bounded by more or less narrow, imposed bands of clay. In these bands as rapid a rhythm is attained as in the dentated ornamentation of the death pattern by means of sunken transverse lines made with finger-nails or some implement, whereby these clay bands acquire a plastic profile. The higher ridges on which the light falls alternate with the deep grooves lying in shadow. **I therefore consider the dentated ornamentation to be a painted imitation of the plastic rhythm, occurring also at earlier epochs, in the bands imposed on the unpainted but ornamented vessels.**

The black bands are replaced by a number of finer black lines without dentations in certain groups belonging to different families, whereby a more delicate and often more elegant effect is achieved. This replacement of the black bands by fine lines is apparently a secondary and later feature. One might perhaps see in this feature an imitation of the incised lines that occur, combined with imposed bands in relief, both in the Ch'i Chia pottery and, less frequently, in the unpainted Pan Shan pottery.

Black-and-red patterned families.

Even a cursory study of the ornamentation in the Pan Shan pottery clearly reveals how this pottery is naturally divisible into a number of décor families. It may of course be asked whether anything is to be gained by such a classification, but it is just as easy to answer: Not only is something, but everything is to be gained hereby. Without this grouping — somewhat near-sighted though it may be — any true analysis of the style and any attempt at correlative dating would be entirely lacking in corroboration. Any effective penetration into the details of the patterns, as also any understanding of the evolution of the style as a whole, is inconceivable without this extremely arduous and detailed work of classification. All comparison with other styles becomes at bottom fruitless unless some order has been created by such labour and a deep insight gained into the intricate maze of patterns.

The décor within the different families varies from vessel to vessel, but the common features are so striking to the eye that it is only after a closer study that the individual variations are observed.

Décor family 1 P.

The family of the horizontal bands.

The simplest decoration of all consists of horizontal bands of approximately similar breadth running round the vessel. In this design the bands are as a rule alternately black and red, being separated from one another by an extremely narrow unpainted line. The black bands are dentated on either side or else on one side only. The red bands are here, as in subsequent families, entire. Vessels possessing this extremely simple décor sometimes have a distinct air of pure classicism about them (K. 5001, Pl. XXXIV, fig. 2). The uniformity of the decoration is sometimes broken by an unexpected vertical line (K. 5007, Pl. II, fig. 3), or by the black bands' being of greater breadth (K. 5208, Pl. I, fig. 7), or by their being reduplicated.

A further change in the general scheme is effected by the broad black bands' being resolved into a whole series of 5—6 narrow black lines. These are without dentation, but above them there succeeds a slightly broader black dentated line (Pl. II, figs. 6—7). Actually, then, these pots possess three horizontal elements of different artistic value: the red bands, the narrow black lines and the broader black dentated bands.

Occasionally we find that the lower border is lacking in these vessels (K. 5025, Pl. I, figs. 9 and K. 5496 Pl. I, fig. 4), but in that case it is replaced by the pattern itself. Otherwise the border consists of any one of the following: 1. a wavy line, 2. two wavy lines, 3. lowest down, a straight horizontal line and above it one or two wavy lines, 4. a primitive spiral and beneath it a black horizontal band (K. 5011, K. 5015 and K. 5014, Pl. II, figs. 5—7), or 5. narrow leaflike spaces[1]) (K. 5024, Pl. XXXIV, fig. 3).

In the high-necked vessels the band ornamentation typical of the family frequently continues up to the upper edge of the neck (K. 5011, Pl. II, fig. 5). In other cases the neck is decorated with: A. series of short angles pointing to the left, bounded alternately by red and black horizontal bands (fig. 52 and K. 5496, Pl. I, fig. 4), B. angles, red bands and trellis pattern made up of single black lines (fig. 53), C. lowest down, a band with high triangular teeth, above that a red band and above that again a trellis pattern (fig. 54), D. below, a serrated band and above that a zigzag

---

[1]) Such "spaces" are usually denoted here by the expression "in ground colour", i. e. the colour of the ware.

pattern bounded by red lines (fig. 55). In the short-necked vessels it is not very often that one finds any external decorative elements: e. g. a black rim or a black trellis-work pattern. On the other hand, there is generally an interior decoration, varying between the following types:

Fig. 52. 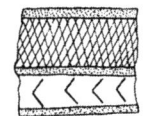 Fig. 53. 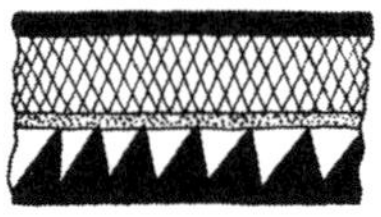 Fig. 54.  Fig. 55.

1. garland pattern (fig. 56) or 2. black semicircles or segments (fig. 57). 3. lines with more or less distinct angular spaces (fig. 58), at best emphasized by red V-and ∧-shaped ornamentations (fig. 59). The actual rim of the neck often (K. 5009, Pl. II, fig. 2) has a row of vertical lines in black (fig. 60), i. e. a rhythm in black and ground colour. Occasionally this lineation may change to a dentated rim at the upper edge of the interior pattern of the neck. In pot K. 5024 (Pl. XXXIV, fig. 3) towards the top of the interior surface runs a garland pattern, and above that a red band as well as a dentated rim as just described (fig. 61).

Fig. 56. Fig. 57.

Fig. 58.  Fig. 59. 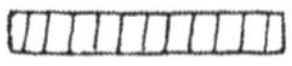 Fig. 60.

There is very closely akin to this décor family a series of vessels having alternating black and red bands, which in this case however are not horizontal (K. 5205, Pl. XIX, fig. 2, K. 5738, Pl. XIX, figs. 3—4, K. 5103, Pl. XX, figs. 4—5 and K. 5505, Pl. XX, fig. 1).

The family comprises vessels of the following types: P. S. IV, V, VII, VIII, IX, XI, XII, XVIII, XX, XXIII, XXIV and XXXI.

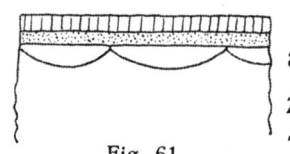

Fig. 61.

As a whole the family must for various reasons be regarded as an early Pan Shan group. Pots with broad and narrow horizontal belts occur even among the unpainted Pan Shan pottery. The simple pattern, the abundance of vessels of primitive manufacture and very irregular shape, the clumsily made spiral borders, the occurrence of vessels without a border, the red colour in some border elements, which occurs only in this and in the third family — a feature indicating that there is still a lack of fixed rules governing the decorative scheme —, the often simple neck ornamentation, the fact that all high-necked vessels of this décor family have very large and well-developed ears with holes (with one exception), and the profile of the necks straight and vertical — all this is evidence that the décor family as a whole is to be regarded as an early group in Pan Shan pottery.

Among the vessels possessing a spiral border can be set up a practically complete type series from the most primitive to more advanced spiral-patterned borders (see Pl. II). It should be observed here that the spiral-patterned border extends over an ever-increasing area as the decorative design is developed and refined. Vessels such as K. 5014 (Pl. II, fig. 7) and K. 5116 (Pl. XXXIV, fig. 6), which close the series, form a transition to the true spiral décor family. It might be asked by way of hypothesis whether it may not be this very form series that indicates the process of evolution from this group to the later spiral group. One circumstance that militates against this hypothesis is that the spiral of the border has been painted black, whereas the spiral group invariably has the true spiral line painted red. However, the colour has actually changed in the vessel showing the most advanced design; for there is a red spiral in the border in K. 5116 (Pl. XXXIV, fig. 6). A circumstance that supports the hypothesis is that the number of spiral nuclei in the more advanced borders is 4, as in the spiral décor group. Vessels with the most primitive spiral borders have more than four spiral nuclei.

Among the vessels of this family the group decorated with a more complicated design — three horizontal elements (red bands, dentated black bands, and narrow black lines) is a later invention; the group thus comprises more advanced vessels. The most recent vessel in the family as a whole is probably the vessel K. 5024 (Pl. XXXIV, fig. 3), in which the ground-colour leaf-border, the low, but nevertheless externally decorated, collar with its trellis-pattern, and, in particular, the direct transition into one another of the red and the black colour, and finally the rare assurance and elegance of the shape, are strong indications of a close affinity to the Ma Chang pottery.

Of the vessels belonging to this family the great majority come from Ning Ting Hsien, one or two from Nien Po Hsien and Ti Tao Hsien and also from Yü Chung Hsien, the last-named belonging to the complex type with three decorative elements. The remainder of this type were bought at Lanchow. The vessels with primitive spiral borders are from the same localities. Of those that came from Ning Ting Hsien the distribution is about equally apportioned between the localities Wa Kuan Tsui, Pan Shan and Pien Chia Kou. A very few vessels have come from Wang Chia Kou.

Décor family 2P.

The zigzag pattern.

This family, which in the material at my disposal consists of only a few vessels (8 in all), is characterized by a décor composed of alternate red and black zigzag bands running round the vessel with interjacent angle-bands (see Pl. III and IV). Occasionally the black bands are replaced by narrow black lines (K. 5225, Pl. IV, fig. 3). Otherwise the bands are dentated either along the top or along the bottom or else along both top and bottom. On the upper and lower sides of the zigzag band there are formed close to the borders triangular fields, filled with black, or both black and red angle-bands. As a rule the space within these angle-bands forms an unpainted triangular field. This may be cleft (fig. 62 and K. 5022, Pl. III, fig. 1) or filled with a trellis pattern[1]).

Fig. 62.

The bottom borders consist of a simple black band, and below it are often one or two black wavy lines.

The low-necked vessels have a garland décor on the interior surfaces of the neck. There is one case of a low-necked vessel having the exterior part of the neck decorated, the ornamentation consisting of a band of left-pointing angle-lines.

The high-necked vessels have a décor on the exterior surfaces of the neck: 1. trellis pattern (fig. 63), 2. trellis pattern on the upper half of the neck, a dentated

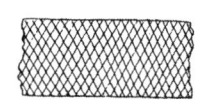

Fig. 63. 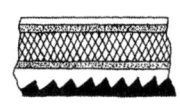   Fig. 64.    Fig. 65.

pattern on the lower half, both executed in black (fig. 64). The halves are separated by a red band. Or 3, a high dentated pattern on the upper half, angle-lines below (fig. 65).

The actual rim of the neck is often decorated with a rhythm in black and ground colour: black lines alternating with an unpainted surface.

The vessels belong to the form types P. S: XVIII, XXIII and XXIV. Only one

---

[1]) K. 5026 (Pl. III, fig. 3). The pot has a trellis pattern in every other triangular field, but as the number of fields is odd, there come at the end two trellis-patterned fields lying adjacent to one another. The painter of the pot has not been far-sighted enough to solve the problem in an artistic manner. Similar irregularities owing to lack of foresight occur not infrequently among the earlier décor families, but not in the more highly advanced vessels.

vessel belongs to the high-necked type P. S: XXIV. Its ears are of medium size without holes and with a scalloped edge. The rest of the high-necked vessels belong to type P. S: XVIII. Vessel K. 5018 (Pl. III, fig. 4) has a plastic decoration ending in a wavy line, just below the rim of the neck on the exterior surface.

The zigzag pattern characteristic of this family is manifestly borrowed from the unpainted but plastically ornamented group of Pan Shan sepulchral vessels (Pl. XX and XXI), which in one form-group (the first) exclusively, and also in other form-groups, has this pattern as an important element, here apparently inherited from earlier epochs. From the decorative point of view, the similarity between the vessels with an unpainted zigzag ornamentation and those belonging to this family is very striking. There is a family parallel to this within the black-patterned dwelling-site group.

The great majority of the vessels would appear to belong to the first of the three divisions of the Pan Shan sepulchral pottery, the early Pan Shan, though not, generally speaking, to the most primitive of its creations. Nevertheless, vessel K. 5023 (Pl. IV, fig. 4), from Ti Tao Hsien, Yang Chia Yai, is extremely primitive. It is highly unskilled work, as regards both painting and design.

Most of the pots belonging to this group are from Ning Ting Hsien, Wa Kuan Tsui, one or two are from Ning Ting Hsien, Pan Shan, and one pot from Ti Tao Hsien.

Décor family 3 P.

The semi-circular pattern.

There is a small décor family in which the area between the upper and lower borders on the body has four groups of alternately black and red semi-circular or curved bands. In most vessels the curves rest on the lower border, occasionally they hang from the upper border (K. 5110, Pl. IV, fig. 5). The innermost part close to the border often forms a small unpainted half-moon. The bands are usually alternately dentated, black or entire, red, but in one or two cases the dentated black bands in the pattern are replaced by a number of thin black lines (K. 5028, K. 5272 and K. 5029, Pl. IV, figs. 6—8) on the analogy of the similar change observed in certain vessels in the first and second décor families.

The lower border may consist of: 1. a plain horizontal band without dentations, and below it a red and a black wavy band, 2. one black wavy band between two black, entire bands, 3. four black wavy bands between two black, entire bands, 4. one red, entire band between two black bands with a dentated edge opposite the red band. The lower borders thus vary considerably in design and, like some of the lower borders in the first family, may also contain red elements.

It is but seldom that there is any ornamentation on the outside of the necks of low-necked vessels belonging to the family (K. 5110, Pl. IV, fig. 5, with a row of crosses). The high-necked vessels have an external neck decoration of the usual types: simple, high, rough dentations or dentations combined with a black trellis band bounded by red lines (fig 66). The actual rim of the neck may be either with or without a rhythmic line executed in black. One of the low-necked vessels possesses large ears with holes (K. 5113, Pl. III, fig. 6) and a dentated edge — a unique case. One of the high-necked vessels (K. 5029, Pl. IV, fig. 8) has no ears; in another high-necked vessel the neck is partly broken off, so that it is impossible to determine whether such decoration was present or not.

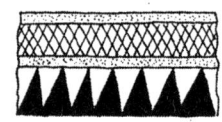

Fig. 66.

Everything seems to indicate that this décor family is one of the earlier families, but the number of vessels is too small to afford us any definite idea on the point. It is quite clearly allied to a group of unpainted Pan Shan vessels ornamented with imposed curved bands. For the rest, the family is apparently divisible into two groups of different values even in point of time: an earlier group with alternating black dentated and red entire bands (in which also the ears are strongly developed), and a later group with black bands replaced by fine lines (in this group ears are usually wanting). The vessels belong to the form types P. S: XXIII, XXIV, XXVIII, and XXIX. They come from Ning Ting Hsien or were bought at Lanchow.

Décor family 4P.

The garland pattern.

Closely allied to the foregoing décor family is a very small group of vessels with alternating black and red bands curved to resemble garlands decorating the surface between the lower and upper borders. The upper edges of the black bands are dentated. In one place they give way to a series of narrower, undentated black lines (K. 5752, Pl. XXXIV, fig. 5) on the analogy of the preceding families. The drawing of the garlands may be done carelessly (K. 5012, Pl. III, fig. 7) or with some precision (K. 5114, Pl. III, fig. 8.)

The lower border consists of a plain black band or a similar band and a black wavy band running above it.

The upper border has in one case a double black dentated band (K. 5752, Pl. XXXIV, fig. 5); otherwise it consists of a plain black band with the upper edge dentated.

Low-necked vessels have no exterior but an interior decoration on the neck (garland pattern). The rim of the neck is with or without a line. The one high-necked vessel belonging to the group is given the usual neck décor consisting of high, thick dentations beneath, and above that a trelliswork band executed in black (Pl. III, fig. 8).

The high-necked vessel has small, scalloped ears with holes.

Owing to the small body of material, the position of this family among the other Pan Shan vessels is difficult to determine. It could hardly belong to the very earliest, nor yet to the more advanced groups. It should be noted that this family likewise possesses examples of the more advanced décor with black bands giving way to finer lines. Only types P. S: XXIII and XXIV are represented in the family.

The vessels were found partly in Ning Ting Hsien and partly in Nien Po Hsien. Some were bought at Lanchow.

Décor family 5P.

The ladder pattern.

One of the smallest families in Pan Shan ware. It is characterized by a décor between the borders consisting of patterns each running obliquely from bottom to top in horizontal rows and resembling primitive ladders (fig. 67). The rows, which may be two or three in number, either succeed one another quite close together or are separated by two bands, the lower one black and dentated, and the upper one red and entire.

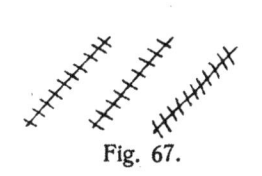

Fig. 67.

In the first case the ladders in adjacent rows lean in opposite directions.

The lower border consists of a plain horizontal band above and a wavy band below.

The neck (in the known cases somewhat low and without ears) is decorated on the outside with wavy bands or crosses and on the inside with garland bands.

The family gives the impression of being primitive. The vessels are of considerable breadth and clumsy in shape. The collars have primitive patterns. Only two vessels of this décor type are known, both being of form type P. S: XXIII, the one purchased at Lanchow (K. 5127, Pl. V, fig. 2), the other at Ning Ting Hsien, Wa Kuan Tsui (K. 5019, Pl. V, fig. 3[1]).

The primitive ladder pattern occurs as a decorative detail partly on the neck and partly on the mantle in a couple of urns belonging to the closely related families.

---
[1]) The latter demonstrates the family's close kinship with family 1P.

Décor family 6P.

Pattern: irregularly scattered circles.

The predominant decoration of this and the two succeeding families consists of plain or concentrically grouped circles; indeed, these families might perhaps be combined into one, but the difference in the manner of distribution of the circle decoration is so significant that its division into three different décor families seems to be fully justified. In the most primitive of these families, the sixth, the circles are irregularly scattered over the otherwise unpainted surface between the borders. They are composed of an outer black circle dentated inwards, and a red circle placed concentrically within it. The innermost space consists of an unpainted surface. Here and there between the circles there are sets of short or long, straight bands, placed either vertically or obliquely, and consisting of two outer black bands, dentated inwards, and between them a red band. In the material at my disposal the family consists of one single pot of form type P. S: XXIII (K. 5040, Pl. XXXV, fig. 1). The lower border is formed by a single straight horizontal band. The pot is low-necked and without ears, and the neck is ornamented (garland) on the interior only. Both the pot and the painting seem to be extremely primitive. The décor is possibly one of the earliest representatives of the Pan Shan pottery. The pot comes from Ning Ting Hsien, Pan Shan.

Décor family 7P.

Pattern: a horizontal row of small circles.

A small group of pots have as their main ornamentation a horizontal row of small circles. The circles may be plain (K. 5489, Pl. VI, fig. 1) or composed of several concentric elements. In the latter case the circles are alternately black dentated and red entire (K. 5125, Pl. V, fig. 6). The central space consists of an unpainted surface. The plain circles are in the row alternately black and red. Along the borders triangular fields may occur, bounded by black or red lines.

The lower border consists of a straight band above and a wavy band below, both black. Interior neck decoration: garland bands. The vessels are of form type P. S: XXIII. A relatively primitive family. Place of origin: Ning Ting Hsien.

Décor family 8P.

Pattern: five large circles.

This likewise represents a small family. There are only three vessels of this type in the material I have had at my disposal. It is characteristic of the group that the zone between the upper and the lower borders is occupied by 5 large circles, consisting of concentric elements, alternating red entire and black dentated circular bands. The centre forms a large circular surface decorated in various ways. Along the borders at top and bottom arise triangular fields between the circles. The innermost circle is red. Outside this red circumference there may be one or three circles. The black circles are broader and more substantial than the red ones. The inner surface is decorated with a trellis pattern (K. 5129 and 5052, Pl. V, figs. 4—5) or with horizontal rows of lines (K. 5053, Pl. V, figs. 7—8). The triangular fields along the borders are undecorated or decorated 1. with curved angle-lines alternately black dentated and red entire, 2. with an X-like ornament (fig. 68).

Fig. 68.

The lower border consists of a straight line above and a wavy line below. The exterior neck decoration varies: 1. spiral pattern combined with dentated bands (K. 5053, Pl. V, fig. 7), 2. a row of crosses (K. 5052, Pl. V, fig. 5), 3. combined rows of angles pointing to the left and above them two dentated bands (K. 5129, Pl. V, fig. 4). Interior neck decoration: garland bands (K. 5052) or a ring of double horizontal lines (K. 5053, Pl. V, fig. 8). The vessels belong only to form type P. S: XXIV, though sometimes with the height of the collars slightly modified (K. 5052 and K. 5053). K. 5052 has no ears. In vessel K. 5053 there are ears scalloped along the edge but otherwise rudimentary, and they are moreover pierced with rudimentary holes. The family has representatives belonging to a fairly early phase of the Pan Shan pottery (early Pan Shan), e. g. K. 5129, though also vessels of a more advanced type, e. g. K. 5053 (middle Pan Shan). The vessels come from Ning Ting Hsien or were bought at Lanchow.

Décor family 9P.

Lancet or elliptical pattern.

A group of pots in which the area between the upper and lower borders is decorated with a vertically placed, oblong lancet-shaped or elliptically shield-like ornamentation, more or less complicated, is perhaps worth classifying as one décor family, though it turns out to be hardly as uniform as the preceding families.

The characteristic ornamentation of the pattern consists either of simple red bands (K. 5100, Pl. VI, fig. 3) or of curved lines placed beside one another in alternate black and red. The interior border-line is red. The areas between the characteristic ornaments are filled with arcs curtailed at top and bottom (K. 5054, Pl. VII, fig. 1) or with horizontal dentated bands with thick dentations pointing upwards (K. 5100, Pl. VI, fig. 3). In this family the black elements have a distinct tendency to greater breadth than the red elements (K. 5042, Pl. VII, fig. 2 and K. 5054, Pl. VII, fig. 1). The lancet-like or elliptical surfaces are sometimes divided by a red vertical line separating two halfmoon-shaped surfaces, which are surrounded by black bands dentated on the outside (K. 5017, Pl. XXXV, fig. 2). These lancet-like or elliptical surfaces are in other cases filled with a trellis pattern (K. 5100, Pl. VI, fig. 3 and K. 5054, Pl. VII. fig. 1), with crosses (one figure in K. 5017, Pl. XXXV, fig. 2[1]) or with primitive chessboard pattern (K. 5042, Pl. VII, fig. 2).

The lower border consists of 1. a plain horizontal line, 2. the same, and under it a wavy line, 3. two plain horizontal lines and between them two wavy bands so arranged that a wave-crest of the lower band and a wave-trough of the upper band meet one another (K. 5054, Pl. VII, fig. 1) — a form of border that has not occurred in any of the foregoing pattern families and clearly represents an advanced feature.

Only pots of the form types P. S: XXIII, XXIV, and XXV belong to this family.

Fig. 69. The collars are decorated either on both sides or on the inner side only. Exterior collar décor: 1. trellis pattern or 2. crosslike ornamentation (fig. 69). Interior collar décor with considerable variation: 1. a thick dentated edge and above it a red band, 2. a ring of garland-like lines, 3. a wedge pattern with red wedges pointing alternately upwards and downwards and separated by black bands of angles. The edge of the collar has black lines in horizontal or vertical rows.

The family appears to comprise vessels both of a more primitive and of a somewhat more advanced type. The most highly advanced vessel is apparently K. 5054 (Pl. VII, fig. 1), with its complicated and artistically well-balanced pattern and its rather fine border. Nor would the urn K. 5100 (Pl. VI, fig. 3) appear to belong to the earlier forms of the Pan Shan pottery.

The majority of the vessels were bought at Lanchow. Some are from Ning Ting Hsien, Wa Kuan Tsui.

---

[1]) Not visible in Pl. XXXV, fig. 2.

Décor family 10P.

Square or check pattern.

One of the largest décor families amongst the Pan Shan pottery is the square- or check-patterned family. It contains various decorative solutions, which are nevertheless easily capable of being combined into one common, closely related group. Of all the families this is one of the most geometrical, but a close study of the pattern shows that straight lines, at any rate in the case of the main design — the square or check pattern — are preferably avoided. This primary pattern is most conspicuous in an urn K. 5031 (Pl. XXXVI, fig. 1), in which the supplementary décor hardly intrudes at all upon the main décor. Between the upper and lower borders are drawn two series of coloured (red or blue) curved bands: one series runs from the top right down towards the left, and another series runs from the top left down towards the right. The curved bands join at the bottom in a distinct angular point or a rounded corner and form, two and two together, a heart- or shield-shaped surface bounded at the top by the upper border. The boundary-lines of these surfaces cross one another, thus forming across the surface of the vessel a network of squares standing on their points. The net has variously one or more meshes (squares) obliquely above one another. The most clearly defined and most beautiful is perhaps the décor in those cases in which there occurs only one square in the vertical direction (K. 5030, Pl. VII, fig. 6 and Pl. XXXVI, fig. 3, also K. 5036, Pl. VIII, fig. 4), but even where two or more squares have been painted above one another this décor may have a good and rich effect (K. 5117, Pl. VIII, fig. 7 and K. 5045, Pl. IX, fig. 8).

As indicated above, the framework of the main design is painted red or blue. In isolated cases the framework may occur alone (K. 5031, Pl. XXXVI, fig. 1). In this urn triangular fields are formed at the top, decorated with a primitive ladder pattern (cf. family 5P), and at the bottom triangular fields (fig. 70) filled with parallel lines.

Fig. 70.

Generally, however, the framework design is accompanied by black bands dentated on the side nearest the framework and forming, inwards, squares and, outwards with the borders, triangular fields, or else combining with one another to form zigzag lines running round the vessel (K. 5038, Pl. VIII, fig. 6) or garland wreaths (K. 5035, Pl. VIII, fig. 2). The triangular fields may leave the ground unpainted (K. 5030, Pl. VII, fig. 6 and Pl. XXXVI, fig. 3) or else be filled with angle-lines in alternate black and red (K. 5085, Pl. XXXVI, fig. 2) or only black, with crosses (K. 5753, Pl. VIII, fig. 1) or with unpainted leaflike ornamentation (K. 5036, Pl. VIII, fig. 4). The triangular fields are also sometimes bisected by a black line (K. 5753, Pl. VIII, fig. 1 above) or filled with a row of slanting black lines. The inner surfaces of the squares may in rare cases be unpainted, but they are generally occupied by a more or less complicated pattern. The most common pattern used for filling up these spaces is a cross, which combined with the black frame forms a window-like ornamentation with four panes. These small panes may be empty or else they are occupied by a large black dot (fig. 71).

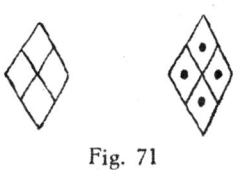

Fig. 71

In other cases the large squares forming the main design are decorated 1. with a fine-meshed trellis pattern in black (K. 5115, Pl. VII, fig 4), or 2. with parallel black lines which in adjacent squares point in opposite directions (K. 5031, Pl. XXXVI, fig. 1), or 3. with small squares filled with similar lines (K. 5030, Pl. VII, fig. 6 and Pl. XXXVI, fig. 3), or 4. with squares lying within one another in alternate colours (K. 5041, Pl. VII, fig. 5), or finally, 5. with a black square in which are lancet-like leaves in the ground colour (K. 5037, Pl. VIII, fig. 3). In a number of the vessels the surfaces of the black elements have a tendency to acquire predominance by reason of their considerable breadth.

The lower border consists of 1. a single straight band or 2. and 3. a straight band, and below it *one*, or in rare cases *two*, wavy bands, or 4. a wavy band between two straight ones. All the elements of the border are black.

The following form types belong to this family: P. S: II, III, XVIII, XXIII — XXV, XXX and XXXIII, i. e. both high- and low-necked pots, jugs and bowls. The family embraces abundant transitional forms between very low- and wide-necked and very high- and narrow-necked vessels.

The low-necked vessels are here frequently painted on the outside of the necks as well. The exterior neck patterns vary considerably: 1. a plain wavy line (K. 5030, Pl. XXXVI, fig. 3), 2. a crown-like dentated band with high, thick dentations (K. 5117, Pl. VIII, fig. 7), 3. alternate broad, red bands and series of narrow, black lines (K. 5034, Pl. VII, fig. 8), 4. trellis pattern, 5. one row of crosses, 6. one row (fig. 72 and Pl. VII, fig. 4) of open double crosses, 7. on the upper half a trellis pattern and on the lower half a high black dentated line with thick dentations, 8. the upper half with a trellis pattern, the lower half with angles having their vertex towards the left. There are a number of other combinations as well. There is an interior pattern on the necks of the low-necked vessels, the most common

Fig. 72.

pattern being the garland in a more or less complicated design. Black dentated bands alternating with red lines also occur (K. 5030, Pl. VII, fig. 6 and Pl. XXXVI, fig. 3, also K. 5035, Pl. VIII, fig. 2[1]). The rim of the neck in the lower-necked vessels is often ornamented with black lines.

The high-necked vessels have ears. In two isolated cases the ears are fully developed although not large (K. 5034, Pl. VII, fig. 8 and K. 5031, Pl. XXXVI, fig. 1). The great majority of the pots in the family have average-sized ears with holes. An occasional vessel has small ears without holes (K. 5036, Pl. VIII, fig. 4). The vessel that came from the large grave at Pien Chia Kou (Pot 5), like all the other high-necked and very advanced pots in this grave, has quite rudimentary ears.

The family has representatives of all ages. Hardly any of the vessels, however, are quite primitive, though possibly vessel K. 5124 (Pl. VIII, fig. 5) is. Vessels of this family have been found in the large Pien Chia Kou grave, which was filled with only advanced vessels (Pot 5, K. 5106). The urns in which the black parts show a tendency to predominate (K. 5035, Pl. VIII, fig. 2 and K. 5036, Pl. VIII, fig. 4) apparently belong to the more advanced vessels in the group (late Pan Shan). Moreover, they also possess a more highly developed supplementary décor, e. g. an elegant garland wreath above the lower border in K. 5035, unpainted leaf pattern in K. 5036[2]), lancet-shaped leaves in K. 5037 (Pl. VIII, fig. 3) and chessboard pattern in K. 5078 (Pl. IX, fig. 6).

Some of the vessels were bought at Lanchow. The remainder are from Wa Kuan Tsui, Pan Shan, Wang Chia Kou and Pien Chia Kou, all in Ning Ting Hsien.

This family, such as it is now represented in the collection of the material at my disposal, appears more than other families to be a geographically limited décor family.

Décor family 11 P.

Spiral pattern.

The main group of Pan Shan sepulchral pottery undoubtedly comprises the very large family with a spiral pattern. In discussing the first décor family we pointed

---

[1]) Vessel K. 5101 (Pl. VI, fig. 7) has as its interior neck décor a dentated band, curtailed at diametrically opposite places, with thick dentations. At the points of curtailment this pattern changes to a series of horizontal lines. In other respects also this urn is very originally and irregularly decorated (the squared pattern is replaced on two opposite sides by triangles and other more irregular geometrical figures). The décor certainly cannot have been executed by an experienced professional potter; it looks rather as if it were an experiment in painting done by an unpractised hand. The earless collar of most unusual shape and medium height likewise seems to indicate that the vessel is a highly individual experiment.

[2]) Vessel K. 5036 (Pl. VIII, fig. 4). The shape of the neck and the decoration on the neck are of a markedly advanced character, identically similar to the advanced form and décor of the neck in the spiral group.

out that there occurred among its vessels a group with a border in which the spiral pattern was the chief element. We also showed how in this group it was possible to follow the gradual evolution of the spiral element to a more elegant and positive design and an ever more and more dominant position. Eventually the spiral border covered more than half of the decorated surface. It was tentatively assumed that this implied a transition to an entirely predominant spiral decoration, which extended over the whole area between the upper and lower borders. In support of this hypothesis as to the origin of the spiral décor the fact may perhaps not unjustifiably be adduced that some of the primitive vessels belonging to the spiral family still have necks decorated with the first décor family's simple alternation between red plain and black dentated lines (K. 5214, Pl. XXXIV, fig. 7). In that case the neck pattern is to be regarded as a last rudiment of the earlier decorative method.

The spiral decoration on the Pan Shan pottery consists, in the case of every vessel, of a single true spiral line. It is coloured (usually red) and runs in more or less sweeping and rotatory curves in a horizontal direction round the mantle of the vessel, thus forming four spiral centres or spiral nuclei (K. 5143, Pl. XI, fig. 6). Amongst the large quantity of vessels of this type I know of only four exceptions to this rule, two urns with five spiral nuclei and two with six (K. 5156, K. 5214, Pl. XXXIV, fig. 7 and K. 5146, Pl. X, fig. 7, also K. 5149, Pl. X, fig. 5).

The choice of four nuclei is no doubt due partly to its being easier to draw two spiral nuclei on either side of the mantle (the vessel is of course divided into two equal sides by the handles), and partly to the symmetry's being more easily appreciated by the eye. Finally, the design may perhaps have been influenced by the fact that, when only four spiral nuclei are painted on the vessel, the space between the spiral line and the border, as viewed from above, appears as a more or less regular square. This no doubt likewise facilitated the painting of the spiral, and besides contributed towards making the vessel attractive to the eye (K. 5155, Pl. X, fig. 4 and Pl. XXXVII, fig. 1, also K. 5143, Pl. XI, figs. 6—7).

The spiral nucleus, which consists of a coloured circular band representing the periphery and inside it a round disc of the unpainted ground surface, may be either small or large, and the ground surface with or without decoration.

The area between the spiral line proper and the lower border is filled with alternate black bands, usually dentated at the top only, and red, entire bands. One or two, and occasionally three, of these bands run round the pot, following the curve and direction of the spiral band and forming rhythmic though unsymmetrical wavy lines. Beneath these bands are formed four likewise unsymmetrical triangular fields filled with the tops of similar lines truncated through the border (unsymmetrical angular bands consisting of curved lines). Here too the bands are alternately red and black. The handles are usually set in two of these triangular fields.

At the top, above the spiral line proper, the latter is followed by one or more bands painted alternately black and red. As indicated above, where there are four spiral nuclei, they form a more or less regular square round the neck (K. 5155, Pl. X, fig. 4). The corners of these squares are frequently extended into a kind of starfish-like arms (fig. 73 and K. 5143, Pl. XI, fig. 6) in consequence of their being compelled to follow the line of the spiral. The upper border and the neck here truncate irregular triangular fields. These consist, in the inmost area, of unpainted surfaces or sometimes have a simple decoration, such as a trellis pattern.

Fig. 73.

In spite of the large number of vessels, there are only a few form types that belong to this family, viz. P. S: XXI, XXIII — XXV, XXVIII, and XXXIII. The main bulk of them consists of types A and B, the large funeral urns, this pattern being very well suited to their broad mantles. In the material at my disposal there are about as many high-necked as low-necked vessels.

The low-necked vessels all have the same interior décor on the neck, the garland pattern, which has thus, as far as regards these vessels and that part of them, supplanted other decorative forms. The exterior surface of the neck of the low-necked vessels is usually undecorated, but when it has a decoration it is of an extremely simple character, a wavy band, a series of crosses, open double crosses or angles pointing left.

The high-necked vessels likewise have sometimes an interior decoration on their necks, but then it is generally an extremely simplified garland band along the rim. Their exterior neck decoration certainly varies somewhat, but it is limited to a small number of decorative forms: 1. spiral bands, 2. trellis pattern, 3. and 4. one or two bands with long points or dentations, 5. on the lower half a band with points or dentations, on the upper half a trellis pattern bounded by red bands (in rare cases the trellis-work is replaced by series of slanting simple lines K. 5143, Pl. XI, fig. 7), 6. a row of squares standing on one of their points.

The lower border is also very simple. It is most commonly the plain horizontal band. The following combination is also common: above, a plain horizontal band, below, a wavy band. Occasionally one finds a wavy band between two plain horizontal bands or a plain horizontal band above two wavy bands.

Thus, in spite of its quantitative superiority, the family is strikingly sparing, one might almost say poor, in the decorative forms supplementing the main design. Indeed, in this case, where the principal design is so mobile and so rich, a sense of artistic economy requires that the subsidiary décor shall not attract too much attention. Some modification of this circumstance appears in the course of time, when the spiral element, though it is certainly emphasized at first, is nevertheless jeopardized and is subsequently brought to a state of dissolution. Then the spiral nuclei and their decoration come more and more to dominate the pattern. But of this more anon.

Likewise *in point of time* this family would appear to assume a central position in Pan Shan pottery. *A number of details all point with one accord to the fact that the family has undergone a distinct evolutionary process during the lifetime of the pattern.* The details whose modification in the course of time can thus be distinctly followed are: the increasingly attractive assurance and elegance characterizing the drawing, the evolution of the spiral nuclei from small, undecorated circular surfaces to large dominating circular fields with a strong, expressive decoration, the equivalence of the red and the black lines during earlier phases and the subsequent increasing breadth of the black bands at the same time as the red lines become narrower and narrower (the pot acquires an increasingly black appearance), and finally the decreasing size and significance of the ears (they either disappear entirely or else turn to small rudiments lacking scalloped edges, true ear-shape and holes). The narrowing down of the red lines, moreover, paves the way for the dissolution of the spiral décor. On an urn such as the late K. 5287 (Pl. XII, fig. 7), the effect of the spiral has been partly conjured away by the pattern between the spiral nuclei passing into a form resembling a cornucopia open at the top. This almost entirely neutralizes the sense of one ornament's immediate and rhythmical continuation into the next. Moreover, the overwhelmingly large spiral nuclei and their ornamentation with its complex chequer design, and the purely rudimentary presence of a death-pattern, indicate that this urn is a transitional form passing into the Ma Chang culture, in which the spiral has disappeared, though the four spiral nuclei are still preserved as large circles filled with patterns of various kinds (K. 5303, Pl. XXII, fig. 5, K. 5304, Pl. XXIV, fig. 1).

The earlier vessels belonging to the spiral family should perhaps include, inter alia, K. 5150, 5177, 5179, and 5163 (Pl. X, figs. 1—3 and 6). Somewhat more highly developed vessels are: K. 5155, 5149, and 5146 (Pl. X, figs. 4—5, 7 and Pl. XXXVII, fig. 1). To the intermediate forms in the group should be referred: K. 5184, 5158, 5164, 5151, 5159, and 5143 (Pl. XI, figs. 1—7). Undoubtedly still more advanced: K. 5140 (Pl. XII, fig. 1). To the most recent and most highly developed in the family belong: K. 5153, 5142, 5141, 5171, 5144 (Pl. XII, figs. 2—6), K. 5193, and 5968 (Pl. XII, figs. 8—9), forming a special group, which I shall discuss later on. The above-mentioned K. 5287 (Pl. XII, fig. 7) should perhaps be placed last in the series.

A number of the pots belonging to the spiral family show a simplification of the elements that belong to the design and supplement the spiral, in that the triangular spaces have been left empty. This provides a small special group within the family. To this belong: Pl. XI, fig. 8 and Pl. XXXVII, fig. 2. In the two last-mentioned vessels, which are otherwise noteworthy for their exquisite colouring, the décor possesses some remarkable details. The spiral nuclei lie somewhat low down on the mantle. Tangentially, or nearly tangentially, to these spiral nuclei, however, there projects a straight tongue (consisting of three bands, one red bounded by two black, which are dentated inwards) from the lower border slanting upwards to the right and ending at the lower black band of the spiral curve (the spiral itself likewise consists here of a red line bounded by two black bands dentated only inwards). Between the spiral and the lower border, this tongue separates two fields, which in the two urns in question are decorated with similar crosses with flat bars across the ends — the heraldic "cross potent" (fig. 74)

Fig. 74.

In one of these urns the upper spaces are likewise decorated with similar crosses. Both the details of the pattern and the individual tone of the colour indicate a very close kinship between the urns. Were they not purchased in different localities, though in the same province, Ning Ting Hsien, one would be tempted to attribute them all to the same artist's hand. The peculiar oblique line running from the bottom left-hand side of the border upwards to the right may possibly recur in one of the very finest members of the spiral family (K. 5144, Pl. XII, fig. 6), which is otherwise not associated with this special little group which I have been discussing here. This special group might be considered to belong to the main bulk of the spiral family.

Another special group is formed by the most advanced vessels (Pl. XII, figs. 2—9). The ensemble has a very black appearance, owing, as has been pointed out above, to the disproportion between the broad black bands and the narrow red lines. All of them possess extremely rudimentary ears. The vessels' silhouettes are elegant, obviously executed by a sure hand. The collars are all attractively curved and are of slightly more than medium height. All are painted on the outside with one of the three following patterns: 1. two rough lines of points, one above the other, 2. wide-meshed trellis pattern, 3. the one half a black band with high points, the other half a band with trellis-work, and between these a narrow red band. The spiral nuclei, which are large, sometimes very large (K. 5144, Pl. XII, fig. 6), are occupied by a vigorously designed decoration, which, as we have pointed out already, jeopardizes the existence of the main décor. The surface of the spiral nuclei is ornamented with one of the following patterns: 1. squares (Pl. XII fig. 2) 2. large crosses and in the angles formed thereby more or less crescent-shaped lines, Pl. XII, figs. 4—5 and fig. 75), 3. chessboard pattern (K. 5193, 5968, Pl. XII, figs. 8—9, K. 5465, Pl. XXXVII, fig. 4), 4. large black squares (fig. 76), or trellised squares surrounded by oblong, unfilled rectangles and in the corners small black squares (K. 5144, 5287, Pl. XII, figs. 6—7) and 5. serpentine lines alternating with rows of thin black lines (fig. 77 and K. 5142, Pl. XII, fig. 3).

Fig. 75.

Fig. 76.

Fig. 77.

The pattern on the vessel K. 5221 stands entirely by itself within this family. The vessel is a bowl of form type P. S: XXI, the outside being unpainted, while the fairly broad upper edge and the whole of the inside are painted. It has a collar that is internally fairly high, decorated with a close-meshed trellis pattern made up of black lines. On the upper rim is an unpainted zigzag band on a black ground. The pattern may possibly be interpreted as two rows of dentations, the points of which face one another. On the bottom of the vessel is seen a red triangle with the points on the sides of the vessel. Outside this red triangle there are two black ones, and outside these again one red triangle, which has a spiral nucleus to the left of the points. It is best to regard the design as a somewhat lifeless spiral pattern. At the top above the spiral triangle are irregular triangular filling-up lines in black (4) and red (1). It is noteworthy that the black lines are not dentated. The absence of dentations is however fairly common in the case of internal painted surfaces with a black and red décor.

Very closely related to the family just described, or connected with it by obvious transitional forms, is a small number of vessels that are from several aspects singularly interesting. They possess either a truncated spiral décor comprising four spiral nuclei placed together in pairs, or else a décor consisting of four circles, likewise in pairs. From the fact of the spiral's being truncated in two places or the circles' being set close to one another in pairs there arise two fresh spaces for decoration of a more individual form. It seems that, either out of boredom at the persistent recurrence of the spiral ornamentation or out of a desire for fresh combinations, one or more artists have endeavoured with a gentle hand to break away from the spiral running round the vessel. In vessel K. 5152 (Pl. XIII, fig. 1) the real spiral line is terminated by the actual spiral nucleus, while the subjacent lines are, after an elegant break in the curve, curtailed by reaching the lower border. The intermediate space is filled up with a tree-like pattern (fig. 78) painted in red. The space between the branches is filled with black, in which the ground surface is partially left unpainted to form narrow, lancet-like leaves. These black surfaces border on the red lines with dentated edges. The artistic effect of the interruption of the spiral is striking. There is something animal-like and draconic in the spiral, particularly the right-hand one. The aspect from one side with the handle and the ear in the median line gives an almost heraldic effect. This effect is still further enhanced in vessel K. 5145 (Pl. XIII, fig. 2), partly by the spiral nuclei, which in the former were empty, being now adorned with a large black dot in the centre, and partly by the fact that the red tree is replaced by a figure which ends at the top in a head-like circle. From the middle of the figure project arms, which appear to grasp the spirals. Below the arms the line representing the trunk continues down to the lower border without any further branches. Three of the spiral's accompanying lines bend upwards around the spiral nucleus, three or four curve downwards towards the border. Beside the figure there are seen, in the upper part, two unpainted leaf-like areas containing a red line, and at the lower end of the figure, close to its base, there are two broken lines, rising upwards and outwards, likewise in red, but accompanied by black dentated bands. In the centre of the head is a large black dot. It would perhaps be over-bold already at this stage to interpret the figure on this urn as an anthropomorphic design; but its animal character has become intensified. So far however the legs are wanting. The action of the figure is clear — grasping the adjacent spiral nuclei. In vessel K. 5068 (Pl. XIII, fig. 3) the spirals on the mantle have disappeared, being replaced by four large circles placed close to one another in pairs and consisting of a number of alternate red and black concentric elements. In the centre is a large black dot, as in the foregoing vessel. This urn is in distinct contact with the spiral family through the neck ornamentation — a spiral pattern with four spiral nuclei. Between the two pairs of circles are placed figures, which now have heads, arms and legs. There is no trace of any leaf ornament. Unfortunately both the figures are badly worn. There are however distinct traces of there having been a black dot in the centre of the circular head. The anthropomorphic

character of the figure is here more clearly seen than in the previous case, although the drawing is very primitive[1]). There can be no doubt as to the affinity of this figure with the previous cases and its development out of them. Inter alia, the legs have evolved out of the original curves of the spiral's accompanying lines. The lines in K. 5145 (Pl. XIII, fig. 2), now isolated from the spiral, have in the urn K. 5068 (Pl. XIII, fig. 3) been entirely joine on to the figure.

This pattern is all the more remarkable for the fact that it is manifestly a transition to the Ma Chang style. For in the latter we find the same pattern, although in such a new guise that one must have first seen the Pan Shan urns before being able to understand the Ma Chang pattern. The affinity between the two patterns will perhaps be most clearly realized if one compares the vessels just mentioned (especially K. 5068) from the Pan Shan pottery with the Ma Chang urn K. 5312 (Pl. XXXIX, fig. 6). The shape of the urn is very much like the urn-form of the Pan Shan style. Between two circles consisting of several concentric elements, and in which both red and black colours are employed, anthropomorphic figures are interposed, which sit on the lower border with legs swung outwards, and have arms pointing sideways and upwards and a head consisting of the large circle that surrounds the neck of the vessel. The arms end in fingers. Even on the elbows and knees there are finger-like projections (Professor Andersson points out that these latter are common in historical Chinese animal ornamentation and are often placed in fantastic positions). The similarities between this and the pattern on the urn K. 5068 are so great and so comparatively complicated that there can be no question of an accidental resemblance. The structure of the two patterns must have had a common origin — the very one, in fact, to which attention has been drawn above. Here are some of the points of resemblance: In both vessels the principal lines of the pattern are painted red. These lines are edged with black. The lower part of the body ends similarly in both ceramic styles: in a fundament or phallus unwarrantably long to belong to a human representation. The arms are directed upwards with identically the same action. The legs are spread out in a practically similar manner, though they are further developed in K. 5312. The neck is short. The head is a circle. The figure is surrounded by two comparatively large circles, which it, so to speak, thrusts away from itself. There are of course dissimilarities. Thus, the number of circles has been reduced from four to two. As a matter of fact, this is easily explained, as the figure now requires more room. Moreover, the connection with the four spiral nuclei, which were the origin of the whole design, has

---

[1]). Cf. the pattern with the anthropomorphic figure on vessel K. 5495 (Pl. XIX, fig. 6). The resemblance is striking. Certain characteristic details are common to both, e. g., the shape of the head and the way in which the body terminates at the bottom.

been lost. The fingers are a new feature. The head is not now placed below the upper border, but the border has itself taken over that rôle.

The main bulk of the vessels of the spiral group in the material at my disposal come from Ning Ting Hsien, one or two from Ti Tao Hsien. Pan Shan, Wa Kuan Tsui, Wang Chia Kou, Pien Chia Kou are well represented. The majority of the vessels of the more advanced group are from Wang Chia Kou and a few from Pien Chia Kou, while an occasional specimen is from P'ai Tzu P'ing, Pan Shan and Kan Liang. A quantity of the vessels belonging to this family, including even one or two of the latter group, were bought at Lanchow.

Décor family 12P.

Pattern: bands running obliquely from the top downward.

(Examples: K. 5080, Pl. XIII, fig. 4, K. 5064, Pl. XIV, fig. 1, K. 5027, Pl. XXXV, fig. 4). A small and fairly uniform décor family has a decoration consisting of alternating broad black fields or bands with dentated edges and between them narrow, entire red bands, all running from the upper border to the left towards the lower border. The black bands have unpainted spaces forming lancet-like leaves (K. 5027) with or without an oblong black smudge in the centre, or else a band ornamented with chessboard pattern is inserted in between the black bands (K. 5064). On the urn K. 5027 each alternate red band is truncated. These truncated bands run from the lower border upwards to the middle of the mantle, but here they suddenly terminate. This gives a more mobile effect.

Only urns of form type P. S: XXIII belong to this group. The outside of the neck is unpainted or else ornamented with a row of left-hand angle-points. The interior of the neck is decorated with alternating black and red horizontal bands or with a garland design. The lower border consists either of a plain band or of a horizontal band and, beneath it, a wavy band.

In the actual arrangement of the bands this décor family follows the decorative traditions from earlier epochs. For a number of roughly made, unpainted vessels of the Pan Shan style possess very similar oblique band-patterns (K. 5454, Pl. XX, fig. 10, K. 5455, Pl. XXI, fig. 9 and K. 5442, Pl. XXXVIII, fig. 6). It is hardly likely however that most of the painted vessels in our collections belong to the earliest representatives of the family; they are more probably fairly late. (The pots have acquired an increasingly black appearance.) The pots were purchased at Lanchow.

Décor family 13P.

Pattern: complicated bow-shaped (arc) or garland design.

(Examples: K. 5224, 5599, 5485, 5111, 5756, Pl. XIV, figs. 5—9). This little décor group, with its curves and its broad black bands, is to some extent related to the more advanced vessels of the spiral group. The whole effect of the design on the vessels is very dark. The pattern consists of halfmoon-shaped red bows or curves, usually two, but sometimes several together, embracing the vessel. These bows start from the top at the upper border round the neck and curve downwards. Above the outer large bow run 1—3 shorter, less curved, red bows. Outside and between the bows are broad, black, sickle-shaped bands, which border on the red elements with dentated edges. Below the points at which the bows meet one another there are irregular triangular fields painted and filled in various ways. The lower border consists of a broad plain line executed in black. The neck: either short or high, always slightly curved outwards at the top and decorated as well on exterior as on interior surfaces. On the interior surfaces of the neck: garland patterns in various designs. On the outside of the neck of the high-necked vessels is a wide-meshed trellis pattern, on that of the low-necked vessels a row of angle-lines with their points towards the left.

Vessels of five form types belong to this family: P. S: XVIII, XXII, XXV, XXX, and XXXIX.

The family clearly belongs to the more advanced groups of the Pan Shan style (late Pan Shan). This is indicated by the soft silhouette of the high collars, as also by the decided predominance of black in the impression created by the vessels, which effect is caused by the broad black bands. The death-pattern system however is still preserved practically throughout the entire family, except that in one or two cases the uppermost inner bows have no black dentations on their upper side. As there are no B vessels among the specimens so far extant, it is not possible to observe the stage of development of the ears.

As ancillary to this décor family we may possibly reckon the vessel K. 5599 (Pl. XIV, fig. 6) of the form type P. S: XXXVIII, though it is perhaps more likely to belong to décor family 1; for on the exterior of the necks there is a decoration based on the design of the first family.

The wreath-like pattern on the body is self-evident as far as this vessel is concerned owing to its double-neck design. The vessel is complicated in form, though it has quite primitive features, such as the pattern on the necks and the ears.

Most of the vessels belonging to the family were bought at Lanchow; two are rom Wang Chia Kou.

Décor family 14P.

Pattern: horizontal rows of lancet-like leaves in ground colour.

A fairly uniform décor family (examples: Pl. XIII, figs. 5—6, Pl. XIV, figs. 10—11) though comprising only a few vessels. The mantles of the pots, bowls (K. 5480, Pl. XIV, fig. 11), and hanging vessels (K. 5104, Pl. XIV, fig. 10) belonging to the family have one or two, sometimes three, series of lancet-like leaves left unpainted on black horizontal surfaces or bands. The leaves are in the vertical plane (K. 5056, Pl. XIII, fig. 6), lying obliquely (K. 5104, Pl. XIV, fig. 10), or standing obliquely (K. 5060, Pl. XXXVIII, fig. 1). The different black bands within which these leaf-like areas appear are usually separated from one another by dentated edges and red, narrow bands. The lancet-like leaves occasionally have an oblong spot in the centre (K. 5480, Pl. XIV, fig. 11). There can hardly be any question here of true cowrie patterns. Vessel K. 5060 (Pl. XXXVIII, fig. 1) has a lower band in which are unpainted lancet-like shapes, and an upper band with unpainted annular surfaces.

Of the low-necked vessels, the bowl K. 5480 (Pl. XIV, fig. 11) and the hanging vessel K. 5104 (Pl. XIV, fig. 10) both possess a band on the inside of the neck with a pattern of points, and above it a very narrow entire band. On the exterior of the neck K. 5480 has a wavy band and K. 5104 a black band with lancet-like leaves in ground colour.

The high-necked vessels have a garland pattern or a plain band on the upper edge of the inside of the neck. On the outside are two pointed bands, one above the other (K. 5060, Pl. XXXVIII, fig. 1, K. 5197, Pl. XIII, fig. 5), or one pointed band and beneath it a series of left-hand angles (K. 5056, Pl. XIII, fig. 6). The ears are sometimes small but provided with holes (K. 5056), and sometimes quite rudimentary and in that case without holes. Vessels of form types P. S: X, XXIII, XXIV and XXXI belong to this family.

The family is certainly in an advanced class (late Pan Shan). The earliest vessel is probably K. 5056, which appears to differ somewhat from the rest in point of décor. The high-necked vessels K. 5060 (Pl. XXXVIII, fig. 1) and K. 5197 (Pl. XIII, fig. 5), like the hanging vessel and the bowl, are more highly developed and, as indeed is evidenced by the finds in the large Pien Chia Kou grave (containing, inter alia, Pot 4, K. 5047), contemporaneous with the most highly advanced black spiral group (Pot 3, K. 5475).

The vessels were bought at Lanchow or in Wang Chia Kou. One comes from the large Pien Chia Kou grave.

Décor family 15P.

Pattern: black spool- or vase-shaped surfaces with a central band (the latter consisting of an unpainted vertical dentated or wavy band, on which is sometimes a red band) alternate on the mantle with narrow beaker-shaped surfaces filled with close-meshed trellis-work.

A uniform and quantitatively fairly rich décor family (Pl. XV). The vase- or spool-shaped black patterns on the mantle — six, or in the very small vessels fewer in number — are sharply delimited on the outside or else dentated along the edges. They are frequently divided into two halves by a red band, upon which the black portions border with dentated edges (K. 5070, Pl. XV, fig. 5). This central element may disappear altogether (K. 5628, Pl. XV, fig. 4). Sometimes its place is taken by a wavy band formed by the ground colour's being exposed on the black surface (K. 5076, Pl. XV, fig. 8) or by a couple of similar wavy bands (K. 5071, Pl. XV, fig. 6). The red band, which in these cases is absent altogether, may in other cases be replaced by a number of narrow, black lines (K. 5088, Pl. XV, fig. 3). In the most artistically executed vessels the black spools are given a more varied pattern in red: crosses (K. 5074, Pl. XXXVIII, fig. 5) or bands with squares passing vertically into one another (K. 5077, Pl. XV, fig. 9). Dots in the ground colour occur in vessels with the more intricate patterns (K. 5074, 5077). Moreover, a characteristic feature of the family is the fact that the lower border invariably consists of a single black horizontal band, and also that the upper border consists, with but a few exceptions, of an inner, black or red band encircling the neck, and outside it a number (3—4) of very narrow, black circles concentric with the band.

To this décor family belong the form types P. S: XV, XIX, and XXVII—XXIX. The majority are small or medium-sized vessels. The high-necked vessels of P. S: XXVII, which are the most common, are usually furnished with necks that are disproportionately high. The pattern on the outside of the neck generally consists of a lower and an upper half, the latter decorated with trellis-work, the former with a band of black points (K. 5071, Pl. XV, fig. 6), a wavy line in ground colour on a dark surface or two black dentated bands bordering on a plain red line (K. 5074, Pl. XXXVIII, fig. 5). The whole of the neck may also be decorated with alternating black and red bands like the design in décor family 1P (K. 5628, Pl. XV, fig. 4).

The strong, closely scalloped ears on the neck, provided with one, and often two, holes, indicate that the high-necked vessels at any rate were held suspended by strings or, more likely perhaps, strong though narrow sinews or straps. The vessels frequently had a thick, oily coating of black or brown, sometimes they have obviously been burnt. It would appear as if the vessels of this family had been used for keeping some kind of oil in, and possibly oil may have been burnt in them.

It is extremely difficult to make any definite statement as to the position of this décor family in relation to the other families or as to its chronology. It is clearly related to the succeeding family, which is certainly to be regarded as a fairly advanced group. The design characteristic of family 15P is, in some of the vessels, very carefully thought out and neatly arranged. Some of the urns with this ornamentation have been executed in a very beautiful, even refined, style (K. 5074, Pl. XXXVIII, fig. 5, K. 5077, Pl. XV, fig. 9). Other features, as for instance the well-developed ears and the high straight necks, are more primitive, but that is perhaps of less consequence here. In this case the ears have been retained, as the specific function of the vessel required them.

Most of the vessels were bought at Lanchow, one or two in Yü Chung Hsien, and one, slightly different from the rest, in Ning Ting Hsien, Pan Shan (K. 5498, Pl. XV, fig. 2).

The group gives the impression of being extremely homogeneous and uniform, and by way of hypothesis it may be asked whether it might not be a geographically uniform group from a hitherto unknown necropolis.

There is however a black-figured group from the Pan Shan area with a similar design (K. 5488, Pl. XV, fig. 1). The red centre band on the spool-shaped surfaces is in these vessels replaced by a series of narrow black lines or by a vertical wavy band, and the borderlines of the beaker-shaped surfaces consist of black instead of red bands.

Décor family 16P.

Pattern: bottle-, gourd-, shoesole-, or pot-like surfaces, filled with a trellis pattern, alternate with pistil- or shield-like surfaces with diverse ornamentation inside them.

This décor family (see Pl. XVI) comprises one of the larger groups of Pan Shan pottery. It is fairly uniform and is obviously related in its pattern to family 15P.

The most characteristic feature of its décor are the bottle-, gourd-, or pot-like surfaces. They are invariably filled with a fine-meshed trellis-work consisting of two sets of narrow, black lines, each running obliquely from the bottom upwards, the one from right to left and the other from left to right. The bottle-like surfaces are 4 to 6 in number. In the more primitively painted vessels belonging to this family the number varies between 5 and 6 surfaces (K. 5055, 5122, Pl. XVI, figs. 1 and 3). Viewed from above, these vessels with their peculiar design look almost like calyxes. In the more advanced vessels the number of bottle-like surfaces is always four, and these when viewed from above form a cross (K. 5048, Pl. XVI, fig. 6). The shape of these trellised surfaces varies both in the more primitive vessels and in the more highly developed ones. In the former case, however, the shapes are more arbitrary: sole-like (K. 5058, Pl. XVI, fig. 2), club-like (K. 5122, Pl. XVI, fig. 3), or irregularly fantastic (K. 5055, Pl. XVI, fig. 1). In the latter case they are definitely and deliberately formed (K. 5050, Pl. XVI, fig. 7, K. 5781, Pl. XXXVIII, fig. 3). Where there are many bottle-like surfaces there is naturally less space available for their complementary figures, which consequently assume a pistil-like form or that of a bulb in section (K. 5058, 5122, Pl. XVI, figs. 2 and 3). Where the bottle-like areas are four in number, their complements are given greater space and become more shield-like (K. 5048, 5050, Pl. XVI, figs. 6 and 7), or sometimes oval (K. 5134, Pl. XVI, fig. 8).

The bottle-like surfaces are bounded on the sides by a red band and by the upper and lower borders. Upon these red bands verge the black complementary surfaces with dentated edges. These black surfaces may be intersected by red bands or contain ground-colour spaces with red contours or otherwise be ornamented with some occasional red element (K. 5057, Pl. XVI, fig. 4). This applies to the more primitive and earlier vessels. In later vessels the red colour is used only as a filling in the leaf-shapes left uncoloured on the black surfaces. In the more advanced vessels there are no red elements whatever on the black surfaces. In the more primitive vessels the decoration on the black fields is somewhat variegated and irregular. There are patterns like pistils or bulbs in section, as also crosses and vertical zigzag bands (K. 5057, Pl. XVI, fig. 4). The fields in K. 5048 (Pl. XVI, fig. 6) very irregularly contain very little black. One group occupying a central position in the family is formed of urns such as K. 5083, 5120 and 5133, in which the black field is bisected by a vertical red band. On either side of it lancet-like leaves following close upon one another are formed of unpainted spaces on the black ground[1]). This leaf-pattern will be remembered from the families 11, 12, 13, and 14. In the more advanced vessels in this family the black surface increases in breadth and force and is filled out with

---

[1]) In some cases these leaves have a red line down the centre from end to end, giving them a somewhat cowrie-like appearance.

only a few, rather large, lancet-like leaves (K. 5781, Pl. XXXVIII, fig. 3) or with a chessboard pattern (K. 5050, Pl. XVI, fig. 7), which is specially characteristic of the immediately succeeding family, though it occurs also in some of the immediately preceding advanced families.

The family so far consists only of vessels of form types P. S: XXIII and XXIV (types A and B). Those more primitive vessels that are high-necked have very high necks, very straight towards the top and with well developed ears. The necks of the advanced high-necked vessels are — exactly on the analogy of the highly developed spiral vessels — somewhat shorter, more curved at the top and of a more elegant shape; they have rudimentary ears. The exterior decoration on the necks of the high- and straight-necked vessels of a more primitive type is divided into two halves. The lower consists of a band of points (K. 5058, Pl. XVI, fig. 2) or left-hand angles. The upper half consists of a band of fine-meshed trelliswork, a red horizontal band forming a border between it and the lower decoration (K. 5058). The exterior neck décor on the more advanced high-necked vessels is a trellis pattern or the two bands of points, the one above the other, which have been characteristic of one or two advanced groups belonging to some of the previous families (K. 5059, 5050, 5134, Pl. XVI, figs. 5, 7 and 8, also K. 5781, Pl. XXXVIII, fig. 3). Low-necked pots have no exterior décor on the neck, unless the red border line extends on to the neck (see Pl. XVI, figs. 1, 3 and 4). The décor on the interior of the neck in the earlier, low-necked specimens varies a good deal: 1. plain bands after the design of the first family, or 2. alternating upper and lower angles with intermediate oblique black lines, or 3. bands of garlands. In the more advanced low-necked vessels bands of garlands. The same occurs also on the upper interior rim of some of the more advanced high-necked vessels (K. 5781, Pl. XXXVIII, fig. 3).

The lower border varies between 1. a plain horizontal band, 2. the same, and beneath it a wavy band, 3. a wavy band between two plain horizontal bands.

This large décor family extends over a considerable part of the Pan Shan ceramic period. A number of the vessels belong to the most advanced forms of the Pan Shan style. The process of development within the family is clearly traceable. Curiously enough, the family has left no traces in the Ma Chang style, at any rate not in the material now at my disposal.

The more primitive vessels come from Nien Po Hsien (Mi La Kou) and from Ning Ting Hsien (Pan Shan and Wa Kuan Tsui). The more advanced are from Ning Ting Hsien (P'ai Tzu P'ing, Pien Chia Kou and Wang Chia Kou).

Décor family 17P.

The surface of the mantle is divided by vertical series of bands (usually two black bands dentated along the inner edges, and between them a red, plain band) into trapeziform fields, generally filled with chessboard pattern.

A group consisting for the most part of smallish vessels and having the entire surface of the mantle divided up into trapeziform fields by triads of vertical bands (see Pl. XVII—XVIII). The breadth of the vertical, black bands may vary considerably: sometimes they are narrow, equivalent to the red bands (K. 5126, Pl. XVIII, fig. 1), in other cases they are particularly broad and dominate the whole design (K. 5084, Pl. XVII, fig, 10). The number of trapeziform surfaces varies between 4 and 8. Certain vessels with 6 and 4 surfaces are particularly attractive (K. 5126, Pl. XVIII, fig. 1, and K. 5097, Pl. XVII, fig. 4). The pattern in the trapeziform areas terminates abruptly at these black bands, and the artist has usually not succeeded in so balancing the design as to round it off neatly as an organic whole or in a fashion pleasing to the eye (K. 5044, Pl. XVII, fig. 5). The ornamentation is however most successful in this respect when the supplementary pattern is less heavy and compact (K. 5097, Pl. XVII, fig. 4). As pointed out above, the most common supplementary pattern is a chessboard design of alternating black and unpainted squares, the latter, consequently, being the colour of the ware itself. The squares may be quadrate (K. 5091, 5084, Pl. XVII, figs. 7 and 10) or rhomboid (K. 5046, Pl. XVII, fig. 9). They are often very small, in other cases fairly large. The black squares are in some cases larger than the light-coloured squares (K. 5625, Pl. XVII, fig. 2). The light squares may have a diagonal line down the centre (K. 5044, Pl. XVII, fig. 5). In one or two exceptional cases half the number of squares are not filled entirely with black paint but are instead given a small-squared mesh design (K. 5091, Pl. XVII, fig. 7). Occasionally all the squares are filled with fine, parallel lines running in opposite directions in each alternate square (K. 5097, Pl. XVII, fig. 4).

Vessel K. 5095 (Pl. XVII, fig. 6) is peculiar, possessing four surfaces with alternate trellis pattern and horizontal rows of pointed bands, the points projecting upwards. In other cases the trapeziform areas are all filled with trelliswork (K. 5257, Pl. XVII, fig. 8). K. 5211 (Pl. XVII, fig. 1) is a very primitive vessel with trellis design.

To this group belong vessels of the form types P. S: VIII, XIII, XIV, XVII, XVIII, XXIV and XXXIII. Vessels of type P. S: XXXIII predominate.

The lower border usually consists of a plain, black, horizontal band, below which, in the case of a couple of the larger vessels, is a wavy band. The beaker K. 5094, a smallish vessel of type Z, has a plain horizontal band and beneath it a wavy band, but in addition it has on the basal surface — a unique case — a series of primitive ladder-patterns painted all round the bottom.

Vessels of the types P. S: XVIII and XXIV have necks ornamented on the exterior with a bisected pattern: above, trelliswork and, below, a band of high points. On the inner rim they have a plain band or a row of short vertical lines. Vessels of type P. S: XXXIII (type Z) usually possess low necks and a slightly expanded mouth. They are in this case decorated on the outside with plain horizontal lines, close-meshed trelliswork or bands of left-hand angles. Where the Z-type vessels' necks are higher they are ornamented with special patterns. They also have a decoration on the inside of the slightly expanded mouth; it is usually a combination of one red plain and one black dentated line, occasionally replaced by a line of points (K. 5097, Pl. XVII, fig. 4) or else a sequence of horizontal lines. The garland pattern also occurs. The inner rim is decorated with a black or red band or with a series of short, vertical lines.

Owing to its chessboard pattern the family is closely akin to several of the more advanced families, particularly the later groups of the spiral pattern family and the bottle-pattern family.

One vessel with large squares comes from the large grave found at Pien Chia Kou. It would appear that the vessels with large chessboard squares are more advanced, and moreover stand in a higher artistic class, than those with smaller squares.

The majority of the vessels were bought at Lanchow, some are from Ning Ting Hsien (Pan Shan, Wa Kuan Tsui, Pien Chia Kou), and one vessel is from Kao Lan Hsien, Kao Ying.

Décor Family 18P.

Pattern: broad, black horizontal bands with unpainted circular surfaces.

A small group of vessels (see Pl. XVIII, fig. 2—3) have as their characteristic décor one or two broad black horizontal zones running round the mantle, and on these zones a large number of small, or a less number of large, unpainted circular surfaces. Where there are two bands they are separated by a narrow red horizontal band on to which the black portions verge with or without dentated edges. For the rest, the décor is fairly individual, and consequently each urn will be discussed here separately.

In the case of urn K. 5082 (Pl. XXXV, fig. 3) there is only one lower, broad horizontal band with large, round unpainted areas. On these latter there is drawn upon the otherwise unpainted ware a series of 7—8 lines pointing obliquely upwards, black in colour and leaning first to the left and then to the right in alternate circles. Above this black band there is a narrow red band, and above that a series of still narrower, black lines running round the vessel. Then comes the upper border. The urn most probably belongs to the earlier or middle phase of the Pan Shan pottery.

Urn K. 5062 (Pl. XVIII, fig. 2) has two broad, black zones with a large number of smaller, more or less circular areas with the ground colour exposed. Most of the circular areas of the upper band are filled with a fine trelliswork. Two irregularly placed circular surfaces have black lines arranged like the spokes of a wheel. The circular surfaces in the lower band have similar wheel ornamentation. The death pattern system is altogether lacking.

In urn K. 5061 (Pl. XVIII, fig. 3) the painter has combined the patterns of this and of the preceding décor family: the upper zone is divided by vertical lines into trapeziform surfaces with a chessboard pattern, while the lower zone is similar to the lower band on the preceding urn.

The lower border on these urns consists of a wavy band, or of a wavy band and under it a plain horizontal line.

The urns so far known that have this pattern all belong to form type P. S: XXIV. They have small ears with or without needle-eye holes and a slightly notched edge. The necks are fairly straight and high, notably in the earliest representative of the family, urn K. 5082 (Pl. XXXV, fig. 3), the exterior of the neck having a bisected decoration, at the bottom a band of points, at the top a broad band of fine-meshed trellis pattern. On urn K. 5082 we find between the very high points a primitive oblique ladder pattern.

To judge from the appearance of the ears and the close relation between the patterns of this family and those of the earlier vessels in the foregoing family (K. 5061, Pl. XVIII, fig. 3) and also of the most advanced vessels of the first décor family, we are probably justified in assuming that the pots of this family belong to the middle and later phase of Pan Shan pottery, though not to its most highly developed groups.

The vessels were bought at Lanchow or Ning Ting Hsien (Pan Shan or Wa Kuan Tsui).

Décor Family 19P.

Rope pattern.

A group that is fairly uniform and full of character — it is however a small one — comprises a series of urns in some degree related in its décor to the first family (see Pl. XVIII, fig. 4—7); for the décor consists of horizontal bands and lines that somewhat resemble those found in the advanced forms of the first décor family, in which the broad, black bands partly give way to series of narrow, black lines. Compare K. 5013 (Pl. XVIII, fig. 4) of this family with K. 5015 (Pl. II, fig. 6) of the first family. Moreover in décor family 19, as in this advanced group within the first family, we can distinguish three elements. The elements are here broad, red bands surrounded by broad, black bands and series of 3—5 narrow, black, dentated lines, whose points usually run obliquely up towards the left and are parallel to one another. These latter lines combined with the points give an impression of rope or string wound round the vessel. A further characteristic feature of the family is the fact that, as in the Ma Chang vessels, the broad, black bands border on the red bands without intervals and without any dentated edge (K. 5282, Pl. XXXVIII, fig. 2, K. 5284, K. 5283, Pl. XVIII, figs. 6—7). An exception to this rule is the pot K. 5020 (Pl. XVIII, fig. 5), in which there occurs a rudimentary dentated edge along the top of the black bands. This pot thus represents a transitional stage. In a number of the vessels, in which we find only two red bands with accompanying black bands, there is between these triads of bands a dominant patterned zone with: 1. squares (K. 5283, Pl. XVIII, fig. 7) or 2. complicated, advanced patterns (K. 5282, Pl. XXXVIII, fig. 2) consisting of squares and triangles and also unpainted, oblong, rectangular areas forming crosses around small, black squares; (this pattern is also generally used to fill up circles in advanced spiral vessels — a border design belonging to late Pan Shan pottery and transferred to the Ma Chang pottery) or 3. circular areas set in rows in large numbers close to one another (K. 5284, Pl. XVIII, fig. 6). The squares, triangles and circles are filled with a fine-meshed trelliswork. In one case the narrow, black lines have no dentated edge (at the lower end of K. 5283). The points of the dentated bands may be somewhat clumsy and fairly high (K. 5020, Pl. XVIII, fig. 5). This latter vessel however is somewhat isolated within the family as regards its pattern and also as regards the exterior and interior design on the neck.

Lower border: Above, a broad, black band, and below, a narrower, wavy band.

These vessels have singularly thin walls; they are light, fairly high and in form approach those of the Ma Chang vessels. They all belong to form type P. S: XXIV, although their necks are only of medium height and slightly expanded at the top, and although they are entirely without ears. The exterior and interior ornamentation on the neck is uniform. The exterior décor is a wide-meshed network of squares, the interior décor consisting of a narrow garland design on the upper rim (Pl. XVIII fig. 7).

The family is in many respects closely related to the Ma Chang pottery. The shapes and silhouettes of the vessels and both the moderate heights of the necks and their elegant forms resemble those of the Ma Chang style and the other advanced Pan Shan vessels. The red bands are painted direct on the black bands. Rope patterns are moreover common in Ma Chang pottery (K. 5299, Pl. XXVI, fig. 7). Both the exterior and interior décor of the necks is the same as that of many other advanced Pan Shan vessels. The lower border as seen in family 19 is part of the orthodox design in vessels of the Ma Chang style, although the rhythm of the wavy band is here far more rapid than that in the Ma Chang style. For the rest, the family is of so uniform a character that one might suspect that it represents a geographical group from a hitherto undiscovered mortuary field. All the vessels were bought at Lanchow.

Individual vessels. Patterns in black and red.

A number of smaller vessels, which are likewise painted black and red, cannot advantageously be grouped in any of the foregoing décor families, but they nevertheless may have certain points of contact with one or more of them. Some of these vessels possess a strongly individual décor, though this fact does not, of course, prevent the possibility of their being isolated representatives of true décor families.

An ornamentation that is very closely akin to that of the first family occurs in the two bowls K. 5205, (Pl. XIX, fig. 2) and K. 5738 (Pl. XIX, fig. 3—4). This ornamentation is painted on the interior surfaces of the vessels. A red cross has its point of intersection in the centre of the bottom of the vessel. The four angles between the arms of the cross are filled with alternate black dentated and red angle-lines of the same breadth. Both are possibly very early Pan Shan vessels.

A similar cross is found on the interior surface of the bowl K. 5206 (Pl. XIX, fig. 1). In the four angles there are angle-lines dentated on the side facing the cross, and filled with a fairly wide-meshed trelliswork. We find the cross again in the bowl K. 5218 (Pl. XIX, fig. 5), but here the angles are filled up with a network of unpainted leaf-shaped surfaces. I conceive this cross design on the interior circular surface of the vessels to be a native invention of a purely ornamental character, comparable with a similar décor in other cultures. Of this I shall have more to say later.

In the bowl K. 5495 (Pl. XIX, fig. 6) there are on its interior surface three arms of a red cross. The two smaller spaces between the arms of the cross are filled with narrow, parallel, black lines running from the outside towards the interior of the bowl. Similar parallel black lines occupy also a part of the remaining space on the other half of the bowl's interior surface. Between the two latter sets of parallel lines is a field occupied by a distinctly anthropomorphic figure. It has a head, consisting of a broad black ring, a backbone ending in a tail, two arms with hands, the latter having five fingers, and in addition ribs and two legs set in too horizontal a plane and provided with five-toed feet. The resemblance between this figure and those already indicated as being anthropomorphic belonging to the décor group of the spiral family, as well as a number of Ma Chang vessels, is striking. The first point we note is the manner of drawing the head simply as a round ring without either nose, eyes or mouth, also the presence of a tail-like appendage below and between the legs. The figure depicted on the vessel we are discussing here has the character of a dead body, i. e. a skeleton. This is indicated both by the clearly differentiated ribs and also by the presence of a tail portion. The painter was not unacquainted with the general appearance of a skeleton and the fate that awaits the dead under ground.

A red cross, though surrounded by black (here actually grey or brown) boundary lines, is found also on the inside and on the bottom of the bowl K. 5220 (Pl. XIV, fig. 2). The angles are in this case filled with a series of parallel horizontal lines. On the outside of the vessel is a garland décor. The rim is black.

The three human heads of burnt clay, which have already been dealt with in the form series, are very extraordinary specimens. The painting of the heads is comparatively simply done. The mantles are in two cases ornamented with the upper part of a spiral pattern, with its typical triangular fields adjacent to the upper border.

In the head K. 5473 (Pl. XIX, fig. 8) the upper border consists of a black circular band, along the upper edge of which are fine dentations. It borders on the broad red band that marks the boundary between neck and body. This red band is quite conventionally placed, similarly to that on the necks of most Pan Shan vessels. The transition between neck and head is also emphasized by a red band. For the rest, the decoration on the neck consists of a series of narrower, black, horizontal bands. The face is encircled by an outer black line, dentated along its inside edge, and an inner red line. The crown of the head and the nape of the neck have a vertical décor consisting of alternating plain, red lines and dentated, black lines of the same breadth. The head undoubtedly belongs to the end of the early or the beginning of the middle period of the Pan Shan pottery and is certainly the most primitive of the three figurines of this kind now known.

In head K. 5472 (Pl. XIX, fig. 7) the upper border consists of a black band of points, the latter being turned upwards. The boundary of the neck and the neck itself, as well as the head, except the face, are decorated with a design resembling that of the first décor family. The red bands are narrower than the black ones. The conventional boundary line has been shifted further down and made thinner. Below the mouth is a series of narrow, vertical lines indicating a beard; beneath the eye is a curved line, on the nose two straight lines, and where the hair begins there is a curved line with the ends bent downwards. On the cheeks a fairly large space has been left between a lower red and an upper black band. The wedge-shaped gaps between the bands are filled up with lines running obliquely upwards, which at the point of the wedge pass imperceptibly into the usual dentations between the bands. The drawing of the face is, in spite of its crude simplicity, forceful and, in its primitive way, expressive. The predominance of the black horizontal bands over the red, the simple, clear-cut décor of the face, the decorative upper border, the shifting of the position of the red boundary line — all indicate an advanced stage of development in comparison with the foregoing figurine. Everything points to the fact that the figurine belongs to the middle period of the Pan Shan style.

In the figurine K. 11.038: 5 (Pl. XIX, fig. 9), which was purchased in Paris, the lower edge of the brim terminates in a border cut out to form points, making the brim into a 19-pointed star. The décor on this brim is "free", i. e. it does not, like that on the brim of the two preceding heads, belong to an excised décor that formed part of the uppermost portion of the mantle of an A or B urn with a spiral pattern, but is manifestly designed specifically for the place on which it is painted. The conventional, red border-line between neck and body occurs here as in the first figurine described, and beneath this band there is a broad, black band dentated along the top. The lower part of the brim is radially divided by vertical red bands, as many in number as the points of the brim though somewhat irregularly drawn, into sectors which at the front are decorated with vertical, black, wavy bands and at the back are filled with wide-meshed black trelliswork. The decoration on the front side (the black wavy bands) is apparently to be interpreted, in keeping with the plastically fashioned snake on the back of the head, as a decoratively simplified snake ornamentation. At the top of the neck is a red band bordering on the head, and between this upper and the lower boundary line is a black décor consisting of a row of black angle-lines running clockwise round the neck — a neck ornamentation well known in the Pan Shan decorative art. The back and the sides of the head are painted with an entirely black ground, leaving at the bottom a free edge above the red boundary line on the neck. The face is practically heart-shaped, bounded by a series of ears — fashioned at the top more like eyebrow ridges — on the cheeks and on the point of the chin, all distinctly ear-shaped with holes and notches. From the jaws, between the pierced horns, runs a broad, red band extending right down over the nose. Around the lower part of the mouth are radiated, scattered black lines. The remainder of the face is ornamented with vertical black lines. Above the eyes are a couple of narrow, horizontal lines, and there is also a similar line beneath the nose. The face is full of character, indeed strikingly drawn with moustaches and beard indicated. On account of its upper border — the conventional red boundary lines — this figurine should possibly, in spite of its greater decorative execution, be placed in the period intermediate *between* the two preceding figurines.

The jug-like vessel K. 5623 (Pl. XIX, fig. 12) has on the exterior of the bowl four circular areas, the outer circumference framed in black, and inside a rose-shaped design in ground colour, in which is a red ring with its outer edge dentated. This ring is filled with black trelliswork. The pattern has a vegetable character. For the rest, on the mantle is painted a fairly coarse-meshed trellis pattern, on the neck black points with the apices downwards, inside the neck a garland decoration. The whole décor of the vessel is very attractive. The vegetable, flowerlike character of the design is manifest. The vessel is no doubt of an advanced type and in point of decorative shape may best be placed with a group of advanced, black-figured vessels with a décor having a floral and animal tendency, which however never becomes definitely naturalistic.

The medium-sized urn K. 5274 has a high neck but no ears, its décor being resolved into a system of fine lines. The vessel belongs to the form type P. S: XXVIII, i. e. there is a sharp line of demarcation between the upper, more horizontal part and the lower, more vertical part of the mantle. The lower edge of the painted area and the line of demarcation between mantle and neck are both emphasized in the décor by fairly broad black bands. The lower half of the mantle has an upper and a lower red line, and between these a series of straight, horizontal lines. The upper half of the mantle is ornamented with a system of gently undulating black lines, and exactly between them a similarly undulating red line. Nearer the neck one red and several black, fine lines encircle the vessel. The exterior of the neck is decorated with a band of four very large black points directed upwards, and beneath the rim, which is turned over, runs a red band. The décor is very closely associated with a number of dwelling-site vessels with an entirely black ornamentation. The shape of the vessel likewise indicates some kinship with this group.

Urn K. 5626 is of about the same size as the preceding one and, indeed, belongs to the same type of vessel. The lower half of the mantle has an under border consisting of three narrow, wavy lines, above which run two broader horizontal lines and between them four finer lines — all executed in black. The top of the upper half of the mantle, round the neck, has an encircling border consisting of an inner series of narrow lines and a thick outer line, all in black. Below this border is a broad, decorated band with fields bounded alternately by concave and convex lines. The fields bounded by red convex lines are filled with a fine-meshed trellis pattern. The black fields bounded by concave lines have horizontal wavy lines in ground colour. The ornamentation on the neck is in this case entirely destroyed. The décor on this pot is associated with that on a number of black-figured dwelling-site vessels, but in all probability the pot belongs to the mortuary style of pottery and to the middle section of the Pan Shan group. It is in particular related to families 15—16.

Vessel K. 5332, a low-necked mug of the form type P. S: XV with a rounded body, has a narrow field of bands lying between the broad, black and plain, upper and lower borders and decorated with angles pointing left. The exterior of the collar has the same design, while the inside of the collar has a double row of black garlands. The border-line between neck and body is red, the rest of the décor black. Rows of angles pointing left frequently occur on the exterior of the necks of earlier pots, as also on the necks of some Ma Chang vessels. The motif is thus common to the Pan Shan and the Ma Chang styles of pottery. Of this I shall have more to say later.

Vessel K. 5352, of form type P. S: XXXII, has a similar field of bands between the upper and lower borders, though decorated with a row of round surfaces each consisting of two circles: the inner circles filled with a fine-meshed trellis pattern. On the neck are unpainted squares standing on one point, in the centre of each a dot, and around that a ring of 6—8 other dots. A red border-line between neck and body. The rest of the décor is black except for a red band on the inside of the neck. Above this band a number of short vertical lines run round the rim. Below the band is a double row of garlands. The upper border is dentated along the top. The surface of the vessel, like that of the Ma Chang vessels, is not very smooth. The ware is similar to that of the Ma Chang group. The vessel is undoubtedly very closely related to the Ma Chang pottery. A number of transitional forms having the same décor, but entirely without the death-pattern system, are closely akin to this pot, but are dealt with under the Ma Chang pottery.

Vessel K. 5344 (Pl. IX, fig. 9), similar in shape to the preceding vessel, has a similar field of bands between the upper and lower borders, though here decorated with a row of rhombi standing on a point and filled with a fine-meshed trelliswork. The exterior of the neck is painted black and is decorated with a fine zigzag line in ground colour. On the inside of the neck is a décor consisting of a row of short, vertical lines along the edge, below it a broad red band, and beneath that a thin, plain, garland pattern. On the border-line between neck and body, though placed on the latter, is a red band. The rest of the décor is black. Along the top of the upper border is a dentated edge. The surface of the vessel is not very smooth, the ware is near to the Ma Chang type. The vessel is undoubtedly very closely related to the Ma Chang pottery. Here, as in the preceding case, there are very closely associated forms dealt with under the Ma Chang pottery.

Vessel K. 5357 (Pl. XIX, fig. 11), also of the same type as the preceding beakers, though having a slightly higher neck, is decorated between the upper and lower borders with black triangles pointing alternately upwards and downwards, and between them oblique bands consisting of three parallel lines in ground colour. The black upper border is not dentated, the top edge, as in the Ma Chang system, joining the red border-line at the neck. The inside of the neck is decorated as in the foregoing vessels. Round the neck's outer rim is a row of black points directed downwards. The ware is typical Pan Shan. The colour however resembles that of the Ma Chang style, dull and grey. A transitional vessel.

The beaker K. 5356 (Pl. XIX, fig. 10) has a décor somewhat akin to that of the first family, although clearly differentiated from it. The border-line between neck and body is broad and red. The rest of the décor is black. The mantle has on the black zone two horizontal wavy lines in ground colour and the upper edge dentated against the red band. On the inside of the neck is a décor of garlands. The ware is typical Pan Shan. The colour somewhat dull. A transitional vessel passing into the Ma Chang style.

HOW THE MA CHANG POTTERY WAS MADE.

The painted Ma Chang pottery is, as we shall show later, associated in many ways with the Pan Shan pottery and must be regarded as an offshoot of the latter. Even as regards the actual manufacture and construction of the vessels, the process has on the whole been identical in both types of pottery.

The quality of the clays used in the manufacture of the Ma Chang ware has — generally at any rate — been fairly good, an admixture of large grains having as a rule been avoided. There are however vessels in which — mainly as a result of subsequent cracking phenomena of the same kind as those caused by unslaked grains in mortar of lime used in modern walls, in this case cracking of terracotta chips owing to the expansion of the grains of lime when they decompose on absorbing water (e. g. K. 5229, Pl. XXXIII, fig. 4) — large grains of lime are found to be mixed up with the clay. The ware generally has a certain small-grained character: indeed, this is characteristic of the Ma Chang ware and has no doubt arisen owing to an admixture of fine sand in the clay. The firing process has been the same as in the case of the Pan Shan vessels, though the degree of temperature has in general been somewhat lower. The surface colour is for the most part slightly paler than that of the Pan Shan pottery, and after firing the ware acquires a softer and more porous texture. Although some of the Ma Chang vessels have a greyer tone than the Pan Shan urns, the Ma Chang pottery never acquires the colourless grey tone and brittle, easily powdering consistency of the Han ware. When being fired, several vessels were piled on top of one another in the kiln, just as in the case of the Pan Shan vessels. This is evidenced by numerous brand-marks, particularly on the larger vessels.

The Pan Shan vessels were built up of rings, which were then daubed over with clay, and it is comparatively easy to follow the traces of the process. In the case of the Ma Chang pottery, however, it is generally very much more difficult to discern any traces left by the constructional process, in spite of the ware of the Ma Chang period being to a certain extent coarser. This is due partly to the absence here of primitive vessels and partly to the fact that special care seems to have been taken to remove all traces. The ring method of construction is however clearly observable, for instance, in vessel K. 5375 (Pl. XXXIII, fig. 5), where the joins between the rings are still distinctly visible. The joins between the broad collar and the body of the vessel are seen in the bowl K. 5323. On the under side of the high-footed bowl K. 5379 the joins are daubed over with clay, it is true, but they are nevertheless easily discernible. We divine — rather than see — that the foot of the vessel is also made up of rings. The rings are specially conspicuous on the inside of the extremely globular urn K. 5981, in which the joins have been left exposed, as also on the outside of the vessel K. 5330 (Pl. XXXIII, fig. 6) on the base, and likewise on the bowl K. 5486. Against a suitable light one can see quite clearly the rings on the outside of the base of the urn K. 5295. Neither in the vessels here mentioned nor in the others belonging to the Ma Chang style of pottery are any traces of a potter's wheel discernible. In extremely rare cases it is possible to observe on the insides of the large pots the two systems of ridges that are characteristic of the insides of the larger Pan Shan vessels, viz. a system of more distinctly marked ridges drawn in a spiral from the bottom right-hand side up towards the left, and a horizontal system of slighter ridges traversing the former. In the case of the Pan Shan pottery, these two systems represented, as I have previously demonstrated, traces of the method of construction. The horizontal ridges constituted the horizontal bands of clay, and the spirally turned ridges were the result of smoothing over, with the fingers or an implement, the joins between the bands by rotating the pot clockwise, the right hand moving anti-clockwise in its interior. The same is the case here. There are still, however, a great many vessels of the Ma Chang style on the insides of which we find only the one system, i. e. the spiral system, as for instance K. 5296, often replaced by furrows running radially from the bottom upwards. In certain cases there is no sign even of this system on the inside, nor is there any hint of rings or ridges on the exterior. As there is no evidence of any "throwing" process in the Ma Chang pottery, and as, on the other hand, the ring construction occurs here in so many cases, I take it for granted that the latter method was generally employed, even in cases in which it has not left any direct external traces. It might be possible in some instances, particularly in the case of smaller vessels, to suspect their having been shaped directly with the hand and without the help of rings — a method of manufacture frequently practised amongst primitive peoples and employed alternatively with the ring method. In the Ma Chang vessels the work of smoothing over the outside surface has been done so thoroughly that except in rare cases the rings cannot be discerned at all. This applies particularly to the mantles, which are here often very round, but the bases too are made very smooth, in many cases far more so than in the vessels of the Pan Shan group. The outer surface seems in the majority of cases to be covered with a thin coating of "slip", i. e. a finer quality of clay than the rest of the ware, this being specially noticeable where a handle has been broken off, as in vessel K. 5327, in which the ring-joints are clearly visible beneath the layer that has fallen away. In this case the surface layer proves to be of a lighter and less warm colour than the inner ware. In one isolated case (Pl. XXII, fig. 8.) this thin surface layer has been applied with a pencil or brush about 2 cm. broad. Its fairly thick bristles have left traces in the form of small parallel, shallow grooves, about a dozen to the centimetre. In this case, then, it can be established that the pencil or brush was in the service of the ceramic artist at least as early as in the later aeneolithic era (see Bibl. 93).

The degree of smoothness on the exterior surface shows a wide divergence from the Pan Shan ideal. In the Pan Shan pottery the surface was smoothed, and even polished, especially on the mantle. In the Ma Chang pottery it is full of tiny holes, grainy and dull, and has a dry effect. This dull effect is so obvious that a single glance at a shard is often sufficient to enable it to be distinguished from the bulk of Pan Shan shards. Under the microscope this grainy and pitted quality in the Ma Chang ware is naturally still more clearly emphasized.

In certain cases the surface has been considerably scratched prior to firing and painting, and this has manifestly been done quite deliberately. The pot K. 5291 may be considered a typical representative of this scratched ware. In this vessel the scratches run in a vertical plane on the neck and spread radially downwards on to the mantle. The vertical scratches are curtailed at the upper edge of the base by a horizontal system of scratches. The scratches are fairly shallow, it is true, but at the same time they are very distinct and were apparently made by small hard grains (fine-grained sand?) being drawn over the surface with the hand. At the same time, slight traces of finger-marks are discernible in the scratched surface. Scratched ware occurs fairly commonly during the Ma Chang period.

Here too the concentric striation on the necks, which is already observed in the Pan Shan material, is of very frequent occurrence, and it is still more clearly marked, particularly on the broad brim of the neck, which is so common a feature of this style. Here, as in the case of the Pan Shan pottery, this concentric striation no doubt arose as a result of the neck's being fashioned with a templet cut out of wood or bamboo.

The handles are affixed to the Ma Chang vessels in the same manner as to the Pan Shan pottery.

Under the bottoms of the vessels there are in some cases clear impressions of woven mats (K. 5452, Pl. XXXIII, fig. 7). These impressions must no doubt be given the same interpretation here as in the case of the unpainted vessels and the pottery decorated in relief.

THE FORMS OF THE MA CHANG VESSELS.

Painted vessels belonging to the Ma Chang style of pottery are far more sparsely represented than the painted Pan Shan vessels.

They show throughout a family likeness to the Pan Shan vessels and are manifestly derived from the most advanced types of Pan Shan pottery. In a number of the different form types there are series of individual vessels which represent transitional forms from late Pan Shan pottery to early Ma Chang pottery.

In the Ma Chang pottery the Pan Shan types are gradually transformed and changed into characteristic shapes, but the number of individuals within each form group is only in a few cases large enough to enable the process of evolution to be distinctly followed. It seems evident however that, as regards both the large and the small vessels, which in their forms are fairly clearly differentiated from one another, simultaneously with the contraction of the number of main types — a quantity of Pan Shan forms die out — there eventually arises within these main types a lively individual variation of a character that, in part, represents fresh conceptions. The form groups decrease in number during the beginning of the Ma Chang period, but for this very reason there clearly emerges a new evolutional process. An urge to create fresh forms undermines the conventional main tendency.

In many respects even the more advanced Ma Chang forms possess certain features in common with the Pan Shan vessels. The flat-bottomed bases like an inverted and truncated cone are characteristic of the great majority of the vessels. Only two types of vessels have a truly distinct foot — a feature indeed that is not possessed by any of the Pan Shan sepulchral vessels.

As regards the upper portion, the Ma Chang vessels possess necks varying between high and low. The number of neckless types is considerably smaller than in the Pan Shan pottery. The variation in the height of the necks of the larger Ma Chang vessels tends towards necks of medium height. The highest neck forms found in the Pan Shan pottery are entirely absent here. The low necks are in some cases still lower than the lowest occurring in the Pan Shan vessels (Pl. XXIV, fig. 2, and Pl. XXXIX, fig. 4). The mouths are in certain cases very narrow (Pl. XXIV, fig. 8). It is a tendency in advanced Ma Chang for the upper part of the neck to expand horizontally into a broad brim (Pl. XXIII, fig. 7, and Pl. XXVI, figs. 4 and 7). The ears found on the high Pan Shan necks have here disappeared entirely, as in the case of the most highly developed forms of late Pan Shan pottery.

Variations in the form of the bodies will be further discussed later on. We find that here, as in other points of detail, the origin from Pan Shan forms is quite obvious.

Ring- or bow-shaped handles with a hole in the centre occur in most types of vessel. The larger vessels usually have two handles diametrically opposed to one another and set slightly below the middle of the body. The handles here tend to be carried somewhat further down than those of the similar Pan Shan vessels; at the same time the loop becomes narrower. Vessels possessing two handles set asymmetrically and resembling the Pan Shan types P. S: XXIX and P. S: XXX do occur, though they are rare (the ceramic type will be found in the annexed diagram as M. C: XI). The smaller vessels generally have two diametrically opposed handles placed on the neck. These handles have a certain tendency to lengthen, and moreover they vary widely both in form and position. Single annular handles are, in certain types of cup and jug, set on the neck (Pl. XXV, fig. 9, and Pl. XXVI, fig. 6) or in the centre of the body (Pl. XXIII, fig. 2.) There are even examples of the massive ridge- and knob-like handles, or rudiments of them (Pl. XXIII, fig 2.)

In the dishes that are provided with a foot there are holes in the foot. The holes are round, two in number, and they lie diametrically opposite to one another slightly above or below the centre of the foot. What has been their purpose? It seems to me most probable that they were used as a primitive suspension arrangement for carrying the sepulchral vessel in the funeral procession. In that case a cord was threaded through the holes, and, the ends being tied together, it formed an excellent handle. The vessel has then hung with the interior surface of the bowl downwards. In discussing these foot-holes, however, we must not forget that Chinese archaic bronze vessels (during the Chou and Han dynasties), in cases in which they possessed ring-shaped feet, often have these feet pierced with holes, round, vertically oblong or cruciform, and invariably in pairs, two diametrically opposed or four placed in the form of a cross round the foot. Here they generally lie higher up on the foot than in our Ma Chang bowls. Among the bronzes it is in the Pan, Lei, Tsun, Ku and Tou forms that these foot-holes occur. A true connection in this respect between the late neolithic material and the bronze material may be presumed to exist, though by no means necessarily so. Should however such a connection really exist, there might conceivably have been a ritualistic significance underlying the holes in the feet of these sepulchral vessels. According to Chinese tradition, the purpose of the holes in the bronze vessels used in ritual is to release spirits that may, quite unintentionally, have found their way beneath the high foot during the sacrificial feast[1]).

In a few vessels we find a central hole in the bottoms (e. g. in the pot Pl. XXII, fig. 3, also in some small beaker-shaped bowls with double handles). This type of holed vessel is thus found among both the larger and the smaller forms. The hole is pierced in the middle, as in modern flowerpots, but it is relatively smaller, having an external diameter of 6—7 mm. It may be cylindrical or conical, with the larger diameter outwards and downwards. It has invariably been pierced after firing. Pots of this kind might conceivably have been used for rinsing small-sized objects, roots or suchlike, but the hole is perhaps too small for such a purpose, and indeed would easily get stopped up. It is also not very likely that we are here dealing with flowerpots; at any rate, a pot shaped like that shown in Pl. XXII, fig. 3 could hardly serve such a purpose. Another possibility is that the vessel was a kind of watering-pot for watering plants placed in rows — and pots of this kind might very well have served that purpose. Finally, there is the possibility of the holed vessel's having been used as a saltcellar[2]).

Below is a list of the forms, classified in groups and types in the same manner as in the case of the Pan Shan sepulchral pottery. As the majority of the vessels belonging to the Ma Chang style of pottery are manifestly derived from the Pan Shan type, I have arranged them in series analogous to the Pan Shan series. Most of the typical series of the Pan Shan style are also represented in the Ma Chang pottery, but the number of types is far smaller, as indeed is but natural considering that the number of known Pan Shan vessels is so far in excess of the quantity of Ma Chang vessels as yet discovered. The profiles of the form types are reproduced in the figures annexed to the text.

Of the first series of form types only two types are represented here, viz. M. C: I and M. C: II, which are to a certain extent refined types evolved from P. S: I and

---

[1]) E. A. Voretzsch: Altchinesische Bronzen, Berlin 1924, p. 74. (See Bibl. 90 a).

[2]) Vessels of a similar kind with one or a few holes in the bottom are known from the Roman Iron Age, from Denmark and from the same epoch in Norway (see Johs Boe: Jernalderens keramik i Norge, Bergen 1931, fig. 243 b and text on p. 156, Bibl. 20 a), also from J. de Morgan's excavations in the Caucasus. (One pot is in the Salle de Morgan in the Museum at St. Germain, France.)

P. S: II respectively. Like the latter, they are without handles. Their profiles are more clearly defined and more highly cultivated than those of the Pan Shan vessels in question. The former vessel is a dish, and the latter a fairly low bowl-form.

Form type M. C: I.

A small dish (fig. 79 and Pl. XXIX, fig. 9) with flat bottom and sides with a straight profile but widening out fairly rapidly. Round the top of the dish is a narrow horizontal brim. The vessel is painted on the inside only.

Form type M. C: II.

A small bowl (fig. 80 and Pl. XXIX, figs. 12 and 13) with a relatively small bottom, from which the bowl widens out fairly rapidly upwards, the sides having a convex profile. The bowl is painted on the inside only: also a band runs round the mouth on the outside. Compared with the bowl P. S: II, the bowl M. C: II is considerably lower.

Of the second form series, the hanging bowls, there is no type in Ma Chang pottery without annular handles, and there are no types with ears. Only one single Ma Chang form can be referred to this series. It is a fairly globular pot with medium-sized mouth, four pairs of holes arranged in the form of a cross round the mouth, and two diametrically opposed ring handles slightly below the middle of the vessel. It is clear that this vessel not only could be held suspended but was intended to be carried by the two annular handles. In the shape of its body the vessel is perhaps most closely akin to the forms P. S: VII and P. S: VIII, particularly the latter. It is however far larger than the vessels in the analogous Pan Shan group.

Form type M. C: III.

A hanging vessel (fig. 81 and Pl. XLI, fig. 1) with globular body, medium-sized mouth without neck or brim, and with a pair of diametrically opposed handles set just below the equatorial plane. The walls of the vessel are pierced with four pairs of fairly large holes placed all in the same plane slightly below the mouth. These pairs of holes sit crosswise around the mouth. The globular body is distended upwards and downwards into a

(I) 96　　　　　　　　　　　　　*Palæontologia Sinica*　　　　　　　　　　　　Ser. D.

M. C. I. K. 5038.
Fig. 79.

M. C. II. K. 5616.
Fig. 80.

M. C. III. K. 5320.
Fig. 81.

M. C. IV. K. 5946.
Fig. 82.

M. C. IV. K. 5360.
Fig. 83.

M. C. VII. K. 5294.
Fig. 84.

M. C. VI. K. 5611.
Fig. 85.

M. C. V. K. 5949.
Fig. 86.

M. C. VIII. K. 5786.
Fig. 87.

M. C. VIII. K. 5309.
Fig. 88.

M. C. VIII. K. 5828.
Fig. 89.

M. C. IX. K. 5979.
Fig. 90.

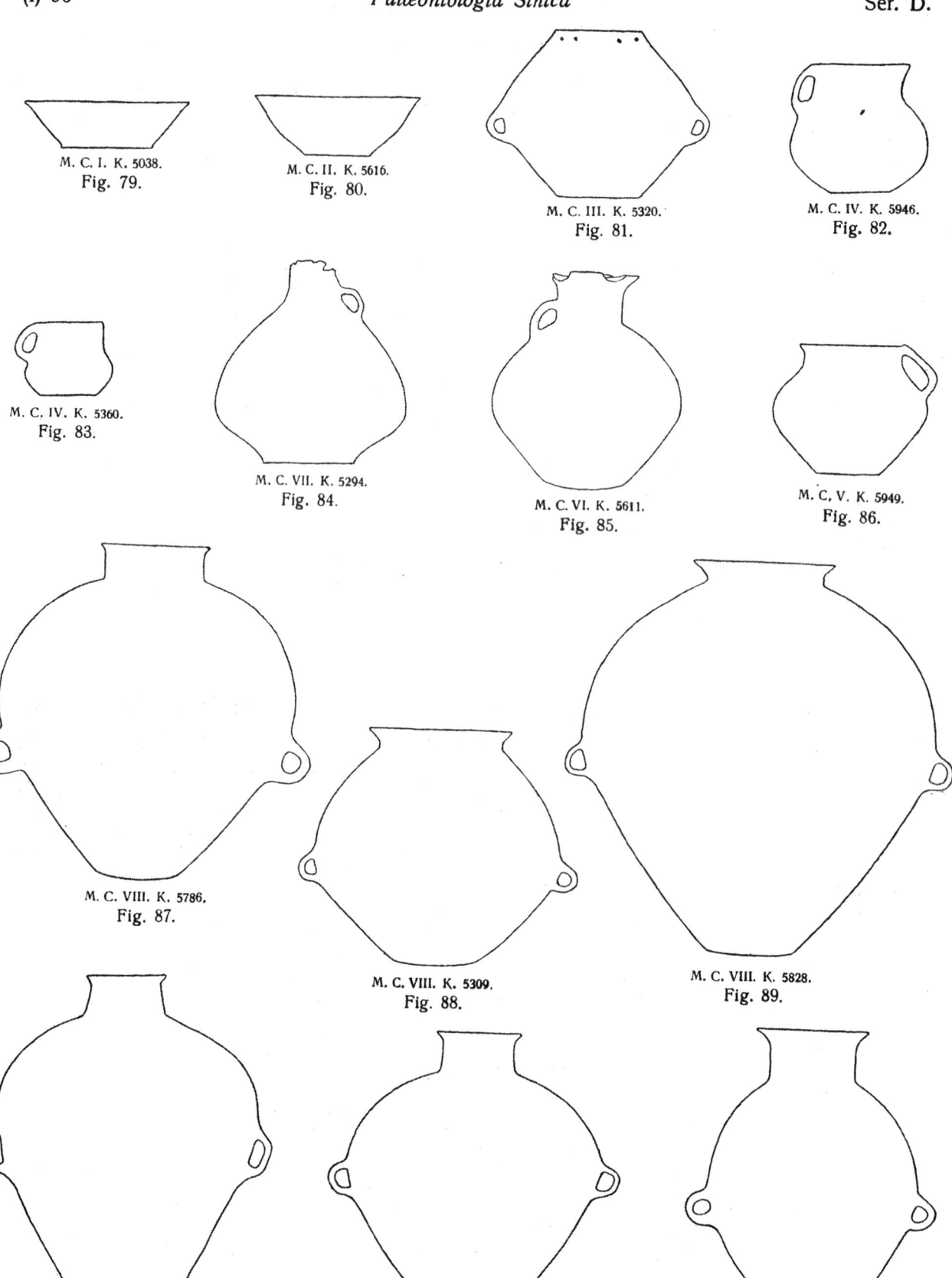

M. C. IX. K. 5755.
Fig. 91.

M. C. IX. K. 5292.
Fig. 92.

slightly conical shape and is then truncated by mouth and bottom. The handles are very sturdy. The pot is painted on the outside only.

The third form series is characterized by the fact that the vessels have an unpaired handle set on the neck and the uppermost part of the body. The series so far contains four different types, all provided with a neck, which however in the case of two of the types merges into the body. In these forms the profile describes a more pronounced curve than in the analogous Pan Shan forms. The types are divisible into cups (M. C: IV) and jugs (M. C: V—VII). The cup M. C: IV is clearly evolved out of the cup P. S: XVI. The jug M. C: V is closely related to the jug P. S: XV but has a better designed handle. The two succeeding forms, M. C: VI —VII, are both derived from the high-necked jugs of the types P. S: XVIII—XIX. In the first of these (M. C: VI) the body has largely retained its form, while the mouth has been given a pronounced brim. In the second (M. C: VII) the widest part of the body has been shifted lower down and the body itself has been given the shape of a pear. How the mouth terminated in this case — whether with or without a brim — it is impossible to determine, as only one specimen of this form of jug has been found so far, and the upper part of the somewhat high neck of our specimen has been broken off.

Form type M. C: IV.

A small cup (figs. 82, 83 and Pl. XXV, figs. 4 and 9), with body low or of medium height and a proportionately high neck. The body's profile is convex, the neck's profile concave. The neck is embraced by a very strong handle, which is attached to the rim of the mouth and to the uppermost portion of the body. The neck is not distinctly differentiated from the body, and may even merge into it to such an extent that its character of a neck almost entirely disappears (Pl. XXV, fig. 9). At the top there may be a suggestion of a brim to the mouth (Pl. XXV, fig. 4). The cup is painted on the outside and also on an inner band round the mouth.

Form type M. C: V.

A medium-sized jug (fig. 86 and Pl. XXX, fig. 9) with small bottom, a markedly globular side, fairly wide neck with a concave profile and the brim of the mouth slightly turned outwards; further, a very large handle fixed at the upper end to the brim of the mouth and at the lower end just above the equatorial plane. Neck and body merge into one another. The outside of the vessel is painted, as is also an inner band round the mouth.

Form type M. C: VI.

A medium-sized jug (fig. 85 and Pl. XXVI, fig. 6) with a fairly small bottom, the body globular or the shape of an inverted pear truncated at the upper and lower ends, high, narrow neck and a handle attached partly to the middle of the neck and partly to the upper part of the body. The top of the neck opens out into a wide brim. The vessel is painted on the outside and also on the inner surface of the brim.

Form type M. C: VII.

A medium-sized jug (fig. 84 and Pl. XXIV, fig. 3) with small bottom, pear-shaped body, high narrow neck and a handle attached partly to the neck a little way above the border-line of the body and partly to the upper portion of the body. The main difference between this jug and the preceding type lies in the shape of the body, the widest portion here lying very low down on the vessel. The jug is painted on the exterior only.

In the Pan Shan pottery the third form series is succeeded by a fourth, comparatively somewhat heterogeneous, group. There are however no obviously related forms in the Ma Chang pottery. I proceed therefore to the following group.

The first two forms of the fifth Pan Shan series (P. S: XXIII and P. S: XXIV) comprised, it will be remembered, the bulk of the material belonging to the Pan Shan sepulchral pottery. That is hardly the case here. It is true that the two types, the low-necked M. C: VIII and the high-necked M. C: IX, both contain a large number of individual specimens, though not in such abundance as M. C: XIV. Obvious transitional forms connect them up with respective types in the Pan Shan material, and their subsequent development can be definitely traced. Besides these two forms there occur also two types of vessel with pairs of handles, which however are asymmetrically placed. The one represents a form closely related to the form type P. S: XXIX, and the other a form closely related to the form type P. S: XXX, and in these both the types M. C: X and M. C: XI undoubtedly have their respective prototypes.

Form types M. C: VIII and M. C: IX.

The Pan Shan types P. S: XXIII, the low-necked pot, and P. S: XXIV, the high-necked pot, (the types A and B) had tended in their latest phase of development towards higher bodies and lower necks. At the same time, the upper half of the vessel had become increasingly rotund and the lower half more and more conically pointed. Similarly, the diameter of the bottoms had diminished. These tendencies are continued in both the types of large pots belonging to the Ma Chang style (see figs. 87—92), the one of which has a low neck and the other a high neck. The average size of these vessels diminishes. Some vessels can hold about 25 litres, while others have a capacity as small as 4 litres. No clear difference is determinable here between the body forms of the high-necked and of the low-necked vessels. The breadth of the body in the earlier Ma Chang vessels, e. g. Pl. XXII, fig. 1 and Pl. XXIII, fig. 1, which still retain the Pan Shan style's dentated edge round the painted upper border, and sometimes also the exterior decoration on the neck, is not much greater than the height: $\frac{\text{breadth of body}}{\text{height of body}} = \frac{38.5}{36}$. Later the bodies increase in height. Some advanced vessels of the Ma Chang period have bodies whose breadth and height are practically the same: $\frac{\text{breadth of body}}{\text{height of body}} = \frac{36.8}{36}$ (Pl. XXIV, figs. 1 and 2) and $\frac{\text{breadth of body}}{\text{height of body}} = \frac{36}{36}$ (Pl. XXIV, fig. 7). In other advanced Ma Chang vessels the height has become greater than the breadth: e. g. Pl. XXXIX, fig. 2, in which $\frac{\text{breadth of body}}{\text{height of body}} = \frac{34}{36}$, and Pl. XXIII, fig. 6, in which $\frac{\text{breadth of body}}{\text{height of body}} = \frac{33}{36}$. These vessels are at the same time markedly hemispherical towards the top, and their bottoms are very small, the diameter being about $^1/_4$ of the greatest diameter of the body. This gives the pots a pronounced breast (Pl. XXII, fig. 6, Pl. XXIV, fig. 2). Others again of the advanced Ma Chang vessels increase still further in relative height. In vessels such as Pl. XXIV, fig. 5, Pl. XXV, fig. 1 and Pl. XXVI, fig. 9, the height far exceeds the breadth. The ratio $\frac{\text{breadth of body}}{\text{height of body}}$ in the first case $= \frac{30}{36}$, in the second case $= \frac{29}{36}$ and in the third case $= \frac{26}{36}$. This means of course that the breast is less emphasized, the upper part of the body is not so spherical, and the shape becomes that of an egg, a plum, or an inverted and extended pear, the point being invariably truncated by the bottom. In another series the vessels retain their pronounced breast, but in this case the pot becomes strongly globular not only in its upper part but in its entirety (Pl. XXIV, fig. 9 and

Pl. XXII, fig. 3), with the obvious result that, the globe being truncated at the top by the neck and at the base by the bottom, the breadth becomes far greater than the height. The ratio $\frac{\text{breadth of body}}{\text{height of body}}$ in both these cases $= \frac{43}{36}$.

Both these variants of the body-form in the form types M. C: VIII and M. C: IX, the high and relatively narrow, and the low and more globular, I regard as being new inventions during the Ma Chang period. The indications are that the globular body probably represents a form that was arrived at and is fairly common in the middle part of the period. The extended narrower type perhaps represents a form that was not evolved until later. In some cases it is no doubt a degenerate variant, possibly also showing a local influence. Several somewhat degenerate vessels of this type come from the locality Ma Pai Tse in Nien Po Hsien. These pots are shaped like an inverted pear. There is a similar vessel from the site Ma Chang Yen, which has given the period its name, but in this case it has a plum-shaped body.

The handles in these two form types are fairly sturdy. The handle's upper point of attachment is generally just below the centre of the body. In a number of advanced vessels it is shifted still further down; moreover, the handle is often set at a more or less oblique angle (see Pl. XXIV, figs. 4, 5 and 6). The two types M. C: VIII and M. C: IX can be fairly clearly differentiated, though there are a few isolated transitional forms between them (Pl. XXIV, figs 6 and 8).

The representatives of the low-necked form type M. C: VIII are somewhat few in number. The mouth of this type is generally wide, its neck is low and widens rapidly upwards to form a brim. The profile of the neck consists of a concave curve. Owing to the paucity of these vessels, the course of development is difficult to determine with any certainty. It is easy to see, however, that the heights of the necks are considerably smaller than those of the late Pan Shan vessels of form type P. S: XXIII. The majority of the vessels of this type preserved in our collection probably belong to the middle and latter part of the Ma Chang system. There is a demonstrable tendency amongst them for the collar part of their necks to become lower and lower and to widen out more and more.

The form type M. C: IX occurs in large numbers; it has a high neck and a relatively narrow mouth. As has already been pointed out, the vessels belonging to this type generally have decidedly lower necks than the Pan Shan vessels of the type P. S: XXIV. Only in one case, (Pl. XXII, fig. 2), is the neck of any considerable height. To judge from the pattern on the mantle and that on the neck, as also from the shape of the body, this high-necked pot would appear to be an early and somewhat isolated individual. In the other vessels the height of the neck varies considerably. The mouths are in general narrower than those in the form type M. C: VIII. The variation is however fairly wide, and vessels of type M. C: IX occur with a mouth as wide as the narrowest forms to be found in type M. C: VIII.

In the Pan Shan vessels of type P. S: XXIV the neck was quite clearly differentiated from the body, whereas among the Ma Chang vessels there is a tendency to let neck and body merge gently into one another. The tendency is patent in the vessels from the Ma Chang Yen site, and still more obvious in the vessels that come from Ma Pai Tsu. The same feature is clearly observable also in the vessel K. 5308 (Pl. XXIV, fig. 5) bought at Lanchow. The tendency represents a feature that is new to sepulchral pottery and belongs to the highly advanced Ma Chang style; moreover, it would appear to have had a strong influence on the pottery of following periods towards an ever-increasing effect of mobility in its silhouette.

The outer profiles of the necks are generally at least slightly concave. The necks of the earliest vessels (e. g. Pl. XXIII, fig. 1) are entirely of the advanced Pan Shan form, but they are without ears. Subsequently the mouth widens out to form a brim, finally acquiring in some cases a quite pronounced breadth (Pl. XXIII, figs. 4, 5 and 7). These pots with brims represent, as compared with the earliest Ma Chang vessels, fairly advanced forms. It is evident, however, that this tendency — at least in Nien Po Hsien — was suppressed during the end of the period, when a marked degenerative process was going on at that site. There then emerges in some cases a new and peculiar type of neck, which narrows down considerably towards the top and then again widens out (Pl. XXIII, fig. 6).

Form type M. C: X.

Small pot or jug (fig. 93 and Pl. XXIX, fig. 6) with fairly large bottom and low, bulbous body, low neck, medium-sized mouth, large annular handle attached to the edge of the mouth and to the upper portion of the body and ending in a point which projects above the plane of the mouth. Just below the widest part of the vessel is a nipple-like rudiment of a ridge handle. The vessel is painted on its exterior, also on the interior of the neck.

Form type M. C: XI.

Medium-sized vessel (fig. 94) with an almost spherical body truncated at top and base by the neck and bottom. The neck is of medium height, and there are two

(I) 102   *Palæontologia Sinica*   Ser. D.

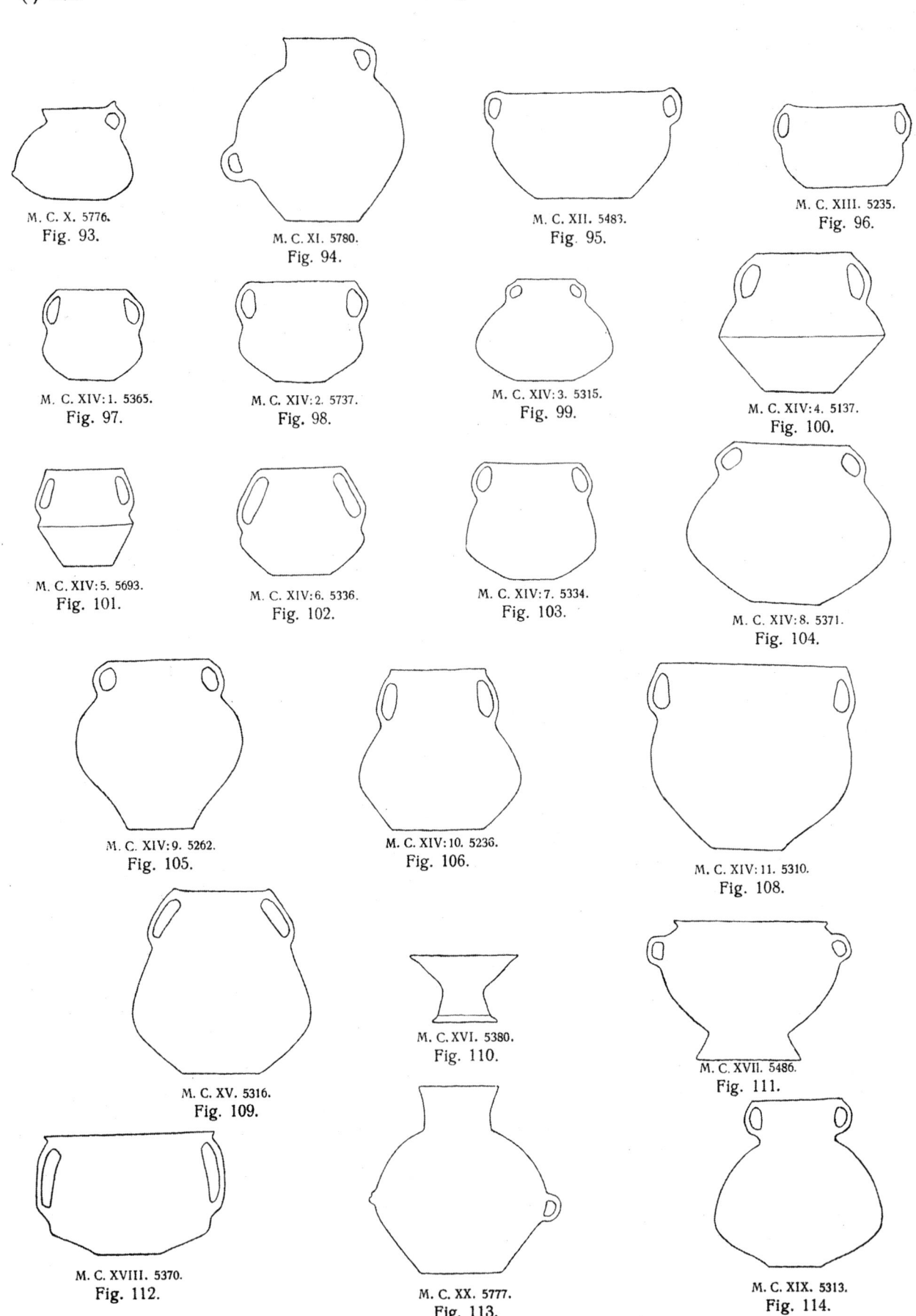

M. C. X. 5776.
Fig. 93.

M. C. XI. 5780.
Fig. 94.

M. C. XII. 5483.
Fig. 95.

M. C. XIII. 5235.
Fig. 96.

M. C. XIV: 1. 5365.
Fig. 97.

M. C. XIV: 2. 5737.
Fig. 98.

M. C. XIV: 3. 5315.
Fig. 99.

M. C. XIV: 4. 5137.
Fig. 100.

M. C. XIV: 5. 5693.
Fig. 101.

M. C. XIV: 6. 5336.
Fig. 102.

M. C. XIV: 7. 5334.
Fig. 103.

M. C. XIV: 8. 5371.
Fig. 104.

M. C. XIV: 9. 5262.
Fig. 105.

M. C. XIV: 10. 5236.
Fig. 106.

M. C. XIV: 11. 5310.
Fig. 108.

M. C. XV. 5316.
Fig. 109.

M. C. XVI. 5380.
Fig. 110.

M. C. XVII. 5486.
Fig. 111.

M. C. XVIII. 5370.
Fig. 112.

M. C. XX. 5777.
Fig. 113.

M. C. XIX. 5313.
Fig. 114.

asymmetrically placed annular handles, the one embracing the neck and the other set on the opposite side of the body just below the equatorial plane. The neck has a concave profile. The handles are very strong, particularly the one on the body. The vessel is painted on the outside, also on an inner band running round the mouth.

The sixth form group belonging to the Pan Shan pottery, which was characterized by double, diametrically opposed handles on the neck, comprised three types of vessels: P. S: XXXI — P. S: XXXIII (the X—Y—Z vessels). Forms analogous to these are found in the Ma Chang style. There are low bowls, akin to the X vessels, of two somewhat different types, M. C: XII and M. C: XIII. The former is of medium size and has no forms of handles other than annular handles. The latter has in addition a projecting, somewhat rudimentary ridge handle, divided into two sections, on the body. These two types are rare. Then comes a form that is very numerously represented — indeed it is quantitatively no doubt the predominant form of vessel in the Ma Chang style — viz. the Ma Chang bowl M. C: XIV, analogous to the Y vessels of the Pan Shan pottery. It shows a remarkable variation, and it is easy to follow its evolution and subdivision into new types of vessels all existing during the Ma Chang period. Finally, a form of large beaker, M. C: XV, is related to the Pan Shan Z type, though substantially modified. This form is also rare.

Form type M. C: XII.

A medium-sized bowl (fig. 95 and Pl. XXVII, fig. 6) with large bottom, low body, the sides widening out upwards and having a convex profile; low neck, not very clearly differentiated, with wide mouth and a concave profile. Two diametrically opposed annular handles embrace the neck. The bowl is painted on its exterior and also on an inner band round the mouth.

Form type M. C: XIII.

A small bowl (fig. 96), with a medium-sized bottom, low body with convex profile, and relatively high neck very indistinctly differentiated and embraced by two diametrically opposed handles. The mouth is wide and has a slight brim. The neck is concave in profile. Between the handles and low down on either side of the body are ridge handles divided into two sections. The bowl is not so closely related to the Pan Shan X type as is the preceding one and forms to a certain extent a transition to the following Ma Chang type. It is painted on the outside, and also on an inner band round the mouth.

Form type M. C: XIV.

A type of bowl that develops during the Ma Chang period into the most important and the most richly varied form of vessels within this style (for figures see the diagram figs. 97—108). Numerically also it assumes a predominant position in Ma Chang pottery.

It obviously originates in the Y type of the Pan Shan pottery, though even within the latter style the Y type showed distinct variations. However, during the Ma Chang period there develops an almost infinite variety. In particular those types that, to judge from their patterns, are of an early date are closely akin to the Pan Shan forms (Pl. XXVIII, figs. 1 and 2, Pl. XXVII, fig. 10 and diagram M. C. XIV: 1). They are of small size. From these ordinary types there evolve forms of vessels of strikingly different kinds.

A number of vessels (e. g. Pl. XXVI, fig. 2 and diagram M. C. XIV: 2) have wider mouths and proportionately higher necks. In shape these vessels to a certain extent resemble the foregoing type M. C: XIII.

In a large number of the vessels the necks are not so clearly differentiated as in the Y vessels of the Pan Shan style — indeed, there is some difficulty in deciding which is neck and which is body. In order to make the term clear I venture *in this case* to regard as neck that part of the vessel which is embraced by the handles. Within this definition, however, it is difficult to include a variation in type such as, for instance, the vessel shown in Pl. XXX, fig. 1. A still more manifestly peculiar form in the same evolutional chain is represented by the vessel reproduced in Pl. XLI, fig. 4 and diagram M. C. XIV: 6. To judge from their patterns, these specialized forms belong to the later phases of the period.

Other forms are transitional from the ordinary forms to vessels with high bodies and high necks, as e. g. Pl. XXVIII, fig. 8. Here neck and body merge into one another with gentle gradations. This specialized form belongs to the period's most highly developed types. A further distinguishing feature of some of these advanced forms of vessel is their size (diagram M. C. XIV: 10). Towards the close of the period the vessels tend to assume ever-increasing proportions, and by the end of the period many of them have already attained to the dimensions of the medium-sized Hsin Tien vessels.

The lower-necked vessels likewise increase in size towards the close of the period (Pl. XXVIII, fig. 5, Pl. XXX, fig. 7 and Pl. XL, fig. 6, diagram M. C. XIV: 9). In these latter short-necked vessels the silhouettes become richer and more varied. The necks assume gently concave lines as they expand outwards (Pl. XXX, fig. 6, Pl. XL, fig. 6), and the bodies show a tendency to become globular or lenticular (Pl. XL, fig. 6 and diagram M. C. XIV: 8).

Strong contrasts are achieved in the shape by narrowing down the neck and giving the body a more and more pronounced lenticular form (Pl. XL, fig. 2). The silhouettes of the bodies are likewise given great variety, the continuity being broken through abruptly secant planes (Pl. XXX, fig. 7). An advance in this respect is observable in such vessels as are shown in Pl. XXIX, figs. 1 and 3, and diagram M. C. XIV: 4 and 5, in which the body to a certain extent acquires a heart-shaped silhouette. A similar silhouette, though without any abrupt breaks, occurs in a vessel such as Pl. XXVII, fig. 7. It is in these latter vessels that the most experienced and imaginative effect is achieved in the silhouette of form type M. C: XIV at the close of the period. It thereby comes into very close touch with the ceramic forms of the Hsin Tien period.

Large bowl forms are evolved by greatly increasing the size of the high-collared but otherwise ordinary Y type from the early part of the period, as e. g. Pl. XLI, fig. 2 and M. C. XIV: 11. These vessels would appear to date from the middle part of the period, as is indicated by both the exterior and the interior patterns and also by the not very highly developed silhouette.

The extreme evolutional forms of the bowl type of vessel described here are sufficiently differentiated to permit of their being referred to different form types. As, however, intermediate links have survived, I have judged it more correct to keep them together in one form type.

Form type M. C: XV.

Beaker or stoup (fig. 109 and Pl. XXVII, fig. 12, one of the handles broken off) with small bottom, high body, widest just above the bottom, low neck and two long handles, the upper end of which is attached to the rim of the neck and the lower end fairly low down on the body. The beaker form manifestly finds its prototype in the Z vessels of the Pan Shan pottery, but the body is considerably higher and the handles much longer. Moreover, the mouth is narrower than in the Pan Shan type. The vessel is painted on the outside, also on the interior of the neck.

So far there have been discovered no form types from the Ma Chang period associated in form with the Pan Shan seventh group of "fancy forms". There are however among the pottery of the Ma Chang period a few new form types that do not occur among the Pan Shan mortuary pottery previously discussed. It is possible that these types were new creations in Kansu during the Ma Chang period or that they were imported into that province during the same era. Further, there is the possibility that they existed amongst the dwelling-site pottery contemporary with the Pan Shan sepulchral pottery, but that it was not until the Ma Chang period that they were included amongst the mortuary paraphernalia. Finally, there is the possibility of the types' actually existing in the Pan Shan pottery though not yet discovered. Two types have an annular foot, M. C: XVI and M. C: XVII. The first of these is a dish standing on a foot, the second is a deep bowl likewise standing on a foot and furnished with two diametrically opposed handles. Ring-footed vessels do not occur in the Pan Shan style; on the other hand, we know the annular foot from the contemporary dwelling-site pottery. It is probable, therefore, that during the Ma Chang period it was borrowed from the dwelling-site pottery. One pot, M. C: XIX, which has a high neck and two handles up on the neck, gives the impression of being a temporary experiment and an extravagant variant of the type of pot M. C: IX. Finally, there are an elegant form of bowl with two long handles (M. C: XVIII), and a unique pot (M. C: XX) with an annular handle and a rudimentary ridge handle, both placed in the equatorial plane.

Form type M. C: XVI.

A small bowl or dish on an annular foot (fig. 110 and Pl. XXIX, figs. 7, 8 and 10). The dish may be flat or deep, and the foot may be more or less distinct from the dish. Usually the foot is widened at the end into a distended ring, and it has generally a couple of fairly large, diametrically opposed holes. In some cases however these holes are wanting. The foot's profile may be either concave or nearly straight. This type of vessel may perhaps have been the prototype of the later "Tou" bowl, a well-known form among the archaic bronze vessels of China. In this type of pottery the upper side of the dish only is painted.

Form type M. C: XVII.

A medium-sized bowl (fig. 111 and Pl. XLI, fig. 6). It has a fairly high annular foot and a body of the same basic type as P. S: III, with wide mouth, the edge forming a brim, and hemispherical in form. Just below the brim of the neck are two sturdy annular handles placed diametrically opposite to one another. The bowl is painted on both the exterior and the interior.

Form type M. C: XVIII.

A medium-sized, fairly high bowl (fig. 112 and Pl. XXX, fig. 11) with a base like an inverted cone, abruptly truncated by the small bottom surface, a vertically straight, fairly high side, wide mouth, the brim of the mouth being clearly differentiated, fairly broad and expanding upwards; two diametrically opposed handles set partly on the brim of the mouth and partly on the side just above the borderline of the base. The shape, with its well-defined, clear-cut outline, is somewhat peculiar. I consider it probable that the form is a new one created during the Ma Chang period. The vessel is painted on both the exterior and the interior.

Form type M. C: XIX.

A small pot (fig. 114 and Pl. XXX, fig. 3) with a lenticular body, high neck with narrow mouth and broad brim to the mouth, and two handles attached partly to the brim of the mouth, partly to the neck just below its middle portion. The shape may be regarded as a curious blend of types M. C: IX and M. C: XIV. Presumably it is a temporary experiment. The vessel is painted on the outside; also a ring is painted round the interior of the mouth.

Form type M. C: XX.

A medium-sized pot (fig. 113 and Pl. XXIII, fig. 2) with fairly large bottom, spherical body truncated by neck and bottom, high neck and two handles set in the equatorial plane, the one an annular handle, the other a rudimentary ridge handle. The pot is clearly derived from the Pan Shan form type P. S: IX. The type is presumably a new one created during the Ma Chang period.

THE PAINTING AND DÉCOR OF THE MA CHANG POTTERY.

In the foregoing we have shown what the Ma Chang pottery has borrowed and inherited from the Pan Shan pottery in regard to construction and form. The affiliation of the Ma Chang pottery to the Pan Shan style stands out with still greater clarity when it comes to painting and décor. In the following we shall have cause to revert again and again to this point, but it should at once be emphasized here that this technical and decorative heritage is in practically every respect utilized in an extremely independent manner and in many ways evolves into something quite foreign to the general spirit of the Pan Shan pottery.

Three entirely different decorative systems are employed in the painted ornamentation of the Ma Chang vessels.

The first system is a direct legacy from the Pan Shan pottery. In it two colours are used, each one covering different parts of the surface, the ware itself appearing here and there as a light ground beneath the décor. The colours are black and red. Both are dull and often powdery and grainy. The black colour may tone off into grey, brown and violet as well as blue, but it has seldom or never that deep, rich, black tone which distinguishes the best black colour in the Pan Shan pottery. The red colour is generally darker here than in the Pan Shan pottery and often changes to violet, less frequently to brown. The painted portions of the surface, owing to the granulation both of the ware and of the paint, which highly refracts rays of light falling upon it, not infrequently have a kind of dewy appearance somewhat like certain forest berries, as for instance, the bog whortleberry. Dull painting of this kind is well-known from other cultures as well.

The second system utilizes only one colour against the ground colour of the ware, but otherwise employs the same "families" of patterns as in the foregoing system. The colour here used is black with the modifications spoken of in regard to the black colour employed in the foregoing decorative system. It generally has a violet or a blue tone. In certain cases one might almost suspect that it is a mixture of a red and a black material, as in K. 5330 (Pl. XXV, fig. 6).

The third decorative system likewise makes use of two colours. The one of these colours here covers the entire decorative surface and serves as a background for the other colour, which in its turn alone provides the decorative design (Pl. XL, fig 3). A coloured ground of this kind is called slip. The rest of the vessel, the undecorated part, generally has no slip. The coloured slip is a new invention of the Ma Chang period and occurs on both large and small vessels belonging to that style. True painted slip is lacking in the Pan Shan pottery which has so far been found, and it is probable therefore that the slip was introduced some way on in the Ma Chang period. As a fully developed material it is a relatively late phenomenon characteristic of the period's more highly and most highly advanced ceramic representatives.

Slip acts to a certain extent in a manner in direct contrast to the texture of the pitted ware and the other thick, powdery paint. It fills in the tiny hollows in the ware and gives the surface a certain polish, which however never approaches the degree of lustre attained in the Pan Shan pottery. In its earliest phase it is thin and pale (K. 5990, Pl. XXIV, fig. 4), though in time it becomes denser and darker, e. g. K. 5979 (Pl. XXIII, fig. 6). It almost invariably has a brownish tone, often with a shade of yellow. Occasionally it acquires a fine, dark purple tinge, e. g. K. 5979.

The active décor, the pattern, is, as mentioned above, painted on the slip and is usually executed in black. It not infrequently happens, however, that in the firing the two paints, the superimposed black and the underlying russet, have melted together, with the result that in such cases the black paint for the most part acquires a brown or violet tone. It often shades off into blue.

The different parts of the vessels are of extreme importance to the decorative scheme and are on the whole the same as those of the Pan Shan vessels. The neck or collar often widens out into an extra broad brim, a new feature of which ready use is made as an area for ornamentation. This particularly applies to the more or less horizontal upper side of the brim. The neck itself is often decorated both on the outside and on the inside. Below the neck comes the breast-like or belly-like part of the vessel, the mantle, here still broader and more predominant than in the Pan Shan pottery and, as in the latter, the most important decorative area. Below the mantle is the base, here too frequently fashioned like an inverted, truncated cone. As in the Pan Shan pottery, it is almost invariably undecorated. Ornamentation is also lacking usually on the bottom surface, though there are cases in which it is decorated. In cases where there is a real foot, that feature is never ornamented. In the larger vessels the handles are without exception undecorated. In the smaller vessels, on the other hand, the décor on the handles is a very conspicuous feature in Ma Chang pottery. The décor on the mantles is often influenced even by the ornamentation on the handles and not infrequently forms an entirely composite design in harmony with it — a decorative feature peculiar to the Ma Chang period and almost entirely unknown in the Pan Shan pottery. The insides and interior bottoms of low and open bowls and dishes are frequently decorated. In vessels of this kind the exterior may or may not have a décor, just as in the Pan Shan vessels of the same type. Dishes standing on a foot are decorated on the inside of the vessel but have no ornamentation on the exterior surface.

The décor in most Ma Chang vessels begins down below with a lower border obviously borrowed from the Pan Shan pottery, though here it is far more conventional. We may recall the rich variations in the lower border of the Pan Shan pottery, particularly during the early and middle phase of that period. Already in late Pan Shan pottery we find that the variations had come to an end and that a certain measure of conventionalism had taken its place. It is the two most common lower borders of the late Pan Shan style that become all-prevailing in the Ma Chang period. Of these borders the one consists of a single fairly broad or narrow, black horizontal band (occasionally replaced by a red band), the other of two bands, both black or in one or two isolated cases red, e. g. K. 5466 (Pl. XXII, fig. 8), one upper broad horizontal band and one lower narrow wavy or garland-like band, sometimes quite graceful and slender. This latter band, which is manifestly derived from the wavy band of the lower border in the Pan Shan pottery and is put in the same place, has a much slower rhythm, with fewer and slower undulations than the Pan Shan band, and is fashioned in the form of a garland rather than in that of a true wave. The difference between the two bands of this type is nevertheless particularly striking and is perceived by the trained eye at the first glance. In the smaller vessels a true lower border is often lacking, its place being sometimes taken by a black surface with a pattern formed characteristically out of the ground colour. One of the most common lower borders of this type is composed of black zones with cowrie chains in ground colour — a design totally unknown in Pan Shan pottery. The point in connection with the lower border described above is of some considerable theoretical importance as it proves that the Ma Chang pottery is a direct descendant of late Pan Shan pottery and is not an earlier off-shoot of it.

In the Pan Shan décor the band bordering on neck and body and the subjacent upper border formed two features that were signally characteristic of the Pan Shan pottery and were in general the most conventional in style. The boundary bands were almost without exception red and in certain exceptional cases might be shifted slightly higher up or lower down. The upper border usually consisted of a single broad black band dentated or pointed along the top. This band might be reduplicated or varied, though it was only in rare cases that any variation occurred. The earliest representatives of the Ma Chang style, e. g. K. 5755 (Pl. XXIII, fig. 1) and K. 5286 (Pl. XXXIX, fig. 1), still have the boundary band and the upper border separate, and the border is still dentated along the top. In the great majority of Ma Chang vessels however the boundary band, which has still retained its red colour, has merged into the upper border, which is likewise still black but has lost its dentated edge. Thus during the Ma Chang period the design on the upper portion of the body is terminated by a broad double band, the upper half of which is red and the lower half black. It is best to transfer the term upper border to this double band, especially as the red portion is now placed for the most part on the body with its upper rim on the lower edge of the neck. In a few small and advanced Ma Chang vessels (e. g. K. 5314, Pl. XXVII, fig. 11, Pl. XL, fig. 6 and K. 5315, Pl. XL, fig. 2) this upper border has been shifted further down and the red band has been surrounded by *two* black bands, one above it and one below it, a characteristic Ma Chang triad, even as applied to other ornamental details. On the vessels ornamented in *one* colour and on vessels with a coating of slip the double band — the upper border — is replaced by a plain horizontal band. In certain cases the upper border is absent altogether.

Even as regards the upper border the Ma Chang pottery has inherited from the Pan Shan pottery. In this respect, as also in regard to the lower border, it is obviously conventional. But the Pan Shan ornamentation had here already acquired a stereotyped form, which is repeated in an orthodox manner throughout the entire period.

In the *larger* vessels the *exterior* decoration on the necks is far more uniform during the Ma Chang period than that on the Pan Shan pots. Here too the Ma Chang ornamentation originates in Pan Shan patterns. On some of the earliest Ma Chang vessels there is painted a wide-meshed trellis pattern, a design well-known from the late Pan Shan vessels. The principal exterior neck pattern, which is discussed below (see K. 5304, Pl. XXIV, fig. 1), is likewise known from the Pan Shan pottery, though now it shows a strong development and wide variation. We find already in early Pan Shan pottery an ornamentation on the neck consisting of black bands of angles pointing to the left, i. e. running clockwise (fig. 115). This neck decoration survives throughout the Pan Shan pottery and occurs, for instance, on the head bought in Paris and also on one of the vessels from the large Pan Shan grave. The angles on the Ma Chang vessels are more roughly, bluntly and nonchalantly drawn (fig. 116). The lower line of the angle is often lengthened while the upper line is shortened (K. 5300, Pl. XXII, fig. 7), the lower and longer line often merging into the red band of the upper border. This ornamentation develops in turn into a row of vertical zigzag bands each having three strokes, e. g. K. 5289 (Pl. XXII, fig. 6) and K. 5293 (Pl. XXVI, fig. 9). The zigzag band may further be given a greater number of strokes (fig. 117). In other

Fig. 115.   Fig. 116.   Fig. 117.   Fig. 118.

cases a horizontal band is drawn through the points of the angles, thereby considerably altering the character of the pattern (fig. 118). A neck décor in any other design is rare in the larger Ma Chang vessels. In one isolated case, K. 5617 (Pl. XXXIX, fig. 2), the angular décor is reduced to a narrow band just below the brim of the neck. In this case a number of plain horizontal lines are painted on the remaining portion of the neck. On one vessel, K. 5295 (Pl. XXII, fig. 2), there is a red band about the middle of the neck, and above it a row of narrow, black dentations directed downwards, with the points resting on the red middle band. The lower half of the neck is decorated with a black band with narrow dentations pointing downwards. On pot K. 5979 (Pl. XXIII, fig. 6) the décor on the exterior of the neck consists of double black zigzag bands.

The exterior décor on the neck of the *smaller vessels* is singularly varied and on the whole very original. The majority of its motifs are new inventions as neck ornamentation, but at the same time they are in many cases patterns transferred from the Pan Shan *mantle ornamentation*. Bands of angles running in a clockwise direction also occur here, but the part they play is a very insignificant one. There are also vertical zigzag bands, e. g. K. 5949 (Pl. XXX, fig. 9). Common designs on the necks of the smaller vessels, on the other hand, are: black horizontal lines varying considerably in number (Pl. XXIX, fig. 1 and Pl. XXV, fig. 5), vertical lines (Pl. XXIX, fig. 3), groups of vertical lines (Pl. XXVII, fig. 5), alternating groups of vertical lines and crosses (Pl. XXV, fig. 9) or vertical lines and vertical rows of dots (Pl. XXV, fig. 4); vertical wavy bands in ground colour, vertical wavy lines or bands in close proximity to one another and with very rapid rhythm (Pl. XXVII, fig. 2), horizontal zigzag bands, horizontal wavy bands, rows of squares filled with trelliswork (Pl. XXVII, figs. 9 and 12), or similarly filled circles, and squares in ground colour on a black surface (Pl. XXV, fig. 3), chessboard pattern (Pl. XXVIII, fig. 1), complicated chessboard patterns (Pl. XXIX, fig. 5) and trelliswork (Pl. XXVII, fig. 10). In the smaller advanced vessels the trellis design has evolved into a network of meshes as in a fishing-net,

(Pl. XXVII, fig. 3). In this case the network consists of a series of horizontal garlands. There are transitional forms between the ordinary wide-meshed trellis pattern and this latter pattern. This fishing-net design frequently covers not only the neck, but also, in very advanced vessels, a good part of the body as well.

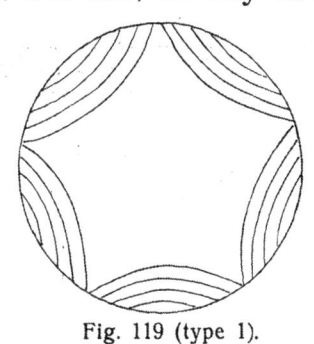

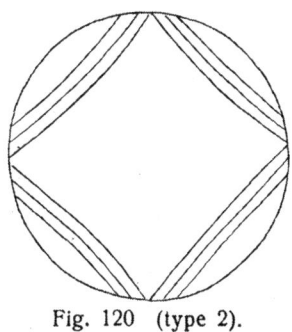

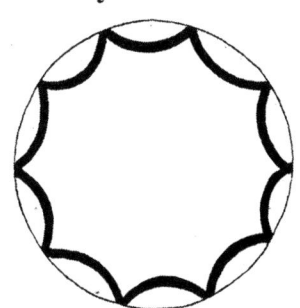

Fig. 119 (type 1). Fig. 120 (type 2). Fig. 121 (type 3).

The great majority of the designs on the exterior of the neck, both of the larger and of the smaller vessels, are purely geometrical, sometimes quite simple and in other cases fairly intricate. Thus, the geometrical tendencies in the Ma Chang style are very conspicuous as far as the exterior neck décor is concerned. Moreover, it may be said that, on the whole, the neck patterns, both in the larger and in the smaller vessels, afford fairly sound clues to the evolution of the Ma Chang pottery. We shall however have more to say on this point when we come to the different décor families.

The interior neck décor is on the whole very uniform and not, like the exterior ornamentation, divided into two groups, one for the large and one for the small vessels. It is extraordinarily easy to trace its origin from the interior neck décor in Pan Shan pottery. In this respect some of the earliest Ma Chang vessels are ornamented with designs of a similar kind to those in a number of the advanced Pan Shan vessels. The décor consists in this case of double, treble or quadruple, narrow black bands of garlands surrounding the interior of the mouth (fig. 119). Similar, though fewer and straighter, bands of garlands occur also in more highly advanced vessels from middle Ma Chang (4 festoons, fig. 120). A still more simplified and rougher design is seen in the apparently advanced though at the same time degenerate pot K. 5980 (Pl. XXIII, fig. 8), one of the representatives of a whole group of degenerate and advanced pots, concerning which more anon (fig. 121). Likewise in late Pan Shan there was another closely related interior neck design consisting of a row of vertical black lines or strokes — a last survival of the death-pattern system of Pan Shan pottery — along the inside edge of the neck, beneath this a narrow red horizontal band, and under that again a few single, double or treble bands of garlands in black. This décor is adopted by the earliest Ma Chang vessels almost without modification (fig. 122). Here however the red band is broader and broadens more and more as time goes on. In the course of development the strokes round the rim tend to merge at the top into a black line or a band dentated along the lower edge (fig. 123). Or again the strokes increase in length (fig. 124). In some advanced two-co-

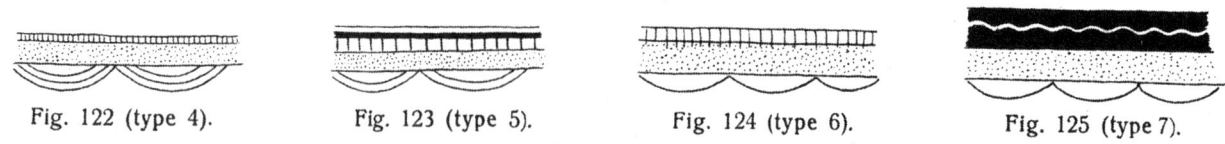

Fig. 122 (type 4).   Fig. 123 (type 5).   Fig. 124 (type 6).   Fig. 125 (type 7).

loured vessels this black band increases in breadth, rhythm being lent to it by a narrow band of short undulations in ground colour showing up against the dark background. The red band still survives below it (fig. 125). In other advanced vessels with a large brim the black band becomes particularly broad and is given a row of round spots in ground colour (fig. 126). Generally speaking, the interior neck décor na-

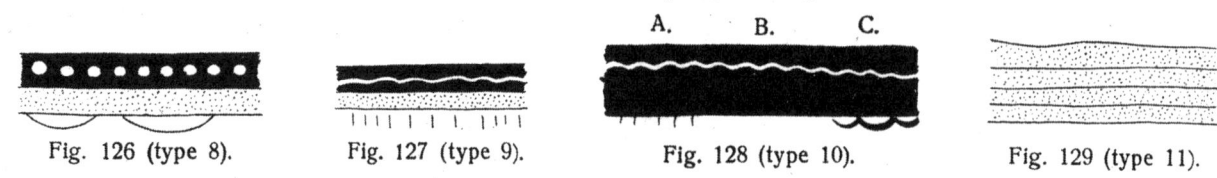

Fig. 126 (type 8).   Fig. 127 (type 9).   Fig. 128 (type 10).   Fig. 129 (type 11).

turally gains in forcefulness and breadth in proportion as the breadth of the brim increases. While this development is going on in the black band, the garland-like lines grow distinctly more and more rudimentary. In the more highly developed vessels, particularly in some of those covered with slip, the lines of garlands are succeeded by black vertical strokes (fig. 127). In the most advanced vessels the neck décor con-

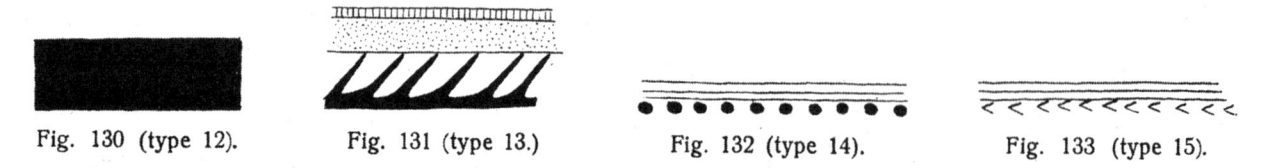

Fig. 130 (type 12).   Fig. 131 (type 13.)   Fig. 132 (type 14).   Fig. 133 (type 15).

sists of a single black band with a wavy band in ground colour, and with or without a dentated edge or garland pattern below (fig. 128), of a few plain black horizontal lines on dark slip (fig. 129) or of one broad horizontal band (fig. 130). In some of the most advanced vessels the border consists of strokes or dentated bands, and along the lower edge a broad red band and beneath that black oblique lines, the lower

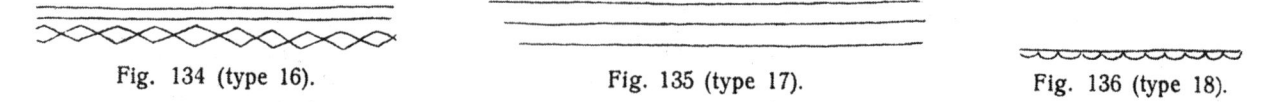

Fig. 134 (type 16).   Fig. 135 (type 17).   Fig. 136 (type 18).

ends joining on to one another round the interior of the mouth (fig. 131). I shall pass over here, for the present, some further late variations in the interior neck décor (figs. 132—137). Of this part of the décor it may be said that it emanates from advanced Pan Shan patterns, its fairly distinct course of evolution proceeding along lines that were quite original as far as the Ma Chang period was concerned.

Fig. 137 (type 19).

Another detail, which is fairly characteristic in its execution in the Ma Chang decorative style, is the ornamentation close to and below the handles of the smaller vessels. In the case of the larger pots the handles are generally placed below or on the lower boundary of the decoration on the mantle, so that they have but little influence on its design. In the small vessels the handles are set on diametrically opposite sides of the usually fairly high neck[1]), and it is natural that they should thus influence the décor both on the neck and on the mantle. This was however not the case in the small vessels of the early Pan Shan period, in spite of the fact that the handles were similarly placed. In late Pan Shan vessels, however, there were instances of the handles' having this effect on the ornamentation of the mantle. In cases where the mantle décor was divided up into trapeziform surfaces the handles were sometimes surrounded by similar smaller trapeziform fields, as e. g. K. 5084 (Pl. XVII, fig. 10). In other cases there was painted beneath and around the handle a horizontal triad consisting of one red and two black bands, the latter dentated along the side adjoining the former. In some of the small vessels of the early Ma Chang period we find this latter décor adopted without any modification, as in K. 5324 (Pl. XXVII, fig. 9), even including the typical dentated edges, as a final relic of the Pan Shan death-pattern system. In slightly more advanced Ma Chang vessels the triad is the same, but the strokes have been eliminated and the colours merge into one another. In a very large proportion of the Ma Chang vessels, particularly those belonging to a late Ma Chang period, the predominant ornamentation on the mantle is completely interrupted below the handles. The mantle décor is thus bisected into two fairly large belts by the narrow square or rectangular fields beneath the handles. These fields are edged with black lines, as in K. 5327 (Pl. XL, fig. 5), or with broad, red bands enclosed in black lines. The fields are in most cases ornamented with a cross. These crosses are typical of the small vessels during the late Ma Chang period (Pl. XL, fig. 6). These fields are also decorated with various other patterns.

To sum up, it may be said of this décor that most of the Pan Shan vessels are entirely without such ornamentation. Some vessels of early Ma Chang style have taken over the rare Pan Shan system as far as concerns the ornamentation round the handles. This ornamentation inherited from the Pan Shan pottery is modified in keeping with

---

[1]) The lower parts of the handles are placed on the top of the mantle.

the Ma Chang system — the last remnants of the vertical stroke design disappear —, but gradually even this ornamentation is altogether replaced by a new decorative system, which is characteristic of the fully developed Ma Chang style.

The handles themselves are undecorated in the case of the large pots. In that of the small vessels there is generally some sort of ornamentation, which may be of two kinds, either plastic or painted. The *plastic ornamentation* belongs especially to the typical transitional period between the Pan Shan and the Ma Chang styles of pottery, though it survives occasionaliy quite far into the Ma Chang period. In earlier vessels it consists of an imposed band with a striated surface, i. e. a direct legacy from the Pan Shan pottery. In certain more advanced vessels, e. g. K. 5349 (Pl. XXVII, fig. 8), the striation is more complicated: the bands merge into the handles in the troughs and not on the crests of the waves. Here too, then, the Ma Chang potter strikingly refashions an inherited tradition. The painted ornamentation is very simple and geometrical, the most common patterns being black horizontal bands and crosses.

As in the case of the Pan Shan vessels, so in regard to the Ma Chang pottery we feel bound to divide up various groups of vessels with similar painted patterns into separate décor families. The predominant pattern amongst the Ma Chang vessels, just as in the case of the Pan Shan vessels, is the pattern on the mantle, and therefore this pattern quite naturally constitutes the décor family's correlating element. The décor families are denoted by ordinal numbers and the letter M: 1 M, 2 M, and so on. This enables them to be easily distinguished from and compared with the Pan Shan décor families 1 P, 2 P, etc.

Décor family 1 M.

The mantle decorated with 4 large circles.

The décor family 11 P, the central décor of the Pan Shan pottery — the family of the spirally ornamented pots — presents, as we have shown above, a clearly defined evolutional series. There the four spiral nuclei grow larger and larger until the remaining space on the vessel becomes so limited that the spiral ornamentation itself is almost entirely expelled. In the course of the transition to the Ma Chang style the spiral band disappears altogether, while the four enlarged spiral nuclei remain, themselves now forming with their supplementary patterns the most effective portions of the whole décor.

It is the 4-circle décor thus evolved that gradually assumes the central position in Ma Chang pottery, as far as the larger vessels are concerned. This pattern becomes as fundamentally important for the study of the evolution of the patterns, and thereby of the relative chronology within the period, as the spiral patterns in Pan Shan pottery. Those links in the chain of development that are preserved are quite sufficient to enable us to reveal in rough outline the tendencies that mark the ornamentation of the period.

The mantle décor in this family consists, as already pointed out above, of four circles filled with patterns. They are symmetrically placed around the mantle and are so arranged that one circle lies above each handle and the two others are inserted between them. A characteristic supplementary décor fills the gaps between the circles. This latter décor is to a certain extent uniform in character, though at the same time it presents a regular evolutional process — an extremely important fact from the chronological point of view.

The supplementary pattern, which extends from the upper to the lower border, serves the purpose of separating two circles placed on a mantle having a surface that is narrower on the upper part than on the lower part. The solution of this constructive and ornamental problem has been worked out in a manner as simple as it

Fig. 138.    Fig. 139.    Fig. 140.    Fig. 141.    Fig. 142.

is natural. In the earliest phase the pattern consists of a boundary line that divides at the bottom end into two curves, which follow the line of the circumference of the adjacent circles. See for instance the pattern forming a "filling" on vessel K. 5755 (Pl. XXIII, fig. 1 right, and fig. 138). A variation of this pattern is achieved by a trifurcation at the lower end, e. g. K. 5311 (Pl. XXIII, fig. 3 and fig. 139). This simple supplementary décor may also be bifurcated at the upper end, as e. g. in K. 5295 (Pl. XXII, fig. 2), a lower angular filling being often added, either single or trifurcate, e. g. K. 5981 (Pl. XXIII, fig. 5 and figs. 140 and 141). The filling-up pattern grows more and more, taking up an ever-increasing amount of space and becoming moreover intricate and ramified. During this process the lower part of the central branch is first bifurcated, e. g. K. 5286 (Pl. XXXIX, fig. 1 and fig. 142). Then the circles are placed a little higher up in order to provide more space for the supplementary décor, e. g. K. 5303 (Pl. XXII, fig. 5 and fig. 143). Here one of the branches is frequently raised above the lower border and is permitted to continue an uninterrupted course concentrically around the elevated circle, e. g. K. 5307 (Pl. XXII, fig. 4

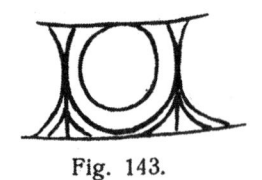

Fig. 143. Fig. 144. Fig. 145. Fig. 146.

and fig. 144). The number of pairs of branches is increased from two to three, e. g. K. 5300 (Pl. XXII, fig. 7 and fig. 145), and occasionally may even amount to four, e. g. K. 5991 (Pl. XXXIX, fig. 3 and fig. 146). This means that the circles are raised further and further away from the lower borders and their relative size on the surface of the mantle is successively reduced. The pattern scheme here exhibits every conceivable intermediate stage; indeed, it must certainly present a chronological series of evolutional phases. The very shapes of the vessels, as well as the patterns on the interior and exterior of the neck, corroborate the evidence provided by the evolutional series that the supplementary pattern has enabled us to follow up[1]).

By reason of the individual ornamentation on the circular surfaces the décor family falls naturally into a number of fairly clearly differentiated sub-families, within which an evolutional process is distinctly traceable. However, even the sub-families represent in themselves to a certain extent different stages in the development of the period's style. One or two of the sub-families are early, another belongs to the middle part of the Ma Chang period, while others again represent late stages. Nevertheless, the members of the sub-families cannot be placed in rows adjacent to but distinct from one another; they rather overlap one another, much as do the pure lines in a population. If dots are made to represent existing pots, and rows of pots to represent sub-families, the interrelation can best be shown graphically by the following simple diagram, in which the dots to the left signify early, and dots to the right late pots:

```
I.    . . . . .
II.         . . . .
III.           .
IV.         . . . . . .
V.                . .
VI.                 .
```

There are thus six different sub-families, but one or two pots that belong to this family but are nevertheless isolated pieces are not included.

---

[1]) An exception is found in the two vessels K. 5979 and K. 5980 (Pl. XXIII, figs. 6 and 8), from Ma Pai Tsu, which may be regarded from the point of view of both shape and colour as advanced though degenerate forms. They possess primitive supplementary patterns. The reasons formerly adduced for considering them to be advanced seem to me to be sufficiently weighty to warrant their being regarded as late pieces, though degenerate even in their decorative design. I shall have more to say on this point when discussing the circle décor.

Sub-family I. An early sub-family, with the circles filled with different kinds of squared network and modified chessboard pattern. Here we find transitional stages between the Pan Shan and the Ma Chang styles. Vessels such as K. 5755 (Pl. XXIII, fig. 1) and K. 5286 (Pl. XXXIX, fig. 1) are from many aspects difficult to place entirely in any one of the groups. The lower border, as well as both the interior and the exterior neck patterns, are typical of the late Pan Shan period. The pattern on the interior of the neck consists of treble or quadruple, narrow, black rows of garlands, that on the exterior of the neck of wide-meshed and very wide-meshed trelliswork. The silhouette of the neck of K. 5755 is entirely of late Pan Shan type, as is also the upper border, which still retains the upper dentated edge. The lower border, on the other hand, is in both cases more of the Ma Chang type. Moreover, the shape of the pots is progressively assuming a Ma Chang form. Ears are entirely absent. The mantle décor is Ma Chang in style, the circles consisting of red and black bands merging into each other. The supplementary pattern between the circles is of an earlier type, and the ware is on the border-line between Pan Shan and Ma Chang ware; in K. 5755 more the former, in K. 5286 more the latter.

In the pot K. 5285 (Pl. XXII, fig. 1) the ware is dull and grainy, and is thus more of the Ma Chang type. The pattern on the exterior of the neck is here of an early Ma Chang style. The mantle décor is at the same stage of development as that on the preceding vessels, and is accordingly of Ma Chang style. Both the upper and the lower borders possess the Pan Shan character, though the design perhaps belongs rather to the Ma Chang type.

In the case of all these three vessels the circles are filled with geometrical squared patterns or modified chessboard patterns with alternating trellis-filled and more simply decorated squares. The squares are in one case filled with crosses, producing a windowpane effect, K. 5286, in another case with black dots, K. 5755, and in the third case with a ladder pattern, K. 5285.

The three pots, K. 5777 (Pl. XXIII, fig. 2), K. 5295 (Pl. XXII, fig. 2) and K. 5297 (Pl. XXII, fig. 3) represent a further step in the direction of the Ma Chang style. They are all small and markedly globular (a Ma Chang feature). All three are made of typical Ma Chang ware. The necks are high and fairly variable, thus representing a Pan Shan feature, although ears are entirely lacking. In all three forms the neck décor, both exterior and interior, is modified Pan Shan ornamentation, but it nevertheless tends towards the Ma Chang style. In this respect, as in a number of others, the pot K. 5297 is evolutionally the furthest advanced. Thus, it is ornamented with a fishing-net design on the outside of the neck, though at the same time it still retains a somewhat primitive supplementary pattern between the circles on the mantle. The dentated pattern, derived from Pan Shan, is retained on the upper border of K. 5777. In the case of the two others, the upper border is painted in typical Ma Chang style with a band consisting of a black rim below and a red rim above. The lower border consists, in all three pots, of a single black horizontal band. The supplementary patterns in the circles are of an intricate geometrical design. As in the three preceding pots, the circles on K. 5777 and K. 5295 are filled with a modified chessboard pattern with trelliswork in each alternate square. Simplest of all is the pattern in K. 5777, in which the lighter squares are ornamented with strokes. The squared pattern in K. 5295 has a design that is reminiscent of the late Pan Shan vessels, particularly as a filling in the centre of the spirals, viz. a modification of the chessboard pattern, with a cross in ground colour around a small central square. In K. 5297 there is a different pattern in each alternate circle. Two circles contain four squares filled with close-meshed trelliswork arranged around a square filled with wider-meshed trelliswork. The other two circles are ornamented with highly complicated, domino-like crosses, all the arms of similar length. Here we already have the deliberate ornamental geometry of the Ma Chang style in its developed form.

The member of this sub-family that has the most pronounced Ma Chang tendencies is the pot K. 5289 (Pl. XXII, fig. 6), with its typical Ma Chang ware and its emphatically breast-like and high form. It may be regarded as a late piece. The décor on the exterior of the neck is advanced Ma Chang (vertical zigzag bands), as are also the upper and lower borders. The circles on the mantle have diminished in size and have been elevated above the lower border. The supplementary pattern between the circles is many-branched, resembling ribs, and at the top is a cowrie pattern set in the vertical plane. The décor inside the circles consists of chessboard pattern, with alternating black squares and squares divided into four small squares. These vessels were all bought at Lanchow.

Sub-family II. The typical features of this sub-family consist of a mantle décor comprising four circular surfaces surrounded by concentric rings. The sub-family is as a whole more advanced than the preceding, for instance K. 5311 (Pl. XXIII, fig. 3), K. 5307 (Pl. XXII, fig. 4), K. 5504 (Pl. XXIII, fig. 4). True transitional types going back to Pan Shan pottery are absent altogether. The majority are medium-sized vessels more or less spherical in shape. The necks range from medium height to high. The brim of the neck is far more pronounced than in the foregoing sub-family. The ware is throughout coarser and of the Ma Chang type. The Ma Chang system of red and black elements is consistently applied throughout. There are no traces whatever of dentations in the exterior décor. There is however a dentated edge round the inside of the mouth in K. 5307. The upper and lower borders are both Ma Chang in character. The pattern on the interior of the neck consists, in the case of two vessels, of a wreath of four festoons, each made up of two or three painted black lines. The décor on the inside of the neck of K. 5307 is broader and more advanced owing to the brim's being larger in this case. Beneath the ring of dentations is a broad red band with a garland-like wreath below it, the festoons consisting of pairs of black lines. There are four festoons. The exterior neck décor consists throughout of a row of angles facing left, the points being intersected by a horizontal band, all executed in black (fig. 147), this, as we have previously shown, representing a somewhat advanced feature. The pattern between the circles is still fairly simple, though in K. 5307 it is already five-branched.

Fig. 147.

The circles themselves consist of a broad band, the outer half of which is black and the inner half violet or blue. In a few vessels there is no inner black terminal contour on this circular band. The circles are filled with black concentric lines. The centre usually has a large black dot. One pot comes from Yü Chung Hsien; the rest were bought at Lanchow.

Sub-family III. There is only one representative — K. 5303 (Pl. XXII, fig. 5) — in the material at my disposal. The four circles are filled with a series of black, nearly horizontal lines, along the upper edge of which are rows of short, black toothlike strokes. The ware is typical of the Ma Chang pottery, as is also the form. The neck has a fairly well pronounced brim. Neck décor and borders the same as in K. 5307 (Pl. XXII, fig. 4). The supplementary pattern between the circles is simpler and in this case merges very distinctly into the circles themselves. The one extant pot is a good representative of the middle Ma Chang style. The vessel is from Chin Hsien.

Sub-family IV. A family with numerous representatives. It is characterized by circles filled with close-meshed trelliswork. The family belongs to the middle and close of the Ma Chang period. The ware is typical of the Ma Chang pottery. A few pots are small and have spherical bodies, e. g. K. 5981, K. 5976 (Pl. XXIII, figs. 5 and 7). Many indications go to show that they are the earliest types of the sub-family. The other vessels are larger and distinctly breasted at the top. The necks of the earlier types are fairly strongly pronounced. In the more advanced forms within the sub-family they are lower. The collars are in the majority of cases well expanded. The patterns on the interior of the neck are advanced, and very broad, and they vary a good deal. The predominant décor consists of a black, strongly dentated line along the upper edge and beneath that a broad red band, and below that again a garland of simple festoons. The dentated line is in rare cases replaced by a wreath of small circular surfaces in ground colour, K. 5976, and instead of the garland there may be bands of angles facing left, K. 5300 (Pl. XXII, fig. 7), or a broad black rim, K. 5991 (Pl. XXXIX, fig. 3). In the advanced forms the breadth of the pattern on the inside of the neck increases considerably. The pattern on the outside of the neck consists, in the least advanced form, K. 5981 (Pl. XXIII, fig. 5), of bands of angles facing left. In the vessel K. 5976 (Pl. XXIII, fig. 7) it consists of similar bands with the points intersected by a horizontal band — the characteristic ornamentation on the exterior of the neck in the preceding sub-family. The décor on the outside of the neck is more advanced in the other vessels and consists of bands of angles which merge at top and bottom into other elements, K. 5991, or whose lower parts are strongly predominant, K. 5300, or else it consists of vertical zigzag bands, K. 5466 (Pl. XXII, fig. 8). The lower borders are typical Ma Chang borders, with slow rhythm and garlands rather than waves. In a couple of cases they are, curiously enough, not black but red. The upper borders consist in one or two cases of pairs of lines, the upper one red and the lower one black. In one case the red line has black elements on either side of it, K. 5617 (Pl. XXXIX, fig. 2). In other cases, again, the upper border has been simplified, either the black or the red band disappearing altogether. The supplementary patterns between the circles show a well-defined evolutionary series running through the different pieces, from relatively simple, K. 5976, to more intricate and very strongly branched forms, K. 5991. The trellis pattern is wide-meshed in the earliest pot and closer-meshed in the others. In the more highly developed forms the circles are relatively small owing to the large amount of space taken up by the supplementary pattern, and they are also raised a good way above the lower border. The mantle of pot K. 5991 is covered with a light-coloured slip — this too an advanced feature. Of the vessels mentioned here, K. 5981 comes from Mi La Kou in Nien Po Hsien, K. 5976 from Yen Chi Kou in Chin Hsien, K. 5617 from Ma Chang Yen in Nien Po Hsien, and K. 5991 also from that locality. The rest were bought at Lanchow.

Sub-family V. A sub-family with only two late representatives, K. 5288 (Pl. XXIV, fig. 2) and K. 5304 (Pl. XXIV, fig. 1). These vessels have three circular surfaces arranged in the form of a clover leaf within each of the four large circles — that is to say, a fairly complicated geometrical pattern. In K. 5304 each of the supplementary circles consists of two black concentric rings, the inner one filled with very fine-meshed trelliswork. In K. 5288 the small circles are separated by a miniature edition of the supplementary pattern on the mantle. In the centre of the large circle the various elements merge together to form a three-armed cross. The vessels are large, their capacity being about 25 litres. They are made of typical Ma Chang ware. The bodies are advanced in form, being very high-breasted at the top. The bases are very small. The necks are low, ending in a fairly strongly pronounced brim. The patterns on the interior of the neck are advanced, broad, and consisting at the top of a broad black ring of dentations with or without a line, beneath that a red band, and below that again a ring of garlands consisting of four festoons of 3—4 rows of garlands. The décor on the exterior of the neck consists of bands of angles facing left (the small space available leaves no room for the other forms that characterize the advanced exterior neck-décor). The upper and lower borders are typical of the period. The supplementary pattern between the circles is made up of many (5—7) branches. The circles are raised above the lower border and are relatively small. Both form and décor indicate throughout that this décor family should be placed very late. Both vessels were bought at Lanchow.

Sub-family VI. Only one representative of this family is preserved, and that is a late piece: K. 5828 (Pl. XXXIX, fig. 4). The circles are filled with a large number of small cowrie patterns placed either horizontally or obliquely, on a black ground. Ware, form and neck are similar to those in the two representatives of the preceding sub-family, as are also the border and the supplementary pattern between the circles. The décor on the outside of the neck is likewise similar, while that on the inside is original. It is very broad and consists of two black lines with a row of dentations between them, and under them a broad violet band. From this band there runs a row of black bands in an oblique downward direction, joining one another along a horizontal band running round the lower part of the inside of the mouth. The circles on the mantle are comparatively small and raised high above the lower border; they also have the usual periphery consisting of two bands, an outer black, and an inner red. The supplementary pattern between the circles has a number of branches. Most of the mantle portion of the pot is covered with a white slip. The vessel was bought at Lanchow.

Miscellaneous pots. Two vessels already mentioned before, viz. K. 5980 (Pl. XXIII, fig. 8) and K. 5979 (Pl. XXIII, fig. 6), are also members of this décor family.

The author regards them as individual types that are hardly representative of entire décor families.

The vessel K. 5980 is very closely related, both as regards manufacture, form and decorative style, to a number of vessels with entirely different patterns, all from Ma Pai Tzu, Nien Po Hsien. These vessels are extremely roughly executed, the shape being extraordinarily poor and irregular, and the surface very uneven and badly fashioned. There is only one colour — blue-black, and that too is coarse. The patterns seem to have been simplified to the verge of primitiveness and are more or less degenerate. The lines are broad and irregular. The shape of these pots is far narrower and more elongated than is otherwise usual in Ma Chang pottery. I regard the group as a local product of a degenerate quality. As far as the pot K. 5980 is concerned, the circles on its mantle are filled with a rough squared pattern with a dab in the middle of each square. Most of the individual patterns on this vessel are simplified or degenerate, as e. g. the upper border, which has been reduced to a single horizontal band, the pattern on the outside of the neck, which is particularly roughly drawn, and that on the inside of the neck, which has become a band of many festoons, painted in a most unskillful fashion. The decorative filling on the mantle between the circles is likewise extremely simplified.

The pot K. 5979 was found on the same archaeological site. It is also of a rough shape and its decoration is not very artistically done, although in this case the lines are thinner and drawn with a surer hand. Its form is unique — a narrow, high base and the shoulder part more spherical in outline. The neck, too, is peculiar, narrowing down towards the top and then widening out into a brim. The mantle is covered with a slip of deep violet red. Two of the circles are filled with a highly complicated geometrical design including a partial chessboard pattern. The other two alternate circles are decorated with trelliswork, which is intersected horizontally by a fairly thick black line and vertically by a band filled with crosses (fig.148). The supplementary décor on the mantle is quite simple. The pot represents a style that is distinctly related to that of the degenerate Ma Pai Tzu vessels mentioned above, though it possesses certain advanced features, as e. g. the dark slip. I regard the Ma Pai Tzu group as a degenerate Ma Chang group, with certain primitive and certain advanced features.

Fig. 148.

Décor family 2 M.

Anthropomorphic patterns usually alternating with circles.

The next largest décor family belonging to the Ma Chang period is also to a certain extent related to the Pan Shan family 11 P. Within the spiral pattern family there was a small separate group, in which the spiral pattern was interrupted in order to make room for an anthropomorphic pattern. The development of this pattern was followed up to a stage in which the spiral nuclei were replaced by four circles with concentric elements. The anthropomorphic figures had become conventionalized into a linear design of the simplest kind. The head consisted of a circle with a dot in the middle, the body of a straight vertical line, and the arms and legs consisted each of two lines forming angles pointing downwards. The legs were attached to the body fairly high up, so that a long tail was formed. If we compare the pictures of the Pan Shan urn K. 5068 (Pl. XIII, fig. 3) with a picture of the Ma Chang vessel K. 5990 (Pl. XXIV, fig. 4) from Ma Chang Yen, we find exactly the same body-line and similarly drawn arms and legs in both vessels. Even the tail is the same. The head however seems at first glance to have disappeared altogether, for the circle now lies in a new position, surrounding the neck of the pot, and represents the boundary-line between neck and body. This is the point of departure in our classification of the Ma Chang family 2 M, and from it the decorative pattern develops in different directions.

As we have demonstrated before, the above-mentioned Pan Shan urn with the complete anthropomorphic pattern may be dated as belonging to the middle Pan Shan group. For the present, apparently, we possess no specimens of this pattern dating from late Pan Shan pottery. This means that, in spite of the fact that the pattern has thus maintained its existence along conservative lines from the middle Pan Shan to the Ma Chang period, and continues throughout the latter, there is still a wide gap in the sequence. The great majority of Ma Chang vessels having this pattern belong to the middle and latter half of the period, as is indicated both by the shapes and by a great many of the decorative details. The borders are typical Ma Chang. The dentation motif is absent altogether. The necks are low and are painted, both on the exterior and on the interior, in an advanced style.

The earliest of these vessels would appear to be pot K. 5990 (Pl. XXIV, fig. 4). In shape it does not differ very widely from the Pan Shan pots, though on the whole its upper part is somewhat spherical. The neck is of medium height and somewhat resembles the necks of late Pan Shan pots, although the brim is undoubtedly larger than that of the latter vessels. The colour of the décor is brownish violet and there is no black anywhere, but a very thin slip instead. The ornamentation on the neck is advanced; on the inside it consists of a broad uninterrupted horizontal band, and on the outside of clumsily painted vertical zigzag bands. A somewhat original and surprising feature of this pot is that there are no circles between the anthropomorphic figures. Instead the pot has four such

Fig. 149.

figures, which merge into one another (see fig. 149). In the other vessels belonging to this family there are, with one exception, circles between the figures.

The shapes of the other vessels with this pattern are typical advanced Ma Chang forms or else entirely original forms (the jug K. 5294, Pl. XXIV, fig. 3). If we except this jug, the rest of the vessels form what is from the most widely differing aspects a good type series, representing the period from the close of middle Ma Chang to the close of late Ma Chang. The necks of the slightly earlier specimens are not particularly high, as e. g. K. 5308 (Pl. XXIV, fig. 5), but in the later vessels we find them becoming lower and lower, e. g. K. 5787 (Pl. XXIV, fig. 7). The bodies belong to the advanced and elongated form, K. 5308, or else they are bulgy towards the top. The most advanced and most bulgy forms within this family, e. g. K. 5787, are comparable with the forms of the most advanced specimens of the preceding family, K. 5288 (Pl. XXIV, fig. 2) and K. 5828 (Pl. XXXIX, fig. 4), in which respect there is complete agreement. The surface of all the vessels is typical Ma Chang. The décor of the neck is generally advanced. *But that is not all. The stages in the development of the décor of the preceding family, which was represented by different advanced sub-families, recurs in one detail in the pattern of the mantle here*, so that complete parallelism is attained between the families and the dates of their respective members. Manifestly the earliest of the pots with an anthropomorphic decoration are those that have as their intermediate and supplementary décor circles extending from the lower handles up to the upper border. *These circles are decorated with the different type-patterns belonging to the sub-family 1 M*, in this case those of 1 M I, e. g. K. 5308 (Pl. XXV, fig. 1), chessboard pattern with every other square black and every other with a window-cross. In K. 5308 the anthropomorphic figure as a whole very much resembles the figure on the vessel discussed above, K. 5990 (Pl. XXIV, fig. 4), as well as that on the Pan Shan vessels, but it has been given three joints (Pl. XXIV, fig. 5), to its legs and "fingers" or "beard" on elbows and knees. A closely related though more advanced stage is represented by the pot K. 5982, in which however the joints on each leg have been increased to four and the number of fingered knees doubled.

In a following group the distinguishing element consists of the concentric circles that we found in sub-family 1 M II. In the earliest pot of this type, K. 5312 (Pl. XXXIX, fig. 6), which is closely related also in form to the 1 M II group, being globular and having an expanded brim, the figure gives a very good anthropomorphic effect. It is in a sitting posture, with extended three-jointed legs, and has fingers on the hands, knees and elbows. Legs and arms are highly modified, as for instance in K. 5298 (Pl. XXV, fig. 2) and K. 5786 (Pl. XXIV, fig. 6), and the anthropomorphic character is very largely obscured.

In a third group, e. g. K. 5301 (Pl. XXIV, fig. 8), we find between the anthropomorphic figures, as in the advanced pots in sub-family 1 M IV, circles filled with trelliswork and raised high up above the border and handles. The legs of these figures have four joints and are so arranged that they join up with the legs on the other side of the circle, that is to say, the figure's legs form a continuous horizontal zigzag system round the pot. The shapes of the pots are here of a highly advanced type.

A fourth evolutional phase is represented by the single pot K. 5309 (Pl. XXIV, fig. 9). It has thin walls, is globular in shape, and the surface of the mantle is far narrower than in the preceding vessels. In this case there has not been room for the anthropomorphic pattern on the surface, and it has been limited to a body with arms only, but these arms are converted into an ornamental zigzag band with fingers on the apices of the angles. This idea of making the pattern fantastically conventional and rudimentary represents a very late Ma Chang stage. The original pattern inside the neck of this late pot is identically the same as that on one of the most advanced members of the preceding décor family — K. 5828 (Pl. XXXIX, fig. 4).

Of all the pots belonging to this décor family the most original in form as well as in décor is the jug K. 5294 (Pl. XXIV, fig. 3). It is covered all over with a dark brown slip. On the neck are well-developed, vertical zigzag bands. Two broad bands resembling laces run in low curves across the two sides of the pot, leaving a triangular space on the front. Within this space an anthropomorphic figure has been drawn with body and neck like a long straight stem, the head surrounding the neck of the vessel, two-jointed legs and three-jointed arms. There are fingers on the hands, on the shoulder, on the knees and on the "tail" (phallus?). Of all the anthropomorphic figures that we possess dating from this epoch, this is the most human in appearance. To judge from the peculiar profile, the shape of the neck and the exterior pattern, as well as the presence of slip, this vessel should probably be dated some time fairly far on in the Ma Chang period.

Vessels belonging to this décor family are all of types M. C: VIII and M. C: IX, with the exception of the jug mentioned above. They come from Ma Chang Yen or else were bought at Lanchow.

Décor family 3 M.
The cowrie pattern.

We find in a number of vessels an almond- or spool-shaped ornament executed in ground colour against a black background and constituting a distinct part of the décor on the mantle. A straight line is usually drawn along the longitudinal axle (fig. 150). Occasionally the straight line in the ornamentation is replaced by a wavy line, in which case the cowrie character of the design stands out very clearly (fig. 151). The ornament also (fig. 152) acquires a fairly distinctive cowrie-like appearance in cases in which the central line is exchanged for a row of dots, as e. g. in the vessel K. 5342 (Pl. XXV, fig. 7).

The general arrangement of the cowrie pattern is usually as follows: a row of horizontal cowrie ornaments combine to form one or more chains (fig. 153) round

Fig. 150.   Fig. 151.   Fig. 152.   Fig. 153.

the vessel, the belt of cowrie ornaments thus generally constituting a border. The cowrie design is particularly often used for the lower border, e. g. K. 5377 (Pl. XXV, fig. 8). Both the upper and the lower borders in the vessel K. 5302 (Pl. XXVI, fig. 4) contain cowrie chains, and there are two cowrie chains on the mantle of vessel K. 5139 (Pl. XL, fig. 4). In one case the cowrie décor is used as an ornament in the decorated fields on the mantle which lie beneath the neck-handles and which are typical of Ma Chang pottery, viz. in the vessel K. 5328, in which each field contains two cowrie patterns pointing obliquely upwards.

A row of cowrie ornaments, set obliquely, constitutes the main décor on the mantle of the beaker K. 5342 (Pl. XXV, fig. 7).

The cowrie pattern also serves as a "filling" in the circles in the décor family 1 M VI, (Pl. XXXIX, fig. 4). The cowrie motif has perhaps been most sparingly employed in the vessel K. 5289 (Pl. XXII, fig. 6), which also belongs to 1 M I, and in which each supplementary pattern between the circles has at the top of it a cowrie ornament set in a vertical plane.

Those members of the first décor family that have the cowrie motif are both markedly advanced, particularly K. 5828 (Pl. XXXIX, fig. 4), which is one of the most typical products of the late Ma Chang style. Of the rest of the vessels ornamented with a cowrie design, perhaps the beaker K. 5342 is the earliest. The Ma Chang system, as far as regards the coloured bands, is in this case well applied, and there is no dentated edge. The ware is typical of the period. The neck is at any rate slightly curved outwards at the top, and its interior décor, broad and forceful in its design, is of a type that resembles Pan Shan. At the same time, the exterior décor on the neck and the band on the handles executed in relief prohibit the dating of the vessel too late. No doubt it belongs to the first third stage of the period.

A small group of beakers and cups within the family permits us to trace fairly distinctly the development of the cowrie chain pattern.

In the earliest of these vessels the cowrie chain consists of a large number (8) of well-drawn and distinctly almond-shaped cowrie patterns (fig. 154), e. g. K. 5354 (Pl. XXVI, fig. 2) and K. 5377 (Pl. XXV, fig. 8). The former of these is ornamented with a pattern on the outside of the neck that is borrowed from the Pan Shan style and is well known from late Pan Shan pottery as a mantle décor, and also from

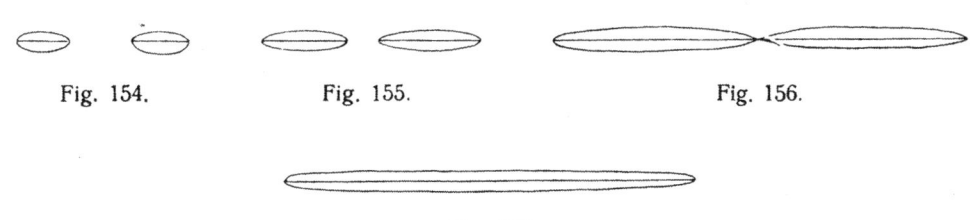

Fig. 154. Fig. 155. Fig. 156.

Fig. 157.

the earliest Ma Chang vessels of the décor family 1 M I, in which it is employed to fill up the space within the circles, e. g. K. 5295 (Pl. XXII, fig. 2). Moreover, it has bands in relief on the handles. The shape of the vessel is however fairly advanced. Both these vessels appear to come within the transitional period between the early and middle Ma Chang epochs.

The other vessels ornamented with a lower cowrie border are painted in one colour only — brownish black. Their inner borders are of an advanced type with wavy bands in ground colour, and their handles are decorated with crosses or with horizontal bands. They exhibit an increasing decadence in the cowrie pattern, the number of cowrie ornaments diminishing first to 5, e. g. K. 5360 (Pl. XXV, fig. 9), then to 4, e. g. K. 5363 (Pl. XXV, fig. 10), and finally to 3, e. g. K. 5358 (Pl. XXVI, fig. 3), while the pattern becomes elongated almost beyond recognition and is far more carelessly drawn. (See figs. 155—157.) For the rest, a feature common to these small vessels is the markedly geometrical patterns on their necks, among which zigzag bands K. 5359 (Pl. XXVI, fig. 1), crosses K. 5360 (Pl. XXV, fig. 9) and straight lines together with geometrical meanders K. 5358 (Pl. XXVI, fig. 3) and K. 5330 (Pl. XXV, fig. 6, belonging to family 15 M), play the most important parts.

The middle-sized M. C: IX vessel K. 5302 (Pl. XXVI, fig. 4), which has a cowrie-patterned upper and lower border and, in the middle of the mantle, a horizontal band with black outside edges and a violet grey middle section, should, owing to the shape of its body, its high and wide-brimmed neck, and both the exterior and the interior decoration on the neck, be placed very close to a vessel such as K. 5976 (Pl. XXIII, fig. 7), dating from the middle part of the period. The pattern on the mantle — series of horizontal lines above and below the middle band — is manifestly a legacy from a string ornamentation in Pan Shan pottery. Here the cowrie chains consist of almost circular spots in ground colour crossed by a black line. The small beaker K. 5139 (Pl. XL, fig. 4) possesses the same kind of cowrie chains and no doubt belongs also to the same period.

Among the vessels with the cowrie design is the small vessel from Yü Chung Hsien, which is ornamented with double cowrie borders. Some of the other small vessels are from Shih Chia Wan and Shan Chuang in Ti Tao Hsien. To this family also belong representatives of the larger pots M. C: VIII and M. C: IX, as well as representatives of the low beakers of the type M. C: XIV and the cups of the type M. C: IV.

Décor family 4 M.

The main decorative design on the mantle consists of horizontal zigzag bands.

This is the décor on a few vessels. Where the pot is painted in two colours, the zigzag band is either divided, according to the Ma Chang system, into a violet middle strip edged with two black strips, e. g. K. 5299 (Pl. XXVI, fig. 7) or else it is multiplicate. In cases in which the décor is executed in a single colour (black) applied to slip, the zigzag bands are in pairs or threes. The family contains distinctly separate groups, but as there are so few vessels it seems to me to be unnecessary to divide them up into sub-families.

The jug K. 5611 (Pl. XXVI, fig. 6) of type M. C: VI is by reason of its size, spherical form etc. closely related to some of the small vessels belonging to the central portions of the décor family 1 M, as e. g. K. 5976 (Pl. XXIII, fig. 7), and should itself no doubt be dated at the same period, the close of the middle Ma Chang. As in the latter piece, the neck here is fairly high and has a pronounced brim. Similarly, the pattern on the inside of the neck belongs in this case too to type 8. The outside pattern consists of a row of very roughly painted angles, which partially merge into the border and into the black-painted brim. In this vessel the mantle has a very broad horizontal zigzag band in two colours. The triangular spaces left at top and bottom are ornamented with black stars.

The pot K. 5299 (Pl. XXVI, fig. 7), of the type M. C: VIII, also dates apparently from the same period. The neck has not so pronounced a brim. The neck motif is of type 5 and the décor on the exterior of the neck is the same as in the preceding vessel. Round the top of the mantle runs a series of degenerate string-pattern bands (derived from late Pan Shan pottery). The lower part of the mantle has a broad zigzag band in slow rhythm, the central strip being dark red. Above and below, the zigzag band forms triangular spaces in ground colour, ornamented with vertical wavy bands, ending at the top in a head-like part and terminating at the bottom in a tail. On the analogy of the décor on the head purchased in Paris, this pattern is perhaps to be interpreted as a snake decoration.

The two vessels described here have a décor that in some measure foreshadows the ornamentation of the Hsin Tien period. The vertical ornament in the latter is of fairly common occurrence, and there too we find the star pattern.

A group that is somewhat isolated from the preceding vessels is composed of two small beaker-like vessels of type M. C: XIV, K. 5329 and K. 5669. The zigzag bands are of the same sort as in the preceding vessels, but the supplementary pattern here consists of triangles filled with trelliswork. The patterns inside the neck are of type 5. There is no pattern on the outside of the neck of K. 5669, while that in K. 5329 consists of rhombi in ground colour. The handles are fairly long and extend from the upper edge of the neck some way down on to the mantle. In the one case (K. 5329) they are ornamented with a band in relief. There are no really satisfactory clues as to the date. The interior neck patterns, the handles and the shape, all point to the latter part of early Ma Chang.

The two vessels K. 5255 and K. 5232, both of type M. C: XIV, are difficult to date. The characteristic pattern consists of 4—5 pairs of thin, black, oblique bands, which in combination, though not separately, form a zigzag pattern. The violet-and-black colouring of the Ma Chang system is very sparingly used here: in K. 5255 it is confined to a triad for the upper border and to a band forming the interior neck pattern, and in K. 5232 only to a triad for the upper border. The pattern on the inside of the neck consists in this case of two black horizontal lines; that on the outside of 3—4 black horizontal lines. The handles are ornamented with crosses (K. 5255) or oblique black lines (K. 5232). Below the handles there are fields containing crosses (K. 5232); in the case of K. 5255 the décor has been destroyed. The vessels very closely resemble those of the Yang Shao pottery, which are decorated in black only.

A group that is sharply distinguished from the four vessels described above, and indeed is pretty well isolated from the larger groups of vessels belonging to the other décor families, is composed of two vessels K. 5292 (Pl. XL, fig. 3) and K. 5293

(Pl. XXVI, fig. 9), of type M. C: IX, both bought at Lanchow. They resemble one another fairly closely, both in form and décor. K. 5292 has more the shape of a plum, K. 5293 more that of an inverted pear. The bodies of both are of the narrowest Ma Chang type. The necks are fairly high and broad-brimmed. Both vessels are covered with a light-brown slip, and the rest of the décor is painted in black with a bluish-brown tinge. In both the inner surface of the brim is ornamented with a broad horizontal band. The décor on the outside of the neck consists of broad vertical zigzag bands. Both vessels have very broad upper borders, the one (K. 5293) entirely filled in, the other having a pair of string-pattern bands. Both vessels possess the typical Ma Chang lower border with very narrow bands of garlands. The mantle of vessel K. 5292 forms one broad zone ornamented with double zigzag pattern, while that of K. 5293 is divided by a broad horizontal band into two zones: the upper with trebled, the lower with single zigzag band. The pots are in all probability highly advanced forms belonging to the late Ma Chang period.

The vessel K. 5290 (Pl. XXVI, fig. 5), also bought at Lanchow, may likewise be referred to this zigzag family. In this pot, however, the zigzag décor is not predominant as in the above-mentioned vessels. It has here been moved up to the upper part of the mantle. The lower, broader zone of the mantle is decorated with a row of almond-shaped ornaments set in a vertical plane and drawn with broad bands on the outside and many narrower bands on the inside. The zigzag band runs horizontally on the upper zone of the mantle, which is separated from the lower zone by a broad horizontal band. The zigzag pattern is supplemented at top and bottom by triangular ornaments filled with wide-meshed trelliswork. The pot is of the form M. C: IX and has a fairly high neck, somewhat contracted at the top, and a broad brim. It is decorated in black with a slightly bluish tone. To a certain extent it resembles, in colour and also in shape, the degenerate vessels from Ma Pai Tzu, which we have already discussed, though it has a more refined profile than they. The décor on the inside of the neck is of type 6, but it is here still more advanced (fig. 158), having thick, widely separated upper strokes. The exterior neck pattern is roughly designed and degenerate. The pot undoubtedly belongs to the latter part of the Ma Chang period. Vessels belonging to this family are of types M. C: VI, IX and XIV. The jug is from Ting Yuan Chien in Yü Chung Hsien. The rest were bought at Lanchow.

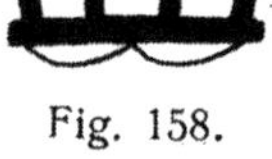

Fig. 158.

Décor family 5 M.

The mantle decorated with a horizontal row of reduplicated rhombi.

A few vessels belong to this family. Only one pot with this pattern, K. 5754 (Pl. XXVI, fig. 8), of type M. C: IX, is preserved in the material at my disposal. To judge from the fairly high and wide-brimmed neck, the small, nearly spherical body and the pattern on the exterior of the neck (type 6), this pot belongs to the middle part of the period. The pattern on the interior of the neck has been destroyed. A horizontal centre band, divided up into a red middle strip and two black outer strips, separates the mantle into two zones: the upper one decorated with crisscross strokes, the lower one with reduplicated rhombi. The other vessels bearing this pattern are small beakers of the type M. C: XIV, and have fairly narrow bands round the mantle decorated with a row of rhombi. The patterns on the inside of the neck indicate a variation in age. The oldest vessel is the low-necked K. 5333 (Pl. XXV, fig. 3), which has an interior neck pattern of type 4 and an exterior neck pattern consisting of a row of small squares in ground colour with black dots in the centre. The following beakers have higher necks. Beaker K. 5362 (Pl. XXV, fig. 5) has a carelessly painted interior neck pattern showing a peculiar variation (fig. 159), that is to say, with a red band above and a black band below, the position of the bands being reversed in relation to the general décor.

Fig. 159.

The décor on the exterior of the neck consists of a series of black horizontal lines. This vessel is somewhat more advanced than the preceding one. The vessel K. 5946 (Pl. XXV, fig. 4) is still more advanced. The pattern on the inside of the neck consists of three black horizontal bands and that on the outside consists of large numbers of vertical lines and vertical rows of dots. The large beaker K. 5234, which is covered entirely with a brown slip, is ornamented on the inside of the neck with a single horizontal band and on the outside with groups of vertical lines. The vessel belongs to the final phase of the period.

Décor family 6 M.

Square décor.

Sub-family 6 M I. Large squares filled with trelliswork, and between them small black squares and rectangles in ground colour, together forming crosses.

Already in the late pottery from Pan Shan we found as a characteristic auxiliary pattern a complicated network of squares filled with trelliswork and surrounded by small black squares (fig. 160) and oblong rectangles in ground colour. This pattern occurred as a filling for the circles in the most advanced spiral vessels, e. g. K. 5287 (Pl. XII, fig. 7), and also in the rope-pattern family, e. g. K. 5282 (Pl. XXXVIII, fig. 2), in which it decorated narrow horizontal zones. In these latter the network of squares was truncated, only one row of squares being left, with supplementary triangles at top and bottom representing the remaining segments of truncated squares. The pattern is inherited by the Ma Chang pottery, in which however the squares are gradually converted into long rhombi filled with trelliswork, and the rectangles become light-coloured slits between them.

Fig. 160.

A number of the vessels belonging to this group are just on the boundary line between the two types of pottery, and it is doubtful in which group they ought to be placed. Such a vessel as K. 5331 (Pl. XL, fig. 1), for instance, displays perhaps more of the Pan Shan characteristics. The dentated ornamentation still survives here both on the upper bands and on the vertical black bands surrounding a red band below the handles. The décor on the inside of the neck has unattached dentations at the top, a narrow red horizontal band and double garlands of four festoons. The pattern on the outside of the neck consists of a row of trelliswork squares. The handles are ornamented with bands in relief. The ware is closer to the Pan Shan type. In the vessel K. 5978 (Pl. XXVII, fig. 1) all the details are similar to those in the preceding vessel, but the ware is now more of the Ma Chang kind, porous and dull on the surface. In K. 5373 the upper black border has merged, in keeping with the Ma Chang system, with the red boundary-line between neck and body. The outside of the neck is decorated with slanting ladders, alternating with rows of angles pointing downwards. Otherwise the details are the same. Vessel K. 5343 (Pl. XXVII, fig. 2) is at the same stage of development, but the exterior neck pattern consists of vertical wavy lines close together and the black band that forms the upper border has increased in breadth. In K. 5353 the band in relief is replaced by a cross. The interior neck pattern is in this case in an advanced style (type 7). The exterior consists of short-waved bands in ground colour. The red and black bands in the upper border have been merged into one. In vessel K. 5345 the shape of body and neck has also undergone a change. The neck is somewhat drawn in towards the top. It has an extremely rudimentary pattern on the inside and its exterior décor consists of groups of black wavy bands. Below the handles are double crosses (fig. 161). The spaces between the rhombi are very narrow and long and the trellis pattern extremely close-meshed, the rhombi large, the black intermediate squares very small. The most advanced vessel in the

Fig. 161.

group, however, is K. 5337 (Pl. XXVII, fig. 3), in which the decorated surface is covered with a greyish brown slip. The neck is attractively designed with an outward concave bend. The handles are decorated with black horizontal bands, and the surfaces beneath them with double crosses. The pattern inside the neck is of a highly advanced type 10 A. That on the outside is a fishing-net design.

The evolutional process within the décor family is thus very clear, being completely analogous to that in the other décor families and extending throughout the entire period.

Sub-family 6 M II. It will be remembered that one of the most characteristic patterns in the Pan Shan décor consisted of a single row of trellised squares. This décor also occurs in typical Ma Chang vessels and is undoubtedly a legacy from the preceding period. The development within this group can be followed up quite analogously to that in the preceding group, although there are fewer vessels of earlier types. In a vessel such as K. 5338 the details are more indicative of the Pan Shan than of the Ma Chang system, but the ware has rather the character of the Ma Chang ware. The upper border still retains its dentated edge along the top. The vessel K. 5315 (Pl. XL, fig. 2) is characteristic in both form and décor, obviously belonging to a phase well on in the Ma Chang period. The low narrow neck with its pronounced outward concave bend, the highly arched body, as well as the nature of the colour and decorative system, all indicate the ornamental style of the Ma Chang pottery. The pattern inside the neck is of miniature design and fairly rudimentary (fig. 162). The pattern outside the neck has along the top three narrow horizontal lines, and, below, groups of vertical wavy bands close together, the waves being in miniature. The handles have horizontal bands. The upper border merges into an advanced form of horizontal string patterns. The squares are filled with close-meshed trelliswork and have black contours. The vessel certainly belongs to the middle of the period. So also does the vessel K. 5228, which however is made of an uncommonly fine and smooth Pan Shan-like ware. Nevertheless, there is no death pattern at all on this vessel. The coloured bands are of a markedly Ma Chang type. Both the outside and the inside of the neck of this vessel have a unique décor. The interior décor consists of trelliswork at the top, forming a narrow band, and below that a broader red band. The exterior décor consists of triangular elements curiously arranged between two black lines (fig. 163). Beneath the handles are black crosses. The vessels K. 5483 (Pl. XXVII, fig. 6) and K. 5367 are made of extremely coarse Ma Chang ware. The former is a very ordinary bowl-shaped vessel of type M. C: XII with patterns of simple design on the inside and outside of the neck. It belongs most probably to the beginning middle-part of the period. The latter vessel has an advanced pattern on the inside of the neck, type 10 B, and on the outside a distinctive, highly developed fishing-net design. The handles are ornamented with horizontal bands, and beneath the handles are crosses. The décor below the neck closely resembles that on K. 5315 just described. The vessel is of later date than the preceding one and belongs to late Ma Chang. The same applies to the vessel K. 5368 (Pl. XXVI, fig. 10), which is covered with a thick coating of brown slip, and the interior neck pattern of which is of type 10 A. The exterior neck pattern is analogous to that on the foregoing vessel, as is also the décor on and below the handles. The string-pattern band is in this vessel replaced by a narrow horizontal band with a row of short vertical lines close together. The shape of the pot, its décor and slip are otherwise very closely similar to those of the most advanced pot in the preceding sub-family, K. 5337 (Pl. XXVII, fig. 3). There is slip in both cases, the interior and exterior of the neck are similarly decorated, and the décor on and beneath the handles is the same. The shape is almost identically the same.

Sub-family 6 M III. The trellis-filled squares are in a row and form a chain through a broad framework.

Two vessels belong to this décor family: K. 5780 and K. 5369 (Pl. XXVII, fig. 4), both made of very coarse ware similar to that of the two vessels K. 5483 (Pl. XXVII, fig. 6) and K. 5367 in the preceding sub-family. The ware differs considerably from that of the other Ma Chang pottery, and it may be that these vessels have the same origin, in which case they may possibly constitute a group from a certain locality unknown to us. The colours on three of these vessels are arranged on the same system, comprising broad red centre strips and narrow black contours. The jug K. 5780, of type M. C: XI, has a square ornamentation on the outside of the neck, the squares being filled with trelliswork. That on the inside has been destroyed in this case. The mantle is divided into an upper and a lower belt, the former having short-waved bands in ground colour on a black background, the latter having the pattern that is typical of the family. In beaker K. 5369 the pattern on the interior of the neck is of advanced design — type 10 A, that on the exterior surface is a manifold zigzag décor. On the handles are horizontal bands, and beneath them are crosses. Here too the surface of the mantle is divided into two belts, the upper one having a row of circular surfaces in ground colour on a black background and the lower one having the design characteristic of this sub-family. It is possible, as I have said, that these two vessels are variants in which local characteristics appear.

Sub-family 6 M IV. This sub-family likewise possesses a small group of pots in which the characteristic pattern consists of filled rhombi. In the material at my disposal there are only three of these vessels: K. 5340 (Pl. XXVII, fig. 5), K. 5322 (Pl. XXVII, fig. 7) and K. 5341. They are of a peculiar beaker-like form with a somewhat heart-shaped silhouette, low bodies and fairly high necks narrowing towards the top, the brims varying in form. Of these vessels, the beaker K. 5322 has obviously the more striking, advanced form. In every case the patterns on the inside of the neck are late: in K. 5340 an extremely rudimentary garland design and in K. 5322 a décor of type 10 B, in K. 5341 a décor of type 10 C. The latter vessels are covered with a thick slip, orange-brown in the case of K. 5322, violet in that of K. 5341. In all three vessels the handles are ornamented with horizontal bands. Beneath the handles there are crosses on the two first-mentioned vessels. K. 5340 has an exterior neck décor consisting of groups of vertical lines between an upper and a lower horizontal band, the latter representing the upper border. The area between the upper and lower borders is decorated with the pattern that is characteristic of the family — a chain of black rhombi. The pattern on the neck of vessel K. 5322 is original and consists of a combination of upper and lower horizontal bands and horizontal lines, between them a chain of filled rhombi, and also triangles filled with parallel lines (fig. 164). This combination is

Fig. 164.   Fig. 165.   Fig. 166.

quite unknown in the Pan Shan style and is a product of the geometrically inventive and experimental decorative art of the Ma Chang period. The upper border (fig. 165) consists of two horizontal bands joined together with broad strokes fairly far apart. Between this and the lower border, which likewise consists of a broad horizontal band, comes the mantle's characteristic pattern. Closely related to the neck pattern on this vessel, though still more geometrically complicated, is that on K. 5341, on the lines of décor family 12 (fig. 166). On each side of the vessel, between the handles, there is a space the chief ornamentation of which consists of two rhombi, each divided into nine small rhombi, alternately black (5) and ground colour (4), the latter with a dot in the middle. The intermediate spaces are filled with trelliswork, the lines being parallel to the sides of the rhombi. These surfaces are crossed in the centre by oblique bands. The principal décor is on a narrow band on the mantle. The beaker is highly advanced.

The three vessels belonging to this sub-family are all late. The most advanced are undoubtedly K. 5322 and K. 5341, which belong to the last products of the period, whose silhouette gives a very mobile effect and whose décor is intricate and geometrical.

The vessels that are members of this décor family are of types M. C: XI, XII and XIV in the form series. Of sub-family I, two are from Ti Tao Hsien, the one from the locality Shih Chia Wan and the other from the place known as Su Chia Yang Hua, one from Mi La Kou in Nien Po Hsien, and one from Yü Chung Hsien. All the rest of the vessels belonging to this décor family were bought at Lanchow.

Décor family 7 M.
A row of trellis-filled circles decorate the mantle.

A fairly large décor family, the members of which are partly transitional types between the Pan Shan and the Ma Chang styles of pottery and partly extend throughout the entire Ma Chang period. The evolutional process exhibits a striking parallelism with that in the first sub-family containing the square décor.

The earliest vessels stand in all respects so near the border-line between the Pan Shan and the Ma Chang ceramic groups that it is difficult to know just how to place them. The family was as we know already fully developed in the Pan Shan period. A vessel like K. 5352 has been classed with the Pan Shan pottery on account of the quality of the ware, the exterior décor on the neck and the dentated edge of the upper border. Indeed, vessel K. 5334 has been placed in the Pan Shan period as the ware is typical Pan Shan and the triad of bands beneath the handles has a dentated ornamentation, and in spite of the fact that the upper border has now merged, in keeping with the Ma Chang system, into the band that forms the boundary between neck and body. Both the pots mentioned here have bands in relief on the handles and also double circles. The former beaker possesses the typical delicate inner border of the Pan Shan style with a dentated ring, a narrow, red horizontal band and a wreath of garlands drawn in thin lines. In the latter beaker the décor on the outside of the neck consists of a band of trellis-filled squares similar in character to the sub-family 6 M III. The beaker K. 5324 (Pl. XXVII, fig. 9) is made of ware of a Ma Chang type; the interior décor on the neck has lost its red horizontal band, the exterior décor on the neck consists of the same squared design as in the foregoing vessel. The triad of bands beneath the handles is dentated, but the upper border belongs to the Ma Chang system. The somewhat high-necked beaker K. 5323 (Pl. XXVII, fig. 10) is of a still more pronounced Ma Chang character, the ware being coarse Ma Chang, while the handles are long, the ornamentation inside the neck is of type 6, that on the outside consists of trelliswork; the upper border is in Ma Chang style and the circles have been simplified, the handles are decorated with crosses on each, and one cross has been placed, as in Ma Chang, beneath the handle, though here beneath only one of them. The beaker K. 5349 (Pl. XXVII, fig. 8) has a neck that becomes narrower towards the top, and very long narrow handles decorated with the band executed in relief that indicates the Ma Chang style, the wave crests appearing as elevated dots and the wave troughs merged into the surface of the handle. The décor inside the neck is of type 6, that on the outside consisting of short-waved horizontal lines in ground colour after the manner of the tenth Ma Chang family. Beneath the handles is a peculiar décor of two red vertical bands bordering a rough trelliswork (fig. 167). On the handles, black horizontal bands are painted in the waves of the bands in relief. The vessel probably belongs to the middle part of the period. The beaker K. 5364 is slightly more advanced; it is of coarse Ma Chang ware, the handles being similar to those in the preceding vessel. The décor on the exterior of the neck consists of a row of black circles filled with trelliswork and a supplementary pattern (fig. 168) between the circles. The interior décor is so far the most highly advanced (type 7). For the rest, the décor is typical Ma Chang.

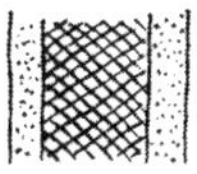

Fig. 167.

Fig. 168.

The two vessels K. 5314 (Pl. XXVII, fig. 11, Pl. XL, fig. 6) and K. 5371 are members of the very extensive late group of the type M. C: XIV. They have large lenticular bodies, low and fairly narrow necks with a concave silhouette. The décor is highly advanced. In vessel K. 5314 the décor inside the neck is considerably more advanced than type 8, though closely related to it; there is no red horizontal band at the lower end, and, as in types 9 and 10, the ring of garlands is replaced by a row of dentations along the lower edge (fig. 169), while the exterior neck ornamentation consists of the fishing-net pattern. The handles are decorated with oblique black lines, and the fields below them are ornamented with crosses. The upper part of the mantle and the upper border have merged into a complex which is bordered, at top and bottom, by triads of horizontal bands after the Ma Chang style. The triads are connected with vertical wavy lines running close together. The band comprising the main décor takes up the lower half of the mantle. The circles are single and are filled with rough trelliswork; they are connected with one another by means of 3—4

Fig. 169.

horizontal lines — an entirely new detail. Vessel K. 5371, which is covered with a painted slip, has an interior neck décor of type 10 A, the fishing-net pattern on the outside of the neck, horizontal bands on the handles, and triads of crosses in the fields beneath them. The pattern in the upper part of the mantle has no red bands, and the horizontal bands are in this case united by narrow vertical lines. Of these two vessels the latter is the more highly advanced and is among the latest products of the period.

Vessel K. 5316 (Pl. XXVII, fig. 12) has as the décor on its mantle two zones containing circles with double peripheries and filled with trelliswork. The zones are separated from one another by a Ma Chang triad.

The vessels all belong to the types M. C: XIV and XV. The majority of them were bought at Lanchow. Beaker K. 5364 comes from Chi Tao Liang in Kao Lan Hsien.

Décor family 8 M.

Characteristic décor on the mantle: band of angles pointing left.

There is only one member of this family in the material at my disposal — a large bowl of a rare and exquisite form, K. 5296 (Pl. XLI, fig. 2).

The pattern inside the neck is of type 4. That on the outside has a row of circles whose outer peripheries have merged into a long chain. The handles are undecorated. The upper border consists of one black and one red band of the Ma Chang style. The characteristic décor is strongly predominant and consists of a row of roughly drawn red angles pointing to the left, their contours being black. These angles have fingers or dentations at the apices and at the ends (cf. the anthropomorphic pattern). From its decorative details the vessel may be presumed to belong to the middle part of the Ma Chang period.

The vessels is one of an advanced special type of M. C: XIV. It was bought at Lanchow.

Décor family 9 M.

Pattern: lines grouped together into bands forming more or less meander-like complexes.

Of all the décor families belonging to the Ma Chang period, this is perhaps the one in which the fanciful, geometrical "jigsaw" design was carried to the greatest lengths. In the beakers of this family the line-motif varies from piece to piece. However, the patterns on the mantle are consistently constructed of series of 3—5 parallel lines, which together make straight bands joined to one another in such a manner as to form an intricate geometrical design composed of different, markedly unsymmetrical meander-like ornaments. Patterns of this character may comprise a dense combination of lines (K. 5376, Pl. XXVIII, fig. 2, and K. 5374) or they may be more widely separated (K. 5989 and K. 5229, Pl. XXVIII, figs. 3 and 4). They are sometimes executed in two colours, K. 5374, sometimes in one colour, K. 5262 (Pl. XXVIII, fig. 5), or in other cases, again, a décor of brown slip is employed, K. 5243 (Pl. XXVIII, fig. 6). On the basis of the various shapes and supplementary decoration it is possible to distinguish between earlier and later vessels within the family. All indications go to show that the earliest belong to the middle of the period and the latest to its close.

Beakers K. 5350 (Pl. XXVIII, fig. 1) and K. 5376 (Pl. XXVIII, fig. 2) are fairly closely related to one another, both as regards their shape and their decorative detail. The patterns on the inside of the neck very closely resemble one another (types 4 and 5), and that on the outside is identical in both vessels: chessboard pattern with alternate black and light-coloured squares with a black dot in the middle. In vessel K. 5350 the meander design is not particularly distinct: against a dark background the bands cross one another in an extremely irregular fashion. In vessel K. 5376 primitive meander shapes show up clearly against the light background. The vessels date from the central part of the period.

We find a distinct meander shape in the linear complexes in beakers K. 5374 and K. 5246, the forms of which are more advanced and in which the ornamentation inside the mouth is of type 9. The décor outside the neck consists in K. 5374 of short-waved, ground-colour horizontal lines on a black background, after the fashion of décor family 10, and in K. 5246 of a few narrow horizontal lines close to the rim. Neck and body are here merged into one. Strictly speaking, the meander pattern in this case constitutes the décor on the lower part of the neck. The very narrow mantle has a décor consisting of a band of almond-shaped ornaments lying horizontally. Vessels K. 5989 and K. 5229 (Pl. XXVIII, figs. 3 and 4) represent still more advanced beaker forms, the décor inside the neck of the first being of type 9, and that of the second consisting of three horizontal lines and below them a row of round dots, type 14. The outside décor on the neck of the former vessel consists at the top of three horizontal lines close together, and beneath them a belt of vertical wavy lines close together (fig. 170), terminating at the bottom in the upper red band of the border. The outside décor on the neck of the latter vessel consists of a row of narrow black triangles, their apices pointing down-

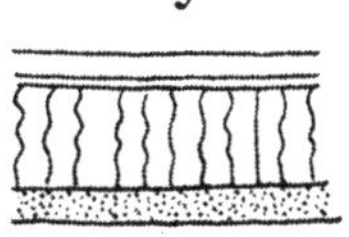

Fig. 170.

wards and their bases merging into a single band. In both these vessels the meander décor is executed in a decorative and logical fashion.

The meander décor is in a way more crude in the two vessels K. 5262 (Pl. XXVIII, fig. 5) and K. 5248, in which however the harmony of the pattern is better preserved. The interior decoration on the neck in the former vessel is of type 10, in the latter it consists of three horizontal lines, and beneath them a row of miniature angles pointing to the left, type 15. The exterior decoration is in the former case a fishing-net design, in the latter case three narrow horizontal lines at the top and groups of vertical lines at the bottom. Both these vessels are highly advanced and, like the vessel K. 5243 (Pl. XXVIII, fig. 6), which is covered with slip, belong to the final products of the period.

Vessel K. 5243 is advanced in shape; on the outside of the neck is a fishing-net pattern, on the handles horizontal bands, below the handles crosses, and on the inside of the neck a décor consisting of two horizontal lines, and beneath them a kind of primitive ring of squares, type 16, all the details thus indicating a very far advanced stage. The characteristic pattern decorates the lower half of the body, and owing to the narrowness of the band the meander décor is truncated and interrupted, though the eye readily combines the details together into a single whole. The upper portion of the mantle has two bands decorated with short vertical lines.

This décor family is as a whole one of the most advanced and is entirely without early representatives. The décor is a typical Ma Chang invention. In the course of development the pattern becomes more distinct and regular. It sometimes reminds one of basket-plaiting, and it is not improbable that the models for some of these and similar geometrical patterns were borrowed actually from the technique of basket-plaiting, in which the material favours, if not necessitates, a regular geometrical treatment of the pattern. The contrast between the spiral bands of the Pan Shan period and the décor on a vessel such as K. 5989 (Pl. XXVIII, fig. 3) could hardly be more marked. Only vessels of form type M. C: XIV belong to this décor family. One vessel is from Nien Po Hsien, Ma Pai Tzu, another from Kao Lan Hsien, 80 li south of Chi Tao Liang. The rest were bought at Lanchow.

Décor family 10 M.

The mantle decorated with horizontal wavy lines with extremely small undulations in ground-colour on a black background, which merges at the top into the upper border, and in the middle into a horizontal Ma Chang triad.

A small uniform group dating from the middle Ma Chang period. The décor is otherwise recognizable as a decorative design from some of the contemporary décor families, e. g. on the necks of the beakers K. 5349 (Pl. XXVII, fig. 8), which is otherwise ornamented with circles, and K. 5374 (meander décor), also on the upper part of the mantle of the jug K. 5780. The interior neck patterns are of type 4 (K. 5372, Pl. XXVIII, fig. 7) and variants of types 9 and 19 (the remainder). The exterior of the necks is decorated with small squares, 6 M I, or with the same ornamentation as that on the mantle; the handles with crosses or horizontal bands. Beneath the handles are crosses (K. 5327, Pl. XL, fig. 5), crosses with 4 dots between the arms, or cowrie ornamentation. The decorative detail, as also the shapes, seem to indicate that the group assumes a central position within the Ma Chang period. There is no evidence to show that different dates can be assigned to the various members of the group, though possibly K. 5372, owing to the décor on the interior of the neck, may be placed somewhat earlier, and K. 5328, owing to the cowrie pattern and its more animated form, somewhat later than the rest.

The vessels are all in the shape of beakers of type M. C: XIV and were all bought at Lanchow.

Décor family 11 M.

The décor divided into horizontal zones on a brownish-red slip. It is composed of narrow black lines and shows considerable variation.

From the systematic point of view this is an extremely important little group of vessels, all of a relatively high beaker shape. The characteristic feature of the group is the thick slip, which we noticed in the case of the late vessels of preceding décor families. The group appears to be very uniform and its members practically all contemporary with one another. There is very little variation in the supplementary patterns, though all the more in the décor on the mantle. We find that, with rare exceptions, the décor on the outside of the neck is throughout the entire group the fishing-net design. In some forms it is composed (fig. 171) of horizontal wavy bands (similar to the patterns of this kind that we have observed before), e. g. in K.

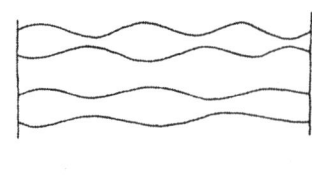

Fig. 171.   5238 (Pl. XXVIII, fig. 9). But there is also another form here, in which the wavy lines (fig. 172) intersect one another like the blades of a pair of scissors, e. g. K. 5237 (Pl. XXVIII, fig. 8).   Fig. 172.

The former system would appear to be the primary one, the latter being a primitive simplification and degeneration of it. The necks are high, and the pattern inside the necks is in all vessels very much simplified; a couple of vessels — K. 5238 (Pl. XXVIII, fig. 9) and K. 5233 — have a garland ornamentation of an extremely simplified kind, (types 18 and 19), and two other vessels, K. 5236 and K. 5237 (Pl. XXVIII, fig. 8) have wavy bands on a dark ground. The rest of the vessels possess a décor of type 17 on the interior of the neck, comprising two or three straight horizontal lines. In all the different vessels the mantle is divided into narrow bands, interrupted by the fields, decorated with crosses, beneath the handles. The ornamentation in these bands varies widely, but the most common pattern is angles, usually with blunt apices, pointing to the right, or, as one might say, running anti-clockwise. In the Pan Shan pottery and in the neck-pattern on Ma Chang vessels, which was borrowed from that style, the direction of the angles was invariably to the left — clockwise. Here it is generally in the contrary direction, e. g. K. 5241 (Pl. XLI, fig. 3). An exception is K. 5240. Single bands of this kind occur on vessels K. 5240, K. 5233, K. 5241 (Pl. XLI, fig. 3), K. 5242 and K. 5236, double bands on the vessel K. 5237 (Pl. XXVIII, fig. 8). Bands of single vertical lines are seen on vessel K. 5238 (Pl. XXVIII, fig. 9), bands of crosses on vessel K. 5240, and a complicated profusion of linear patterns on K. 5236. On the vessels K. 5233 and K. 5237 there are bands of cowrie-like patterns of a most degenerate type.

As I have indicated above, this décor family belongs to the close of the period and, both in form and in design, shows a distinct resemblance to the pottery of the Hsin Tien period, in which geometrical combinations of similar kinds, partly against a brown slip, are common. Moreover, the larger beakers belonging to this group have dimensionally reached the height of the medium-sized Hsin Tien vessels, and are closely related to them in form. *There is every probability that it is vessels of just this type that represent the evolutional basis of the Hsin Tien pottery.* The decorative motifs on these vessels are manifestly degenerate. The vessels are all of type M. C: XIV. The majority were bought at Lanchow. One is from Yü Chung Hsien (K. 5242).

Décor family 12 M.

The surface of the mantle has one or two zones decorated with rhombi, which are divided into small squares, usually four.

A small group of vessels (3 only).

On the mantle of vessel K. 5319 (Pl. XXIX, fig. 4) there are two zones decorated with the characteristic pattern, and on the rest there is only one zone. The zones on K. 5319 are separated and bounded by triads after the Ma Chang system, the upper one merging into the upper border and the pattern on the exterior of the neck, which consists of a much reduced string design. The patterns on the inside of the neck are here a rudimentary garland design, type 18. Both the handles and the fields beneath them are decorated with crosses. Vessel K. 5950 has an upper border after the Ma Chang system, ornamented with a red edge above and a black edge below. Two horizontal lines of type 17 form the décor on the interior of the neck. Vessel K. 5137 (Pl. XXIX, fig. 3) has a plain upper border and an interior neck décor consisting of a horizontal wavy line in ground colour on a black band, type 10 B. The exterior neck pattern on the former vessel consists of groups of vertical lines, that on the latter vessel of vertical bands set close together. The handles of the former pot are ornamented with crosses, those of the latter with horizontal bands. Both of these pots are of a highly advanced form, the latter having an irregular, heart-shaped profile. Beaker K. 5319 is of a more ordinary shape. K. 5137 has a brown slip beneath the décor. In K. 5319 and K. 5950 the characteristic décor stands out against a dark background. In the beaker K. 5137 the band that constitutes the characteristic décor is filled with triangular surfaces covered with parallel lines (fig. 173). The connection between this pattern and the exterior neck décor on a couple of very advanced forms, K. 5322 (Pl. XXVII, fig. 7) and K. 5341, belonging to sub-family IV of the square-décor family, is manifest here. In the

Fig. 173.

pottery of the Hsin Tien period there often occur triangular elements filled up in this manner against a brown slip. Vessel K. 5137 in particular is very far advanced in every respect. The other two vessels are more difficult to place, but K. 5319 presumably belongs to the middle part of the period, and K. 5950 to its close. The vessels are all of form type M. C: XIV and were all bought at Lanchow with the exception of vessel K. 5950, which comes from Hsia K'o, Ya Tzu Tsui, in Chin Hsien.

Décor family 13 M.

Horizontal and vertical lines.

A small uniform group of three beakers of form type M. C: XIV, possessing wide mouths, low bodies and high necks, has this décor. The décor is painted on a thin, brownish violet slip. In all three vessels the décor is carried out in a violet blue colour. Necks and bodies merge more or less imperceptibly into one another. The handles of two of the vessels are somewhat long and affixed vertically, while in the third they are short and more annular. The silhouette of the bodies is more or less broken, this being most marked in vessel K. 5375 (Pl. XXIX, fig. 2). The décor on the interior of the necks consists of a dark band in the form of a carelessly painted row of garlands (type 19). The handles are adorned with horizontal bands. On the neck of K. 5693 (Pl. XXIX, fig. 1) is a series of narrow horizontal lines. The low body of this vessel is ornamented with a narrow band of long, narrow, filled-in spots. On the neck of K. 6124 are groups of vertical lines, and on its body a series of horizontal lines. Vessel K. 5375 has on either side of the neck a field divided into two rectangles. Each of these contains two bar ornaments consisting of 4 horizontal lines and one vertical line. The bars alternate as in the sketch, the whole design acquiring to a certain extent the character of a series of dominoes.

Fig. 174.

The members of this group — all belonging, as already pointed out, to form type M. C: XIV — are so closely related to one another in ware, colour, form, and décor that they might all have been made at the same date by the same artist. They are all highly advanced and belong to the final phase of the Ma Chang period. Vessels K. 5693 and K. 6124 were both found during excavations at Ma Chang Yen, Loc. 4, Sk. 1. The third was bought at Lanchow.

Décor family 14 M.

On the mantle a narrow band with black almond- or walnut-shaped dots.

A small group consisting of three vessels. They all possess very similar and advanced Ma Chang forms with low bodies and very high necks somewhat tapering upwards and then widening into a brim at the top (advanced M. C: XIV types) and two diametrically opposed long and narrow handles (the shortest in K. 5365, the longest in K. 5336, Pl. XLI, fig. 4). The mouths are of medium size. Vessel K. 5365 has a very broad décor on the inside of the neck, consisting above of a narrow black horizontal band with a wavy line in ground colour, beneath that a broad, red horizontal band, and below that again a double band of garlands in black — in fact, a décor that is quite unique. The exterior neck décor consists here of two horizontal lines at the top, and below them four wavy bands, all in black. Vessel K. 5336 has an interior neck décor of type 14 and an original exterior neck décor, consisting of vertical bands composed of wavy lines, and between them a miniature chain (fig. 175) composed of cowrie-like links. Vessel K. 6167 has an interior neck décor of type 17 and an exterior one consisting of groups of vertical lines. Both the vessels K. 5365 and K. 6167 have an upper border consisting of a black line below and a red line above, whereas K. 5336 has a horizontal triad bounded by two black lines. The bands that contain the characteristic motif are low down. In K. 5365 the spots are more walnut-shaped, in the other two they are more almond-shaped. Both form and décor indicate that the vessels belong to the latter part of the period. One vessel was found in Ning Ting Hsien, Wang Chia Kou, another in Ti Tao Hsien, Shan Chuang; the third was bought at Lanchow.

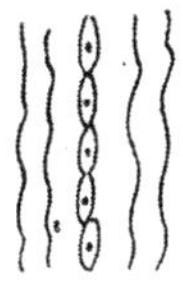

Fig. 175.

Décor family 15 M.

A horizontal band with an indented meander constituting the main pattern on the mantle.

A small group of vessels having on the mantle a horizontal geometrical meander (fig. 176), which is well known from the technique of rush-plaiting. There are squares above and below the meander filled with trelliswork. The vessels are all of very similar specialized forms of type M. C: XIV, the bodies are spherical and have low necks, the exterior profiles of which are concave. Necks and bodies merge gradually into one another. The colour of the décor is a blackish blue. The interior décor of the neck is the same, type 10 A. The exterior décor consists, in the case of vessels K. 5326 (Pl. XXIX, fig. 5) and K. 5330 (Pl. XXV, fig. 6), of a network of squares according to décor family 6 M I, i. e. trellis-filled rhombi and crosses in ground colour. The handles are ornamented with horizontal bands. Below the handles of K. 5326 are double crosses and below those of K. 5330 is an indented meander in the vertical plane. The upper part of the mantle has narrow bands, in K. 5326 with short wavy lines and in K. 5330 with double rows of dots separated by a horizontal line. In K. 5330 the indented meander consists of a band in ground colour with a separate outer contour

Fig. 176.

running round the squares, and in K. 5326 of a black band along which runs a row of spots in ground colour. Vessel K. 5330 has a cowrie border along the bottom.

These vessels are closely related to one another in every possible respect — not only in form and colour but also in the décor as a whole and in its details. They certainly belong to the same epoch and are presumably from the same locality. The markedly geometrical character of the décor, as well as the form and colouring of the vessel, indicate a late phase of the Ma Chang period, though possibly they do not belong to the close of that period. As already mentioned above, they belong to type M. C: XIV and were all bought at Lanchow.

Décor family 16 M.

Geometrically ornamented dishes.

A small group of dishes of types M. C: I, II and XVI is decorated on the upper surface only. The décor is geometrical throughout and is derived in all except one case from the cruciform design used in Pan Shan pottery for the round upper surface of the dish, with the centre of the cross in the middle of the bottom of the dish. The exception is the "tou"-formed dish K. 5379 (Pl. XXIX, fig. 8), which possesses a décor of trelliswork executed entirely in black. The lines forming the trellis design intersect one another at right angles, so that here too a series of crosses of a sort is formed. The rim of the dish is in this case entirely black. Perhaps the simplest of the other kindred decorative forms is the ornament on the "tou" bowl K. 5381 (Pl. XXIX, fig. 7), in which the arms of the cross are bent to the right and form a distinct swastika. The swastika is red with black contours, which coincide at the top with a black ring round the dish. This ring has a band of black bars running radially round its outer edge. We find this black ring with its band of bars recurring in the "tou" bowl K. 5380 (Pl. XXIX, figs. 10 and 11). The cross occurs here too and is complicated in "jigsaw" fashion by angles with their apices pointing upwards between the arms of the cross, and short bars parallel with them outside each angle. All these figures have black contours with a red line down the middle. Of a still more complex "jigsaw" design is the décor on the dish K. 5382 (Pl. XXIX, fig. 9), in which the cross again occurs. Where the arms of the cross meet there is formed a square (fig. 177) with a small cross in the middle. The sectors between the arms of the cross are decorated with an intricate network of bars. In each sector these bars form two squares (fig. 178), which cross one another, and the points of

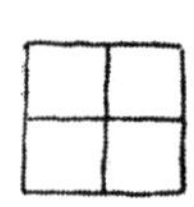

Fig. 177.

which lie on the outer rim of the dish. The rectangle thus formed in the angle of the cross is bisected by a bar. All these bars are red with thin black contours. Between the bars are formed a number of narrow rectangular surfaces divided longitudinally by a thin line and ornamented with two rows of dots. The rim of the bowl is decorated with a large number of small crosses (fig. 179). The geometrical "jigsaw" design is here carried to extreme lengths.

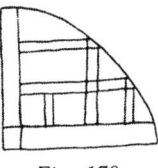

Fig. 178.

The somewhat deep dish K. 5616 (Pl. XXIX, figs. 12 and 13) also has a cross as its main décor. The arms of the cross are united at the rim of the dish by a broad circular band. In each sector is a triangular meander (fig. 180) consisting of double lines.

Fig. 179.

The décor on all these dishes is markedly geometrical. Hardly anywhere in this pottery is the involved geometrical design so deliberately cultivated as here. The origin of the ornamentation on these dishes is apparently the plain cross décor found on the Pan Shan dishes. It is extremely difficult to date these dishes owing to the small number of pieces and the peculiar decorative conditions. For the form is without any of those supplementary motifs that are usually found in other families and which otherwise offer obvious points of comparison. The studied and almost mathematically worked out geometry of these designs indicates however a highly evolved Ma Chang style. Vessel K. 5616 was found in a grave at Nien Po Hsien, Ma Chang Yen, Loc. 4, Sk. 2, Pot 2. The other mortuary urns found in locality 4 are strongly advanced both in form and décor. The slip that we find on the other vessels occurs also here. This vessel may therefore be dated at the close of the period on stronger grounds than the others.

Fig. 180.

Individual vessels.

Besides those previously mentioned, there are a number of vessels belonging to Ma Chang pottery the mantles of which have a predominant décor of an individual character. The supplementary décor, on the other hand, is frequently the same in these as in the other vessels. They cannot be grouped under any of the families described above. Nevertheless, it must be assumed that they are in many cases representatives of a larger number of vessels and true décor families, in which case it is quite by chance that they should have come to the material at my disposal as the sole representatives of their characteristic pattern. In many instances their pattern is very closely related to the décor families discussed above, and in the majority of cases their Ma

Chang character is patently evident, thanks not only to the nature of the ware but also to the colour and style of the décor, the pattern of the supplementary décor, as well as the formal peculiarities of the characteristic pattern. To insert these vessels, with their marked individuality, into their respective chronological places within the period is possible in certain cases owing to their form and supplementary décor, while in others it is quite impracticable. To enable us to do so we should require a far greater number of representatives possessing the characteristic décor.

The mantle of K. 5339 (Pl. XXX, fig. 1) of type M. C: XIV, from Tao Sha Hsien, Ka Tu Ma Kou, is divided into trapeziform fields separated by a Ma Chang triad, each side of the vessel having three such fields. In each field the inner contours of the trapeze are twofold and executed in black, the innermost containing trelliswork. The handles and the fields beneath them are ornamented with oblique black bands. The décor on the inside of the neck is of type 4, that on the outside consists of bands of angles pointing left.

In the case of the pot K. 5313 (Pl. XXX, fig. 3), which is of an original shape (form type M. C: XIX), the mantle is decorated with a series of swastika-like crosses after the Ma Chang triad system. Adjacent crosses join on to one another at the top, while at the bottom they merge into the lower border or are fashioned into arms (fig. 181) bent so as to form one or two distinct angles and with or without hands. The crosses, which are five in number, differ somewhat from one another and represent, so to speak, different stages of development of crosses provided with hands and, in part, resembling a swastika. It seems reasonable to suppose that some symbolism lies behind this pattern, which is of a somewhat menacing nature. There is no ornamentation on the handles. The décor on the inside of the neck is of type 4, that on the outside consists of a series of black horizontal bands joined to one another by vertical stems near the handles. The supplementary décor on the pot indicates that it can belong neither to the earliest nor to the most recent of the Ma Chang products. It was presumably made during the middle phase of the period. The pot was bought at Lanchow.

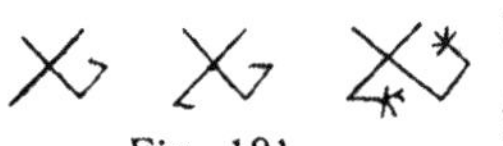

Fig. 181.

K. 5355 (Pl. XXX, fig. 2). Here the characteristic pattern consists of groups of 3—4 vertical, black wavy lines with short, rapid undulations. The upper border is a regular Ma Chang triad. The pattern inside the neck is closely related to type 5; the black and the red bands, however, have changed places, and there is no dentated line. The pattern on the outside of the neck is composed of groups of vertical lines. The outermost line in each group has rows of horizontal strokes (fig. 182), alternately at top and bottom. The handles are ornamented with horizontal bands. The patterns both on the exterior of the neck and on the mantle are original. That on the former is more typical of the experimental, geometrical style. The vessel, which is of the ordinary M. C: XIV form, was bought at Lanchow.

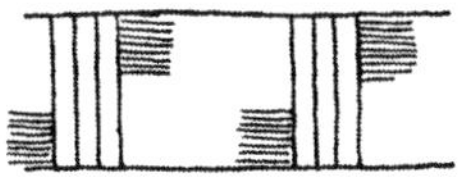

Fig. 182.

K. 5346 (Pl. XXX, fig. 4). In this small beaker, which is of type M. C: XIV and comes from Ti Tao Hsien, Su Chia Yang, the characteristic pattern on the body consists of a row of small round dots in ground colour on a broad, black band which has no border along the lower edge, and along the upper edge merges into the red boundary-line between neck and body. The décor on the outside of the neck likewise merges into this red boundary-line at the bottom and consists of a line-pattern motif, two bands of lines below and one above. These two groups of bands are separated by a narrow red band. The interior décor consists of a black dentated edge uppermost, then follows a broad red horizontal band, and below that a black band with groups of suspended vertical lines. The handles are ornamented with black horizontal bands.

K. 5737 (Pl. XXX, fig. 5). The characteristic pattern on the mantle of this beaker consists of a row of smallish rings in ground colour on a black background. The pattern inside the neck is a primitive form of type 13, specially suitable here owing to the width of the mouth and the neck's proportionally considerable height, also to the fact that it widens out to a certain extent. The pattern outside the neck is a network of squares with black dots in them and in the triangular fields formed at top and bottom. The handles are decorated each with three vertical lines. The black ground forming the pattern on the mantle merges at the top into the red boundary-line between neck and body. The shape is a specialized form of type M. C: XIV. The vessel was bought at Lanchow.

K. 5320 (Pl. XLI, fig. 1). This piece, of type M. C: III, which approaches in form to a hanging vessel, has a mixed décor. It has no neck. The décor on the mantle is divided into three zones, the two upper ones separated by a Ma Chang triad, the two lower by a horizontal band with one black and one red edge. The uppermost zone is decorated with groups of vertical lines, 3—8 in each group, and so placed as to come between holes pierced through the wall of the vessel. There are 8 of these holes, and they are arranged in pairs round the mouth. The middle zone is decorated with sloping lines in groups forming a false zigzag band. Between these groups are formed triangular fields with dots in their centres. The nethermost zone is ornamented with a row of squares in ground colour on a black ground, similar to décor family 12 M. The squares have a cross in their centres, which divides each of them into four small squares, in which are black dots. The vessel was bought at Lanchow.

K. 5317 (Pl. XXX, fig. 7) belongs to the group of the largest vessels of form type M. C: XIV dating from the Ma Chang period. It is particularly interesting owing to the meander pattern on its mantle. The vessel is so far the earliest known vessel from China with a frieze consisting of a number of formally arranged meanders. The décor on the mantle is divided into two zones bisected by the fields, which are decorated with crosses, below the handles. The upper zone consists of a broad dark band, in which is a row of round spots in ground colour with dark dots in their centres. The two halves of the lower, broader zone are decorated with a meander design consisting of three meanders combined in a highly original fashion. The meander furthest to the left merges into the middle meander towards the top, while that furthest to the right merges into the middle one towards the bottom. The meanders are horizontal and elongated. The décor constitutes one of the symptoms that indicate the period's interest in mathematically geometrical decoration and fully harmonizes with other "jigsaw"-like and geometrically influenced decorative forms dating from that period. *Owing to this fact and to the extremely original manner in which the meanders are combined, I consider that the décor on this vessel originated independently in Kansu without being influenced by other Western meander forms.* The size and form of the vessel (with a clearly differentiated base) indicate that it should be placed late in the Ma Chang system. The same indication is given also by the décor on the interior of the neck, according to type 10 B, as well as by its exterior décor: groups of slightly undulating, vertical lines. The vessel was bought at Lanchow.

K. 5490 (Pl. XXX, fig. 6). This vessel is of medium-sized M. C: XIV form, with a low neck merging gradually into the body, and is characterized by a miscellaneous décor on the mantle entirely in black over a thin brownish-red slip. The décor on the mantle consists of two broad horizontal zones, the upper one containing vertical wavy lines very close together, the lower one divided on each side into three squares, the middle square filled with a chessboard design, the two on either side of it with a meander filled with trelliswork. These horizontal zones are bisected into two parts by the reduplicated cross-décor below the handles. The network pattern on the exterior of the neck, which partly extends down to the upper part of the body, as also the pattern of type 10 C on the interior of the neck, the brown slip, the shape of the vessel and the ornamentation on the body, all indicate the close of the period. The vessel was bought at Lanchow.

K. 5321 (Pl. XXX, fig. 8). A beaker of type M. C: XIV, bought at Lanchow. It is fairly large and has a wide mouth and two handles, the upper edge of which projects slightly above the rim of the mouth. Otherwise, both in form, surface treatment and décor, it is a somewhat roughly executed piece. Its décor bears a fairly close resemblance to patterns belonging to décor family 11 M, but there is no slip whatever. Two colours are employed, black and dark red. The neck is decorated, both on the inside and on the outside, with black horizontal lines. The ornamentation on both neck and mantle is divided into two parts by the décor on, beside and below the handles. The décor on the mantle is bounded at the top by a black-and-red double band, and at the bottom by a triad, of which the central strip is red and the two outer strips black. Similar triads, though in the vertical plane, also bound the décor below the handles. The surface of the mantle has a broad zone divided into triangles, which are filled with narrow black lines running parallel to the right-hand sides of the triangles. Beneath the décor on the mantle is an ornamentation that is original as a border, consisting of angles pointing right. The pot is one of the advanced forms belonging to the period. Its décor with the filled triangles recurs in that of the Hsien Tien period, though in a somewhat modified form.

K. 5244 (Pl. XXX, fig. 10). This beaker, which is covered with a dark reddish-brown slip, also has a mantle décor related to that in family 11 M. The décor is executed only in black against the red slip. The ornamentation on the outside of the neck consists of groups of vertical lines, that on the inside of three horizontal lines. The décor on the mantle is bounded at top and bottom by black horizontal bands. Vertical bands likewise bound the fields below and around the handles. The mantle is decorated at the top with vertical lines and narrow horizontal lines, and at the bottom with entirely filled-in rectangles resting on the lower band. The beaker is advanced in point of shape (oval, somewhat saddle-shaped mouth) and décor (interior neck décor, exterior mantle décor, slip etc.).

K. 5776 (Pl. XXIX, fig. 6). The small jug K. 5776, of form type M. C: X, is of a highly original design as regards both form and decoration; nevertheless, its décor offers clear evidence of its belonging to the Ma Chang group. The mantle is decorated with ovals in the vertical plane, consisting of triads in black and red surrounded by fairly narrow, black curves and filled with pairs of curved lines. The mantle is bounded at the top by a black-and-red double band and at the bottom by a red band. The décor on the inside of the neck consists at the top of a black band of wavy lines in ground colour, and at the bottom of a red horizontal band merging into the upper one. The jug is undoubtedly from an advanced phase of the period. It was bought at Lanchow.

K. 5370 (Pl. XXX, fig. 11, Pl. XLI, fig. 5). This bowl, of form type M. C: XVIII, is unique both in form and décor. It is decorated on the outside with two ornaments, one on either side of the vessel. This ornament consists of two volutes, one below to the left and one above to the right, also an arm at the left upper end without a volute. The pattern is designed in an abstract, floral-animal style. The volutes terminate inwards with finger-like dabs. The end part of the arm is also provided with fingers (a hand). Finally, the arms of the pattern have a dentated edge at the top. For the rest, the pattern has a black contour and red central parts. Close to the hand are one or two smallish black rings. Each of the handles is ornamented with three circles in ground colour on a black surface, and in these circles are patterns resembling bird's tracks. On the inner edge of the vessel is a row of ground-colour rings on a black surface. The inside of the vessel is decorated with ⌠ and ⌡ shaped double volutes with black contours and red medullary parts.

The décor on this bowl, the Ma Chang character of which is obvious, is however very peculiar. Here all geometrical elements are banned, being replaced by a more animated movement and a rhythm akin to that of the central Pan Shan pottery, both the mortuary urns (the spiral pattern group) and the dwelling-site vessels possessing a similar abstract, floral-animal character. The vessel would appear to be either the work of an artist with original and creative ideas or else an isolated representative of some purely local pottery works producing during the Ma Chang period. I am inclined to think the latter to be the more probable. The vessel was bought at Lanchow.

K. 5486 (Pl. XLI, fig. 6). A singular bowl of type M. C: XVII. Unfortunately its décor is partially destroyed, particularly on the inside; it is however sufficiently distinct to show clearly the Ma Chang character of this vessel, which was bought at Lanchow. The whole of its surface is covered with a light-brown slip, and it is decorated in two colours, dark brown and reddish violet. The surface is Ma Chang in character, dull and slightly granular. The exterior is decorated with a broad brownish-black zone containing a series of rings in ground colour, drawn concentrically in twos. Lower down on the outside of the vessel is a garland-like border and higher up is a red band merging into the black zone. The décor inside the vessel is badly damaged. It is possible to observe, however, that at the top is a dark-brown zone, then a red band, which merges into both the upper and the lower brownish-black zone. This latter is ornamented with a row of circular surfaces in ground colour. The vessel appears to belong to the last phase of the Ma Chang period, as is indicated particularly by its well-constructed foot and its well-executed and quite mobile silhouette.

THE DIFFERENT CERAMIC FORMS SUMMARIZED.

It does not fall within the scope of this investigation to try to determine whether the painted ceramic material that I have been dealing with here is from the technical and artistic point of view based mainly on loans from Western cultures or whether it is on the whole autochthonous. It does not however appear to be so isolated as to exclude altogether the possibility of its having connections in various quarters. However that may be, my investigations have produced many indications that the great highway that runs through Chinese culture, the evolution of art as a whole, is of a manifestly individual character. The proper way to confirm this would be, I think, first of all to ascertain, if possible, the course of this evolution, and to discover — again if possible — what has developed, from natural conditions and quite logically, out of the peculiarities of landscape, climate and race. It is only after that that we can discuss the question of loans and relationships. In any case, the most important point is to study the measure of continuity existing in the material we have available.

As regards the two early bodies of material dealt with in this work and named after the places Pan Shan and Ma Chang Yen, in my view and so far as an exhaustive analysis of the material can reveal with any measure of validity, they represent material that shows a distinct line of continuity, in which the evolution of forms and designs proceeds along organic lines and is determinable in its different phases.

From the standpoint of form, these two ceramic groups are of extraordinary interest, seeing that they comprise a number of component links and a limited, yet typical, section of a single chain of development. In the present work I have dealt only with the different groups of mortuary pottery within these bodies of material. The segregation of this part of the ceramic material is justified by the fact that, on Professor Andersson's showing, the domestic pottery and the mortuary pottery are differentiated both in their forms and in their colouring and decorative design. This is however true only in a general way. There are exceptions to the rule, and they clearly demonstrate the contemporaneity of the material in our possession.

The Pan Shan mortuary pottery, as compared with the dwelling-site pottery from the same period, represents to a certain extent a more primitive entity, that is to say, as regards both the forms and the decorative designs that occur during the period. The mortuary pottery was originally borrowed from the dwelling-site pottery, but as the burial customs gradually acquired a more and more pronounced ritualistic character, which eventually left its mark also on the mortuary pottery, and the dwelling-site pottery became rapidly enriched as a result of its being called upon to meet multifarious and increasingly complicated and specialized needs, the two types of pottery showed an ever wider divergence. The former has represented, so to speak, the more conservative and restricted requirements of the dead established by forms and dogmas, and the latter the greater wealth and variation of animate life.

Primitive forms occur in the Pan Shan mortuary pottery, on the one hand, as a principal component amongst vessels made of unpainted ware and, on the other hand, as a quantitatively predominant part of the painted forms of pottery. In the foregoing chapters I have already made a complete inventory of these primitive forms, and I shall therefore refrain from dwelling further on the range of types they represent. Among these form types we have so far found no trace of any imitations of natural vessels or of the shapes of skin vessels, vessels cut out of wood or made of basketwork. The primitive types represent basic ceramic forms arisen primarily out of the incidences of material, technique and the dictates of necessity.

Other less primitive forms also occur in both the above-mentioned kinds of pottery. In the painted Pan Shan pottery we find a series of elegant forms created by artists possessing a refined appreciation of the material they used. I regard them as belonging to a second and higher "stratum" in this culture. All indications go to show that they were created by native potters.

A third "stratum" containing examples both of the painted and of the unpainted group is represented by a number of original forms, fancy forms, concerning which it is premature, owing to the small number of specimens, to express an opinion with any degree of certainty as to their origin and development. At any rate they presuppose the existence of a fairly advanced cultural stage.

It is possible to trace — in a number of cases with many evolutional phases — a process of development of the forms of vessels belonging to the Pan Shan pottery. The development is particularly clear in those forms of which a considerable number of vessels are representative. Some of the most important forms of vessels pass direct into Ma Chang forms, and these are manifestly in process of development during that period.

The evolution of the Pan Shan style of pottery is most clearly apparent in the types A and B (the form types P. S: XXIII and P. S: XXIV). The bodies undergo a distinct transition from a form with the upper part like a slightly flattened hemisphere and the lower part like an inverted and truncated cone to a higher form, of which the upper part is markedly rotund and the lower part more pointed, and which has a smaller bottom (often approaching the shape of an inverted pear, truncated at the lower end by the bottom and at the upper end by the neck). This advanced form of body is very closely related, indeed, represents a transition, to two typical forms of Ma Chang vessels (the form types M. C: VIII and M. C: IX). The high necks of the B vessels, which start by being stiff and practically straight, become in the course of development more and more elegant, more or less concave in silhouette, while they widen out more towards the top, finally acquiring a form closely related to those of the necks of the earlier Ma Chang vessels. Simultaneously with this change in form the ware itself tends to grow thinner, and the pots become, on the whole, lighter in weight, while parallel with these developments we find a transformation and reduction of the ears that were inherited from the unpainted group, and which are placed diametrically opposite to one another on the rim of the high-necked B vessels.

The ears on the B vessels were originally particularly strong; they were provided with holes and were of really practical use as a means of attaching strings or sinews to the vessels. They were notched along the edges. Subsequently their size gradually diminishes, the holes disappear, as also the notched edge. Finally they are reduced to insignificant rudimentary appendages. In the most highly advanced Pan Shan vessels they are absent altogether, as also in the Ma Chang vessels. As to the use to which these ears were put, not even in the case of the very earliest vessels is it possible to suppose that they had anything to do with carrying the vessel. They are too thin and too ineffectively attached to be imagined as serving the purpose of a fastening to take strings or straps. As a matter of fact, the function of supporting the vessel is served by the sturdy annular handles attached to the middle of the body, and which have been used for carrying or lifting. The A and B pots are true processional pots, presumably borne on the heads of those taking part in the procession in which the dead was conveyed along the route from the home up to the necropolis situated high up on the hills. The small ears are most likely connected with the necessity, owing to its somewhat narrow mouth, of tilting the vessel when filling it, or else were used for attaching a lid of some perishable material. The gradual reduction in the size of the ears simultaneously with the widening-out of the neck towards the top is probably to be interpreted as the result of a struggle between tradition and transferred function. Indeed, the widened neck is itself capable of holding in place a cord bound round it. Moreover, from the very beginning the low-necked A vessels, which had collars that widened out at the top, were — except in two isolated cases — without ears. In the hanging vessels the suspensory function of the ears is quite self-evident.

The Ma Chang culture absorbs the advanced A and B forms of the Pan Shan pottery and rapidly modifies them to a quite considerable extent. The result is the creation, firstly of a type with a still more breast-like body and a still smaller basal diameter, and secondly of two new forms of vessel, the one possessing smaller, lower and more spherical bodies, and the other with higher bodies resembling more the shape of a plum. The advanced Pan Shan necks of these A and B vessels are taken over by the early Ma Chang style, and their concave profiles become still more pronounced. In the Ma Chang type M. C: VIII the low A necks develop at the top an increasingly emphasized brim round the mouth and at the bottom a tendency to merge gradually into the body. Both these circumstances serve to enrich the silhouette effect of the profile. This richer silhouette that we find in the Ma Chang pottery is of great importance for the further evolutionary process up to the Hsin Tien and Ssu Wa Shan forms. The tendency is already obvious here. The high-necked B vessels likewise acquire a richer curvature in their profiles and a more emphasized brim. The ears, which had already been lost during the late Pan Shan epoch, were never subsequently revived in the Ma Chang forms.

Out of the Pan Shan period's form type P. S: XXIII (type A) has originated its form type P. S: XXIX through the transfer of one of the handles from the body up to the neighbourhood of the neck or to a position embracing the neck. Out of this form type a specialized form has probably arisen by reducing to insignificance the annular handle on the body — usually to an upward turned ridge handle (K. 5110, Pl. IV, fig. 5). A similar specialized form has emanated from type B on lines analogous to this specialization out of type A. Thus, form type P. S: XXX is in the same relation to B as P. S: XXIX is to A. Type P. S: XXX generally has an annular handle attached partly to the neck and partly to the body, and another annular handle attached to the middle of the body. A rudimentary ear on the front of the neck of vessel K. 5102 (Pl. IX, fig. 5) is further evidence of the probability that this was the course of development. In certain vessels the annular handle on the body is converted into a ridge handle. The somewhat specialized Ma Chang forms M. C: X and M. C: XI have evolved out of the Pan Shan forms P. S: XXIX and P. S: XXX. The most advanced of these Ma Chang vessels likewise have a silhouette effect that is richer in certain respects.

When once we have realized the reduction of the Pan Shan vessels P. S: XXIX and P. S: XXX down to the disappearance of the ridge handles on these pots, we arrive at the ceramic types P. S: XV and P. S: XVIII. However, we are perhaps not justified in insisting too strongly upon bringing the form series to such a fine point of distinction. P. S: XV and P. S: XVIII, which certainly have some affinity to types A and B, need not necessarily have sprung from the intermediate form series. Perhaps they rather belong merely to the same cultural "stratum" in the form series, i. e. they have arisen simultaneously in the same milieu but out of different conditions and different needs. This explains both their general similarity and their peculiar divergences.

In the Pan Shan pottery it is possible to trace an evolutional process in both the form type P. S: XXX and the form type P. S: XVIII. In both cases it is primarily the necks that change. At the outset they are stiff and straight (K. 5223, Pl. IV, fig. 1); later they acquire a more curved and mobile profile. During the middle part of the period they show considerable variation, particularly in the matter of height (K. 5502, Pl. VI, fig. 6, and K. 5625, Pl. XVII, fig. 2). In the course of the later phases of the Pan Shan style the top widens out in an elegant though not too strongly emphasized manner (K. 5224, Pl. XIV, fig. 5, and K. 5756, Pl. XIV, fig. 9). Thus, the process of evolution here is analogous to that of form type P. S: XXIV (type B).

Even when it comes to the continued development of these two forms in the Ma Chang period we can trace the tendency towards an ever-increasing enrichment of the silhouette, in spite of the small number of Ma Chang specimens of these types (e. g. M. C: VI, see K. 5611, Pl. XXVI, fig. 6) in which there is a brim to the neck. The brim is even transferred, though on a restricted scale, to Ma Chang dishes of type M. C: I, e. g. K. 5382 (Pl. XXIX, fig. 9).

Very complicated is the group that embraces the closely related Pan Shan types X, Y, Z (the form types P. S: XXXI, XXXII and XXXIII). They are all characterized by the fact that they possess two diametrically opposed annular handles, fastened at the top to the edge of the collar and at the bottom to the body close to the collar. In their early stage they are bowl- or beaker-shaped and have a comparatively small bottom.

Vessels Y and Z in particular occur in large numbers. We find primitive vessels, whose forms are somewhat indefinite and which assume a central position between types X, Y and Z.

From these primitive vessels there develop, each along lines of its own, the types X, Y and Z. In both type Y and type Z it is possible to a certain extent to trace the course of development up to the most strikingly differentiated types.

In type Y the body becomes in the evolutionary process proportionally lower and increases in rotundity. The neck grows higher, in individual specimens very high. The annular handles are enlarged. The mouth diminishes in width in proportion to the body.

In type Z the vessel increases in height, the neck grows shorter but takes on a more elegant curve, its transition into the body becoming more gradual and the mouth slightly narrower. The widest part of the body is transferred to a somewhat lower plane. In the latest part of the Pan Shan period type Z has attained an extremely elegant and attractive form (K. 5044, Pl. XVII, fig. 5, and K. 5046, Pl. XVII, fig. 9).

All three types are taken over by the Ma Chang pottery (the form types M. C: XII—XV), in which the first is divided into two types M. C: XII—XIII, and the middle one plays an almost predominating part (M. C: XIV). The few vessels originating in type Z (M. C: XV) all undergo substantial modifications in the direction of Ma Chang.

Type Y (M. C: XIV) is, as we have already mentioned, quantitatively the predominating vessel of the Ma Chang period. It acquires a very wide scope of variation and provides a whole series with true specialized forms possessing extraordinarily mobile silhouettes. Vessels with more or less saddle-shaped, oval mouths are also constructed (K. 5362, Pl. XXV, fig. 5), manifestly foreshadowing the form of vessel that occurs somewhat rarely in the Hsin Tien period but is entirely predominant in the Ssu Wa Shan period. Some of these advanced forms of ceramic type M. C: XIV increase in size until they become a kind of tureen, thus emerging from the ranks of the small vessels into those of the medium-sized vessels. In this too we find a tendency that becomes highly significant for the development of ceramics during the Hsin Tien epoch.

In the Pan Shan types X, Y and Z the upper parts of the annular handles are invariably attached to the actual edge of the collar. In some of the related Ma Chang vessels there is a tendency to shift the point of attachment slightly below the edge of the collar. Among the associated vessels of the Hsin Tien period we find two distinct types, the one with the annular handles attached to the edge of the vessel, and the other with the upper point of attachment considerably below the rim of the collar[1]).

It is not possible to show a direct transition from the large pots of the Ma Chang period evolved out of types A and B to the larger vessels of the Hsin Tien period[2]). True, the large Hsin Tien vessels, like the majority of the Ma Chang vessels, have a higher base than the Pan Shan vessels, but the profiles of the pots differ widely from one another and hardly justify the assumption that the one has originated from the other. The necks of the Hsin Tien vessels are higher, generally fairly wide, and they pass direct into the somewhat flat or concave mantle. In the Ma Chang vessels the necks are clearly differentiated, have a narrow mouth and a mantle that is strongly arched. In order to conceive of a transition between types A and B via the Ma Chang form types M. C: VIII and M. C: IX to the Hsin Tien vessels, we must assume that an intermediate link — one or more intermediate periods — is missing. This assumption is perhaps supported in some measure by the evolution of the decorative patterns, which in certain respects exhibits a fairly distinct gap just here. Moreover, it may be assumed in further explanation of this fact that powerful influences from foreign cultures were making themselves felt at this epoch. However, in discussing the X, Y and Z groups' descendants in the Ma Chang ceramic family we cannot omit to point out a third reasonable explanation of the new form in the large Hsin Tien vessels. Apart from the diametrically opposed annular handles attached to the widest portion of the body, we are not entirely unacquainted with the profile of the large Hsin Tien pots. As a matter of fact, it occurs in the *smaller* Hsin Tien vessels also, and, as I have pointed out above, their form can in turn be traced without difficulty from the X—Y—Z group of the Pan Shan style, with a number of Ma Chang forms as intermediate links. The Hsin Tien pottery, so extraordinarily orthodox even as regards the painted décor, has established for its ceramic forms one single dominant type of profile, although in the heavier vessels the points of attachment of the annular handles have for safety's sake been shifted further down. Even in the smaller Ma Chang vessels, as I have also mentioned before, the handles are somewhat mobile in the vertical plane in relation to the body, neck and the rim of the mouth. The same applies to the Hsin Tien pottery. Some vessels are in the form of a well-designed amphora with long handles extending from the rim to the body of the vessel, others possess considerably shorter handles with the upper point of attachment in the middle of the neck, while others again have still smaller

---

[1]) See Bibl. 6. Pl. IV.
[2]) Id. cit. Pl. III, fig. 2.

handles fastened at the point of transition between body and neck. It may be cited as further evidence that the large Hsin Tien vessels had this origin, that, besides the lower pair of annular handles, some large vessels from this culture have at the top, in a similar position to those of the X, Y and Z vessels, and in the same plane, an additional pair of smaller and weaker handles. In vessel K. 5435 this upper pair of handles has degenerated into a purely rudimentary state.

A few new forms occur amongst the Ma Chang vessels, the most interesting being the vessels M. C: XVI, and M. C: XVII, which are provided with a ring-foot. In Pan Shan mortuary pottery the ring-foot is so far unknown; on the other hand, we find it in the Pan Shan dwelling-site material. It is evident, therefore, that it is not a Ma Chang invention but was borrowed from earlier dwelling-site forms. The facts go to show that the Ma Chang mortuary pottery had not altogether lost touch with the forms used in everyday domestic life, but — at any rate in rare cases — received impulses from it and borrowed from it.

Some of the Pan Shan forms and their successors in the Ma Chang pottery that we have discussed here may be the prototypes of part of the richly varied Chinese pottery, and even of some bronze forms, during far later epochs. The very earliest prototypes of the potter's art are preserved throughout the ages with a large measure of continuity, this being, moreover, in full accord with China's cultural constitution, with its characteristically conservative tendencies.

In this connection I will draw attention to only a few important and illuminating facts. (See Bibl. 45, 47—49, 51, 61, 68, 72, 80 and 82.)

Plain bowls and dishes whose forms are related to types P. S: I, II and III survive in unglazed material produced during the Han dynasty, in glazed forms of the Tang dynasty, and they subsequently live on in dainty and fragile porcelain produced during the Sung and Ming epochs. Hemispherical tureen forms of types P. S: XX and P. S: XXII also still survive in the best Chinese forms, both amongst ceramic products and amongst metal vessels. The tendency to the disproportionate enlarging and lengthening of the necks that is so typical of Chinese pottery had already begun to show itself quite distinctly in the Pan Shan material (P. S: XVIII and P. S: XIX).

The Ma Chang bowl with a circular foot and the Ma Chang dish with a circular foot (M. C: XVI and M. C: XVII) both recur in the bronze form Tou, in the Chou pottery and in that of far later dynasties.

As late as in the Tang dynasty there occur types in which spouts are attached similarly to the ceramic types P. S: XXXIV and P. S: XXXV, among the above-mentioned fancy forms. Vessels related to the curious form types P. S: XXXVII and P. S: XXXVIII are found in the pottery used by the patrician class, e. g. in the Ming dynasty, and are still used in China as chamber-pots for men.

The comparison can doubtless be carried further on this point, but such extensive research as it would necessitate is not within the scope of this work.

SUMMARY REVIEW OF THE DÉCOR ON THE PAN SHAN AND MA CHANG POTTERY.

The décor on the painted mortuary pottery from the Pan Shan hills exhibits a distinct evolutional process.

The simple and, one might almost say, naive, geometrical décor — not mathematically worked out — which had already been cultivated in earlier ages, when the art of painting the vessels was not yet introduced or was at any rate exceedingly rare, continues in the Pan Shan pottery to develop along two different lines: on painted and on unpainted vessels.

The geometrically decorated, unpainted group consists of a type of pottery that, although quantitatively inferior, is nevertheless preserved throughout the entire period of the Pan Shan style as an important component of the mortuary pottery. The décor on this unpainted pottery is to a certain extent related to that of the Ch'i Chia pottery. However, the technique of the unpainted Pan Shan pottery is more primitive than that of the Ch'i Chia pottery, and its designs are less refined than the best specimens of the latter style, although the elements are often similar. I regard this primitiveness in the unpainted Pan Shan as degeneracy, as compared with the Ch'i Chia pottery. However, there can hardly be any absolute association between the ceramic styles of the two cultures[1]). We find degeneration going on to a certain extent in the unpainted pottery during the evolution of the Pan Shan style. The advanced graves contain a very decadent form of this pottery.

The "kindergarten" style of the geometrically decorated group found among the painted vessels represents an *early* phase in the development of Pan Shan pottery. On the whole it possesses the same types of pattern as the unpainted group. The plastic notches are translated into a painted form by means of a dentated device that forms almost a radical element of the painted Pan Shan patterns. Professor J. G. Andersson has styled this dentated system the death pattern. The death pattern consists in most of the black bands' having a dentated edge bordering on plain red bands.

---

[1]) This applies only to Pan Shan pottery and Ch'i Chia pottery.

The rhythm achieved by notching in the unpainted group is thus preserved by means of this dentate design in the painted vessels.

The primitive geometrical décor on the Pan Shan mortuary urns is made up of a relatively small group of elements: horizontal bands or zones, curtailed curves or semicircles, horizontal zigzag bands and curvilinear bands, lines bounded at top and bottom by horizontal lines and running obliquely downwards from the top. Undoubtedly the predominant element, as far as the unpainted pottery is concerned, is the zigzag band, which indeed is of common occurrence also in the painted mortuary pottery. In the painted primitive group there are added — as a direct expression of the newly acquired technique of decorating in colour — crudely drawn circles and spirals. Even at this stage curtailed curved elements are arranged round the interior of the neck into a garland-like décor. Red is used now and then in the lower border too. The principal pattern employed for the ornamentation of the mantle consists of horizontal bands or, more correctly perhaps, zones, painted alternately in black and red.

The rectilinear character of the geometrical décor becomes rapidly modified in the course of its further development. The freedom afforded by the technique of painting in contrast to the scratching of the engraver's point, which has at the same time to be pressed in and moved forwards, or to the laborious method of applying strips of clay, is discovered and exploited. Rigidity of expression disappears. The artist enjoys the rich possibilities of his newly acquired technique. The rhythms become manifold, also broader and more mobile. The reaction against the stiff designs of the preceding style gives rise to curved lines and complicated curves. Straight lines are banished altogether when it comes to painted décor, and are only retained in the case of the still surviving, unpainted mortuary pottery. The patterns grow animated and playful. A whole series of fresh elements arise. Spools and shapes like bulbs in section, bottle-, gourd- or vase-like ornaments, upright lancet-shaped leaves, squared patterns, whose lines, however, on closer inspection turn out to be curved, also circles and spirals — these are the patterns that generally adorn the mantle.

The mantle design that is predominant during this phase of the development is a red horizontal spiral line, and, running alongside it on either side, one or more unsymmetrical wavy lines in black and red. The red spiral line has four spiral centres, though in a few exceptional cases it has more than four. The spiral centres are originally small and without any supplementary decoration. The spiral décor is worked up into a rich "orchestration" of the surface of the mantle. Some of the most richly decorated vessels in Kansu pottery are created about this time.

During this period, the spool and bulb designs, as well as the bottle patterns, are not drawn in any stereotyped manner but show lively variation from vessel to vessel.

The black colour increases somewhat in significance and in quantity, becoming entirely predominant as far as the lower border is concerned, which now, following conventional lines, has only two elements to choose from and ring changes upon, viz., the plain horizontal band and the wavy horizontal band. The décor on the exterior of the neck varies, but the predominant pattern in the high-necked vessels has an upper portion, usually embracing slightly more than half of the neck, that is covered with a fine-meshed trelliswork and bounded at the bottom by a red horizontal band, and beneath that a zone comprising a black, dentated band of broad and thick points directed upwards. The décor on the interior of the neck still consists of a vigorous garland design.

We find the patterns described above still surviving during the later stages of the Pan Shan period, but their decorative treatment becomes more clearly defined and purer. New designs are created, inter alia, lancet-like leaves in ground colour slanting downwards from the top, grouped horizontal dentated bands or string patterns in ground colour, also broad bands, or rather zones, containing rows of crosses and circles. The style gains in delicacy and sureness of touch, but the wealth of ornamentation diminishes. The predominance of the black elements becomes more and more conspicuous. The black bands pass into broader, black surfaces, while the red bands become narrower and narrower. Elements that were formerly subordinated to the whole design are now magnified and assume the rôle of giving to the vessel its distinctive character. Thus, in the spiral pattern family for instance, the spiral nuclei grow to such a size that the space required for the unsymmetrical wavy lines that accompany the spiral is materially diminished. Their number has therefore to be reduced. Within the spiral nuclei are painted animated and variegated patterns, among others the chessboard pattern. This chessboard décor becomes increasingly popular as a "filling" in other décor families as well. Lancet-like shapes in ground colour are also a favourite supplementary element at this phase.

A black horizontal band, considerably broader than in earlier vessels and usually to a large extent merging into other elements, constitutes the most frequently occurring lower border at this time. Below this broad band may run a (usually far narrower) horizontal wavy band. The décor inside the neck now consists of a garland band, generally simplified and painted with thin lines. The décor outside the neck consists, in the high-necked vessels, either of fine-meshed trelliswork or of two horizontal dentated bands with high points, the one placed close up against the other, and together covering the entire surface of the neck. The dentations along these bands are well shaped and pointed, and they are directed upwards.

During this last phase in the development of the Pan Shan pottery the "death pattern" system partially disappears, and in many cases the black elements border on the red elements, without dentations and usually without an intermediate strip of ground colour.

Even in the immediately preceding phase of the Pan Shan pottery the otherwise continuous spiral pattern has in some vessels been cleft in two. This leaves two pairs of spiral nuclei, the components of each being joined to one another but not to the other pair by means of the spiral line. Between these pairs is inserted on either side a linear ornament. Out of this originally quite inorganic ornament there gradually evolves a highly conventionalized anthropomorphic figure. At first it is given only head and arms, but later on legs are added. The figure is then in a sitting position. At the same time the spiral nuclei are converted into concentric circles, against which the forearms rest, or rather are pressed or thrust. The circles are large and are placed in pairs without any intermediate space. There are no traces of fingers on these figures in Pan Shan pottery, nor any features. There is usually a black dot in the middle of the head. The conventionalization of the design is thus carried to extremes. As there are only a few vessels of this Pan Shan type still extant it is impossible to follow the evolutional process throughout. The vessel that shows the greatest advance along these conventionalized lines belongs to the middle phase of the Pan Shan period.

As already stated above, the Ma Chang pottery is a scion of the Pan Shan pottery. This is very clearly demonstrated by the classified series of forms and patterns. The final phase of the Pan Shan ceramic style joins on to the initial phase of the Ma Chang pottery, and every indication goes to show that the former is directly renewed in the latter, that is to say, that the Pan Shan pottery ceases at the point at which the Ma Chang pottery starts.

The Ma Chang pottery applies three different decorative methods to its painted mortuary urns. The first method — the two-colour décor — is a direct legacy from that employed in the two-colour Pan Shan pottery. The second method, in which the décor is delineated against a coloured ground, employs the slip system, which had already been invented during the Pan Shan period, though it was then utilized in connection with thin clay slip and in very rare cases with white slip, but never with dark coloured slip. The third method deals with *one* dark colour, but this would appear, quite frequently at any rate, to consist of a mixed colour, something between black and violet or red. We find then that, in the matter of painting, the Pan Shan inventions are exploited during the Ma Chang period with a greater appreciation of their possibilities. The dark, painted slip hardly occurs until during the middle part of the Ma Chang period, and it is used most extensively in the latest phase of that style. During late Ma Chang it becomes very dark and dense. It is probable that the method was transferred more or less directly from the Ma Chang to the Hsin Tien pottery, in which it appears partly as an entire coating of slip used as a background to the patterned décor, partly as a zone slip confined to certain horizontal portions of the décor.

Elements in the painted Pan Shan décor are often directly assumed by the Ma Chang pottery, though modified to suit its own purposes.

In the late Pan Shan pottery the death-pattern system underwent considerable limitations, being succeeded in the Ma Chang pottery by a new system. In the earliest Ma Chang material there are often found here and there rudiments of the death-pattern system in the occasional retention of a dentated edge, this being particularly common in connection with the upper border. But these dentated edges disappear, and it is typical of advanced Ma Chang pottery that black bands and red bands (or such colour variants as take the place of the latter) merge into two-striped bands (double bands) or three-striped bands (triads). The double bands consist of one black strip and one red strip. The triads consist of one red central strip edged with black strips of similar breadth or narrower. The triads are typical of the middle part of the Ma Chang period and of late Ma Chang.

The border-line between neck and body is taken over by the Ma Chang pottery, as also the upper border, but these two elements are here merged into one double band, which assumes the function of an element forming the upper boundary of the décor on the mantle. Later on the new upper border is sometimes varied and takes the form of a Ma Chang triad.

The décor on the exterior and interior of the neck exhibits a lively yet logical variation during the Ma Chang period, and this fact has an important bearing on the relative chronology. That on the interior of the neck (which is common to the larger and to the smaller vessels) is largely influenced, of course, by the fact that in Ma Chang pottery the top of the neck is fashioned into a wide brim. This widening of the neck into a brim and its effect on the décor on the interior of the neck are particularly striking in middle Ma Chang pottery and the beginning of late Ma Chang. The evolution of the interior neck décor has been clearly described earlier (pp. 113—115). In Ma Chang the exterior neck patterns differ somewhat in the larger and in the smaller vessels. As to the former, they adopt to a certain extent the exterior neck décor found in the late Pan Shan pottery, including the trellis pattern, which in Ma Chang already in the earliest phase of the period has become considerably wider in mesh. Another exterior neck element adopted by the large Ma Chang vessels from the neck décor of the Pan Shan style is the left-pointed angle pattern, which in the Ma Chang vessels develops strikingly with a wealth of variation.

Of the exterior neck patterns on the smaller vessels, the "fishing-net" pattern deserves special mention. Originally, perhaps, it is a refined substitution for the wide-meshed trelliswork décor and may be constructed in various ways, firstly, with rows of garlands one above the other, indeed in somewhat primitive fashion (K. 5297, Pl. XXII, fig. 3), secondly with horizontal wavy bands (K. 5490, Pl. XXX, fig. 6), the latter system being capable of achieving a highly elegant effect. Both these systems belong to the close of the middle Ma Chang and to late Ma Chang. During late Ma Chang the pattern ultimately assumes a form that is both simplified and degenerate, the wavy lines crossing one another like the blades of a pair of scissors (K. 5241, Pl. XLI, fig. 3).

The lower border in late Pan Shan pottery was restricted to two variants, the first consisting of a broad, black horizontal band, the second of a similar, often somewhat narrower band, and below that a black wavy band. Both these forms are inherited by the Ma Chang pottery and become orthodox forms in that style, though the lower wavy band undergoes some change in the process. It assumes a slower rhythm and the individual waves become lower and longer. In this respect also it is possible to discern the course of development quite clearly, beginning with more Pan Shan-like curves and ending in a design that becomes more and more characteristically Ma Chang.

The Pan Shan mantle décor is largely taken over during the beginning of the Ma Chang period. Thus, the anthropomorphic pattern, for instance, which has been discussed above in connection with the Pan Shan pottery, is adopted in the course of the Ma Chang period. So too the final product of the spiral décor — the four-circle décor — as also the zigzag, string-pattern, square and cross décor on dishes etc. But all these different patterns are strikingly modified in the Ma Chang pottery, undergoing a regular evolution with parallel phases within different decorative schemes. Perhaps the most interesting and illuminating development is that traceable in the anthropomorphic series, in the four-circle décor and also in the cross décor on dishes.

The anthropomorphic pattern was an invention of the middle Pan Shan period, from which a number of variants are preserved which throw much light on this design, though unfortunately no representatives of the pattern in late Pan Shan have been discovered so far. It crops up again, however, during the Ma Chang period, although in a somewhat altered form. This anthropomorphic pattern is assiduously cultivated during the Ma Chang period. The head now consists of a circular line surrounding the neck of the vessel. The two figures are broader and take up a good deal of space on the pot's surface, with the result that the number of circles has to be reduced from four to two, one on either side of the vessel. The arms sometimes possess hands with fingers. Fingers are also placed on elbows and knees. The legs have two joints to start with, but later they are given three or four, in which case the anthropomorphic character of the figure partially disappears. During the advanced Ma Chang period the organized and anthropomorphic pattern is once more resolved into a purely inorganic system of lines. The pattern thus originates in a geometrical system of lines, gradually acquires a strongly decorative organic effect, but is then again reduced to a purely geometrical linear effect. This decorative process that we find reflected at such early epochs may to a certain extent be regarded as typical of the method of creating patterns, even in Chinese later styles. The Chinese artist does not like to create his designs after the naturalistic method. He is quite keen to adopt an organic form, but in doing so he gives his imagination free play with its designs and usually from the very outset gives it a strictly conventionalized character. Later artists and copyists vary this stylized pattern and carry the tendency to conventionalism still further, sometimes misinterpreting the motif of the pattern, with the result that the original pattern is often difficult to elucidate. The decorative process that has here been described from the Pan Shan and Ma Chang mortuary pottery possesses very obvious parallels in the Pan Shan dwelling-site pottery.

As already pointed out, there is every indication that the four-circle décor of the Ma Chang period was a legacy from the Pan Shan spiral décor with four spiral centres. The transition was referred to when we discussed the Pan Shan pottery. In the pattern thus handed down there occurs as a detail an originally somewhat insignificant element serving the function of separating the circles. This subsidiary décor increases fairly rapidly in area and decorative significance, and as this development proceeds the size and decorative importance of the circles diminish. Accordingly, in the Pan Shan pottery we see them increasing, and in the Ma Chang pottery again decreasing in size. In late Ma Chang the partitive element has gradually been fashioned into a peculiar kind of rib design. Thanks to certain common features in the supplementary decoration inside the circles on the pots ornamented with the anthropomorphic patterns and the four-circle décor, it is possible to trace a definite connection between the evolutionary phases of these two groups.

The décor on the dishes of the Ma Chang period is derived from the cross décor on the Pan Shan dishes. In Ma Chang pottery this décor is transformed in a most involved manner into a geometrical "jigsaw" pattern. This complicated design is executed quite deliberately and has a certain abstract mathematical character. In middle and late Ma Chang a similar complicated geometrizing of patterns also occurs in ceramic groups other than dishes, and an abundant series of patterns is evolved. In its tendency it is one of the most striking reactions against the Pan Shan style's undulating and unconventional linear designs. In these patterns the straight lines and the circular lines gradually assume a completely predominant rôle, and the decorative solutions frequently arise out of purely geometrical problems. Out of straight lines are constructed triangles, squares and rhombi, and the circles are fashioned into concentric ornaments (this indeed is already very common in Pan Shan dwelling-site pottery) and circles in which, for instance, three small circles are inscribed (Pl. XXIV figs. 1—2). In the course of this period of experimenting with geometrical patterns a number of extremely important ornaments are discovered: it is now, for instance, that the swastika and the meander emerge. Vessel K. 5313 (Pl. XXX, fig. 3) actually demonstrates various stages in the evolution of the swastika, while in vessel K. 5381 (Pl. XXIX, fig. 7) it is seen in its fully developed form. The meander occurs in a number of half-finished and not fully complete experimental forms in décor family 9, reaching a highly individual state of completion in vessel K. 5317 (Pl. XXX, fig. 7), which is so far unique. In these cases it is obvious that there is no need to have recourse to any theory that the swastika and the meander were imported. They were both invented in the East quite independently in the course of experiments with geometrical forms.

Besides the patterns dealt with above, mention should also be made of a pattern that is manifestly a representation of the cowrie shell. In the Pan Shan pottery there are patterns possessing a somewhat similar contour, but scarcely any design that is an obvious reproduction of a cowrie. Nor is the cowrie décor in Ma Chang associated in any way, either in its disposition or in its composition, with the leaf- or spool-shaped patterns in ground colour that we find in the Pan Shan décor. The cowrie décor is a new invention of the Ma Chang period and is one of its most characteristic decorative details. There is ample evidence that this pattern was invented fairly far on in the period, the vessels decorated with a cowrie ornamentation belonging to the middle and late parts of the period. In certain cases, however, the pattern clearly degenerated during Ma Chang (see the series of small beakers decorated with the cowrie pattern).

The painted slip indicates a direct transition from the Ma Chang to the Hsin Tien pottery, as also does the geometrization that we find gaining predominance in the design. Some of the typical elements in the Hsin Tien pottery had already been invented during the Ma Chang period, as e. g. the band of triangles filled with parallel lines, the short-waved horizontal line, which is one of the most typical Hsin Tien elements, and the snake and star ornaments, both known in late Ma Chang, though not so common as in the Hsin Tien vessels. From the point of view of pattern, the Ma Chang style has obviously influenced the Hsin Tien pottery. Nevertheless, it is self-evident in this respect that strikingly novel features arise in Hsin Tien, and that true intermediate links are so far wanting.

MARKS ON THE PAINTED PAN SHAN AND MA CHANG POTTERY.

Both in the Pan Shan and in the Ma Chang pottery we find occasional instances of painted mortuary vessels having marks on them that are not directly associated with the otherwise quite coherent décor with which the vessels are ornamented. With a very few exceptions[1]), the same colours are used for these marks — black and reddish violet — as those in which the rest of the décor is painted[2]). After the vessel had been built up and the ware dried, the marks were painted on prior to baking. Marks of this kind are placed either on the bases or on the bottoms of the vessels — in the case of the Pan Shan vessels on the bases only, in that of the Ma Chang vessels either on the bases or on the bottom surfaces.

In some cases these marks below the décor proper are not very distinct in outline (see the Pan Shan vessel K. 5970, fig. 185 and Pl. VI, fig. 2); moreover they are spread about in irregular fashion on the basal surface. Marks of this shapeless kind and with this obviously fortuitous location (see the Pan Shan vessel K. 5214, Pl. XXXIV, fig. 7) have certainly not been put there with any deliberate purpose but are splashes of paint made unintentionally or through carelessness prior to baking. It looks sometimes as if they were the result of wiping the paint off spatulas (or brushes) and occasionally smeared fingers (fig. 185 and K. 5970) on to the, from the decorative point of view, unimportant base.

Fig. 185.

---

[1]) In the two exceptions K. 5015 (fig. 183 and Pl. II, fig. 6) and K. 5786 (fig. 184) the marks are painted with a black colour of an entirely different consistency from that otherwise used: the paint is dull and flaky; moreover it is thinner and has not soaked into the ware. In vessel K. 5015, which is a Pan Shan mortuary vessel painted in two colours, the contrast between the two black paints is very distinct, and in vessel K. 5786 the paint with which the mark was made is black and flaky, whereas the rest of the décor on the vessel is painted with a dark brownish violet colour, which has coalesced better. In both cases, then, it is a question of a flaky, superficial black paint, which could hardly have been applied to the ware prior to baking. I think it is not impossible that this painting, which is not burnt into the ware, has been applied in more recent times.

Fig. 183.

[2]) As to the black paint — the great majority of the marks are black — this fact has been established as a result of an investigation made at the State Testing Laboratories. Samples of black paint were taken from vessel K. 5039, partly from the décor and partly from the mark on the base. The analysis of these substances showed that the paint on both the décor and the mark contained considerable quantities of manganese and iron, the oxides of which constituted the colouring matter.

Fig. 184.

On pot K. 5464 (Pl. XXXVII, fig. 2) there is a large mark on the base, painted with the same black-brown colour as that used for the rest of the décor on the pot — used there in conjunction with red paint. The mark has a broad interior surface, and indeed somewhat resembles a running animal, a pig or short-legged dog. In my view, however, the mark was certainly never intended to be a real drawing. Besides, the outline is far too ill-defined; in fact, the whole figure is too shapeless. It would be indeed strange if the painter of the décor on this pot, who was almost a master of his art — the vessel is of rare elegance and its colouring extremely well balanced, indeed it is one of the most exquisite creations of the Pan Shan style — should when marking the vessel have so debased his art as to execute such a poor drawing. The mark in this case is hardly a drawing done as an exercise (see below) but seems to have been the result of an attempt to clean the brush or stick by moving it rapidly to and fro over the same spot.

In one or two other instances from the Pan Shan pottery it is obviously a decoration, which, though having no connection with the rest of the décor, nevertheless serves to ornament the base. In the great majority of cases this base has been left entirely unpainted, perhaps for the reason that, from the artistic point of view, the vessels were thereby divided tectonically into strongly contrasting parts, or perhaps for the reason that mortuary pottery was intended to be viewed from above (by a crowd of people assembled round the excavated grave, possibly also by spirits). We find such a decoration on vessels K. 5015 (fig. 186 and Pl. II, fig. 6) and K. 5094. On vessel K. 5015 are five small, black ring-shaped marks, placed at about equal distances from one another within a zone on the base a little below the plain lower border (see drawing). Here it can hardly be anything but a piece of pure decoration, in which an original-minded potter has by way of experiment broken away from the traditional decorative scheme (see footnote 1, p. 174). There is no reason in this instance to regard these rings as being some kind of script or ideograph. Much the same reasoning applies to pot K. 5094 (see fig. 187). Here the basal surface is unusually narrow, and the décor on the mantle — forming part of a design that requires special breadth of treatment — has to extend far down towards the plane of the bottom. This mantle décor terminates below in a lower border, which consists of a straight horizontal band and beneath it a wavy band. Below this horizontal border the base is decorated with six primitive ladder patterns, composed of a vertical line crossed by 5—6 horizontal strokes of varying length. The pattern is well known from the other forms of primitive painted Pan Shan décor. Décor family 5 has similar

Fig. 186.

Fig. 187.

patterns, though in that case they are placed obliquely. Several other primitive vessels have this pattern as a supplementary ornamentation on the exterior of the mantle and the neck.

As to the black mark on the base of pot K. 5146 (fig. 188 and Pl. X, fig. 7), which is exceptionally complicated, indeed perhaps the most complicated of all the marks that are so far known to us, as well as the likewise black mark on the base of the Pan Shan vessel K. 5160 (see fig. 189), it is my strong impression that we are here concerned with exercises in drawing, the artist testing his colours and implements before starting on the actual decoration of the pot. He has been trying the suppleness of his hand and testing how the surface of the pottery takes the colour, and in doing so he has let the marks, so to speak, run off the stick or brush on to the ware without any conscious design in his mind and without giving any deliberate significance to the mark he made. The drawing is therefore a kind of practice sketch. In both these marks it is the death-pattern system in a somewhat simplified form that is the most important element, as it is in the rest of the decoration on this vessel. I quite recognize, however, that even in this case they may be owner's marks or ideographs.

The two marks on the base of the Ma Chang pot K. 5990 (fig. 190 and Pl. XXIV, fig. 4) differ somewhat in character. The narrow, straight line that lies in an oblique position just above the bottom plane is, as its shape clearly shows, nothing more than a smear caused by a falling drop of paint. The other mark, on the other hand, was undoubtedly made deliberately. The left portion of it comes into contact with the garland element of the lower border, the darker-coloured arcs of which cut clean across it, which proves quite clearly that the mark was painted before the garlands and probably, too, before the rest of the décor on the pot. It would appear therefore to be a drawing done by the artist "to get his hand in", though he did it somewhat too high up on the base, so that it clashed with the rest of the décor.

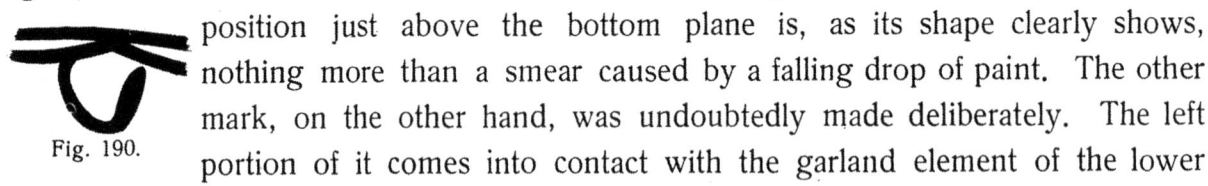

The view may of course be put forward that the other marks are also nothing but similar practice drawings, but that is undoubtedly too facile an interpretation. Unfortunately the body of material available is too small and the circumstances attending the discovery of the vessels are too uncertain to enable us to give any definite interpretation of these marks.

None of the vessels found in the large grave in Pien Chia Kou have any mark on base or bottom, and only one vessel dating from the Ma Chang period that belongs to a collection of pieces from a grave — unfortunately not excavated by Professor Andersson himself. This latter vessel is the small beaker K. 6124 found in the locality that gives its name to the period, Ma Chang Yen, in Nien Po Hsien. To this grave belongs another small beaker, K. 5693 (Pl. XXIX, fig. 1), of very similar ware, shape, quality of the paint and decoration, these two beakers being obviously twin vessels; also a larger pot, K. 5617 (Pl. XXXIX, fig. 2), made of a quite dissimilar kind of ware, and the painting and quality of the colour of which differ considerably from those of the smaller vessels. The two smaller vessels are manifestly a pair, and it is to be presumed that the statement that they come from the same grave is correct. On the other hand, the statement that the larger vessel is also one of the objects found in that grave appears to me somewhat doubtful. Beaker K. 6124 has a violet cross (fig. 191) on the bottom (the whole pot is painted in violet). The other small beaker has no such mark, nor has the larger pot K. 5617. This would seem to imply that pots from the same grave of the Ma Chang period may differ in his respect, the one having a mark on base or bottom and the others having no such mark. In the case of the Pan Shan pottery this is also true to a certain extent, judging from the fact that there are no absolutely identical marks, and that similar marks are extremely rare on the numerous pieces of Pan Shan pottery acquired by purchase. This lot of purchased vessels consists in all probability of a conglomerate of pots from plundered graves containing objects of a similar nature to those found in the Pien Chia Kou grave (that is to say, each grave containing a quantity of vessels). Thus, in both the Pan Shan and the Ma Chang pottery the marking was probably not done on all the pieces of pottery in a grave but was confined to a certain number of individual vessels. This would imply that the marks are hardly ownership marks. One would suppose that, had there been any such ownership mark or ideograph, it would have been painted on all the pots in the grave[1]). I consider it probable, therefore, that the majority of these marks are potter's marks, made either in order to denote the person who has manufactured the vessel or else as a record of work performed. In the former case, then, the potter would only have signed his product now and then, when he felt inclined to do so. In the latter case the marks might denote, for instance, a number — the tenth vessel, the twelfth vessel, or whatever it might be — or else the last vessel of a completed series, e. g. the set of vessels in one grave. The latter interpretation would only be applicable on the assumption that the potter was not a member

Fig. 191.

---

[1]) As is the case e. g. in Egyptian prehistoric pottery. (Flinders Petrie).

of the dead person's family but traded his product to them in the way of barter or for cash.

Of the remaining marks, two Pan Shan marks and one Ma Chang mark consist of a plain straight line, in all three cases however drawn in a different direction, though all on the bases. The line on the Pan Shan pot K. 5120 (fig. 192) is vertical, that on the Pan Shan vessel K. 5158 (fig. 193 and Pl. XI, fig. 2) is an oblique line pointing upwards from left to right, while that on the Ma Chang pot K. 5983 (fig. 194) is drawn horizontally.

On the base of the Ma Chang vessel K. 5466 (fig. 195) are three oblique lines, pointing upwards and combined to form one mark.

Fig. 192.   Fig. 193.   Fig. 194.   Fig. 195.   Fig. 196.   Fig. 197.   Fig. 198.

On both Pan Shan and Ma Chang vessels, cases are known of marks consisting of a long stem with a shorter branch projecting at right angles from (about) the middle of it. In the case of the Pan Shan vessel K. 5140 (fig. 196 and Pl. XII, fig. 1) the stem is drawn vertically and the branch horizontally. In that of the Ma Chang vessel K. 5317 (fig. 197 and Pl. XXX, fig. 7) the stem is practically horizontal and the branch vertical.

The mark that occurs most frequently is the cross. It is found both in Pan Shan and in Ma Chang pottery. In the former it is placed, like all other marks, on the base; in the latter it occurs on the bottom only K. 6124 (fig. 191), K. 5786 (fig. 184 and Pl. XXIV, fig. 6), K. 5323 (fig. 198 and Pl. XXVII, fig. 10).

A standing cross with the one stem pratically vertical and the other practically horizontal is seen in the Pan Shan vessel K. 5057 (fig. 199 and Pl. XVI, fig. 4).

Fig. 199.   Fig. 200.   Fig. 201.   Fig. 202.   Fig. 203.   Fig. 204.   Fig. 205.

Crosses drawn with less care are those on the Pan Shan vessels K. 5034 (fig. 200 and Pl. VII, fig. 8) and K. 5151 (fig. 201 and Pl. XI, fig. 4). In the former vessel the vertical stem is aslant, while the other stem is horizontal. In the latter vessel the two stems slope somewhat towards the vertical and horizontal plane respectively, and the horizontal stem is a good deal shorter than the vertical one. Of the Ma Chang crosses, that on the bottom of pot K. 5323 (fig. 198 and Pl. XXVII, fig. 10) is noteworthy, as two of its arms are considerably shorter than the other two. Each of these shorter arms belongs to a different stem.

Rather like a cross, though far too irregular to be really intended as such, is the mark on the base of the beaker K. 5243 (fig. 202 and Pl. XXVIII, fig. 6), which has somewhat the silhouette of a bird in flight.

On the Ma Chang vessel K. 5364 (fig. 203) there is a mark on the bottom in the shape of a ring.

On the base of the Pan Shan vessel K. 5184 (fig. 204 and Pl. XI, fig. 1), which has a spiral décor, is a mark consisting of a ring and, projecting from its centre, a straight line pointing obliquely upwards to the right. Finally, there is on the base of the Pan Shan vessel K. 5035 (fig. 205 and Pl. VIII, fig. 2) a mark that is somewhat reminiscent of a snake. We have now gone through all the marks found in this pottery.

In their construction all these marks are, with a few exceptions, extremely simple. I have dealt with the exceptions above. As compared with the other patterns on the vessels, the marks, regarded as drawings, are exceedingly primitive. Moreover, they are indifferently done, being often painted with extreme carelessness. They apparently represent attempts at a record of words and figures, that is to say, a primitive form of writing.

EXAMPLES OF PAN SHAN AND MA CHANG POTTERY IN LITERATURE OR IN PRIVATE COLLECTIONS.

Professor J. G. Andersson's discovery of the prehistoric cultures in China has found a resounding echo in the domain of European and Far Eastern research, and a large body of literature has already grown up dealing with the problems connected with the new discoveries. I propose to devote the last few pages of this treatise to a Bibliography of at least the most important of these works.

As my book is intended to be a monograph on the Pan Shan and Ma Chang pottery styles, my chief purpose being to record the results of a technical investigation of the material and to analyse its forms and patterns, as well as, wherever possible, to determine its relative chronology, and as the understanding between Professor Andersson and myself was that I should not discuss in detail the absolute chronology nor compare the Yang Shao (including Pan Shan) and the Ma Chang pottery with other Eastern and Western ceramic types, I am here naturally not concerned either with the literature dealing with these aspects of the material at my disposal. On the other hand, it was important, from the point of view of this treatise, that I should endeavour to incorporate in the scheme that was drawn up at its inception some of the Pan Shan and Ma Chang material that has come to light since Andersson's discoveries and is now preserved in various museums and in the hands of private collectors and antique dealers. In dealing with this subject, however, I shall confine myself to such material as has already been published, to vessels discussed and illustrated in books, scientific journals and newspapers, and to material otherwise placed at my disposal in the form of photographs. This latter body of ceramic material forms part of three important collections of Kansu pottery in particular — those owned by Messrs. Wannieck, of Paris, by Messrs. Loo, also of Paris, and by the art dealer Herbert Mueller, of Peking. One or two pots belong to the firm of China Bohlken, of Berlin, and to the Swede, Mr. Yngve Laurell, of Peking. Five pots belong to the Ethnographical section of the Riksmuseum in Stockholm. Four of them are of Pan Shan type, the fifth is of Ma Chang type.

One or two specimens from the material that has been placed at my disposal have already been reproduced in various quarters either from Professor Andersson's publications or else, by permission of the Museum of Far Eastern Antiquities, from our own original photographs (see Bibl. e. g. 21, 46, 67 and 73). Further, with the aid of these photographs, or after a close study of the Kansu material that we have exhibited, certain authors have discussed at some length the manner in which that culture evolved. Professor Osvald Sirén has undoubtedly gone most deeply into the subject — in his book "A History of Early Chinese Art. I. The Prehistoric and Pre-Han Periods" (see Bibl. 82). He reproduced, inter alia, three of our most exquisite Pan Shan pots and two of our Ma Chang vessels (I shall revert later on to one or two other reproductions in Sirén's book). Moreover, he gives a brief, but on the whole adequate, account of the development of these styles. Nevertheless, his use of the term "calabash form" for our types P. S: XXIII and P. S: XXIV is, in my view, improper, or at least misleading, seeing that actually none of our form types can be traced back to natural calabash forms. On the other hand, Sirén's observation that in the Yang Shao pottery (including our Pan Shan material) there is an entire absence of metal-like types (which, however, undoubtedly occur in the Ch'i Chia material) is quite correct. He points out, moreover, that unpainted pottery decorated in relief found in the Pan Shan material exhibits more primitive features than the painted pottery, and this is an extremely significant observation. Indeed, this patent fact forms the very basis of the relative chronology that I have traced in my treatise.

Two Pan Shan pots, both of form type P. S: XXIII, have been presented by the Museum of Far Eastern Antiquities to the British Museum, and were reproduced by R. L. Hobson in the British Museum Quarterly (see Bibl. 50). One of them is very closely related to the pot illustrated in this treatise in Pl. VIII, fig. 2, and its predominant black bands and its elegant drawing make it one of the most advanced and exquisite vessels belonging to Décor Family 10P. The other pot is also illustrated in my work (Pl. XVI, fig. 3) and is one of the most primitive examples of Décor Family 16P.

The material of which Professor J. G. Andersson has himself published a description in "Preliminary Report on Archaeological Research in Kansu" in 1925 (see Bibl. 6) has had to remain in China, and belongs, unless otherwise stated, to The Geological Survey of China. Professor Andersson has himself given an exhaustive account of it, and I am confining myself here to incorporating it in the system worked out in this treatise, and going through it here plate by plate.

The Pan Shan material shown in Pl. I, belonging to Mr. Hsü Ch'êng Yao, extaoyin of Tsinchow, contains a somewhat original form of cup in fig. 1 a and b, the ear on which is placed unusually low down. The cup is otherwise most closely akin to the form type P. S: XIV and has a pattern that is typical of Décor Family 15P. The small pot shown in fig. 2 is of form type P. S: XXVII and belongs to Décor Family 3P. The vessel shown in Pl. III likewise belongs to form type P. S: XXVII; it possesses the large, deeply notched ears that are generally characteristic of this form type and the pattern that is typical of Décor Family 15P. The vessels in Pl. VI—Pl. VIII are all very ordinary both in shape and pattern and belong either to the low-necked form type P. S: XXIII or to the high-necked type P. S: XXIV. Those in Pl. VI both belong to the spiral-pattern family 11P. The upper one is an advanced vessel, the lower one a somewhat early form. Of the two vessels in Pl. VII the one belongs to Décor Family 3P (fig. 1) and the other to the squared pattern family 10P (fig. 2). The vessel shown in Pl. VIII is typical of the most advanced specimens of Décor Family 16P. Finally, the vessel in Pl. IX, fig. 1, is an elegant and late representative of the bowls belonging to form type P. S: XXXI and Décor Family 17P.

Thus, these vessels fall naturally into both the form scheme and the pattern scheme worked out in this treatise.

The head in Pl. XIX, fig. 9, which is discussed and reproduced in this work, has, as I have already pointed out, been carefully studied by Alfred Salmony (see Bibl. 75). It is also reproduced and analysed by Carl Hentze (see Bibl. 46). I have already discussed the conclusions drawn by Alfred Salmony. Hentze's far-reaching hypotheses lie far beyond the scope of my work. In H. Th. Bossert's "Geschichte des Kunstgewerbes" (see Bibl. 22), this head has been incorrectly included amongst the pottery of the Copper Age.

The Kansu material preserved in museums abroad and in private collections and available in the form of reproductions and photographs is fairly comprehensive. It belongs to the Ch'i Chia epoch, the funerary pottery of the Pan Shan area and to material found on contemporary dwelling-sites. Further, it belongs to the Ma Chang and Hsin Tien periods. Examples of the Ch'i Chia and the Hsin Tien ceramic styles I shall here pass over altogether, and shall merely describe in a few words the dwelling-site material of the Yang Shao era from Kansu, of which only occasional specimens have been found. It is therefore only the Pan Shan and Ma Chang material that I shall discuss in any detail.

The two vases belonging to the Musée Cernuschi and reproduced by Ardenne de Tizac (see Bibl. 12), Pl. XXII and XXIII, are both black-figured dwelling-site vessels of the Yang Shao era from Kansu. One of them has two diametrically opposed handles and is of a form that in the main coincides with type P. S: XXVIII; the other is without handles and differs in that respect from all forms of high-necked mortuary vessels. The décor on the upper part of the mantle of the vessel with handles consists of concentric arcs resembling those in Décor Family 3P, and in other decorative respects also this vase is very closely related to a funerary vessel such as that illustrated in Pl. IV, fig. 8. The vessel without handles is ornamented with a vigorous spiral décor. Both are good examples illustrating the fact that the dwelling-site vessels sometimes very closely resemble the mortuary vessels in form and décor.

Even before the Wannieck Collection was dispersed I had an opportunity of studying a number of photographs taken of it, and recently too I have studied on the spot the pieces that are now left. I propose to pass over here altogether the ordinary types (of the form types, P. S: XXIII and XXIV, and the Décor Families 1P, 2P, 3P, 4P and, to a great extent, 11P, and finally 16P), as also the ordinary vessels in the possession of Messrs. Loo, seeing that they contain no novelties. The vessels of a more unusual character I shall discuss each in its own place. A bowl from this collection is reproduced in "L'Illustration" (see Bibl. 13). Sirén has likewise reproduced it in his above-cited work (Bibl. 82) in Pl. I C, as also Bossert in P. 17, fig. 1 (Bibl. 22). It has an entirely black décor, which consists of a highly conventionalized animal or possibly anthropomorphic pattern. The form is most closely akin to type P. S: III, but its mouth is slightly wider. The conventionalism is at the same stage as that in the anthropomorphic figures on the vessels shown in Pl. XIII and the calyx on the vessel reproduced in Pl. XIX, fig. 12. The bowl would appear to be contemporary with the advanced Pan Shan pottery, although it undoubtedly belongs to the dwelling-site group.

We should also doubtless count among the dwelling-site vessels of the Yang Shao era from Kansu the pot described by Dr. Lucian Scherman (see Bibl. 78, Abb. 1). Its form differs altogether from those types of form with which we have become familiar from the Pan Shan mortuary vessels, and the ornamentation is entirely in black. The oval-shaped termination at the lower end is peculiar, but through this feature the pot is related to a number of vessels with pointed bottoms known to us through fragments found on Yang Shao dwelling-sites. The décor is related to the patterns characteristic of Décor Family 3P, though it is perhaps more elegant.

Finally, a jug reproduced in H. d'Ardenne de Tizac's "L'Art chinois classique", Pl. 24 a (see Bibl. 12), likewise belongs to the dwelling-site group of vessels. The reproduction unfortunately does not indicate the colour of the paint used in the design, nor whether there is any slip. It certainly cannot be attributed to the funerary pottery of the Pan Shan or Ma Chang periods; rather, certain features of the painting would appear to indicate that the jug should be dated later than the dwelling-site pottery contemporary with the Pan Shan pottery. In order however to decide this point it will be necessary to study the piece more closely.

It is unfortunate that neither in the above-mentioned article in "L'Illustration" (Bibl. 13) nor in Bossert's work (Bibl. 22, P. 17, fig. 4) are the reproductions of a small, peculiar vase with two very long handles and three diminutive feet as distinct as one would wish. The shape differs from that of the Pan Shan and contemporary dwelling-site pottery, but it is somewhat more closely akin to certain highly advanced Ma Chang forms, and most closely perhaps to some Hsin Tien forms. The décor resembles a number of patterns found on dwelling-site pottery of the Yang Shao period in Kansu, though it does not entirely coincide with them. It has but little in common with the Ma Chang patterns, nor does it resemble the Hsin Tien patterns. This little vase, which undoubtedly possesses certain features characteristic of the Kansu pottery, is a piece that is so far practically unique of its kind. I assume that it is a dwelling-site vessel of somewhat later date — contemporary, perhaps, with pottery of the advanced Ma Chang style.

The great majority of the Pan Shan vessels preserved in the various museums and private collections consists of fairly large low- and high-necked mortuary urns belonging to the form types P. S: XXIII and P. S: XXIV, that is to say, the most important and the most commonly found types of funerary vessels in the material that I have had at my disposal. As far as the published material is concerned, the variation of these types keeps, on the whole, within the bounds already laid down for these form types. Most of the vessels, that is to say, are of quite ordinary shapes.

Of the low-necked mortuary urns (type P. S: XXIII), that in the Sirén Collection [Ars asiatica, 1925: The Plate on the fly-leaf (see Bibl. 17)] and the two vessels, once the property of the art dealer A. Förstner, of Vienna (Op. cit. figs. 2—3), and accounts of which were published in "Mitteilungen der Anthropologischen Gesellschaft in Wien" (see Bibl. 36), are very early Pan Shan forms, as also are a vessel belonging to the Louvre and reproduced in the article in "L'Illustration" (see Bibl. 13) (the fig. furthest to the right in the upper row) and a vessel (Abb. 2) preserved in Munich and described by Scherman in the article quoted above (see Bibl. 78). The necks of all these vessels are very low, widening rapidly towards the top, and they have a fairly straight profile. Moreover, the vessels are ornamented with well-known patterns of early types. Sirén's vessel has an extremely beautiful horizontal band décor (Décor Family 1P). The mantles of the two vessels in Vienna, and that

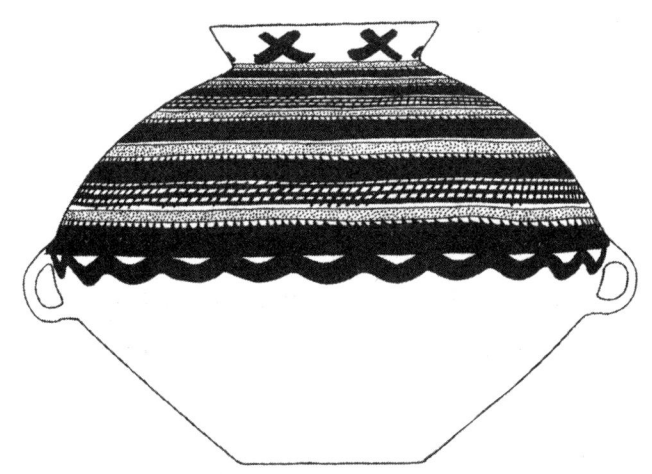

Fig. 206
Wannieck Collection, Paris.

Fig. 207
Ethnographical department of the Riksmuseum, Stockholm.

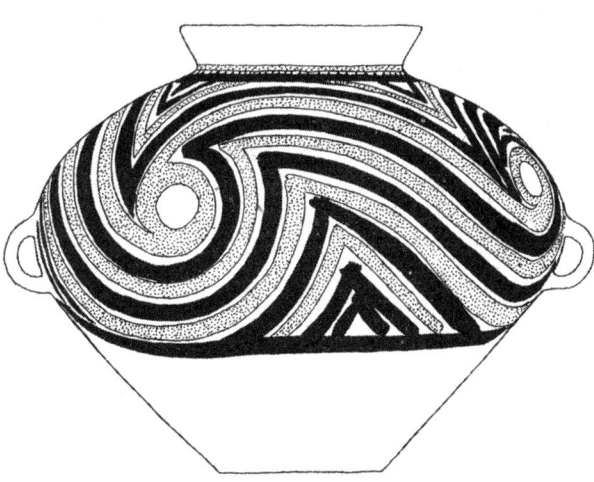

Fig. 208
Wannieck Collection, Paris.

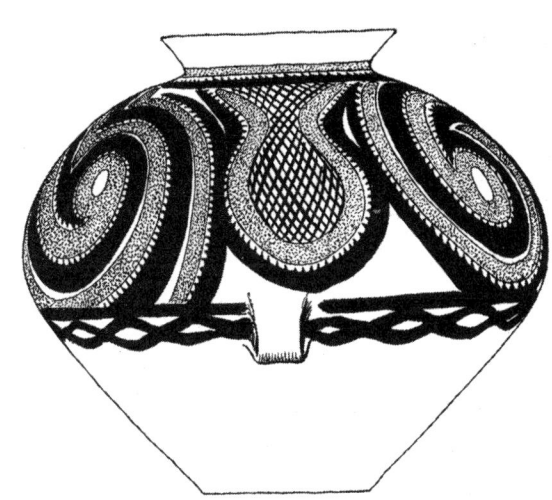

Fig. 209
Wannieck Collection, Paris.

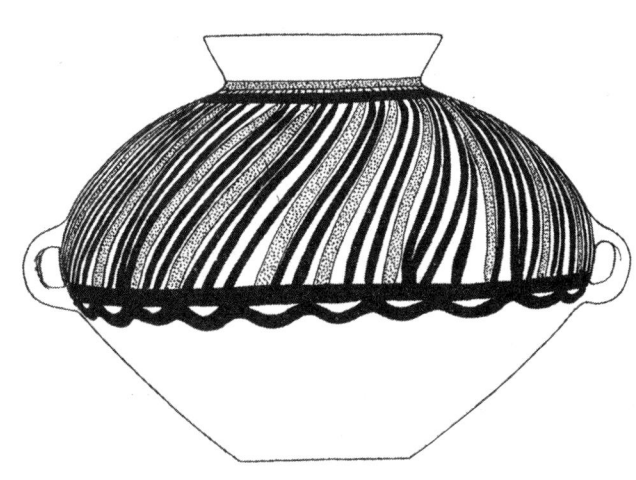

Fig. 210
Wannieck Collection, Paris.

Fig. 211
Mueller Collection, Peking.

of the Munich vessel, are covered with early spiral patterns, in which the black and red elements are of equal value, the spiral nuclei being small and undecorated (Décor Family 11P). The same applies to the Louvre vessel. A pot in the Museum für Völkerkunde, Berlin, reproduced in "Ostasiatische Zeitschrift" as an illustration to an article by Professor J. G. Andersson (see Bibl. 8), is quite a good example of the shape characteristic of type P. S: XXIII during the latter part of early Pan Shan. The shape of the neck is somewhat vague and the breadth of the body unusually large. In regard to its pattern, this pot is also a member of the spiral family 11P. The red and black elements are still of fairly equal value, but on the top of the mantle the black dentated band has been replaced by a series of black lines — in its way an advanced feature in the earlier décor families. The spiral nuclei are still small.

The Wannieck Collection originally contained a number of somewhat early vessels of type P. S: XXIII, the patterns of which show quite unique variations. I have reproduced four drawings of such Wannieck urns. The first of these (fig. 206), which belongs to Décor Family 1P, is original insofar that in a couple of places there have been inserted, between black and red bands, black lines crossed obliquely by short strokes. Another urn (fig. 208), which belongs to the spiral-patterned vessels (Décor Family 11P), is entirely without the death pattern. A third (fig. 209) belongs to the same family, but here the spiral pattern is divided into two, as in the urns reproduced in Pl. XIII, figs. 1 and 2, but in the latter cases there is inserted between the pairs of spirals a bottle pattern characteristic of Décor Family 16P. In this urn, therefore, the character of the design is somewhat mixed. The fourth urn (fig. 210) has a peculiar pattern on the mantle, somewhat akin to Décor Family 12P. The mantle is covered with narrow bands running at an oblique angle, and among them single red bands alternate with series of 2—4 black ones. The black bands are not accompanied by the death pattern, and the pot is therefore reminiscent of the spiral-patterned vessel we have just discussed out of the same collection. It should be observed, however, that the upper border is dentated along the top edge facing the red marginal band between neck and body. The shapes of body and neck as well as the patterns argue in favour of these vessels being dated fairly early.

Another fairly early vessel is an urn of the same form type and of Décor Family 10P, formerly belonging to Mr. Herbert Mueller, of Peking. Its décor consists of a row of squares with red contours (fig. 211). These squares are filled with series of black squares inserted one inside the other and built up of narrow lines. The urn is a so far unique example of black dentated bands' being replaced by series of black lines even in the square-patterned family.

Three somewhat more advanced vessels, dating apparently from middle Pan Shan, are reproduced in Bossert's "Geschichte des Kunstgewerbes", p. 16, figs. 4—6 (see Bibl. 22). These too were once in the Wannieck Collection. The shape of their bodies and the height and profile of their necks vary a good deal, as do also the patterns. On the whole, however, the necks are somewhat higher and the profile of the necks more concave. The black elements in the design are to a certain extent predominant. The vessel shown in fig. 4 has a garland pattern (Décor Family 4P) and is closely related decoratively to the high-necked pot shown in Pl. III, fig. 8. In both cases the décor displays a certain finicking touch in the drawing. The pot shown in fig. 5 belongs to Décor Family 10P, the square-pattern family. That in fig. 6 has a spiral pattern.

One fairly original, low-necked mortuary urn, likewise of the P. S: XXIII form type, (in the Wannieck Collection), is somewhat vague in shape. It is here reproduced in fig. 212. The décor lacks precision and figural distinctness and indicates an unpractised hand. The ornamentation of the vessel cannot be referred to any of the décor families categorized in this work.

Messrs. China Bohlken, of Berlin, have sent to the Museum of Far Eastern Antiquities a photograph of a vessel of form type P. S: XXIII (see fig. 213). The principal décor on the mantle consists of a single row of square patterns, the innermost squares bisected by a vertical red line — so far as I am aware, a unique form of our Décor Family 10P. The originality of this décor is enhanced by the fact that in the triangular fields formed between the squares and the lower border are drawn circles in ground colour, which are likewise bisected by vertical lines. The shape of the urn indicates early Pan Shan. The décor, however, would appear to be somewhat advanced, so that it would be reasonable to date the pot at the transitional period between early and middle Pan Shan.

The four Pan Shan urns belonging to the Ethnographical Department of the Riksmuseum in Stockholm are all ordinary specimens of form types P. S: XXIII or P. S: XXIV. One is of Décor Family 10P (square patterns) one of the Décor Family 11P (spiral patterns) one of the Décor Family 16P (bottle patterns). The fourth belongs to the Décor Family 9P (oval pattern) but is unique, the oval being filled with a vertical zigzag band (fig. 207). It is perhaps a little later than the others, which may be dated early, or from the beginning of the middle Pan Shan.

A mortuary urn apparently belonging to the middle Pan Shan and of the same form type as the foregoing urns is reproduced in Pl. III in an album published by The Imperial Household Museum of Tokyo (see Bibl. 85). It is a pot of the Décor Family 11P, i. e., ornamented with spirals. The black elements predominate and the

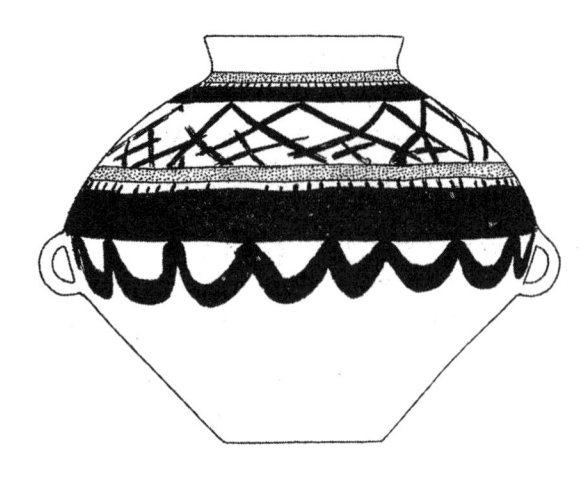

Fig. 212
Wannieck Collection, Paris.

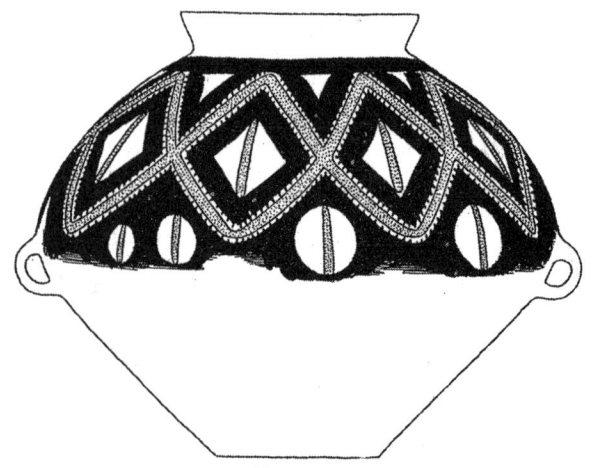

Fig. 213
China Bohlken, Berlin.

Fig. 214
Wannieck Collection, Paris.

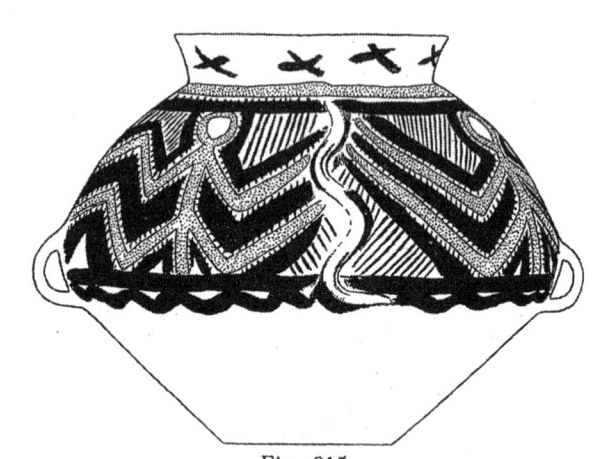

Fig. 215
Royal Ontario Museum of Archæology.

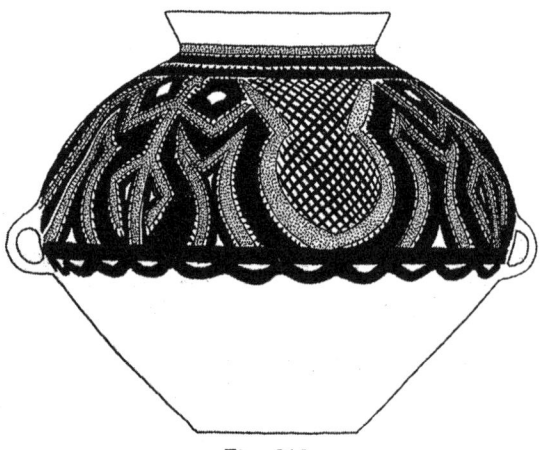

Fig. 216
The Louvre, Paris.

Fig. 217
Mueller Collection, Peking.

medium-sized spiral centres are ornamented with plain crosses. Closely related vessels are reproduced in our Pl. XI.

The décor on three pots from different collections resembles the anthropomorphic patterns reproduced in Pl. XIII. These pots demonstrate in a surprising manner that the anthropomorphic décor is not confined to Pan Shan pots ornamented with spirals and circles, but that it already occurs even in Pan Shan pottery as a dominant décor, e. g. on an urn, fig. 214, belonging to Messrs. Wannieck, also on one belonging to The Royal Ontario Museum of Archæology and reproduced by Yetts in "Indian Art and Letters" (Bibl. 92). The figure on the Wannieck vessel is extremely primitive, like that in our Pl. XIII, fig. 2. The circular disc representing the head is bisected by a vertical line. The anthropomorphic figure on the Ontario vessel is of a more clearly defined shape and bears a stronger resemblance in some respects to the figure in Pl. XIII, fig. 3, the legs of which are distinctly drawn. There is something more ape-like than human about the figure on the Ontario vessel (fig. 215). An original variant of this anthropomorphic shape is found in a vessel belonging to the Louvre, in which the figure is more elongated, the position of the legs is quite out of the ordinary, and the head is quite small, somewhat triangular in shape (fig. 216) and filled in with black paint. It is difficult to place the pots in chronological order. They probably belong to the transitional period between early and middle Pan Shan.

In the Japanese publication quoted above (Bibl. 85) there is reproduced in Pl. II (the lower figure) a low-necked pot of the form type P. S: XXIII. It is ornamented with three broad black horizontal bands with circular areas in ground colour (our Décor Family 18P of a more definite design than hitherto). The bands are separated from one another by narrow, red horizontal lines. The pot might possibly be of a somewhat earlier date than those dealt with under Décor Family 18P and probably belongs to middle Pan Shan. A vessel once in the possession of Herbert Mueller, of Peking (fig. 217), belongs to the same décor family. The shape of the body here approaches those of the Ma Chang pots. The vessel has a neck of medium height and is without ears, and is therefore, so to speak, on the border-line between the form types P. S: XXIII and P. S: XXIV. The principal decorative element on the mantle is a broad black band containing a row of circular areas in ground colour, each one of them decorated with 5—6 crescent-shaped spots, these, too, being well-known as a decorative detail on the highly advanced vessels ornamented with spirals. Both form and décor indicate that this vessel should be dated very late.

The high-necked vessels of type P. S: XXIV, both early and more advanced forms, are likewise described in literature, and also occur in private collections. I regard

Fig. 218
Loo Collection, Paris.

Fig. 219
Wannieck Collection, Paris.

Fig. 220
Wannieck Collection, Paris.

Fig. 221
Kunstindustrimuseum, Copenhagen.

Fig. 222
Kunstindustrimuseum, Copenhagen.

Fig. 223
Mueller Collection, Peking.

as one of the more primitive a vessel in the possession of Messrs. Loo, of Paris, the ornamentation on the mantle of which conforms to Décor Family 1P (it is original insofar that the lower black bands are without dentated edges); it is shown here in fig. 218. The straight stiff neck, the large, deeply notched ears and the primitive pattern on the mantle, all point to the fact that this vessel should be dated extremely early. A somewhat smaller vessel of the same type of form, belonging to Madame Wannieck, has a neck the height of which, in proportion to the rest of the vessel, reaches a maximum within this type. In view of the somewhat smaller ears, with their slight notching, and the simple yet clear and beautifully drawn spiral pattern on the mantle (Décor Family 11P), this vessel should perhaps be dated somewhat later, though within the early Pan Shan group (fig. 219), than the vessel just mentioned. A high-necked urn in the possession of Förster, of Vienna (see Bibl. 36), the neck of which is somewhat rigid in profile, is undoubtedly early (form type P. S: XXIV, Décor Family 11P). The pot illustrated in "Tafel 1" in Max Sauerlandt's "Das Museum für Kunst und Gewerbe in Hamburg 1877—1927" (see Bibl. 77) is of somewhat later date. Among other things, the ears on this vessel are somewhat rudimentary and the spiral centres have already increased in size (the same form type and décor family).

A high-necked Wannieck urn (type P. S: XXIV), decorated all over with a ladder pattern (fig. 220), is a member of Décor Family 5P. Owing to the rudimentary ears it should not be dated too early, although the shape of the neck and the decorative design forbid its being placed in the late Pan Shan period. The pattern assumes a highly refined form on this urn.

Perhaps the most original décor on any of the vessels discussed here is that on an urn of the same form-type as the foregoing ones in the possession of the Kunstindustrimuseum, Copenhagen (fig. 221). It has a body that is not very advanced in shape, and a fairly narrow neck widening out somewhat towards the top and having a practically straight profile. Ears are absent altogether. The pattern on the mantle consists of a band running in whorls throughout its breadth (death-pattern system). The effect of this design is fantastic and the decorative invention may fairly be regarded as original. As to its date, the vessel is rather difficult to place merely with the aid of a photograph. It probably belongs to the middle period of the Pan Shan style. Another vessel belonging to the Kunstindustrimuseum in Copenhagen and of the same form type is very closely related in the shape of the body, profile of the neck, shape of the ears (very small rudiments), and pattern on neck and mantle (Décor Family 16P), to the pot reproduced in Pl. XVI, fig. 8. It differs from the latter (see fig. 222) in the ovals' being in this case filled with spool-shaped elements in ground colour covered with drop-like dabs. Possibly the Copenhagen pot is somewhat more advanced than the vessel reproduced by us. It is certainly from the late Pan Shan. Another vessel that should no doubt be referred to the same décor family is one preserved in the Mueller Collection in Peking, of the same form type. To judge from both form and décor, it is an advanced vessel (fig. 223). The neck, on which are extremely small rudimentary ears, possesses the slightly concave profile and pattern (double horizontal bands with thick, high dentations) characteristic of the advanced vessels. The scutiform fields on the mantle are also filled with a series of similar dentated bands. Horizontal dentated bands of this kind represent as a decorative filling an advanced pattern, (see Pl. XII fig. 7 and Pl. XVII fig. 6), which occurs also, in a slightly different design, as a supplementary pattern in the circular décor of the Ma Chang period (Décor Family 1M, see Pl. XXII fig. 5). The pot is undoubtedly an example of very advanced late Pan Shan.

An urn illustrated by Dr. H. C. Gallois (Bibl. 38, fig. on p. 176) has a neck of medium height. Its shape is transitional between P. S: XXIII and P. S: XXIV. To judge from the shape of the neck, the highly rudimentary ears, the medium-sized spiral centres filled with chessboard pattern (the spiral pattern belongs to Décor Family 11P) and the complete predominance of the black decorative elements, this vessel is advanced (late Pan Shan), if it is not actually a product of the very latest stage of that era.

Probably contemporary with this latter vessel is that illustrated in Pl. I of the Japanese work already cited (Bibl. 85). It too has extremely rudimentary ears, and a neat chessboard pattern as a supplementary ornamentation in the scutiform fields between carefully drawn bottle-patterns (Décor Family 16P). Of a still more advanced style is a vessel reproduced as H. 700 on p. 90 of the Catalogue of the Sunglin Collection (Bibl. 83). It is one of the most advanced representatives of the spiral family, as is shown by the shape of the neck, the pattern on the neck, the breadth and predominance of the black elements, and a very well executed chessboard pattern (cf. Pl. XII in the present work).

A vessel of very great interest from several points of view — still of the same type of form — is in the possession of the Museum für Kunst und Gewerbe, Hamburg; it has been reproduced in various publications, in Forschungen und Fortschritte, 1928 (see Bibl. 76), in the above-cited Geschichte des Kunstgewerbes (Bibl. 22), and in the Hamburg Museum's Jubilee Publication (see Bibl. 77) in "Taf. 2", likewise already mentioned above. Its pattern — bottle ornaments and scutiform fields filled with leaf-pattern — manifestly belongs to Décor Family 16P, but the pot's downward-tapering form, the wide-brimmed neck of medium height and the pattern on the neck, as well as the vaguely drawn lines of the long festoons on the lower border, all indicate that the vessel should be dated at the transitional period bordering on Ma Chang. Nevertheless, the pattern is so far unknown from that period. Unfortunately the reproduction does not show clearly whether the pot has a polished surface like the Pan Shan vessels or a duller surface like that of the vessels from the Ma Chang period.

Other vessels belonging to the Pan Shan ceramic style from Kansu and reproduced in available literature or otherwise in photographic form are of form types P. S: XVIII, XXVII, XXIX and XXX. No new form type arises, and the types that do occur have an exterior form of a very ordinary character.

In the already cited paper by Yetts (Bibl. 92), which contains illustrations of Pan Shan pottery preserved in the Royal Ontario Museum of Archæology, Pl. I, there is a jug (fig. A) of form type P. S: XVIII. It exhibits both the form and the décor of early types. The neck is formal and straight and curtailed in primitive fashion at the top. The ornamentation consists of a horizontal band décor (Décor Family 1P), which continues right up to the edge of the neck.

In the Japanese work already cited (Bibl. 85) there is illustrated in Pl. II (the upper figure) a pot of form-type P. S: XXVII. The decorative designs on both neck and mantle are practically orthodox with that form type (Décor Family 15P), and the pot's figural details and décor are almost identical with those reproduced in our Pl. XV, fig. 3. In the above-mentioned catalogue published by the Devine Galleries (Bibl. 83) there is a pot of the same form type and about the same pattern on the mantle (Décor Family 15P), viz. H. 705, p. 90, the only difference being that in this case the entire neck is covered with a trellis pattern. In the article in "L'Illustration" (Bibl. 13), the jug shown in the middle row of reproductions belongs to type P. S: XXIX and to Décor Family 11P. It should probably be referred to the first part of the period. In "Transactions of the Oriental Ceramic Society", London, (Bibl. 88) there is an illustration of a Pan Shan jug of form type P. S: XXVIII and of Décor Family 3P (hanging semicircular pattern). It now belongs to the British Museum (given by Mr. Oppenheim). It may be dated in the middle Pan Shan group.

In the June number of the Panthéon, 1928, (Bibl. 14), Ardenne de Tizac has published photographs of some Kansu urns. His views as to their chronology are however somewhat misleading. Among other things, he has unfortunately given a Hsin Tien urn as an example of the earliest period, whereas it actually belongs to period 4; a Ma Chang vessel is dated subsequent to it, and a couple of typical Pan Shan vessels (period 2) are placed last. The Pan Shan vessel reproduced in Abb. 4

Fig. 224
Wannieck Collection, Paris.

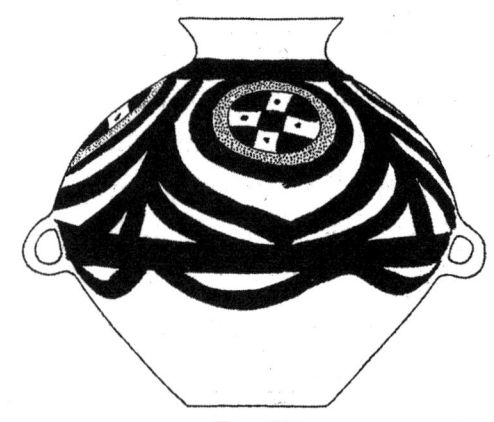

Fig. 225
Wannieck Collection, Paris.

Fig. 226
Laurell Collection, Peking.

Fig. 227
Wannieck Collection, Paris.

Fig. 228
Wannieck Collection, Paris.

is of type P. S: XXX and has a décor that is to a certain extent peculiar. Apparently the neck was once far higher than it is now — as is obvious from the pattern on the neck —, the upper portion of the neck having been broken off and the jagged edge now made smooth. The décor, consisting of horizontal rows of bands with very pronounced dentations, is in all essentials associated with the late Pan Shan ornamentation, and the division into four trapeziform fields justifies its being referred to Décor Family 17P. We find an analogy in the vessel illustrated in Pl. XVII, fig. 6, in which however this dentated ornamentation is confined to two of the trapeziform fields on the vessel.

After this brief summary, it may be said of all the examples of Pan Shan vessels that I have found mentioned in literature or with which I have become acquainted through photographs, that they permit remarkably well of classification in the categories of form and pattern drawn up by me. As regards the patterns, there are a number of individual variations and one or two unique designs, but even these are undoubtedly related to the dynamic Pan Shan style and utilize black and red elements in the "death-pattern system". On a few urns there are no dentations on the black bands (figs. 208 and 210). On the basis of the foregoing study of the subject, the vessels, with but few exceptions, permit of being dated in relative chronological order with a fair measure of certainty.

We are acquainted also with a comparatively large number of Ma Chang vessels through literature and photographs of specimens preserved in private collections. Our knowledge, however, does not by any means cover a group comparable in quantity with the number of Pan Shan vessels of which accounts have been published.

The forms that characterize these vessels belong to types already known to us, viz. M. C: VIII, IX, XIV, XVI and XIX. We are also acquainted, on the whole, with the patterns, although an occasional detail is found to be a novelty.

The predominant form of vessel amongst the material here in question is the type M. C: VIII. Type M. C: IX is far more rare. As regards the décor, in pots of these two form types Décor Family 1M predominates. There are representatives of one or two of its different sub-families. A couple of pots belong to this family, though they possess a décor of a more individual character. The Wannieck Collection contains two pots belonging to sub-family I (both of type M. C: VIII), neither of which are of quite early date (figs. 224 and 225), though they are not of a particularly advanced type either. In the above-mentioned article in the Panthéon by Ardenne de Tizac (Bibl. 14) a pot is reproduced of type M. C: IX and belonging to Family 1M, sub-family II (Abb. 2). The shape of the neck and the pattern indicate at least a relatively early date.

Mr. Yngve Laurell, of Peking, has in his collection an urn of type M. C: VIII (fig. 226) and Décor Family 1M, but it possesses an original supplementary décor in the four circles, viz. a large number of small circles in ground colour. The body of the urn is more or less spherical, the neck is short and has a slight brim, the decorative element between the circles is considerably ramified. All these features point to the vessel's being dated at the middle, if not in quite a late, phase of the Ma Chang period.

Another pot — from the Wannieck Collection (fig. 227) — is considerably more advanced than any of the vessels just discussed, as is indicated by its short, wide-brimmed neck and the highly ramified décor between the circles. The supplementary décor is original, consisting of a cross with uniform arms, and between them four dots. The cross is composed of a black outer contour, dentated along the inner edges, and a violet cruciform line within it. This shows that during the late Ma Chang period ceramic artists experimented with a reversion to a decorative system on the lines of the death pattern. As far as I know, this case is unique. The urn in the Ethnographical Department of the Riksmuseum in Stockholm is a late example of form type M. C: VIII and Décor Family 1M.

Finally, there is in the Wannieck Collection a probably fairly advanced vessel of type M. C: VIII. It has a large belly and a very narrow mouth. The décor on the mantle consists of a kind of string pattern above, and of a single row of squared network below. While this décor is of a pronounced Ma Chang style, it nevertheless has a markedly individual character. The almost flag-like pattern inside the squares lends an air of originality to the whole design. (See fig. 228.)

In "Asiatische Kunst, Ausstellung Köln 1926" (see Bibl. 74) Alfred Salmony has published illustrations of a Ma Chang vessel (Taf. 73—74) in the possession of Ch. Vignier, of Paris. It is of type M. C: VIII and Décor Family 2M. The round disc between the two figures is filled with somewhat original double semicircular patterns, the contours of which are in ground colour. For the rest, the vessel very closely resembles the vessels reproduced in our Pl. XXIV. It is also reproduced in Ipek 1927 to illustrate an article by Herbert Kühn (p. 32, Abb. 2) (see Bibl. 59). Here Kühn wrongly attributes the vessel to the Hsin Tien period. Sirén publishes in his above-cited work (Bibl. 82) an illustration of a vessel of type M. C: IX (op. cit. Pl. V, A) having a lower zone filled with a zigzag pattern (Décor Family 4M). The vessel is very ordinary in every respect.

There is exhibited in the Louvre (E. O. 2760) a vessel belonging to the rare form type M. C: XIX and to the décor family representing the anthropomorphic patterns.

Accounts of some vessels of type M. C: XIV have already been published. In the article in the Panthéon (Bibl. 14), which we have cited several times, a vessel is reproduced (Abb. 5) with two rows of rhomboids filled in with paint (Décor Family 6M, IV). Further, we know of a vessel (belonging to Madame Wannieck and reproduced in the article in "L'Illustration" (Bibl. 13), which is decorated with horizontal wavy bands in ground colour and below that a chain of cowries — so far an original combination of patterns representative of Décor Families 3M and 10M. Finally, in the catalogue of the Devine Galleries is reproduced a vessel that is manifestly covered with a brown slip, decorated on the neck with a fishing-net pattern and on the mantle with a design representative of Décor Family 11M. It is somewhat difficult to date the last-mentioned vessels with any degree of certainty, but the latter is probably a very advanced vessel dating from the end of the period.

In Pl. V of Sirén's work cited above there is a somewhat roughly designed bowl on a foot; it is of type M. C: XVI. The décor on its upper surface is of a strongly Ma Chang character — a triangular figure with arms radiating from it and terminating in 4—5 fingers. This décor is manifestly associated with the anthropomorphic décor of Family 2M and with the swastika pattern that was discussed in the chapter on the Ma Chang décor, and which likewise terminates in fingers.

The Ma Chang pieces mentioned in this chapter extend in some measure our knowledge of the patterns of the Ma Chang ceramic style, but the novel features we have pointed out conform remarkably closely to the Ma Chang style on the whole.

BIBLIOGRAPHY.

1. ANDERSSON, J. G., An Early Chinese Culture. (Bulletin of the Geological Survey of China, no. 5, 1923.)
2. ——, A Prehistoric Village in Honan. (The China Journal of Science and Art, vol. I, 1923, pp. 508—512.)
3. ——, The Cave-Deposit at Sha Kuo T'un in Fengtien. (Palæontologia Sinica, series D., vol. I, fasc. 1. Peking 1923.)
4. ——, Arkeologiska studier i Kina. (Archæological Studies in China.) (Ymer, vol. XLIII, 1923, pp. 189—247.)
5. ——, Arkeologiska fynd i provinsen Kansu. (Archæological discoveries in the province of Kansu.) (Ymer, vol. XLIV, 1924, pp. 24—35.)
6. ——, Preliminary Report on Archæological Research in Kansu. With a note on the physical characters of the prehistoric Kansu race by Davidson Black. (Memoirs of the Geological Survey of China, series A, no. 5, 1925.)
7. ——, The dragon and the foreign devils. Boston 1928.
8. ——, Prähistorische Kulturbeziehungen zwischen Nordchina und dem näheren Orient. (Ostasiatische Zeitschrift, N. F., vol. V, 1929, pp. 49—52.)
9. ——, On Symbolism in the Prehistoric Painted Ceramics of China. (Bulletin of the Museum of Far Eastern Antiquities in Stockholm, vol. I, 1929, pp. 65—69.)
10. ——, Den gula jordens barn. Stockholm 1932. (English edition: Children of the Yellow Earth. London 1934.)
11. —— & FRANZ, L., Archäologische Studien in China. Aus dem Schwedischen übersetzt und mit einem Nachtrage versehen von L. FRANZ. (Mitteilungen der Anthropologischen Gesellschaft in Wien, vol. LIV, 1924, pp. 60—82.)
12. D'ARDENNE DE TIZAC, H., L'Art chinois classique. Paris 1926.
13. ——, Découverte de céramiques peintes datant de cinq mille ans. (L'Illustration, no. 4405, 6/8 1927. Cf. The Illustrated London News no. 4609, 20/8 1927, pp. 315 and 318, An unknown Neolithic culture in China?.)
14. ——, Neolitische Töpfereien aus China. (Panthéon, 1928, pp. 311—313.)
15. ARNE, T. J., Die neuen Steinzeitfunden in China. (Ostasiatische Zeitschrift, N. F., vol. I, 1924, pp. 309—311.)
16. ——, Painted Stone Age Pottery from the Province of Honan, China. (Palæontologia Sinica, series D, vol. I, fasc. 2. Peking 1925.)
17. ARS ASIATICA, VOL. VII, Documents d'Art Chinois de la Collection OSVALD SIRÉN. Publiés avec une préface de M. RAYMOND KŒCHLIN, sous la direction de M. HENRI RIVIÈRE avec la collaboration de S. ELISSÉËV, G. MUNTHE, O. SIRÉN. Paris & Brussels 1925.
18. BISHOP, C. W., The Neolithic Age in Northern China. (Antiquity, vol. VII, 1933, pp. 389—404.)
19. V. BISSING, FR., Prähistorische Töpfe aus Indien und aus Ægypten. Munich 1911.

20. BLACK, DAVIDSON, The Human Skeletal Remains from the Sha Kuo T'un Cave Deposit in comparison with those from Yang Shao Tsun and with Recent North China Skeletal Material. (Palæontologia Sinica, series D, vol. I, fasc. 3, Peking 1925.)
20 a. BOE, J., Jernalderens keramik i Norge. Bergen 1931.
21. BOGAEVSKI, B. L., Раковины в расписной керамике китая, крита и триполья, (Известия государственной академии истории материальной культуры, vol. VI: 8—9, Leningrad 1931).
22. BOSSERT, H. TH., Geschichte des Kunstgewerbes. Vol. III, Berlin, Vienna, Zürich 1930.
23. BRITISH MUSEUM, A Guide to the Pottery & Porcelain of the Far East. London 1924.
24. BUSHELL, ST. W., Chinese Art. 3rd edition. London 1921.
25. BUXTON, L. H. D., Early Man in China. (Man, vol. XXV, 1925, pp. 17—21.
26. CHRISTIAN, V., Die Beziehungen der Altmesopotamischen Kunst zum Osten. (Wiener Beiträge zur Kunst und Kultur Asiens, vol. I, 1926, pp. 41—62.)
27. v. DUHN, F., »Canope». (EBERT: Reallexikon der Vorgeschichte, vol. II, pp. 266—268.)
28. FORRER, R., »Töpferei»—»Töpferscheibe». (Reallexikon der prähist., klassischen und frühchristlichen Altertümer, pp. 830—832, Stuttgart 1907.)
29. FRANCHET, L., Céramique primitive. Paris 1911.
30. FRANKE, O., Die prähistorischen Funde in Nordchina und die älteste chinesische Geschichte. (Mitteilungen des Seminars für orientalische Sprachen an der Friedrich-Wilhelms Universität zu Berlin, vol. XXIX: 1, 1926, pp. 99—114.)
31. FRANKFORT, H., Studies in Early Pottery of the Near East, vol. I, Mesopotamia, Syria and Egypt and their earliest interrelations, vol. II, Asia, Europe and the Ægean and their earliest interrelations. London 1924—1927.
32. FRANZ, L., Eine Höhle in China mit steinzeitlichen Kulturresten. (Speläologisches Jahrbuch, vol. IV, Vienna 1923, p. 128.)
33. ——, Die neuen Ausgrabungen J. G. ANDERSSONS in China. (Mitteilungen der Anthropologischen Gesellschaft in Wien, vol. LIV, 1924, p. 202.)
34. ——, Review of ARNE: Painted Stone Age Pottery etc. (Mitteilungen der Anthropologischen Gesellschaft in Wien, vol. LV, 1925, p. 285.)
35. ——, Review of ANDERSSON: Preliminary Report etc. (Mitteilungen der Anthropologischen Gesellschaft in Wien, vol. LVI, 1926, pp. 248—249.)
36. ——, Neolithische Tongefässe aus China in Wien. (Mitteilungen der Anthropologischen Gesellschaft in Wien, vol. LIX, 1928/29, pp. 26—28.)
37. ——, Die älteste Kultur Chinas im Lichte der neuesten Ausgrabungen. (Anthropos, vol. XXIV, 1929, pp. 313—317.)
——, Cf. ANDERSSON, J. G.
38. GALLOIS, H. C., Præhistorisch chineesch aardewerk. (Dienst voor Kunsten en Wetenschappen, Mededeelingen, vol. II, 1929, pp. 176—177.)
39. GROUSSET, R., Les civilisations de l'Orient, vol. III, La Chine, Paris 1930.
40. GÖTZE, A., Das neolithische Gräberfeld von Walternienburg, Kr. Jerichow I. (Jahresschrift für die Vorgeschichte der sächsisch-thüringischen Länder, vol. X, 1911, pp. 139—166.
41. ——, Der Schlossberg bei Burg im Spreewald. (Prähistorische Zeitschrift, vol. IV, 1912 p. 314.)
42. ——, »Töpferei». (EBERT: Reallexikon der Vorgeschichte, vol. XIII, pp. 328—334.)
43. HALOUN, G., Seit wann kannten die Chinesen die Tocharer oder Indogermanen überhaupt? vol. I, Leipzig 1926.
44. HAMADA, K., P'i-Tsu-Wo, Prehistoric Sites by the River Pi-liu-ho. (Arcæologia Orientalis, I.) Tokyo & Kyoto 1929.

Bibliography

45. HANNOVER, E., Pottery and Porcelain, a Handbook for Collectors, vol. II, The Far East. London 1927.

   HARADA, Y. & J., Cf. Tokyo.

46. HENTZE, C., Mythes et symboles lunaires. Antwerp 1932.
47. HETHERINGTON, A. L., The Early Ceramic Wares of China. New York 1922.
48. HOBSON, R. L., Chinese Pottery and Porcelain. London and New York 1915.
49. ——, The George Eumorfopoulos Collection. Catalogue of the Chinese, Corean and Persian Pottery and Porcelain, vol. I—VI. London 1925—1928.
50. ——, Neolithic Pottery from Kansu. (The British Museum Quarterly, vol. IV, 1929, pp. 41—42).
51. —— and HETHERINGTON, A. L., The Art of the Chinese Potter. London 1923.
52. ——, RACKHAM, B. and KING, W., Chinese Ceramics in Private Collections. London 1931.
53. HŒRNES, M. and MENGHIN, O., Urgeschichte der bildenden Kunst in Europa. Vienna 1925.
54. IZIKOWITZ, K., Calabashes with Star-Shaped Lids in South America and China. (Comparative ethnographical studies, vol. IX, Gothenburg 1931, pp. 130—133.)
55. KARLGREN, B., Review of ANDERSSON: Arkeologiska studier i Kina, An early Chinese culture, The cave-deposit etc., Arkeologiska fynd i provinsen Kansu. (Litteris, an International Critical Review of the Humanities, published by the New Society of Letters at Lund, vol. I, 1924, pp. 142—153.)
56. KASHIWA, O., Review of H. SCHMIDT: Prähistorisches aus Ostasien. (Journal of the Anthropological Society of Tokyo, no. 458.)

   KŒCHLIN, R., Cf. Ars Asiatica.

57. KÜHN, H., Die Beziehungen zwischen Mitteleuropa und China in Neoliticum und in der Bronzezeit. (Ipek 1927, pp. 198—199.)
58. ——, Review of HUBERT SCHMIDT: Prähistorisches aus Ostasien. (Ipek, 1927, pp. 102—103.)
59. ——, Neolithische Funde in China. (Ipek, 1927, pp. 95—96.)
60. KÜMMEL, O., Die ältesten Beziehungen zwischen Europa und Ostasien nach den Ergebnissen neuerer Ausgrabungen in China. (Deutsche Forschung, Part 5, 1928, pp. 112—121.)
61. LAUFER, B., Chinese Pottery of the Han Dynasty. Leiden 1909.
62. LIANG, S. Y., New Stone Age Pottery from the Prehistoric Site at Hsi-Yin Tsun Shansi, China. (Memoirs of the American Anthropological Association, no. 37, 1930.)
63. MASPERO, H., La Chine antique. (Histoire du Monde publiée sous la direction de M. E. CAVAIGNAC, vol. IV.) Paris 1927.
64. ——, Les origines de la civilisation chinoise. (Annales de Géographie, 1926, pp. 135—154.)
65. MENGHIN, O., Die ethnische Stellung der ostbandkeramischen Kulturen. Tocharer und Hettiter. (L'Académie des Sciences d'Ukraine, no. 76, Hruschewsky-Festschrift, Kiew 1928.)
66. ——, Zur Steinzeit Ostasiens. (Festschrift für P. W. SCHMIDT, Vienna 1928, pp. 908—942.)
67. ——, Weltgeschichte der Steinzeit. Vienna 1931.
68. MÜNSTERBERG, O., Chinesische Kunstgeschichte, 2 Aufl. Esslingen a. N. 1924.
69. NELSON, N. C., Archæological Research in North China. (American Anthropologist, vol. XXIX, 1927, pp. 177—201.)
70. NIPPGEN, J., Une civilisation primitive en Chine. (La Géographie, vol. XLII, 1924, pp. 512—517.)

   OSIMA, Y., Cf. Tokyo.
   PELLIOT, P., Cf. SALMONY, A.

71. PFEIFFER, L., Die Werkzeuge des Steinzeit-Menschen. Jena 1920.

   RIVIÈRE, H., Cf. Ars Asiatica.

72. Rücker-Embden, O., Chinesische Frühkeramik. Leipzig 1922.
73. Rydh, H., On Symbolism in Mortuary Ceramics. (Bulletin of the Museum of Far Eastern Antiquities in Stockholm, vol. I, 1929, pp. 71—120.)
74. Salmony, A., Asiatische Kunst. Ausstellung Köln 1926. Bearbeitet von A. Salmony mit Anmerkungen von Paul Pelliot. München 1929.
75. ——, Eine neolithische Menschendarstellung in China. (Ipek, 1929, pp. 31—34.)
76. v. Sauerland, M., Zwei neolithische Tonurnen aus China im Museum für Kunst und Gewerbe in Hamburg. (Forschungen und Fortschritte, Nachrichtenblatt der Deutschen Wissenschaft und Technik, vol. IV, 1928, pp. 353—354.)
77. ——, Das Museum für Kunst und Gewerbe in Hamburg 1877—1927, Hamburg 1929, pp. 33—34.
78. Scherman, L., Neolithische Tonurnen aus China in deutschen Museen. (Forschungen und Fortschritte, vol. V, 1929, pp. 49—50.)
79. Schmidt, H., Prähistorisches aus Ostasien. (Zeitschrift für Ethnologie, vol. LVI, 1924, pp. 133—157.)
80. Schmidt, R., Chinesische Keramik von der Han-Zeit bis zum XIX. Jahrh. Frankfurt a. M. 1924.
81. Seger, H., Die Steinzeit in Schlesien. (Archiv für Anthropologie, N. F., vol. V, 1906, pp. 116—141.)
82. Sirén, O., A History of Early Chinese Art, vol. I. The Prehistoric and Pre-Han periods. London 1929.
——, Cf. Ars Asiatica.
83. Sunglin (Mueller, H.), Collection of Chinese Art and Archæology, Catalog of exhibition, New York 1930.
84. Teilhard de Chardin, P., Le néolithique de la Chine d'après les découvertes du dr. Andersson. (L'Anthropologie, 1926. Vol. XXXVI, pp. 117—124.)
85. Tokyo, Imperial Household Museum. Relics of Han and Pre-Han Dynasties. Catalogue of the exhibition held in May 1932. Published by the Otsuka Kogeisha with a preface by Y. Osima and with descriptive notes by K. Yashima & Y. Harada and an English resumé of the descriptive notes by J. Harada. Tokyo 1932.
86. Torii, R., Études archéologiques et ethnologiques. Populations Préhistoriques de la Mandchourie Méridionale. (Journal of the College of Science, Imperial University of Tokyo, vol. XXXVI, Art. 8. Tokyo 1915.)
87. —— & K., Études archéologiques et ethnologiques. Populations primitives de la Mongolie Orientale. (Journal of the College of Science, Imperial University of Tokyo, vol. XXXVI, Art. 4. Tokyo 1914.)
88. Transactions of the Oriental Ceramic Society 1925—1926, pp. 11—12. London 1926.
89. Toscanne, P., Études sur le serpent, figure et symbole dans l'antiquité élamite. (Délégation en Perse, Mémoires publiés sous la direction de J. de Morgan, vol. XII, pp. 153—228.) Paris 1911.
90. Umehara, S., On the Prehistoric Painted Pottery from China. (Journal of the Anthropological Society of Tokyo, no. 464.)
90 a. Voretzsch, E. A., Altchinesische Bronzen. Berlin 1924.
Yashima, K., Cf. Tokyo.
91. Yetts, P., Painted Neolithic Pottery in China. (Burlington Magazine, vol. XLVII, 1925, pp. 308—310.)
92. ——, Archæology in China. (Indian Art and Letters, vol. IV: 2, 1930, pp. 1—5.)
93. ——, Chinese Origins. (The Times, May 2, 1934.)

CATALOGUE

of the Pan Shan and Ma Chang vessels in the Museum of Far Eastern Antiquities, Stockholm [= S], National Geological Survey, Peking [= P] and the Kulturhistoriska Museet, Lund, Sweden [= L], which are not reproduced in the plates.

No.	Preserved in	Provenience [B. = bought]	Form type	Décor Fam.	
K. 5002	P	Lanchow, B.	P. S. XXIV	1P.	
K. 5004	P	Ning Ting Hsien, Pien Chia Kou, B.	P. S. XXIII	1P.	
K. 5005	P	Lanchow, B.	P. S. XXIV	1P.	
K. 5016	P	Lanchow, B.	P. S. XXIII	1P.	
K. 5032	P	Ning Ting Hsien, Pan Shan, B.	P. S. XXIII	10P.	
K. 5047	S	Ning Ting Hsien, Pien Chia Kou, The large tomb, Pot 4	P. S. XXIV	14P.	
K. 5049	P	Ning Ting Hsien, Pan Shan, B.	P. S. XXIII	16P.	
K. 5051	S	Ning Ting Hsien, Wa Kuan Tsui, B.	P. S. XXIV	16P.	
K. 5072	P	Lanchow, B.	P. S. XXVII	15P.	
K. 5073	P	Lanchow, B.	P. S. XXVII	15P.	
K. 5079	P	Ning Ting Hsien, P'ai Tzu P'ing, B.	P. S. XXIV	16P.	
K. 5083	P	Ning Ting Hsien, Wa Kuan Tsui, B.	P. S. XXVII	15P.	
K. 5087	P	Ning Ting Hsien, Pan Shan, B.	P. S. XXIII	10P.	
K. 5089	P	Lanchow, B.	P. S. XXVII	15P.	
K. 5093	P	Lanchow, B.	P. S. XXXIII	17P.	
K. 5094	P	Lanchow, B.	P. S. XXXIII	17P.	
K. 5098	P	Ning Ting Hsien, Wa Kuan Tsui, B.	P. S. XXIII	15P.	
K. 5099	P	Ning Ting Hsien, Wa Kuan Tsui, B.	P. S. XXXIII	17P.	
K. 5106	S	Ning Ting Hsien, Pien Chia Kou, The large tomb, Pot 5	P. S. XXIV	10P.	
K. 5107	S	Lanchow, B.	P. S. XXXIII	17P.	
K. 5108	P	Ning Ting Hsien, Wa Kuan Tsui, B.	P. S. XXIII	18P.	
K. 5118	P	Ning Ting Hsien, Pan Shan, B.	P. S. XXIV	1P.	
K. 5120	S	Ning Ting Hsien, Wa Kuan Tsui, B.	P. S. XXIV	16P.	
K. 5121	P	Lanchow, B.	P. S. XXVII	15P.	
K. 5128	S	Ning Ting Hsien, Pan Shan, B.	P. S. XXIII	16P.	
K. 5130	P	Ning Ting Hsien, Pan Shan, B.	P. S. XXIV	16P.	
K. 5131	P	Ning Ting Hsien, Wa Kuan Tsui, B.	P. S. XXIV	16P.	
K. 5132	S	Ning Ting Hsien, Wang Chia Kou, B.	P. S. XXIV	16P.	
K. 5133	P	Lanchow, B.	P. S. XXIV	16P.	
K. 5135	P	Nien Po Hsien, Mi La Kou, B.	P. S. XXIII	16P.	
K. 5136	S	Ning Ting Hsien, Wa Kuan Tsui, B.	P. S. XXIII	16P.	
K. 5147	L	Ning Ting Hsien, Pa'i Tzu P'ing, B.	P. S. XXIV	11P.	
K. 5148	S	Ning Ting Hsien, Wang Chia Kou, B.	P. S. XXIII	11P.	
K. 5156	P	Ning Ting Hsien, Pan Shan, B.	P. S. XXIV	11P.	
K. 5157	P	Lanchow, B.	P. S. XXIV	11P.	
K. 5160	S	Ning Ting Hsien, Pan Shan, B.	P. S. XXIII	11P.	
K. 5161	P	Lanchow, B.	P. S. XXIV	11P.	
K. 5162	P	Ning Ting Hsien, Wa Kuan Tsui, B.	P. S. XXIV	11P.	
K. 5166	P	Ning Ting Hsien, Wang Chia Kou, B.	P. S. XXIII	11P.	
K. 5167	S	Ning Ting Hsien, Wang Chia Kou, B	P. S. XXIV	11P.	
K. 5170	P	Ning Ting Hsien, Pien Chia Kou, B.	P. S. XXIV	11P.	
K. 5172	P	Lanchow, B.	P. S. XXIV	11P.	
K. 5173	P	Ning Ting Hsien, Pan Shan, B.	P. S. XXIII	11P.	
K. 5174	P	Lanchow, B.	P. S. XXIII	11P.	
K. 5175	P	Ning Ting Hsien, Wa Kuan Tsui, B.	P. S. XXIII	11P.	
K. 5176	P	Lanchow, B.	P. S. XXIII	11P.	
K. 5178	P	Ti Tao Hsien, B.	P. S. XXIII	11P.	
K. 5180	S	Ning Ting Hsien, Wa Kuan Tsui, B.	P. S. XXIII	11P.	
K. 5181	P	Ning Ting Hsien, Pan Shan, B.	P. S. XXIII	11P.	
K. 5182	P	Lanchow, B.	P. S. XXIII	11P.	
K. 5183	P	Ning Ting Hsien, Wa Kuan Tsui, B.	P. S. XXIV	11P.	
K. 5189	P	Ning Ting Hsien, Pien Chia Kou, B.	P. S. XXII	1P.	
K. 5190	P	Ning Ting Hsien, Pan Shan, B.	P. S. XVIII	1P.	
K. 5192	S	Lanchow, B.	P. S. XXXII	17P.	
K. 5209	S	Yü Chung Hsien, B.	P. S. XV	17P.	
K. 5210	P	Ning Ting Hsien, Wa Kuan Tsui, B.	P. S. XVIII	11P.	
K. 5212	P	Ning Ting Hsien, Pan Shan, B.	P. S. XXX	16P.	
K. 5221	S	Lanchow, B.	P. S. XXI	11P.	
K. 5228	S	Lanchow, B.	M. C. XIV	6M.	Subfam. II
K. 5230	P	Lanchow, B.	P. S. XVIII	13P.	
K. 5231	S	Lanchow, B.	M. C. XIV	9M.	
K. 5232	P	Ti Tao Hsien, Shih Chia Wan, B.	M. C. XIV	4M.	

No.	Preserved in	Provenience [B.=bought]	Form type	Décor Fam.
K. 5233	P	Lanchow, B.	M. C. XIV	11M.
K. 5234	S	Lanchow, B.	M. C. XIV	5M.
K. 5235	S	Lanchow, B.	M. C. XIII	Indiv. déc. M.
K. 5236	P	Lanchow, B.	M. C. XIV	11M.
K. 5240	S	Lanchow, B.	M. C. XIV	11M.
K. 5242	S	Yü Chung Hsien, B.	M. C. XIV	11M.
K. 5245	P	Lanchow, B.	M. C. XIV	Indiv. déc. M.
K. 5246	P	Kao Lan Hsien. S. 80 li Chi Tao Lin	M. C. XIV	9M.
K. 5248	P	Lanchow, B.	M. C. XIV	9M.
K. 5251	P	Yü Chung Hsien, B.	P. S. XV	The décor defect.
K. 5255	S	Lanchow, B.	M. C. XIV	4M.
K. 5274	S	Lanchow, B.	P. S. XXVIII	Indiv. déc. P.
K. 5281	S	Lanchow, B.	P. S. XXIII	11P.
K. 5310	P	Lanchow, B.	M. C. XIV	7M.
K. 5325	S	Kao San Hsien, Kao Ying, B.	M. C. XIV	7M.
K. 5328	P	Lanchow, B.	M. C. XIV	10M.
K. 5329	S	Lanchow, B.	M. C. XIV	4M.
K. 5332	S	Lanchow, B.	P. S. XVI	Indiv. déc. P.
K. 5334	P	Lanchow, B.	M. C. XIV	11M.
K. 5338	P	Lanchow, B.	M. C. XIV	6M. Subfam. II
K. 5341	P	Lanchow, B.	M. C. XIV	6M. Subfam. IV
K. 5345	P	Ti Tao Hsien, Shih Chia Wan, B.	M. C. XIV	6M. Subfam. I
K. 5347	S	Ti Tao Hsien, Su Chia Yang Hua, B.	M. C. XIV	The décor defect.
K. 5348	S	Lanchow, B.	M. C. XIV	10M.
K. 5351	P	Lanchow, B.	P. S. XXXII	1P. [Indiv. déc.]
K. 5352	S	Lanchow, B.	P. S. XXXII	Indiv. déc. P.
K. 5353	S	Lanchow, B.	M. C. XIV	6M.
K. 5361	P	Lanchow, B.	M. C IV	Indiv. déc. M.
K. 5364	S	Kao Lan Hsien, Chi Tao Liang, B.	M. C. XIV	7M.
K. 5365	P	Ti Tao Hsien, Shan Chuang, B.	M. C. XIV	14M.
K. 5366	S	Lanchow, B.	M. C. XIV	6M.
K. 5367	S	Lanchow, B.	M. C. XIV	6M Subfam. II
K. 5371	P	Lanchow, B.	M. C. XIV	7M.
K. 5373	P	Lanchow, B.	M. C. XIV	6M. Subfam. 1
K. 5374	S	Lanchow, B.	M. C. XIV	9M.
K. 5378	P	Lanchow, B.	M. C. XIV	Indiv. déc. M.
K. 5461	S	Nien Po Hsien, Ma Chang Yen. Loc. 3. Sk. 1. Pot 2	P. S:r: IV	Without déc.
K. 5474	S	Ning Ting Hsien, Pien Chia Kou, The large tomb, Pot 1	P. S. XXIII	11P.
K. 5475	S	Ning Ting Hsien, Pien Chia Kou, The large tomb, Pot 3	P. S. XXIII	11P.
K. 5476	S	Ning Ting Hsien, Pien Chia Kou, The large tomb, Pot 8	P. S. XXXIII	17P.
K. 5477	S	Ning Ting Hsien, Pien Chia Kou, The large tomb, Pot 6	P. S. XXIV	11P.
K. 5482	S	Ning Ting Hsien, Wa Kuan Tsui, B.	P. S. XXVII	15P.
K. 5493	P	Ning Ting Hsien, Pan Shan, B.	P. S. XIII	17P.
K. 5500	P	Ning Ting Hsien, Pan Shan, B.	P. S. XV	15P. [Indiv. déc.]
K. 5501	P	Nien Po Hsien, Ma Chang Yen, B.	M. C. XIV	11M.
K. 5503	S	Lanchow, B.	M. C. XIV	6M.
K. 5618	P	Kao Lan Hsien, Ta Shih Chüan, Pot 1. B.	P. S. XXXII	1P. [transition to M. C.]
K. 5619	P	Chin Hsien, B.	P. S:r:1	Déc. in relief 3.
K. 5621	P	Nien Po Hsien, Ma Chang Yen, B.	P. S. XVIII	1P.
K. 5626	S	Lanchow, B.	P. S. XXVII	Indiv. déc. P.
K. 5656	P	Lanchow, B.	M. C. XIV	4M.
K. 5669	P	Lanchow, B	M. C. XIV	4M.
K. 5695	S	Nien Po Hsien, Ma Chang Yen. Loc. 4, Sk. 2, Pot 3	Indiv. form	Indiv. déc.
K. 5758	S	Ning Ting Hsien, Wa Kuan Tsui, B.	P. S. XXIII	11P.
K. 5780	P	Lanchow, B.	M. C. XI	6M. Subfam. III
K. 5795	S	Ning Ting Hsien, Pien Chia Kou, The large tomb, Pot 2	P. S. XXIV	16P.
K. 5797	S	Ning Ting Hsien, Pien Chia Kou, The large tomb, Pot 7	P. S. XXIV	11 P.
K. 5807	P	Ning Ting Hsien, Pien Chia Kou, B.	P. S. VII	1 P.
K. 5809	S	Ning Ting Hsien, P'ai Tzu P'ing. Sk. 3, Pot 2	P. S:r:IV	Without déc.
K. 5950	P	Chin Hsien Hsia K'o, Ya Tsu Tsui	M. C. XIV	12M.
K. 5969	S	Ning Ting Hsien, Pien Chia Kou, B.	P. S. XXXIII	17P.
K. 5982	P	Nien Po Hsien, Ma Chang Yen, Excavated	M. C. IX	2M.
K. 5983	P	Nien Po Hsien, Ma P'ai Tzu, B.	M. C. IX	4M. + 6M.
K. 5984	P	Nien Po Hsien, Ma Chang Yen, Excavated.	M. C. IX	3M.
K. 5985	S	Nien Po Hsien, Mi La Kou, Hei T'ou Chuang, B.	P. S. XVIII	11P.
K. 5988	P	Nien Po Hsien, Ma P'ai Tzu, B.	M. C. XIV	Indiv. déc.
K. 6124	S	Nien Po Hsien, Ma Chang Yen. Loc. 4, Sk. 1	M. C. XIV	13M.
K. 6167	P	Chin Hsien, S. 3 li. Ma Men Kou, E. $^1/_2$ li Po Tzu Cheng	M. C. XIV	14M.

PLATE. I

PLATE I.

Painted vessels of the Pan Shan style, Yang Shao period, bought in Kansu.
(Figs. 1—8, 10—14, = ¹/₄, fig. 9 = ²/₉ of natural size.)

Fig.	No.	Preserved in	Provenience	Height cm.	Diam. of Body cm.	Diam. of Mouth cm.	Diam. of Bottom cm	Thickness of the ware cm.	Form type	Décor Fam.	Style
1	K. 5112	S[1])	Ning Ting Hsien, Pien Chia Kou	11.8	17.0	14.2	7.0	0.5	P. S. XI	1 P.	Early
2	K. 5614	S	" " " Wang Chia Kou	12.5	19.3	12.0	7.0	0.5	P. S. XX	1 P.	"
3	K. 5484	P[2])	" " " Wa Kuan Tsui	12.4	19.0	10.0	8.5	—	P. S. XII	1 P.	"
4	K. 5496	S	" " " " " "	17.0	12.2	4.5	6.0	0.6	P. S. XVIII	1 P.	"
5	K. 5977	P	Nien Po Hsien, Mi La Kou, Hei T'ou Chuang	22.8	18.3	7.2	9.0	0.8	P. S. XVIII	1 P.	"
6	K. 5207	S	Lanchow	16.8	14.5	5.8	7.0	0.4	P. S. XVIII	1 P.	"
7	K. 5208	P	Ning Ting Hsien, Pan Shan	19.0	15.6	6.0	6.0	0.5	P. S. XVIII	1 P.	"
8	K. 5492	S	" " " " "	13.4	12.6	5.0	6.5	0.5	P. S. XVIII	1 P.	"
9	K. 5025	S	" " " " "	23.0	29.0	23.0	11.2	0.8	P. S. IV	1 P.	"
10	K. 5219	P	Ti Tao Hsien, Yang Chia Yai	11.5	16.0	14.5	8.0	—	P. S. V	1 P.	"
11	K. 5105	S	Ning Ting Hsien, Wa Kuan Tsui	10.5	15.0	14.5	6.0	0.4	P. S. V.	1 P.	"
12	K. 5090	P	" " " Pien Chia Kou	10.5	17.7	12.0	9.3	—	P. S. VII	1 P.	"
13	K. 5010	P	Lanchow	12.5	20.5	16.7	7.3	—	P. S. XXXI	1 P.	"
14	K. 5615	S	Ning Ting Hsien, Wang Chia Kou	10.4	17.5	9.5	9.5	0.5	P. S. IX	1 P.	"

Fig. 1. Vessel with a large handle. The handle is annular and is divided vertically into two lobes. The ware is brown with warmer-coloured spots. Surface smooth. The décor is in black with brown shading, and dark brown. The colours are but little differentiated. The upper edge of the black bands is dentated.

Fig. 2. Vessel with two horizontal handles. The ware is pale brownish with warmer-coloured spots. Surface smooth, not polished. The décor is in black with brown shading and violet. The two lower bands are black, the uppermost violet.

Fig. 3. Vessel with a large handle. The ware is yellowish brown. Surface smooth. The décor is in two colours, which however are somewhat difficult to distinguish from one another. The one colour is thinner (black), the other more substantial (dark brown). The wavy band at the lower end is black. Then follow three series of double bands, the lower black, the upper dark brown and smooth. The actual margin has had an ornamentation of radial black lines. The handle is decorated on the outside with a number of roughly painted squares.

Fig. 4. Jug with a fairly high neck and one handle, which is broken off. The ware is a light brownish red brick-colour. The surface is rather pitted, not polished. The rings in the neck are extremely well defined (Cf. Plate XXXI: 1). The décor is in black, of a somewhat poor quality, and reddish violet. The black bands are dentated on the upper edge.

Fig. 5. Jug with a high neck and one handle. The ware is a warm brown. The surface not very smooth, slightly polished. The neck has concentric striations at the top. The décor, in greyish black and dark violet, starts at the lower end with two horizontal bands, an upper one, violet, and a lower one, black. The rest of the mantle surface is ornamented with three pairs of horizontal bands on the death-pattern system. The black bands are dentated. The outside of the neck is ornamented with a trellis pattern in black. Both ornamentation and shape extremely primitive.

Fig. 6. Jug with a high neck and one handle. The ware is of a dirty reddish brown. The surface fairly smooth, polished. The ring method of construction is easily discernible on the inside of the neck. The décor in black with a brown tinge and dark brownish violet, the colours not being strongly differentiated. It starts at the lower end with a wavy black band. For the rest, the mantle is decorated with bands on the death-pattern system. There are two groups of three bands each. Of these, the two lower ones are black and dentated along the top, and the upper one is violet. Round the upper exterior part of the neck runs a broad violet marginal band followed by four black horizontal lines, and below that a band of black angles.

---
[1]) S = The Museum of Far Eastern Antiquities, Stockholm.
[2]) P = The National Geological Survey of China, Peking (Peiping).

PALÆONTOLOGIA SINICA. SER. D. VOL. III. FASC. 1.

PALMGREN: Kansu mortuary urns.

Pl. I.

Fig. 7. Jug with a high neck and one handle. The ware is an attractive brownish red, very light coloured. The surface fairly smooth, highly polished. The décor is in black and red, both clear colours. The ornamentation is on the horizontal death-pattern system, starting below with a narrow, red horizontal band, followed by three pairs of black and red bands, the former dentated along the upper edge. The outside of the neck has at the upper end a red border, and below this a black band. The wavy band lowest down on the neck is black. Black dashes on the rim of the neck. Inside the neck at the top is a black band with its upper edge dentated. From the lowest black band on the surface of the mantle two drops of paint have run down on to the basal surface.

Fig. 8. Jug with a high neck. A large handle has been affixed to the middle of the neck and the upper part of the mantle, but it is now broken off (Cf. Plate XXXII: 6). The ware is brick-red with lighter-coloured spots. The surface smooth, not very highly polished. The décor is in black and brownish red. The lowest wavy band is black, the upper red. The bands above with dentations are black, the other red. The pattern must be regarded as being on the whole fairly primitive, on account of the red element in the lower border. The three black horizontal lines above a black band dentated along the upper edge appear to indicate that black horizontal lines may be substituted for red bands on the death-pattern system.

Fig. 9. Vessel with a very wide mouth. Below the equator two knob- or ridge-handles with a triangular profile. The ware is light brick-coloured brownish red. The surface smooth and dull. The inside of the vessel plainly shows its construction in horizontal bands and how they have been welded together with the aid of the fingers (Cf. Plate XXXI: 3). The décor in black and violet red. At the border-line between neck and body is one red band. The rim of the neck is ornamented with radial black lines, the inside of the neck with groups of narrow, black bands, slanting now in one direction, now in another. The groups are separated by bands of angles in red pointing alternately upwards and downwards. Beneath, this décor terminates in a broad, black horizontal band.

Fig. 10. Vessel with a low collar, widening out slightly towards the top. In the middle of the body two diametrically opposed knob-handles. The ware is pale reddish yellow. The shape somewhat primitive. The décor is in two colours, both of poor quality, the one black, the other very dark brownish red, blackish red or lighter brownish red. The lowest band is red. Above are two black bands. The band on the border-line between neck and body is red. The outside of the neck is ornamented with a black, wavy band. On the inside of the neck are narrow black bands slanting alternately to left and right. The different series are separated by broader, red bands.

Fig. 11. Vessel with a low neck and two diametrically opposed handles, consisting of a disc attached to the side of the bowl, the handle's curved edge turned upwards and roughly erose. The rim of the mouth is sharply truncated. The ware is brownish red and smooth. The décor is in black with a brownish tinge and dark violet. The inside of the neck contains a zigzag band in ground colour on a black background, the rhythm being rapid and irregular.

Fig. 12. Vessel shaped like a bowl. There are no handles, ears or neck. Round the rim of the vessel, about 7 mm. from the edge, is a ring of holes. Around the holes on the inside are raised rings, showing that the holes were made in the soft clay from the outside. The ware is light brownish red. Surface smooth, polished. The décor is in thinnish black and thicker dark violet. The painting was undoubtedly done after the holes had been pierced, and the points of the pattern have been inserted within the narrow spaces between the holes. On the inner side of the rim is a series of vertical markings, broad at the top and narrowing down to a point. Otherwise the inside of the vessel is undecorated. Half of the vessel is still covered with a thick coating of lime, which has been preserved in order to show what the vessels sometimes looked like before being cleaned.

Fig. 13. Vessel with a low neck and two diametrically opposed handles affixed to the neck and the body. The outside of the pot polished. No traces of "throwing". The décor in black and dark brownish violet. The handles are decorated with a network of lines. The inner surface of the neck is decorated with a garland pattern. Five vertical violet lines are joined together by arcs in black and violet.

Fig. 14. Bowl or ampulla. At the top round the mouth are 13 ears placed radially. These ears have large holes and notched edges. They have manifestly served the purpose of suspending the vessel. The ware is pale reddish brown, with spots of a stronger brick-red colour. The surface is smooth and not very highly polished. The décor in two colours, somewhat closely akin to one another, black with a brown tone and blackish violet. At the lower end a violet band. Then follows a broad, black band and then a violet band. The two dentated bands round the mouth are black. The rim is violet.

PLATE. II

PLATE II.

Painted vessels of the Pan Shan style, Yang Shao period, bought in Kansu.
(Figs. 1, 3—7 = ¹/₆, Fig. 2 about ¹/₄ of natural size.)

Fig.	No.	Preserved in	Provenience	Height cm.	Diam. of Body cm.	Diam. of Mouth cm.	Diam. of Bottom cm.	Thickness of the ware at the neck, cm.	Form type	Décor Fam.	Style
1	K. 5008	P	Lanchow	27.1	28.2	14.5	11.3	—	P. S. XXIII	1 P.	Early
2	K. 5009	P	Ning Ting Hsien, Pien Chia Kou	19.5	25.5	14.4	10.4	—	P. S. XXV	1 P.	—
3	K. 5007	S	Lanchow	32.5	37.0	17.5	13.0	0.7	P. S. XXIII	1 P.	Early
4	K. 5021	S	Ning Ting Hsien, Wa Kuan Tsui	45.8	40.4	13.3	16.0	0.8	P. S. XXIV	1 P.	,,
5	K. 5011	S	,, ,, ,, ,, ,, ,,	34.3	29.8	9.2	11.3	0.8	P. S. XXIV	1 P.	,,
6	K. 5015	S	,, ,, ,, ,, ,, ,,	38.9	41.9	17.7	14.3	0.6	P. S. XXIII	1 P.	Early or middle
7	K. 5014	S	Lanchow	26.6	31.1	20.5	13.5	0.8	P. S. XXIII	1 P.	Early or middle

Fig. 1. Vessel with a low neck and two handles.
The ware is reddish yellow, porous and somewhat grainy. No concentric striations are discernible.
The décor is in black and a strong brownish red.

Fig. 2. Vessel with a low neck and two handles, one broken off.
The ware is of a light colour, not very porous. The surface is polished. There are concentric striations inside the neck, though they are very irregular.
The décor is in black and reddish brown.

Fig. 3. Vessel with a low neck and two handles.
The ware is a light reddish brown, moderately porous. The exterior of the vessel is polished. The interior surface of the neck is concentrically, though irregularly striated.
The décor is in black and red, the latter with a tinge of blue-violet. The interior of the neck is decorated with black vertical lines sloping somewhat irregularly in either direction.

Fig. 4. Vessel with a high neck, originally with two large ears pierced with holes. Two handles.
The ware is a light brownish red. The exterior of the pot is highly polished. There are no concentric striations. The neck is very unsymmetrical (Cf. Plate XXXI: 2).
The décor is in black and brownish red. The primitive spirals are black.

Fig. 5. Vessel with two handles and a high, narrow neck, ending in a turned-over edge, beneath which are two ears. The ears are without holes.
The ware is a light reddish brown. The surface polished.
The décor is in black and red.

Fig. 6. Vessel with a low neck and two handles.
The ware is a light reddish brown, somewhat redder below. The exterior of the mantle is highly polished. There are concentric striations on the inside of the neck.
The décor is in black and reddish brown. On the otherwise undecorated basal surface of the urn are five round rings painted in black without any polish.

Fig. 7. Vessel with a wide mouth, low neck and two handles.
The ware is light, toning into grey and pink. The surface is polished. There are no concentric striations.
The décor is in black and reddish brown. The handles function as spiral nuclei. The two series of lines above consist of a red lower band, 4—5 black, narrow lines, and, uppermost, a black band dentated along the upper edge. At the top, on the boundary of the neck, is a red band. The exterior surface of the neck is decorated with a series of black drops on the turned-over edge. These drops are in part continuations of the interior ornamentation of the neck. Beneath the turned-over edge is a black band. The inside of the neck is decorated in black with 4 vertical lines and between them 5—6 garland lines (concentric arcs).

PALÆONTOLOGIA SINICA. SER. D. VOL. III. FASC. 1.

PALMGREN: Kansu mortuary urns. PL. II.

PLATE. III

PLATE III.

Painted vessels of the Pan Shan style, Yang Shao period, bought in Kansu.
($^1/_6$ of natural size.)

Fig.	No.	Preserved in	Provenience	Height cm.	Diam. of Body cm.	Diam. of Mouth cm.	Diam. of Bottom cm.	Thickness of the ware at the neck. cm	Form type	Décor Fam.	Style
1	K. 5022	P	Ning Ting Hsien; Wa Kuan Tsui	33.1	38.1	19.7	14.5	—	P. S. XXIII	2 P.	Early
2	K. 5757	S	„ „ „ „ „ „	29.0	35.2	17.0	15.0	0.8	P. S. XXIII	2 P.	„
3	K. 5026	S	„ „ „ „ „ „	27.0	33.6	16.2	11.8	0.7	P. S. XXIII	2 P.	„
4	K. 5018	S	Lanchow	28.8	32.8	15.7	11.2	0.5	P. S. XXIII	2 P.	„
5	K. 5039	S	Ning Ting Hsien, Wa Kuan Tsui	35.5	42.5	17.2	14.5	0.7	P. S. XXIII	2 P.	Middle
6	K. 5113	P	„ „ „ Pan Shan	28.0	35.0	18.6	15.3	—	P. S. XXIII	3 P.	Early
7	K. 5012	P	Nien Po Hsien, Mi La Kou	33.2	40.2	18.5	12.9	—	P. S. XXIII	4 P.	„
8	K. 5114	S	Lanchow	36.5	34.4	9.4	10.7	—	P. S. XXIV	4 P.	Middle

Fig. 1. Vessel with a low neck and two handles.
The ware is light grey with a tinge of red. The exterior of the pot is polished. Traces of striation on the neck.
The décor is in black and reddish violet. The colours are strong. The three lowest bands are black. Above these is a zigzag décor consisting of a fairly broad black band, dentated along the upper edge, and above that a narrower, reddish violet band.

Fig. 2. Vessel of a primitive form. The mouth is somewhat oval. Two handles.
The ware is brownish red. The surface smooth, not very well polished.
The décor, in black and violet with a blue tinge, starts below with a black horizontal band. On the boundary of the neck is a violet band. Below this are three horizontal bands on the death-pattern system, the middle one violet and the others black. The lowest black band is dentated along the top, the upper one along both edges.

Fig. 3. Vessel with a low neck and two handles.
The ware is a light brownish grey colour. The surface is smooth and slightly polished.
The décor, in brownish black and violet red, starts with two black bands. Below the red boundary-line between neck and body is a black horizontal band. The garland décor on the interior of the neck consists of black bow-shaped fields and below them red festoons. On the base is a brand-mark with an impresssion made by the paint from another pot.

Fig. 4. Vessel with two handles, a fairly low neck and a wide mouth, the rim of which is turned over, forming a contour of rapid undulations. At the edge of the neck there are two rather small notched ears, which are without holes.
The décor is in black and greyish violet, the latter colour very thin.

Fig. 5. Vessel with a low neck and two handles.
The ware is reddish brown, hard and fairly coarse. The surface of the mantle is smooth but not polished.
The décor is in black and dirty red. For the rest, there are two brand-marks on the base, both showing a trellis pattern. The band at the boundary of the neck is red and below it is a black band. The artist has obviously drawn the red zigzag line without adequate calculation, as the ends cross one another close up to one of the handles, and the artist has here been compelled to abandon the original decorative scheme as far as the black supplementary décor is concerned. In this case we are able clearly to follow how the drawing was done. First of all the red zigzag line was drawn, starting on the lower part of the mantle at one of the handles, the line being carried obliquely upwards to the upper border. Then line after line of the zigzag band has been applied entirely free-hand, although the artist has succeeded in drawing the lower triangular fields all of fairly equal breadths. He has then passed the other handle without being able or caring to place it symmetrically in relation to the décor. The zigzag line has been continued and has finally reached the region of the second handle, when the artist has discovered that the remaining space was too small to allow the completion of the decorative scheme at the point

PALÆONTOLOGIA SINICA. SER. D. VOL. III. FASC. 1.

PALMGREN: Kansu mortuary urns.

Pl. III.

A. BÖRTZELLS TRYCKERI A. B. STHLM

where the zigzag line starts. He accordingly decided simply to abandon the pattern scheme as originally designed and to let the ends of the zigzag line cross one another. Subsequently the upper and lower triangular fields were ornamented with black bands, whose inner edges nearest the red zigzag line are dentated, the centres of the triangles being filled with lancet-like leaves in ground colour. Where the zigzag lines have crossed one another there have arisen two oblong fields of quite different shape, into which the supplementary design would not fit. The artist has hurriedly filled each of these oblong fields with a black ladder pattern. The outer edges of the patterns facing the red lines are dentated. Two of the adjacent upper triangular fields are either wholly or partially undecorated. Tiny black lines ornament the broad rim of the neck. The interior of the neck is ornamented with a garland pattern consisting of red bands, and below them black bands dentated along the upper edge. Between the festoons are suspended broad red bands.

Fig. 6. Vessel with a low neck. Attached to the neck are two ears with notched edges and a hole in the middle. Ears are a rare exception in this form type. Two handles.

The ware is a light reddish colour. The exterior of the pot is polished. There are concentric striations on the neck, but they are not symmetrical.

The décor, in black and red, starts with two wavy bands, the under one black and the upper one red followed by a black horizontal band.

Fig. 7. Vessel with a low neck and two handles.

The ware is dense, light-coloured and not very porous. There are irregular, yet to a certain extent concentric, striations on the inside of the neck.

The décor, in black and dark reddish brown, starts with a straight and a wavy band in black. Above these are four pairs of garland bands. Of each pair the lower one is red, the upper one black and dentated. On the border-line between neck and body is a red band. The interior of the neck is ornamented with five vertical lines, and between them double festoons.

Fig. 8. Vessel with two handles and a high neck partially broken off. Two ears are attached to the rim somewhat obliquely in relation to the plane of the handles. They are slightly reduced, irregularly notched and provided with small holes. The two handles are ornamented with a plastic décor consisting of an imposed vertical wavy band.

The ware is reddish brown. The mantle surface is smooth and polished.

The décor, in black and dark red, starts with and terminates in black horizontal bands. The band on the boundary of the neck is red. The bands of garlands are in red and black. The décor on the neck is black except for the uppermost band, which is red.

PLATE. IV

PLATE IV.

Painted vessels of the Pan Shan style, Yang Shao period, bought in Kansu.
($^1/_4$ of natural size.)

Fig.	No.	Preserved in	Provenience	Height cm.	Diam. of Body cm.	Diam. of Mouth cm.	Diam. of Bottom cm.	Thickness of the ware at the neck. cm.	Form type	Décor Fam.	Style
1	K. 5223	S	Ning Ting Hsien, Pan Shan	23.5	20.5	6.5	9.0	0.4	P. S. XVIII	2 P.	Early
2	K. 5222	P	" " " Wa Kuan Tsui	13.2	13.5	5.2	5.5	0.5	P. S. XVIII	2 P.	Early or middle
3	K. 5225	S	Yü Chung Hsien	18.5	16.0	6.8	8.0	0.5	P. S. XXVII	2 P.	Middle
4	K. 5023	S	Ti Tao Hsien, Yang Chia Yai	20.4	25.2	12.5	11.0	0.5	P. S. XXIII	2 P.	Early
5	K. 5110	S	Lanchow	16.0	22.2	13.2	10.3	—	P. S. XXIX	3 P.	"
6	K. 5028	P	Ning Ting Hsien, Pan Shan	27.0	24.0	8.3	9.0	0.6	P. S. XXIV	3 P.	Early or middle
7	K. 5272	S	Yü Chung Hsien	14.5	14.0	5.3	6.5	0.4	P. S. XXVIII	3 P.	Middle
8	K. 5029	S	Lanchow	24.8	21.5	6.2	11.5	0.7	P. S. XXIV	3 P.	"

Fig. 1. Jug with a high neck and one handle.
The ware is a warm, light reddish brown. The surface is smooth and slightly polished. Concentric striations inside the neck. The method of constructing the neck in rings is easily discernible on the inside.
The décor is in black and reddish violet.

Fig. 2. Jug with a narrow neck and one handle.
The ware is a light brick-coloured brownish yellow. The surface is smooth and polished.
The décor is executed in a thinnish and somewhat badly worn black paint, and a brownish red paint, which covers the surface well.

Fig. 3. Vessel with a high neck and two handles.
The ware is a reddish brown colour. The surface is rough, with strongly marked striations on the lower part.
The décor is in two colours, black of a greyish tone and liver-brown.

Fig. 4. Vessel with a low neck and two handles. The vessel is very primitive both in the way in which it is fashioned and in the way in which it is painted, being no doubt the work of a person quite unskilled in the potter's trade, or else a mere beginner.
The ware is grey with a slight reddish tone, coarse and of inferior workmanship.
The décor is in two paints of a very similar colour, black grey and violet grey, the colours being so alike in tone that they almost merge into one another. The band on the boundary of the neck is black. On the interior of the neck is a very primitive black garland motif with a violet dab of paint in the middle of each festoon.

Fig. 5. Vessel with a low neck and a handle. On the side diametrically opposite to this handle is another short handle with an upward-turned silhouette. Its upper edge is notched.
The ware is hard-baked, somewhat flamey, the colour being a strong red. The surface is polished. A thin superficial coating easily flakes off.
The décor is in black (of a somewhat grey tone) and reddish brown. The black paint is grainy and easily falls off.

Fig. 6. Vessel with two handles and a high, straight neck. As a good deal of the neck is broken it is not possible to say whether there were any ears.
The ware is a light reddish brown. The surface is smooth and polished. On the inside of the neck one can easily discern the rings of which the neck is constructed.
The décor is in black (of a somewhat greyish tone), and an uneven brownish red colour. The lower border consists of a red band between two black bands. On the top zone of the body are two horizontal bands, the lower one black, with dentations along the top edge, and the upper one red.

PALÆONTOLOGIA SINICA. SER. D. VOL. III. FASC. 1.

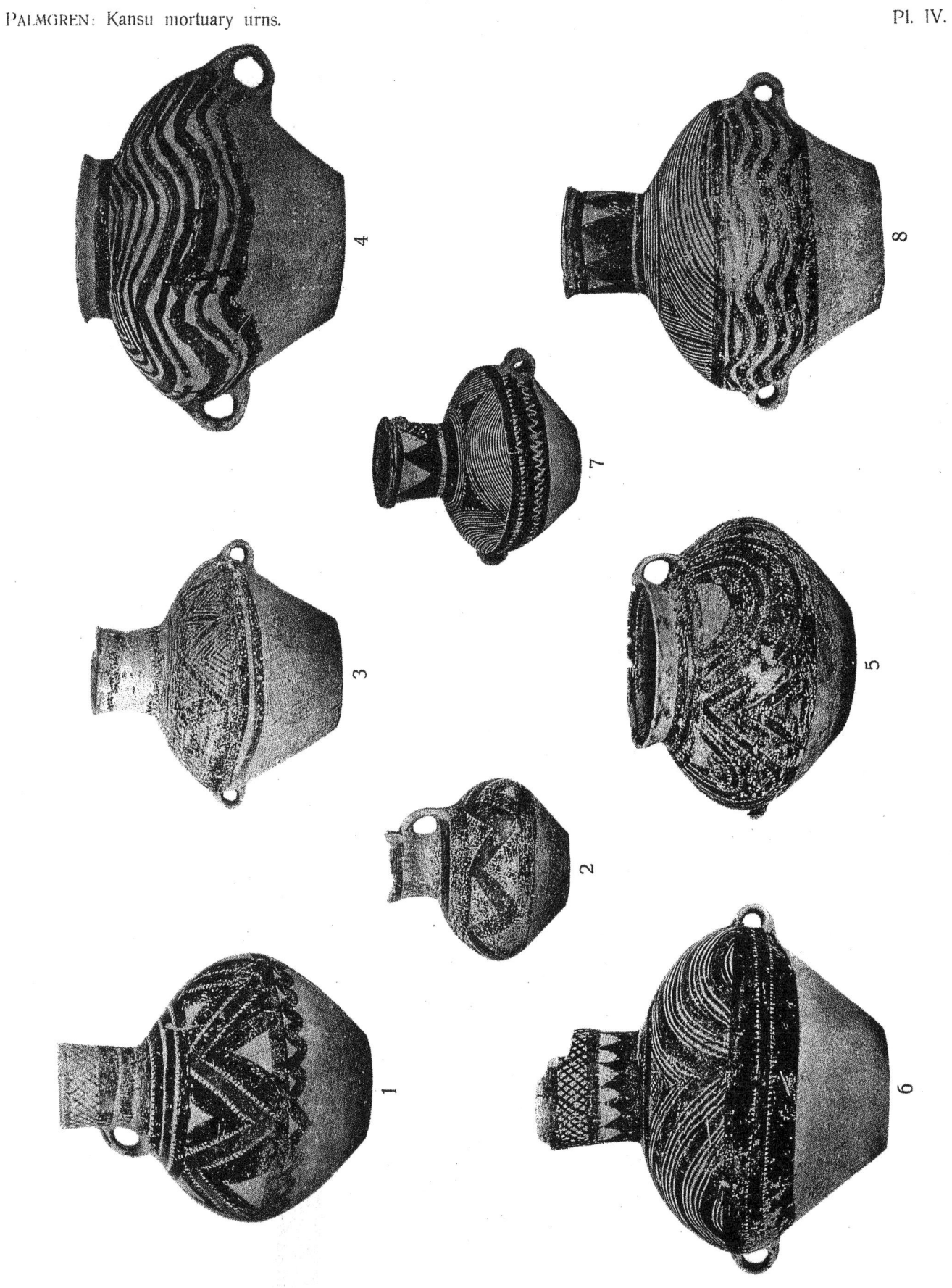

PALMGREN: Kansu mortuary urns.

Pl. IV.

A BÖRTZELLS TRYCKERI A.B. STHLM.

The arcs between these borders consist of red bands and black lines. The trelliswork and the points on the neck are black, the two horizontal bands red.

Fig. 7. Vessel with a high neck and two handles. Two miniature ears with notched edges and two holes each are placed at the rim.

The ware is reddish brown, the colour of brick. The surface is smooth and polished. The method of constructing the neck in rings is discernible on the inside.

The décor is in black and violet.

Fig. 8. Vessel with a high neck and two handles.

The ware is a light greyish brown and fairly coarse. The surface is smooth but not polished. The décor is in black and red of a dull and dirty tone.

PLATE. V

PLATE V.

Painted vessels of the Pan Shan style, Yang Shao period, bought in Kansu.
(¹/₆ of natural size.)

Fig.	No.	Preserved in	Provenience	Height cm.	Diam. of Body cm.	Diam. of Mouth cm.	Diam. of Bottom cm.	Thickness of the ware at the neck, cm.	Form type	Décor Fam.	Style
1	K. 5081	P	Ning Ting Hsien, Pan Shan	35.0	39.0	9.0	14.5	—	P. S. XXIV	2 P.	Early or middle
2	K. 5127	P	,, ,, ,, Wa Kuan Tsui	30.2	37.0	17.0	14.7	—	P. S. XXIII	5 P.	Early
3	K. 5019	S	Lanchow	32.6	40.0	16.5	15.0	0.7	P. S. XXIII	5 P.	,,
4	K. 5129	P	,,	37.7	38.7	8.5	14.2	—	P. S. XXIV	8 P.	,,
5	K. 5052	S	Ning Ting Hsien, Pan Shan	32.8	38.0	14.0	14.7	0.5	P. S. XXIII	8 P.	,,
6	K. 5125	S	,, ,, ,, ,, ,,	30.0	35.2	13.5	14.5	—	P. S. XXIII or XXIV	7 P.	,,
7—8	K. 5053	S	,, ,, ,, Wang Chia Kou	37.0	38.2	13.8	14.5	0.6	P. S. XXIV	8 P.	Middle

Fig. 1. Vessel with two handles and a neck which now has an uneven, broken edge, but which was presumably fairly high.
The ware is greyish brown with a red tone. The surface is smooth and polished.
The décor is in two very similar colours. The one is black but very thin, the other is black-brown.

Fig. 2. Vessel with two handles and a low neck without ears.
The ware is brownish red. The surface smooth.
The décor is in dark red and black.

Fig. 3. Vessel with two handles and a low neck, irregularly fashioned, as indeed is the entire vessel, which has a somewhat primitive appearance.
The ware is brown. The surface of the mantle is smooth but not very highly polished.
The décor in two very similar colours: black (with a brown tone) and violet (also with a brown tone).

Fig. 4. Vessel with two handles a high narrow neck, which is broken.
The ware is a light reddish brown. The surface is smooth.
The décor is in black and reddish brown.

Fig. 5. Vessel with a low neck and two handles.
The ware is a beautiful reddish brown, of a somewhat lighter colour on one side.
The décor is in black and pale greyish violet.

Fig. 6. Vessel with the neck completely broken off, and two handles.
The ware is hard-baked and of a fairly light reddish brown colour. The surface of the mantle is smooth and polished. The method of building up the body in rings is very clearly seen, particularly on the base.
The décor is in two colours, black and dark reddish violet.

Figs. 7—8. Vessel with two handles and a neck of medium height, with two rudimentary ears at the rim. The edges of the ears are notched and the holes are only simulated.
The ware is reddish brown, fairly light in colour. The surface is smooth and slightly polished. There are concentric striations at the top of the neck. On the basal surface the construction of the vessel in rings is very clearly discernible (Cf. Plate XXXII: 2).
The décor is in grey-black and dark brownish violet. The lower border is black. The band at the top of the mantle is violet, and below it is a black border with the upper edge "nipped" all round. The circles are black with the inner edge dentated; they alternate with narrower violet circles. The short lines in the middle of the circles are black. The true spiral line on the neck is violet. Black angle-lines, dentated along the edge facing the violet spiral line, join the latter at top and bottom. The interior of the neck is decorated with long black lines placed in pairs, the one below the other, round the mouth.

PALÆONTOLOGIA SINICA. SER. D. VOL. III. FASC. 1.

PALMGREN: Kansu mortuary urns.

Pl. V.

PLATE. VI

PLATE VI.

Painted vessels of the Pan Shan style, Yang Shao period, bought in Kansu.
($^1/_4$ of natural size.)

Fig.	No.	Preserved in	Provenience	Height cm.	Diam. of Body cm.	Diam. of Mouth cm.	Diam. of Bottom cm.	Thickness of the ware at the neck. cm.	Form type	Décor Fam.	Style
1	K. 5489	P	Ning Ting Hsien, Wa Kuan Tsui	19.0	22.5	15.0	8.4	—	P. S. XXIII	7 P.	Early
2	K. 5970	P	" " " " " "	23.7	19.7	7.2	8.7	—	P. S. XXX	7 P.	"
3	K. 5100	P	Lanchow	20.8	28.5	15.5	10.5	—	P. S. XXV	9 P.	Middle
4	K. 5043	P	"	22.8	23.2	8.4	7.4	—	P. S. XVIII	10 P.	Early
5	K. 5629	P	Ning Ting Hsien, Pan Shan	24.8	23.4	8.5	8.6	—	P. S. XXX	10 P.	"
6	K. 5502	S	Lanchow	19.8	20.5	10.0	9.0	0.5	P. S. XVIII	10 P.	Middle
7	K. 5101	S	Ning Ting Hsien, Wang Chia Kou	26.0	28.0	15.6	13.0	—	variation of P. S. XXIII	10 P.	"

Fig. 1. Vessel with a low neck and two handles.
The ware is a fairly light, warm reddish brown and hard-baked. The surface not very smooth. The collar is somewhat irregular. The vessel is fashioned in a primitive way.
The décor is in crimson and black. The painting gives the impression of being primitively done. The colours are thin.

Fig. 2. Vessel with a high neck and two handles unsymmetrically placed.
The ware is a light reddish brown, hard-baked. The surface of the mantle is polished. There are striations on the neck.
The décor is in black and bluish violet. On the undecorated base are some scattered splashes of colour of an irregular oblong shape. The horizontal band below is black. The mantle décor terminates at the top in two pairs of horizontal bands. Of each pair the lower band is black and dentated along the top edge, and the upper one is violet. In each circle are four concentric elements, black dentated bands and violet circular bands alternating.
The dots in the centres are black. The two horizontal bands on the neck are violet, the points and the trelliswork black.

Fig. 3. Vessel with a low neck and two handles.
The ware is brownish red in the break, the surface brownish yellow, that of the mantle being polished. The neck shows distinct concentric striations.
The décor is in black and reddish violet.

Fig. 4. Vessel with a high neck and one handle.
The ware is brownish red, the mantle smooth.
The décor is in black and dark violet red.

Fig. 5. Vessel with a high neck and two handles unsymmetrically placed.
The ware is brownish red, the surface smooth.
The décor is in black and dark reddish violet. The horizontal line and the wavy line below are black. The band on the boundary-line between neck and body is violet and the band below it is black. The contours of the squares and the small angle lines above the lower border are violet, but the other parts of the mantle décor are black. The colours on the neck are the same as in fig. 2.

Fig. 6. Vessel with a very high neck and one handle.
The ware is a pale reddish brown brick colour. The surface is smooth and polished. There are concentric striations at the top on the exterior of the neck.
The décor is in black and dark violet toning into blue.

PALÆONTOLOGIA SINICA. SER. D. VOL. III. FASC. 1.

PALMGREN: Kansu mortuary urns.

Pl. VI.

Fig. 7. Vessel with a fairly high neck and two handles.

The ware is greyish brown. The surface smooth. There are striations on the collar, but they are very irregular. There is a lack of sureness about the shaping of the vessel, as regards both body and neck.

The décor is in two not very different colours, black and brownish black, the latter colour denser than the former. The vessel's ground colour shows through the black paint, giving it a greyish tone. The painting is very irregular and primitive, obviously executed by an unsure hand and a clumsy artist. The dentated band on the interior of the neck is interrupted in two places by a garland décor in black.

PLATE. VII

PLATE VII.

Painted vessels of the Pan Shan style, Yang Shao period, bought in Kansu.
(Figs. 1, 2, 4—9 = 1/6, fig. 3 = 2/9 of natural size.)

Fig.	No.	Preserved in	Provenience	Height cm.	Diam. of Body cm.	Diam. of Mouth cm.	Diam. of Bottom cm.	Thickness of the ware at the neck. cm.	Form type	Décor Fam.	Style
1	K. 5054	S	Lanchow	32.3	40.8	16.4	14.2	0.7	P. S. XXIII	9 P.	Middle
2	K. 5042	S	,,	32.0	37.0	—	12.5	0.5	P. S. XXIV	9 P.	Early or middle
3	K. 5109	P	,,	24.0	28.0	14.5	11.5	—	P. S. XXIII	10 P.	Early
4	K. 5115	S	Ning Ting Hsien, Wa Kuan Tsui	30.8	37.2	17.2	14.2	0.6	P. S. XXIII	10 P.	Middle
5	K. 5041	S	,, ,, ,, Pan Shan	33.0	30.0	8.3	13.5	0.7	P. S. XXIV	10 P.	Early or middle
6	K. 5030	S	,, ,, ,, ,, ,,	29.0	34.0	16.7	13.5	0.7	P. S. XXIII	10 P.	Middle
7	K. 5033	P	,, ,, ,, ,, ,,	31.1	37.0	16.5	15.0	—	P. S. XXIII	10 P.	,,
8	K. 5034	S	,, ,, ,, Wa Kuan Tsui	31.2	29.0	8.0	10.0	0.5	P. S. XXIV	10 P.	Early or middle
9	K. 5123	S	Lanchow	34.0	40.0	18.7	13.8	0.6	P. S. XXIII	10 P.	Middle

Fig. 1. Vessel with a low neck and two handles.
The ware is brown with warmer coloured patches. The surface is smooth, not very highly polished. There are concentric striations all over the neck, real furrows being visible on the lower part.
The décor is in black and bluish violet.

Fig. 2. Vessel with two handles; the neck has been broken off. To judge however from the existing hole the neck was high and had a fairly narrow mouth.
The ware is a greyish red brick-colour and flamey. The surface smooth and polished.
The décor is in black and a beautiful dark red with a brown tone.

Fig. 3. Vessel with a low neck and two handles. The vessel is carelessly fashioned and primitive.
The ware is grey, slightly toning to brown. The surface is polished.
The décor is in black and violet blue.

Fig. 4. Vessel with a fairly low neck and two handles. The mouth is wide.
The ware is grey with warm red patches. The surface is not particularly smooth.
The décor is in black with a brown tinge and black with a blue tinge.

Fig. 5. Vessel with a high neck and two handles. Owing to considerable damage to the upper part of the neck it is not possible to decide with any certainty whether the vessel had any ears.
The ware is hard and brown, the surface smooth and polished (Cf. Plate XXXII: 1).
The décor is in two very similar colours, greyish black and very dark violet.

Fig. 6. Vessel with a low neck, made in somewhat primitive fashion, and two handles.
The ware is a light brownish grey with paler and warmer patches. The surface is smooth and dull.
Regarding the décor see Plate XXXVI: 3.

Fig. 7. Vessel of irregular shape with a low neck and two handles.
The ware is a greyish-yellowish brown. The surface is smooth.
The décor is in black and dark brownish red.

Fig. 8. Vessel with a high, straight neck, provided at the top with two smooth-edged ears which are fairly broad and are pierced with holes. Two handles, one broken off.
The ware is a greyish brown and somewhat coarse.
The décor is in two colours, black and violet.

Fig. 9. Vessel with a low neck and two handles.
The ware is light brown. The surface is smooth and polished.
The décor is in black and violet.

PALÆONTOLOGIA SINICA. SER. D. VOL. III. FASC. 1.

Palmgren: Kansu mortuary urns.

Pl. VII.

PLATE. VIII

PLATE VIII.

Painted vessels of the Pan Shan style, Yang Shao period, bought in Kansu.
($^1/_6$ of natural size.)

Fig.	No.	Preserved in	Provenience	Height cm.	Diam. of Body cm.	Diam. of Mouth cm.	Diam. of Bottom cm.	Thickness of the ware at the neck. cm.	Form type	Décor Fam.	Style
1	K. 5753	S	Ning Ting Hsien, Wang Chia Kou	21.0	27.0	13.7	10.0	—	P. S. XXV	10 P.	Middle
2	K. 5035	B[1]	Lanchow	34.2	41.0	18.5	14.5	—	P. S. XXIII	10 P.	Late
3	K. 5037	S	„	35.2	41.5	19.3	14.0	0.6	P. S. XXIII	10 P.	„
4	K. 5036	P	Ning Ting Hsien, Pan Shan	38.0	38.0	14.5	14.0	—	P. S. XXIV	10 P.	„
5	K. 5124	S	Lanchow	37.7	36.3	9.7	12.7	0.6	P. S. XXIV	10 P.	Early
6	K. 5038	P	Ning Ting Hsien, Pan Shan	33.7	35.8	15.0	17.5	—	P. S. XXIII	10 P.	„
7	K. 5117	S	„ „ „ „ „	33.6	40.0	16.8	16.0	0.7	P. S. XXIII	10 P.	Middle

Fig. 1. Vessel with a low neck and two handles.
The ware is a light greyish brown, hard-baked. The outer surface is smooth and polished.
The décor is in black and blue violet.

Fig. 2. Vessel with a relatively low neck and two handles.
The ware is a light reddish brown brick-colour. The surface of the mantle is polished.
The décor is in black and blue violet, the surface of the latter paint being quite glossy.

Fig. 3. Vessel with a low neck and two handles.
The ware is brown. The surface smooth and slightly polished. At the base of the neck are oblique, incised lines.
The décor is in black and bluish violet.

Fig. 4. Vessel with a fairly high neck, which has two small rudimentary ears without holes and with a plain edge. Two handles.
The ware is a pale greyish red. The surface is polished. There are concentric striations at the top of the neck.
The décor is in black and red with a violet tinge.

Fig. 5. Vessel with a very high straight neck with two diametrically opposed ears of quadrilateral shape. They are small, with notched edges and merely simulated holes. Two handles.
The ware is brown with greyish patches. The surface smooth and polished.
The décor is in black with a brown tone, and very dark brownish red.

Fig. 6. Vessel with a low neck and two handles.
The ware is a light brownish red. The surface is polished.
The décor is in black and reddish brown. The latter colour is not of very good quality.

Fig. 7. Vessel with a rather low neck and two handles.
The ware is reddish brown. The surface is smooth and polished. There are concentric striations at the top of the neck.
The décor is in greyish black and dark violet.

---

[1] British Museum, London.

PALÆONTOLOGIA SINICA. SER. D. VOL. III. FASC. 1.

PALMGREN: Kansu mortuary urns.

Pl. VIII.

A. BÖRTZELLS TRYCKERI A. B. STHLM

PLATE. IX

PLATE IX.

Painted vessels of the Pan Shan style, Yang Shao period, bought in Kansu.
(¹/₄ of natural size.)

Fig.	No.	Preserved in	Provenience	Height cm.	Diam. of Body cm.	Diam. of Mouth cm.	Diam. of Bottom cm.	Thickness of the ware at the neck. cm.	Form type	Décor Fam.	Style
1	K. 5096	P	Lanchow	17.5	25.5	14.7	10.7	0.5	P. S. XXXIII	10 P.	Middle
2	K. 5479	P	Ning Ting Hsien, Wa Kuan Tsui	16.7	22.0	14.2	8.0	—	P. S. XXXIII	10 P.	,,
3	K. 5526	S	Lanchow	13.0	24.0	23.0	9.0	0.5	P. S. III	10 P.	,,
4	K. 5967	S	Ning Ting Hsien, Wang Chia Kou	22.5	22.5	10.6	7.5	—	P. S. XVIII	10 P.	,,
5	K. 5102	S	Lanchow	21.0	24.5	10.0	9.0	0.5	P. S. XXX	10 P.	Late
6	K. 5078	S	,,	23.0	26.0	8.5	9.0	0.4	P. S. XXIV	10 P.	,,
7	K. 5119	P	Ning Ting Hsien, Pan Shan	20.9	22.2	7.0	8.5	—	P. S. XVIII	10 P.	,,
8	K. 5045	S	,, ,, ,, Wang Chia Kou	19.3	23.3	15.0	9.0	0.6	P. S. XXXIII	10 P.	Early or middle
9	K. 5344	P	Lanchow	10.8	14.0	9.0	5.2	0.4	P. S. XXXII	indiv. déc. P.	Late

Fig. 1. Vessel with a very low neck and two handles.

The ware is a light reddish brown. The surface of the mantle is polished. The neck is striated. The marks left by the fingers can easily be seen on the inside.

The décor is in black and bluish violet, both colours being quite glossy. The interior of the neck is decorated at the top with a plain garland décor consisting of a number of small festoons made up of one or two curved lines.

Fig. 2. Vessel with a wide mouth and two handles.

The ware is a strong brownish red brick colour. The exterior of the vessel is much pitted.

The décor is in black and dark brownish violet. The surface is considerably worn, particularly on the base, so that it is difficult to observe how the lower part of the décor terminated.

Fig. 3. Fragment of a vessel.

The ware is brown with greyish patches. The surface smooth.

There is no décor on the exterior of the vessel. Its interior is decorated in black and red. The narrow light-coloured bands are red.

Fig. 4. Vessel with a high neck and one handle.

The ware is a light brownish red. The surface smooth and polished.

The décor is in two colours, black and brownish red. There is also a light coating of clay, a slip, over the mantle.

Fig. 5. Vessel with a neck of medium height and two unsymmetrically placed handles.

On one side of the brim is a small rudimentary ear, serving in this case as a lip.

The ware is a bright red brick-colour, of a somewhat lighter tone at the bottom. The surface is smooth and slightly polished. There are concentric striations on the brim of the neck.

The décor is in black and brownish red.

Fig. 6. Vessel with two handles and a high neck, the top of which is broken off. Pieces still remaining at the top indicate that it once widened out into a brim. A couple of holes drilled just below the edge indicate that it had already been broken and bound together in ancient times. There is a circular piece missing out of the bottom (Cf. Plate XXXII: 9).

The ware is hard and firm, the colour a very light reddish brown. The surface smooth and highly polished.

The décor is in black and reddish violet.

Fig. 7. Vessel with a high narrow neck and one handle.

The ware is a pale greyish brown, the surface smooth and polished. The neck is still covered with a thick film.

The décor is in deep black and dark violet brown (chocolate brown).

PALÆONTOLOGIA SINICA. SER. D. VOL. III. FASC. 1.

PALMGREN: Kansu mortuary urns.
IX.

Fig. 8. Vessel with a low neck and two handles.

The ware is a reddish brown with a grey patch on the lower part. The surface is smooth and polished.

The décor is in black and bluish violet.

Fig. 9. Vessel with a low neck and two handles.

The ware is greyish brown, the surface smooth and dull.

The broad band just below the boundary of the neck and the band on the inside of the neck are violet; the rest of the décor is in black.

PLATE. X

PLATE X.

Painted vessels of the Pan Shan style, Yang Shao period, bought in Kansu.
(Figs. 1—5 and 7—8 = $1/6$, fig. 6 = $2/15$ of natural size.)

Fig.	No.	Preserved in	Provenience	Height cm.	Diam. of Body cm.	Diam. of Mouth cm.	Diam. of Bottom cm.	Thickness of the ware at the neck. cm	Form type	Décor Fam.	Style
1	K. 5150	S	Lanchow	30.8	25.0	8.0	10.8	0.5	P. S. XXIV	11 P.	Early
2	K. 5177	P	Ning Ting Hsien, Pien Chia Kou	31.1	35.8	17.0	11.5	—	P. S. XXIII	11 P.	,,
3	K. 5179	P	,, ,, ,, Pan Shan	31.2	35.9	16.0	12.0	—	P. S. XXIII	11 P.	,,
4	K. 5155	S	,, ,, ,, ,, ,,	42.5	43.0	17.5	14.0	0.8	P. S. XXIV	11 P.	Early or middle
5	K. 5149	P	,, ,, ,, ,, ,,	37.0	40.8	19.0	12.7	—	P. S. XXIII	11 P.	Middle
6	K. 5163	S	,, ,, ,, Wa Kuan Tsui	46.8	44.0	10.5	14.5	0.8	P. S. XXIV	11 P.	Early
7	K. 5146	S	,, ,, ,, Pan Shan	46.0	41.0	9.5	14.0	0.6	P. S. XXIV	11 P.	,,
8	K. 5168	P	,, ,, ,, Wa Kuan Tsui	36.0	32.6	8.5	11.0	—	P. S. XXIV	11 P.	,,

Fig. 1. Vessel with two handles and a high neck, on which are two large ears, notched and pierced with holes.

The ware is brown with warmer-coloured patches. The surface, smooth and somewhat polished. On the inside of the neck the vessels construction in seven rings is clearly seen.

The décor is in black and red. This décor is one of the most primitive in the spiral family.

Fig. 2. Vessel with a short, wide neck and two handles.
The ware is red with greyish flamey patches. The surface is smooth.
The décor is in black and violet, the black being dull.

Fig. 3. Vessel with a low, wide neck and two handles.
The ware is brownish red and the surface smooth. The shape is irregular.
The décor is in black and dark red.

Fig. 4. Vessel with four large ears round the mouth, a small hole pierced in each. Two handles.

The ware is partly a light, and partly a warm, brown colour. The surface smooth. There are concentric striations at the top of the neck. It is fairly easy to distinguish on the lower part of the base the rings of which the pot is constructed. There are brand-marks in four places on the pot, two on the mantle and two on the base (Cf. Plate XXXII: 8).

With regard to the décor see Plate XXXVII: 1.

Fig. 5. Vessel with a low neck and two handles.
The ware is a light brownish red. The surface is smooth.
The décor is in black and dark brownish red, the black colour being somewhat thin.

Fig. 6. Vessel with two handles and a very high neck, which has two large ears with holes pierced through the middle.

The ware is a greyish brown, with warmer and clearer patches; there is also a large spot burnt quite grey with a semi-glazed, uneven surface covered with a slag-like substance, manifestly spoilt in the baking. For the rest, the surface is smooth but not polished.

The décor is in black and violet, the violet having sometimes a reddish, sometimes a bluish, tone. On the glazed spot the colours are quite spoilt, the violet is grey and the black is greyish brown. There are black lines on the rim of the neck.

Fig. 7. Vessel with two handles and a very high neck, which has two ears pierced with holes.
The ware is a warm, light brown. The surface smooth and not very highly polished. The method of construction in rings can be distinctly seen on the base.

PALÆONTOLOGIA SINICA. SER. D. VOL. III. FASC. 1.

PALMGREN: Kansu mortuary urns.

Pl. X.

A. BÖRTZELLS TRYCKERI A. B. STHLM

The décor is in black and reddish violet. On the base, in the centre of the figure, is a black mark consisting of two black bands, the upper one dentated, the lower one wavy.

Fig. 8. Vessel with two handles and a high neck. The latter has two large ears, which are pierced with holes in the middle.

The ware is light brown. The surface smooth and polished.

The décor is in black and dark red.

PLATE. XI

PLATE XI.

Painted vessels of the Pan Shan style, Yang Shao period, bought in Kansu.
(Figs. 1—6, 8 = ¹/₆, fig. 7 = ²/₁₃ of natural size.)

Fig.	No.	Preserved in	Provenience	Height cm.	Diam. of Body cm.	Diam. of Mouth cm.	Diam. of Bottom cm.	Thickness of the ware at the neck. cm.	Form type	Décor Fam.	Style
1	K. 5184	P	Ning Ting Hsien, Pan Shan	33.0	38.0	18.0	13.5	—	P. S. XXIII	11 P.	Middle
2	K. 5158	P	,, ,, ,, ,, ,,	33.8	37.4	15.5	14.7	—	P. S. XXIII	11 P.	,,
3	K. 5164	P	,, ,, ,, Wa Kuan Tsui	38.7	37.4	10.7	15.1	—	P. S. XXIV	11 P.	,,
4	K. 5151	S	,, ,, ,, Pan Shan	39.0	38.0	10.5	14.5	0.6	P. S. XXIV	11 P.	Early or middle
5	K. 5159	S	,, ,, ,, Wa Kuan Tsui	32.6	40.0	18.5	13.5	0.5	P. S. XXIII	11 P.	Middle
6—7	K. 5143	S	,, ,, ,, Pan Shan	40.0	41.3	13.0	17.0	0.7	P. S. XXIV	11 P.	,,
8	K. 5154	P	,, ,, ,, ,, ,,	35.1	36.7	16.5	13.0	—	P. S. XXIII	11 P.	,,

Fig. 1. Vessel with a low neck and two handles.
The ware is brownish red of a fairly light tone, and the surface smooth.
The décor is in black and dark brown. Below, on the unpainted base is a mark or signature consisting of a ring and a straight line.

Fig. 2. Vessel with a medium-sized neck and two handles.
The ware is reddish brown. The surface smooth. The vessel has been unevenly baked.
The décor is in black and brown. The base has a straight black band running obliquely upwards.

Fig. 3. Vessel with a high neck, which has two small ears without holes. Two handles.
The ware is a light reddish brown. The surface is smooth and polished. There are concentric striations on the upper part of the neck.
The décor is in black and very dark violet.

Fig. 4. Vessel with a high neck, which has two ears with notched edges and holes. Two handles.
The ware is a light brick-red with brighter coloured flames. The surface is smooth and slightly polished. It is very distinctly seen from the interior of the neck that the vessel is built up of eight or nine rings.
The décor is in black and violet, toning now into red and now into blue. On the middle of the base, exactly between the two handles on one side, is a red cross, the lower arms of which are considerably shorter than the upper ones.

Fig. 5. Vessel with a low neck and two handles.
The ware is a warm brown with greyer patches. There are concentric striations on the outside of the neck at the top. On the top part of the base, close to the lower border, is a large brand-mark just between the handles. An indentation is discernible in the convex surface, as well as a change in both the colour of the ware and the tone of the fired black paint, and finally an impression of a trellis pattern, which does not form part of the decorative design of this vessel. For further comment, see the discussion on Plate XXXII: 8.
The décor is in black and violet, the latter taking on now a brown and now a blue shade.

Figs. 6—7. Vessel with two handles and a high neck, which has two ears with simulated holes.
The ware is a warm brown, the surface smooth and polished. There are concentric striations at the top of the neck.
The décor is in black and violet black, the latter colour darker than the former.

Fig. 8. Vessel with a low, wide neck and two handles.
The ware is a light reddish brown. The surface is smooth and polished.
The décor is in black and violet blue. The colours are extremely beautiful against the pale, clear surface of the vessel.

PALÆONTOLOGIA SINICA. SER. D. VOL. III. FASC. 1.

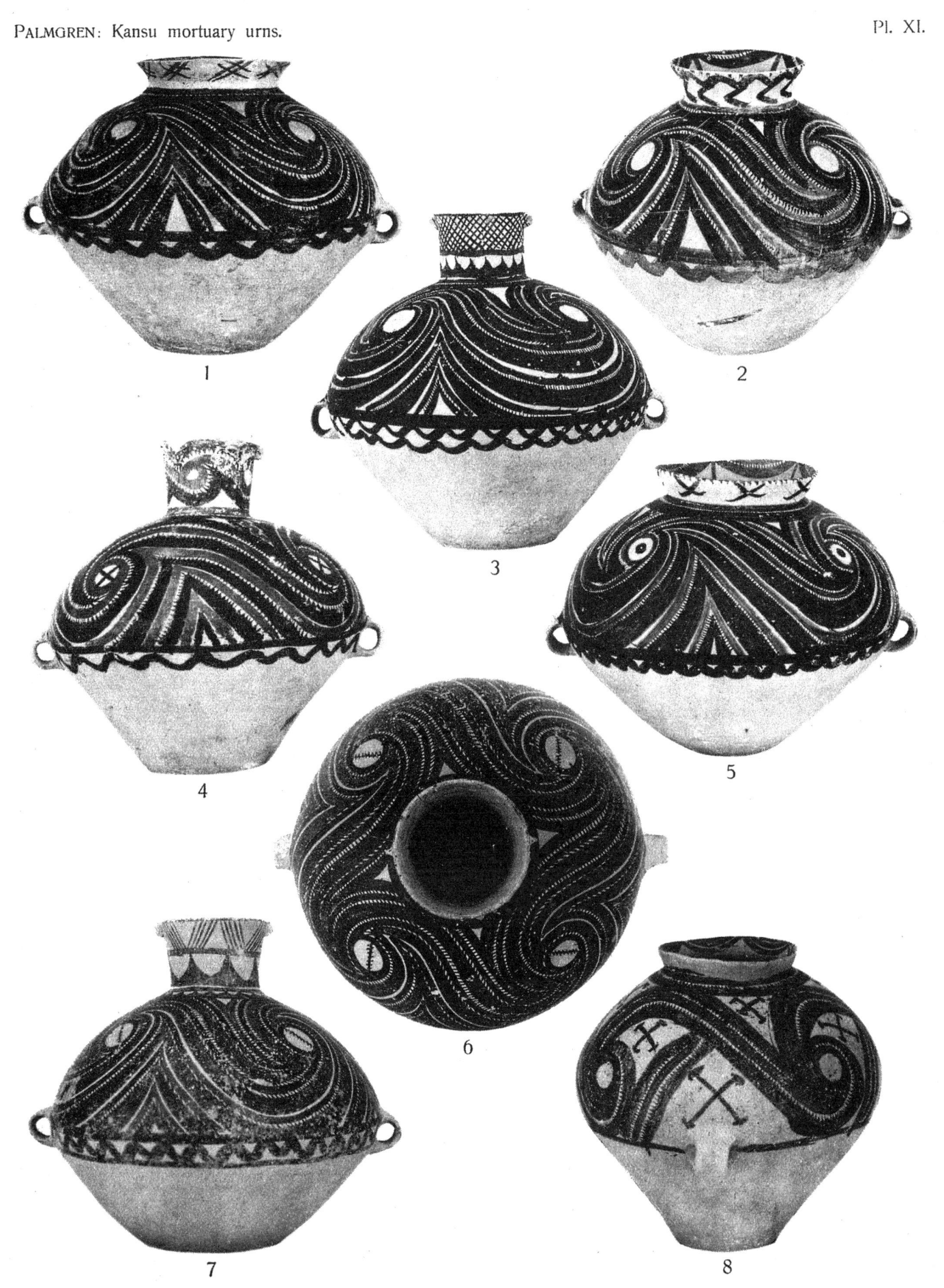

PALMGREN: Kansu mortuary urns.

Pl. XI.

A BÖRTZELLS TRYCKERI A.B. STHLM

PLATE. XII

PLATE XII.

Painted vessels of the Pan Shan style, Yang Shao period, bought in Kansu.
(Figs. 1—7 = ⅙, figs. 8—9 = ²/₉ of natural size.)

Fig.	No.	Pre-served in	Provenience	Height cm.	Diam. of Body cm.	Diam. of Mouth cm.	Diam. of Bottom cm.	Thickness of the ware at the neck. cm.	Form type	Décor Fam.	Style
1	K. 5140	S	Ning Ting Hsien, Pan Shan	34.4	38.7	16.5	13.0	0.8	P. S. XXIII	11 P.	Late
2	K. 5153	S	Kan Liang, 45 li SE of Lanchow	32.7	34.0	11.6	10.3	0.5	P. S. XXIV	11 P.	”
3	K. 5142	S	Ning Ting Hsien, P'ai Tzu P'ing	36.0	36.0	12.8	13.5	0.6	P. S. XXIV	11 P.	”
4	K. 5141	P	” ” ” Wang Chia Kou	38.4	38.1	13.8	13.5	—	P. S. XXIV	11 P.	”
5	K. 5171	P	” ” ” ” ” ”	39.7	38.6	12.7	13.5	—	P. S. XXIV	11 P.	”
6	K. 5144	P	Lanchow	39.0	42.0	13.0	13.0	—	P. S. XXIV	11 P.	”
7	K. 5287	S	”	44.5	42.3	15.5	13.5	0.6	P. S. XXIV	11 P.	”
8	K. 5193	S	Ning Ting Hsien, Pan Shan	16.6	18.4	12.5	8.5	0.4	P. S. XXXIII	11 P.	”
9	K. 5968	P	” ” ” Wa Kuan Tsui	16.7	22.4	12.6	8.8	—	P. S. XXXIII	11 P.	”

Fig. 1. Vessel with a low neck and two handles.
The ware is brownish red. The surface is smooth and slightly polished. Concentric striations on the inside of the neck.
The décor is in black and red. There is on the unpainted base a red mark consisting of a vertical stem and a horizontal branch projecting from the middle of it, and half as long as the stem.

Fig. 2. Vessel with two handles and a neck of medium height, and which has two rudimentary ears without holes.
The ware is brownish red, the surface smooth and polished. There are strong concentric striations on the neck.
The décor is in black and brownish violet, the former colour very predominant.

Fig. 3. Vessel with two handles and a neck of medium height, and which has two ears just below the rim (one is broken off). The ear has no hole and its edge is notched.
The ware is a warm brown, the surface smooth and polished.
The décor is in black and bluish violet.

Fig. 4. Vessel with two handles and a fairly high neck, which has two small ears without holes.
The ware is light brownish red to reddish brown.
The décor is in black and reddish brown.

Fig. 5. Vessel with two handles and a fairly narrow neck, which has two small rudimentary ears without holes.
The ware is light greyish to light red. The surface is smooth. The neck is striated at the top.
The décor is in black and brownish red, the black being very intense.

Fig. 6. Vessel with two handles and a neck of medium height, and which has a pair of extremely small rudimentary ears. These ears are not extended longitudinally, but are shaped like a small square nipple.
The ware is a light brown. The surface is smooth and polished. The neck is striated.
The décor is in violet and black.

Fig. 7. Vessel of an extremely advanced shape, which is very closely allied to the form of the Ma Chang style. It is worth noting that there are no ears on the neck of this, the most advanced, Pan Shan urn. Two handles.
The ware is brown. The surface is smooth and not very highly polished. There are concentric striations at the top of the neck. The method of construction of both neck and base in rings can be easily seen.
The décor is in black brown and red. The true spiral line is red, all the other elements being black brown. The spiral lines form an ornament resembling a cornucopia. This extremely characteristic

PALÆONTOLOGIA SINICA. SER. D. VOL. III. FASC. 1.

PALMGREN: Kansu mortuary urns.

Pl. XII.

feature differentiates the décor on this pot from the décor of a spiral type on all the other pots at my disposal. This spiral décor is undoubtedly the most advanced of them all. It is not a far step from this to the complete resolution of the spiral into four large circular fields.

Fig. 8. Vessel with a low neck and two handles.

The ware is a warm brown with reddish patches. The surface is smooth and polished. The neck has concentric striations on its upper exterior and lower interior.

The décor is in black with a brown tone and reddish violet.

Fig. 9. Vessel with a low neck and two handles.

The ware is fine and of a light reddish brown colour. The outer surface is polished. There is a small hole in the bottom.

The décor is in black and greyish violet.

PLATE. XIII

PLATE XIII.

Painted vessels of the Pan Shan style, Yang Shao period, bought in Kansu.
(¹/₆ of natural size.)

Fig.	No.	Preserved in	Provenience	Height cm.	Diam. of Body cm.	Diam. of Mouth cm.	Diam. of Bottom cm.	Thickness of the ware at the neck. cm.	Form type	Décor Fam.	Style
1	K. 5152	S	Lanchow	37.0	39.0	17.0	13.5	—	P. S. XXIII	11 P.	Middle
2	K. 5145	S	„	36.0	40.2	17.5	13.8	0.6	P. S. XXIII	11 P.	„
3	K. 5068	P	„	42.7	38.0	12.0	15.0	—	P. S. XXIV	(11 P.)	„
4	K. 5080	S	„	32.8	38.8	15.0	15.0	0.5	P. S. XXIII	12 P.	„
5	K. 5197	S	„	28.0	28.4	11.2	9.0	—	P. S. XXIV	14 P.	Late
6	K. 5056	P	„	34.9	31.7	10.6	11.0	—	P. S. XXIV	14 P.	Middle

Fig. 1. Vessel with two handles and a low neck, which has ears at the upper edge. The ears have holes and notched edges.
The ware is a warm reddish brown. The outer surface is smooth and polished.
The décor is in black and brownish red.

Fig. 2. Vessel with a low neck partly deformed in the process of baking. Two handles.
The ware is greyish brown. The surface is smooth and slightly polished. On the exterior of the base it is possible to see the method of construction in rings.
The décor is in black and violet, the former manifestly predominant, and starts with a broad lower border consisting of three black bands. The mantle is decorated with two spiral lines, each containing two spiral nuclei. Between the spirals on the one side is a field filled with a chessboard pattern, the squares being in black and in ground colour. On the opposite side (see fig.) the spirals are separated by a décor of a manifestly anthropomorphic character. A violet vertical stem is crowned with a circle, which has a black dot in the middle. The interior of the neck is decorated with garlands consisting of four festoons, which are separated from one another by plain suspended bands in violet. In one place this band is replaced by a violet vertical band enclosed by two pairs of black vertical lines. Each festoon consists of a black wavy band, and above it a violet band dentated along the upper edge.

Fig. 3. Vessel with a high neck, which has two smallish ears pierced with holes and with notched edges. Two handles.
The ware is brownish red and the surface smooth and polished.
The décor is in black and brownish red.

Fig. 4. Vessel with a fairly low neck and two handles. During the firing process, when the ware was still somewhat soft, the pot was given a hard knock, which caused a large dent at the top of the mantle above one of the handles. There are a few slight and smaller dents to the right of the large one. Moreover, as a result of this knock or pressure — it is of course conceivable that the dents were produced by too heavy pressure applied for a lengthy period — the collar of the neck is badly misshapen, and its upper edge now runs like a switchback round the mouth. When the accident occurred, the wall of the pot was in part sufficiently soft to give way to the pressure without breaking. In other places, notably in the deepest part of the main dent, there have arisen breaks and cracks, which can be seen on the outside and also felt on the inside. In one place there is actually a small hole. Those places in which there are cracks show even to this day that they were harder baked than those places that gradually gave way to the pressure, a fact that indicates that the accident occurred during the actual baking process. The small hole is sufficiently large to show that the vessel can hardly have been used to contain a liquid. The fact that, notwithstanding its violent deformation, the vessel was still utilized for mortuary purposes indicates that it was nevertheless regarded as valuable.
The ware is grey with smallish red spots, and is hardly more than half-baked. The surface is smooth and polished. There are concentric striations at the top of the neck.
The décor is in brownish black and dark reddish violet. The band of the boundary of the neck and the narrow oblique lines are violet; all the rest of the décor is in black.

PALÆONTOLOGIA SINICA. SER. D. VOL. III. FASC. 1.

Palmgren: Kansu mortuary urns.   Pl. XIII.

On the interior of the neck are three bands, the middle one violet and the other two black and dentated along the edge nearest the violet band.

Fig. 5. Vessel with a neck of medium height, and which has two rudimentary ears. Two handles.
The ware is reddish brown with brighter red spots. The surface is smooth and polished. The neck is striated at the top.
The décor is in black and dark brownish violet, the former colour being entirely predominant.

Fig. 6. Vessel with a high neck, which has two ears of medium size pierced with small holes.
The ware is a light brown. The surface is smooth.
The décor is in black and red.

PLATE. XIV

PLATE XIV.

Painted vessels of the Pan Shan style, Yang Shao period, bought in Kansu.
(Figs. 1, 2, 4—11 = ¹/₄, fig. 3 = ¹/₃ of natural size.)

Fig.	No.	Preserved in	Provenience	Height cm.	Diam. of Body cm.	Diam. of Mouth cm.	Diam. of Bottom cm.	Thickness of the ware at the neck. cm.	Form type	Décor Fam.	Style
1	K. 5064	P	Lanchow	23.4	26.8	13.5	9.0	—	P. S. XXVI	12 P.	Late
2	K. 5220	P	„	13.3	20.3	18.0	6.3	—	P. S. XXXV	Indiv. déc. P.	Middle
3	K. 5217	P	„	7.6	11.2	11.0	5.5	0.4	P. S. XXXI	4 P.	Middle or late
4	K. 5951	S	„	18.8	18.8	5.7	8.0	0.5	P. S. XVIII	4 P.	Middle
5	K. 5224	S	„	14.5	16.2	8.0	6.5	0.5	P. S. XVIII	13 P.	Late
6	K. 5599	S	Ning Ting Hsien, Wa Kuan Tsui	24.0	25.2	5.5	10.0	0.5	P. S. XXXIX	(13 P.)	Early
7	K. 5485	P	Lanchow	16.9	22.7	16.2	9.5	0.6	P. S. XXII	13 P.	Late
8	K. 5111	P	Ning Ting Hsien, Wang Chia Kou	16.7	22.2	14.4	10.0	0.5	P. S. XXV	13 P.	„
9	K. 5756	S	Lanchow	27.2	28.5	10.0	9.5	0.5	P. S. XXX	13 P.	„
10	K. 5104	S	Ning Ting Hsien, Pan Shan area (?)	10.7	17.0	12.0	9.0	0.8	P. S. X	14 P.	„
11	K. 5480	P	Lanchow	13.4	19.8	13.0	9.5	—	P. S. XXXI	14 P.	Middle

Fig. 1. Vessel with a low neck and two handles.
The ware is reddish brown with a grey tone. The surface of the mantle is polished.
The décor is in black and dark violet.

Fig. 2. Vessel with a spout and two handles.
The ware is reddish brown, the surface smooth.
The décor is in black and violet. The black is frequently very thin and greyish. The décor on the outside is in black. On the bottom of the vessel (inside), in the middle, is a cross, the arms of which continue up the sides of the vessel to the inside rim of the mouth. In the angle formed between these arms are broad black bands closely following the lines of direction of the violet arms of the cross. The spaces between these black bands are filled with narrower, horizontal lines also in black. The upper edge is ornamented with a broad violet horizontal band, covering the turned-over rim. Below the spout the black paint has run and forms a vertical streak extending some way down on to the basal surface.

Fig. 3. Vessel with a relatively high neck and two handles.
The ware is a very light greyish brown with warmer-toned patches. The surface is smooth and polished.
The décor is in dark brown with a red tinge. On the interior of the neck is a broad horizontal band dentated at the top and having at the bottom a row of small dashes close together. Along the rim of the neck is a very narrow band. One of the handles is decorated with an X, the other with four horizontal bands.

Fig. 4. Jug with a high and narrow neck and one handle.
The ware is somewhat coarse, pale greyish brown in colour, with warmer-toned patches. The surface is fairly smooth.
The décor, in black and greyish violet, is advanced. The band at the boundary of the neck is greyish violet, and the lines in the centre of the festoons are violet; all the rest of the décor is in black. The ornamentation on the neck is completely destroyed.

Fig. 5. Vessel with a high neck of an advanced shape and one handle.
The ware is a pale brown with warmer-toned patches. The surface is smooth and polished. There are concentric striations at the top of the neck.
The décor is in black and dark brown.

Fig. 6. Vessel with two handles and two necks, each having two rudimentary ears. The ears have neither notched edges nor holes and are of quite different size, the inner ones smaller than the

PALÆONTOLOGIA SINICA. SER. D. VOL. III. FASC. 1.

PALMGREN: Kansu mortuary urns.

Pl. XIV.

outer ones. The form of the vessel is very peculiar and elegant; there is no other like it in the collection of prehistoric pottery at my disposal. The two necks make it particularly easy to pour out of, as the air passes in through the one neck and the liquid out through the other.

The ware is a light brownish red brick-colour. The surface is smooth and slightly polished.

The décor is in black and reddish violet with blue tones. The black bands are dentated along the upper edge and somewhat broader than the violet ones.

Fig. 7. Vessel with a short neck, a wide mouth and two handles of a ridge or disc shape, the contour being concave on the upper side and convex on the under side.

The ware is secondarily dirty, its colour that of brick with a brown ground-tone. The surface is smooth and polished.

The décor is in black and a colour shading from violet to a dirty brownish red.

Fig. 8. Vessel with a short neck, a wide mouth and two handles.

The ware is a light reddish brown with warmer-coloured patches. The surface smooth and polished. Concentric striations at the top of the neck.

The décor is in black and reddish brown.

Fig. 9. Vessel with a high neck and two unsymmetrically placed handles.

The ware is brownish red with warmer-coloured patches. The surface is smooth and polished. Concentric striations at the top of the neck.

The décor is in black, which dominates, and in dark reddish violet.

Fig. 10. Vessel with a row of 22 ears placed vertically on the equatorial line. They are all pierced with holes and have notched edges. The brim of the vessel has 28 holes, viewed from above. Of these however no more than 22 are pierced right through. Presumably the holes as well as the ears have been used for suspending the vessel by strings' being threaded through the ears and then passed through the holes. The strings were then probably passed downwards through the next hole and then threaded through the next ear.

The ware is brownish red, the surface smooth.

The décor is in black with a brown tone and dark greyish violet.

Fig. 11. Vessel with a wide mouth and two handles.

The décor is in black and dark violet. The violet is so dark that it can only with difficulty be distinguished from the black colour.

PLATE. XV

PLATE XV.

Painted vessels of the Pan Shan style, Yang Shao period, bought in Kansu.
(¹/₄ of natural size.)

Fig.	No.	Preserved in	Provenience	Height cm.	Diam. of Body cm.	Diam. of Mouth cm.	Diam. of Bottom cm.	Thickness of the ware at the neck. cm.	Form type	Décor Fam.	Style
1	K. 5488	P	Ning Ting Hsien, Pan Shan	15.4	14.7	5.0	9.5	—	P. S. XXVII	15 P.	—
2	K. 5498	L¹)	,, ,, ,, ,, ,,	12.8	15.4	17.8	7.3	—	P. S. XV	15 P. (indiv. déc.)	—
3	K. 5088	S	Lanchow	22.0	20.7	7.5	9.0	0.6	P. S. XXVII	15 P.	—
4	K. 5628	S	,,	20.2	18.2	7.0	7.0	0.5	P. S. XXVII	15 P.	—
5	K. 5070	P	,,	23.5	20.5	7.5	7.3	—	P. S. XXVII	15 P.	—
6	K. 5071	P	,,	22.8	23.0	8.0	9.2	—	P. S. XXVII	15 P.	—
7	K. 5069	S	,,	23.2	21.0	7.0	8.3	0.5	P. S. XXVII	15 P.	—
8	K. 5076	P	,,	18.5	22.7	13.0	12.0	0.5	P. S. XV	15 P.	—
9	K. 5077	S	,,	20.5	26.0	17.0	10.5	0.7	P. S. XXIX	15 P.	—

Fig. 1. Vessel with a high neck without ears. Two handles.
The ware a pale reddish brown. The surface is smooth.
The décor in black is very primitive but of the same type as the black- and red-patterned forms belonging to family XV. The turned-over rim is entirely black, both inside and outside.

Fig. 2. Vessel, the neck of which is broken off. It once had a handle, also now broken off. The handle was attached to the neck and the upper part of the body.
The ware is a fairly light reddish brown and hard-baked. The surface of the mantle is smooth and polished.
The décor is in black and violet red.

Fig. 3. Vessel with a high neck, having two ears just below the rim, which is turned over and forms a narrow brim. The ears are deeply notched and are pierced with holes near the bottom. The lower edge of the brim is also finely notched. Two handles.
The ware is a brown brick-colour. The surface is smooth.
The décor is in black and brown, the black predominating.

Fig. 4. Vessel with a high neck, which has two ears with a hole in the middle. Two handles.
The ware is the colour of brown leather. The surface is smooth and highly polished.
The décor is in black and brownish red.

Fig. 5. Vessel with a high neck, which has two ears pierced with holes. Two handles, one of them broken off.
The ware is a pale brown and the mantle polished.
The décor is in black, which covers the surface well, and reddish brown.

Fig. 6. Vessel with a high neck, which has two large ears pierced with holes. Two handles.
The ware is reddish brown, the surface smooth and polished.
The décor is in strong black and reddish violet, the latter not very distinctive.

Fig. 7. Vessel with two handles and a high neck, which has two large ears with holes. These strong ears with their large holes have undoubtedly been used for the attachment of sinews for the purpose of suspension or for fastening a stopper of wood or other material. The method of construction of the neck with five rings is clearly discernible.
The ware is brown of a reddish and somewhat sombre tone. The surface is smooth and polished.
The décor is in black and brownish red.

---

¹) L = Kulturhistoriska Museet, Lund, Sweden.

PALÆONTOLOGIA SINICA. SER. D. VOL. III. FASC. 1.

PALMGREN: Kansu mortuary urns. Pl. XV.

Fig. 8. Vessel with a short neck, a wide mouth and a large handle.

The ware is a light brick colour, with some stronger red patches. The surface is smooth and polished.

The décor is in black and brownish red. The surface of the vessel has been in part badly damaged by weathering (some of it is completely worn away), and in part blackened by smoke or some dark oily substance. This makes the pattern difficult to observe in parts.

Fig. 9. Vessel with a short neck, a wide mouth and two unsymmetrically placed handles.

The ware is reddish brown with warmer-coloured patches. The surface is smooth and polished. There are concentric striations on the inside of the collar.

The décor is in black and reddish violet.

PLATE. XVI

PLATE XVI.

Painted vessels of the Pan Shan style, Yang Shao period, bought in Kansu.
(¹/₆ of natural size.)

Fig.	No.	Preserved in	Provenience	Height cm.	Body cm.	Mouth cm.	Bottom cm.	Thickness of the ware at the neck cm.	Form type	Décor Fam.	Style
1	K. 5055	S	Ning Ting Hsien, Pan Shan	33.5	40.6	16.6	14.0	0.7	P. S. XXIII	16 P.	Early
2	K. 5058	S	” ” ” ” ”	41.3	36.5	10.8	12.5	0.5	P. S. XXIV	16 P.	”
3	K. 5122	B¹)	Lanchow	30.4	35.4	17.0	11.5	—	P. S. XXIII	16 P.	”
4	K. 5057	P	Ning Ting Hsien, Pan Shan	30.3	38.7	16.2	11.2	—	P. S. XXIII	16 P.	Early or middle
5	K. 5059	S	” ” ” P'ai Tzu P'ing	35.6	35.5	11.6	13.0	0.7	P. S. XXIV	16 P.	Late
6	K. 5048	S	Lanchow	37.5	38.4	9.0	13.7	0.5	P. S. XXIV	16 P.	Middle
7	K. 5050	S	Ning Ting Hsien, Wang Chia Kou	40.0	39.0	13.0	14.5	0.7	P. S. XXIV	16 P.	Late
8	K. 5134	S	” ” ” ” ” ”	28.5	27.8	9.2	10.7	0.5	P. S. XXIV	16 P.	”

Fig. 1. Vessel with a low neck and two handles.
The ware is an attractive, light brownish red with greyer patches. The surface is smooth and polished.
The décor is in black and violet.

Fig. 2. Vessel with two handles and a high neck, which has two ears pierced with holes.
The ware is brownish red with redder and paler black patches. The surface is smooth and slightly polished.
The décor is in black and brownish red.

Fig. 3. Vessel with a low neck and two handles.
The ware is a reddish brown brick-colour. The outer surface is smooth and polished.
The décor is in black and dark red with a brown tone.

Fig. 4. Vessel with a low neck and two handles.
The ware is a light reddish brown with a smooth painted surface.
The décor is black and reddish violet. On the interior of the neck is an ornamentation of segments or festoons in black and red. On the unpainted surface below is an ideograph or a signature in the form of a cross made in red.

Fig. 5. Vessel with a high neck, which has two rudimentary ears without holes. Two handles.
The ware is reddish brown of a fairly light colour. The surface is smooth and polished. Concentric striations on the top of the neck.
The décor is in black and violet, the former strongly predominant, as in the case of most advanced vessels with rudimentary ears.

Fig. 6. Vessel with a high neck, which has two rudimentary ears pierced with holes and slightly notched along the edges. Two handles.
The ware is reddish brown. The surface is smooth and slightly polished.
The décor is in grey-black and dark violet. On the lower part of the base just above the bottom are three black, oblong patches in a horizontal direction.

Fig. 7. Vessel with a neck of medium height and which has two rudimentary ears with smooth edges and without holes. Two handles.
The ware is brownish red and hard. The surface even and polished. Concentric striations at the top of the neck.
The décor is in black and bluish violet.

Fig. 8. Vessel with a high neck, which has two very rudimentary ears. Two handles.
The ware is a warm brown. The surface is smooth and well polished. There are concentric striations at the top of the neck, particularly on the inside.
The décor is in black and violet red, the former being strongly predominant.

---
¹) B = British Museum, London.

PALÆONTOLOGIA SINICA. SER. D. VOL. III. FASC. 1.

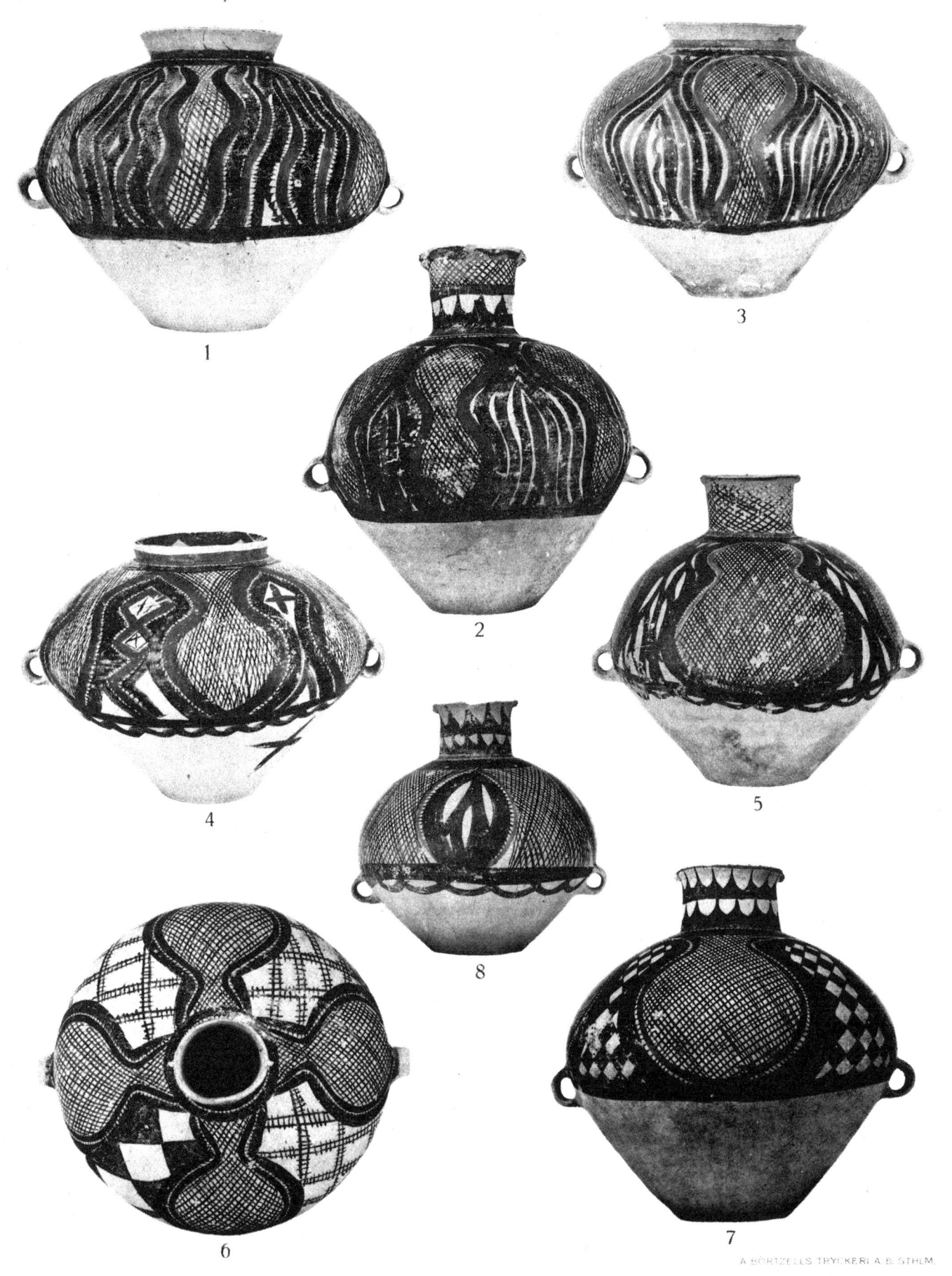

PALMGREN: Kansu mortuary urns.

PL. XVI.

PLATE. XVII

PLATE XVII.

Painted vessels of the Pan Shan style, Yang Shao period, bought in Kansu.
(Fig. 1 = ¹/₃, figs. 2—11 = ¹/₄ of natural size.)

Fig.	No.	Preserved in	Provenience	Height cm.	Diam. of Body cm.	Diam. of Mouth cm.	Diam. of Bottom cm.	Thickness of the ware at the neck cm.	Form type	Décor Fam.	Style
1	K. 5211	P	Ning Ting Hsien, Wa Kuan Tsui	11.9	10.8	5.4	6.5	0.4	P. S. XVIII	17 P.	Early or middle
2	K. 5625	S	,, ,, ,, Pan Shan	25.1	24.7	9.0	9.5	—	P. S. XVIII	17 P.	Middle
3	K. 5610	S	Kao Lan Hsien, Kao Ying	15.4	18.3	12.0	7.5	0.6	P. S. XIV	17 P.	Middle or late
4	K. 5097	P	Lanchow	18.5	22.0	14.0	9.0	—	P. S. XXXIII	17 P.	Late
5	K. 5044	P	Ning Ting Hsien, Pan Shan	19.0	23.0	15.0	8.6	—	P. S. XXXIII	17 P.	,,
6	K. 5095	S	Lanchow	15.5	21.5	13.5	8.3	0.5	P. S. XXXIII	17 P.	,,
7	K. 5091	P	,,	11.0	15.8	10.0	—	0.4	P. S. XXXIII	17 P.	,,
8	K. 5257	P	,,	8.5	10.2	2.9	5.0	—	P. S. XVII	17 P.	,,
9	K. 5046	S	Ning Ting Hsien, Pan Shan	16.0	18.8	12.5	7.0	—	P. S. XXXIII	17 P.	,,
10	K. 5084	S	Lanchow	19.0	25.0	15.0	9.5	0.4	P. S. XXXIII	17 P.	,,
11	K. 5191	S	,,	10.6	17.8	11.2	7.5	—	P. S. VIII	17 P.	,,

Fig. 1. Jug with one handle and a high neck. In the bottom is a large round hole.

The ware is brownish red, with here and there patches of a stronger brick-colour. The surface is smooth but not very highly polished.

The décor on the vessel is now in a very poor state, the colours rather difficult to distinguish, one violet black and less weathered, the other greyish brown, thinner and more worn away.

Fig. 2. Jug with a high neck and one handle.

The ware is reddish brown, with redder patches. The surface is smooth and polished. The neck is striated at the top.

The décor is in black and dark brownish violet, the latter covering the surface better than the former.

Fig. 3. Vessel of mug-like form with one handle.

The ware is a brownish red brick-colour, with brighter and paler patches. The surface is smooth but not very highly polished. There are marked concentric striations on the neck.

The décor is in black with six narrow vertical lines in dark brown. On the interior of the neck are two horizontal bands, the upper one brown and the lower one black and dentated along the top.

Fig. 4. Vessel with a short neck, a wide mouth and two handles.

The ware is greyish brown, a somewhat pale colour. The surface of the mantle is highly polished.

The décor is in black and dark violet red. The interior of the neck is decorated with a red band, and below it a dentated band with high points.

Fig. 5. Vessel with a short neck, a wide mouth and two handles.

The ware is smooth and its colour brownish red, the mantle polished.

The décor is in black and dark violet red.

Fig. 6. Vessel with a short neck, a wide mouth and two handles.

The ware is reddish brown. The surface is smooth and polished. There are concentric striations on the neck. On the inner surface of the vessel are clearly visible the ridges and grooves, running obliquely from the bottom upwards in an anti-clockwise direction, which were formed when the rings were moulded together.

The décor is in black and violet, both covering the surface well.

Fig. 7. Vessel with a relatively wide mouth and two handles.

The ware is a dirty greyish brown. The surface is smooth and polished.

The décor is in two colours, black and violet red.

PALÆONTOLOGIA SINICA. S'ER. D. VOL. III. FASC. 1

PALMGREN: Kansu mortuary urns.

Pl. XVII.

Fig. 8. Vessel with a narrow mouth and one handle.

The ware is a brownish red brick-colour, in parts toning into yellowish brown. The surface is smooth and polished.

The outer surface of the vessel is entirely covered with a slip, a pale greyish brown coating applied by dipping the vessel into a light-coloured solution of clay. Painted on this slip is a décor in black and dark brownish red. There has been a narrow red band round the rim of the mouth, and the narrow vertical lines are red; the rest of the décor on the mantle surface is in black. On the handle is a red band running vertically down it. The décor in black is not so clear; presumably there have been three horizontal bands in black.

Fig. 9. Vessel with a short neck, a relatively wide mouth and two handles.

The ware is thin and fine, the colour a pale reddish brown. The surface is smooth and polished. There are striations on the collar.

With regard to the décor see Plate XXXVIII : 4.

Fig 10. Vessel with a short neck and two handles, one of which, however, is broken off; one can easily see from the upper surface of the break that the handle was partly hollow and that it was attached by being merely pressed firmly on to the smooth surface of the neck.

The ware is light brown with warmer-coloured patches. The surface is smooth and polished. There are concentric striations on the outside of the neck.

The décor is in black and reddish violet. The band on the boundary of the neck and the six vertical, narrow lines on the mantle are violet; the rest of the décor is in black. The rim is decorated with a narrow black band, dentated along the inner edge. Below these dentations on the interior of the neck is a violet band, from which is suspended a delicate décor of black garlands. Each festoon consists of two to four narrow arcs.

Fig 11. Vessel with a wide mouth. Just beneath the widest part of the vessel are two round, stud-like excrescences diametrically opposite to one another. Just below the mouth is a series of holes in pairs, used for the purpose of suspension.

The ware is a light reddish brown colour and fine in texture. The outer surface is smooth and polished.

The décor is in black with narrow vertical lines in violet.

PLATE. XVIII

PLATE XVIII.

Painted vessels of the Pan Shan style, Yang Shao period, bought in Kansu.
($^1/_6$ of natural size.)

Fig.	No.	Preserved in	Provenience	Height cm.	Diam. of Body cm.	Diam. of Mouth cm.	Diam. of Bottom cm.	Thickness of the ware at the neck. cm	Form type	Décor Fam.	Style
1	K. 5126	S	Ning Ting Hsien, Pan Shan	37.5	38.5	13.5	14.0	0.5	P. S. XXIV	17 P.	Middle or late
2	K. 5062	P	,, ,, ,, ,, ,,	31.8	27.9	8.8	11.5	—	P. S. XXIV	18 P.	Middle or late
3	K. 5061	S	Lanchow	36.5	34.5	10.0	13.5	0.4	P. S. XXIV	18 P.	Middle or late
4	K. 5013	S	,,	45.8	42.5	14.8	13.0	—	P. S. XXIV	19 P.	Late
5	K. 5020	P	,,	40.7	38.0	13.5	11.4	—	P. S. XXIV	19 P.	,,
6	K. 5284	S	,,	37.0	36.5	10.5	11.5	0.6	P. S. XXIV	19 P.	,,
7	K. 5283	P	,,	32.1	29.0	10.2	9.9	—	P. S. XXIV	19 P.	,,

Fig. 1. Vessel with a high neck, which has two ears at the rim. The ears have dentated edges but no holes. Two handles.

The ware is reddish brown. The surface smooth and polished.

The décor, in black and very dark violet, starts at the lower end with a black border consisting of a wavy band below and a straight horizontal band above. Where the neck begins is a violet horizontal band and beneath that a black upper border, dentated along the upper edge. Between these borders the surface of the mantle is divided into six fields filled with chessboard patterns. The exterior of the neck has the same décor as fig. 3.

Fig. 2. Vessel with a high neck which has two small, purely decorative ears dentated along the edge and without holes. Two handles.

The ware is light brownish red. The surface polished.

The décor is in black and reddish violet of good quality.

Fig. 3. Vessel with a high neck having two slightly different ears with dentated edges and only an indication of a hole. Two handles.

The ware is reddish brown. The surface smooth, slightly polished.

The décor is in black and bluish violet, the former colour predominating.

Fig. 4. Vessel with a neck of medium height and without ears. Two handles.

The ware is light, greyish-reddish brown. The surface is carefully smoothed, but unpolished. There is concentric striation on the neck.

The décor is in black with a brown tint and red with a violet tint. The interior of the neck is edged with a narrow, black band of garlands.

Fig. 5. Vessel of an advanced shape, akin to that of the Ma Chang vessels. The vessel has a neck of medium height and without ears. Two handles.

The ware is greyish, with a slight tinge of red. The outer surface is polished. There is a distinct concentric striation on the upper part of the neck.

The décor is in black and reddish violet. The inside of the neck has a line of garlands, the interior of these garlands being ornamented with vertical lines.

Fig. 6. Vessel of a highly advanced shape and in form approaching that of the Ma Chang style, neck of medium height and without ears. Two handles.

The ware is a fairly light brown. The surface is smooth and polished. At the top, on the collar, concentric striation is distinctly visible.

The décor is in black, with a brown tone, and dark red.

Fig. 7. An advanced vessel with a fairly high neck without ears. Two handles.

The ware is greyish, with a slight tinge of red. The outer surface is highly polished. Regular concentric striation is seen on the upper part of the neck.

The décor is in black and reddish violet. On the inner side of the neck is a wreath of plain black garlands.

PALÆONTOLOGIA SINICA. SER. D. VOL. III. FASC. 1.

PALMGREN: Kansu mortuary urns.

Pl. XVIII.

PLATE. XIX

PLATE XIX.

Painted vessels of the Pan Shan style, Yang Shao period, bought in Kansu and, in one case, in Paris. (¹/₄ of natural size.)

Fig.	No.	Preserved in	Provenience	Height cm.	Diam. of Body cm.	Diam. of Mouth cm.	Diam. of Bottom cm.	Thickness of the ware cm.	Form type	Décor Fam.	Style
1	K. 5206	P	Ti Tao Hsien, Yang Chia Yai	8.0	—	13.5	6.5	—	P. S. II	Indiv. déc. P.	Early
2	K. 5205	P	Ning Ting Hsien, Wa Kuan Tsui	8.5	—	16.5	8.3	—	P. S. II	Indiv. déc. P. (1 P.)	,,
3—4	K. 5738	S	,, ,, ,, ,, ,, ,,	10.0	17.5	16.5	7.0	—	P. S. XXXIV	Indiv. déc. P. (1 P.)	,,
5	K. 5218	S	,, ,, ,, ,, ,, ,,	8.0	18.6	17.5	8.0	0.5	P. S. II	Indiv. déc. P.	—
6	K. 5495	S	,, ,, ,, ,, ,, ,,	10.5	19.8	19.0	9.5	0.5	P. S. II	,, ,, ,,	Early or middle
7	K. 5472	S	,, ,, ,, Pan Shan area	14.8	—	—	—	0.5	P. S. XL	,, ,, ,,	Middle
8	K. 5473	S	,, ,, ,, ,, ,, ,,	12.5	—	—	—	1.0	P. S. XL	,, ,, ,,	—
9	K. 11038:5	S	Paris	13.0	—	—	—	—	P. S. XL	—	—
10	K. 5356	P	Lanchow	10.4	11.2	7.0	5.3	0.4	P. S. XXXII	Indiv. déc. P.	Late
11	K. 5357	S	,,	9.8	11.8	7.5	5.6	0.3	P. S. XXXII	,, ,, ,,	,,
12	K. 5623	S	,,	15.6	18.0	10.0	8.5	0.6	P. S. XV	,, ,, ,,	,,

Fig. 1. Bowl without handles.
The ware is coarse, of a pale brownish red. The bowl is decorated on the inside only. There are two colours, both of fairly poor quality, the one greyish black, the other very dark violet. A violet cross forms the décor, its arms meeting in the centre of the bottom and continuing up the sides to the rim. In the angles between the arms of the cross are black lines likewise forming angles and dentated along the edges nearest to the violet arms. Inside the angles is a filling of close-meshed trelliswork, also in black.

Fig. 2. Bowl without handles.
The ware is a soft brownish red. Surface rough.
Décor, on the inside only, in black and dark red.

Figs. 3, 4. Bowl with a short spout and one annular and two ridged handles.
The ware is a fairly light, warm reddish brown. The interior surface is smoother than the exterior. The rings of which the vessel is built up are clearly visible.
The décor is in black and violet blue.

Fig. 5. Bowl without handles.
The ware is of a light brick-colour. The surface rough. The rim shows concentric striation.
Only the inside is decorated. The cross is in dark reddish violet, the network in black.

Fig. 6. Bowl without handles.
The ware is of a pale brownish red brick-colour. The surface not very smooth and not polished.
The décor is in greyish black and dark violet. On the exterior of the vessel, just above the bottom, is a broad thin black mark shaped like a Z. At the upper end not far from the rim are a number of irregular violet spots that have run down from the violet-coloured rim. On the interior is a broad T-shaped violet band; the rest of the décor is in black. A human skeleton forms the most significant décor.

Fig. 7. Lid (?) in the shape of a human head.
The ware is a brownish red brick-colour. The inner surface has a stronger tone. The outer surface is fairly smooth and polished. One can very easily see that the head is built up in rings, which are particularly distinct on the inside of and beneath the head. On the exterior of the head are visible the marks of an ear, which has now disappeared, and of two horns or plaits projecting from the front of the head. The parts that have disappeared were once pressed against the smooth surface of the head, in which however no depressions or furrows were made for their attachment (Cf. Plate XXXII : 5).

PALÆONTOLOGIA SINICA. SER. D. VOL. III. FASC. 1.

PALMGREN: Kansu mortuary urns.

Pl. XIX.

A. BÖRTZELLS TRYCKERI A.B. STHLM.

The points on the disc below are cut out of the wet clay prior to colouring and baking. The face was originally terminated at the sides by a pair of ears with notched edges and large holes in their centres. Mouth and eyes are represented by holes pierced in the shape of horizontal slits.

The décor, in black with a brown tint and dark violet, is very closely related to that of the common Pan Shan pots. It seems as if the disc was simply cut out of the upper part of a vessel. It has the same vaulting and it seems possible, to judge from the colours of the points of the disc, that they have been cut out of an already painted pot with a somewhat primitive spiral design.

Fig. 8. Lid (?) in the shape of a human head.

The ware is of a brownish red brick-colour, but the outer surface has a stronger tone and is fairly smooth and slightly polished. The method of construction is clearly discernible. There have been two horns on a small base, now broken off just above where they were fastened on to the head. The face has weaker and more feminine features than that in fig. 7.

The décor is in black and reddish violet. The breast-portion gives the impression of having been cut out of the upper part of the mantle of a pot decorated with a spiral pattern.

Fig. 9. Lid (?) in the shape of a human head.

The ware is that usually found in Pan Shan, brownish red brick-colour with a somewhat paler surface. The construction in rings is very easily discernible. On the sides of the face are five small ear-shaped projections dentated along the edge, forming eyebrows, ears (pierced with holes) and a beard (likewise pierced with a hole). On the front of the skull is a pair of hornlike projections with drilled round, deep, vertical canals, which do not entirely penetrate the wall of the head. Between the horns, but slightly further back, there starts a meanderlike band, raised in high relief, obviously representing a snake, which terminates at the front end in a head with open jaws, the other end coiling over nape and neck and terminating in a tail on the rear edge of the disc. The points of the star-shaped breast-portion were fashioned in the wet clay prior to painting.

Fig. 10. Vessel with two handles, a fairly high neck and a narrow mouth.

The ware is light brownish. The surface smooth, slightly polished.

The décor is in black and reddish violet. On the borderline of the neck is a violet band. The décor of the surface of the mantle is black. The rim and the points on the exterior of the neck are black. On the interior of the neck is a décor of garlands consisting of black curves, three or four in each festoon. The décor is here painted "anti-clockwise", i. e. from left to right. Insufficient space is allowed for the last festoon.

Fig. 11. Vessel with two handles and a high neck with a fairly wide mouth. The handles are ornamented down their centres with imposed strips.

The ware is light-coloured, brown. The surface smooth and polished. Concentric striation towards the top of the neck.

The décor is in black and dark reddish violet. There is a dentated edge round the inside rim of the neck. Below this, on the interior surface of the neck, a violet horizontal band with a black line of garlands below it.

Fig. 12. Vessel with a fairly wide mouth and a large annular handle.

The ware is a dark orange brown. The surface smooth and highly polished (presumably varnished at some more recent period).

The décor, in black and dirty violet, starts at the lower end with a violet band. At the upper end the décor on the mantle terminates in a black horizontal band. Between these bands there is a black trellis-work pattern with four black circular surfaces containing flowery patterns in ground colour and violet, with a black trellis-work pattern in the centre. Round the top of the neck, outside, is a band of black triangles pointing downwards. The rim of the neck is black. Inside the neck is a band of garlands composed of five festoons. Each of these festoons consists of two or three narrow lines, the upper or middle one violet, the rest black.

PLATE. XX

PLATE XX.

Painted vessels of the Pan Shan style, Yang Shao period, bought or excavated in Kansu; figs. 2, 3 bought in Paris.

(Figs. 1—3, 7, 9, 11, 12 = 1/6, fig. 8 = 1/3, figs. 4—6, 10 = 2/9 of natural size.)

Fig.	No.	Preserved in	Provenience	Height cm.	Diam. of Body cm.	Diam. of Mouth cm.	Diam. of Bottom cm.	Thickness of the ware at the neck. cm.	Form type	Décor Fam.	Style
1	K. 5505	P	Ning Ting Hsien, Wa Kuan Tsui	23.7	31.8	5.5	9.5	0.4	P.S. XXXVII	1 P.	Early
2—3	—		Bought in Paris. Belongs to Mr. A. Hellström, Mölndal, Sweden	33.0	38.7	17.0	13.0	0.5	P.S. XXXVI	10 P.	Middle
4—5	K. 5103	S	Lanchow	13.0	15.7	3.2	7.7	0.4	P.S. XXXVIII	Indiv. déc. P.	Early
6	K. 5608	P	Kao Lan Hsien, Kao Ying	9.8	13.0	5.6	6.8	0.5	P. S:r: VII	—	—
7	K. 5451	S	Lanchow	11.2	16.0	7.0	7.0	0.5	P. S:r: I	Relief 3	—
8	K. 5458	P	T'ien Shui Hsien, Yang Chia Po	9.0	9.0	6.5	5.0	0.4	P. S:r: IV	Relief 3	—
9	K. 5444	P	Lanchow	17.0	19.0	10.4	10.0	—	P. S:r: II	Relief 3	—
10	K. 5454	S	Yü Chung Hsien	14.3	13.5	10.0	8.0	0.5	P. S:r: V	Relief 2	—
11	K. 5791	S	Ning Ting Hsien, Pien Chia Kou, The big tomb, Pot 11	18.8	21.3	11.5	9.5	0.5	P. S:r: III	Relief 3	—
12	K. 5796	S	Ning Ting Hsien, Pien Chia Kou, The big tomb, Pot 12	24.0	26.7	14.5	10.3	0.8	P. S:r: III	Relief 1	—

Fig. 1. Vessel with a broken spout and with two handles, each divided into three lobes. Five ears pierced with holes and notched edges are placed horizontally on the borderline between roof and body.

The ware is of a light brownish-yellow brick-colour. The surface smooth and polished.

The décor is in black and dark red.

Figs. 2, 3. Vessel with a low neck, two handles and two projections on the upper surface. They are shaped like a spout, which however is closed at the lower end by the external plane of the body's surface. Each of them has at the top two small diametrically opposed holes. Presumably the object of these projections has been either purely ornamental (e. g. to hold some kind of plumes of a perishable nature, which were fixed into the depressions in the cups and fastened by a cord or sinew passed through the holes) or else they were used for attaching a lid. The form is unique.

The ware is brownish red. The surface of the mantle very smooth.

The décor is in black and reddish brown. The inside of the neck has had a décor, now destroyed.

Figs. 4, 5. Possibly a small chamber-pot for men. With a large spout. The vessel is presumably from a child's grave as its capacity is too small for an adult person. It possesses three ears set horizontally up on the sides of the vessel. These ears have a notched edge and a large hole in the centre. The spout also had originally two radial ears, but they are now partially broken off.

The ware is brownish grey. The surface not very smooth but slightly polished.

The décor is in black and red.

Fig. 6. Vessel with a spout and one handle.
The ware is brownish grey, the surface rough.
The vessel is entirely undecorated.

Fig. 7. Vessel with two ridge-shaped ears placed vertically and diametrically opposite to one another just below the low neck. The edges of the ears are notched. The narrow brim is also notched along the edge.

The ware is rough and of a warm grey colour. The surface is granulated. The method of building up the vessel with rings can be distinctly seen from the inside.

The vessel is decorated in relief, narrow notched bands being applied, which by throwing shadows into the furrows produce a dark effect against a light ground. The notching of the bands is in complete accord with that of the brim and the ears.

PALÆONTOLOGIA SINICA. SER. D. VOL. III. FASC. 1.

PALMGREN: Kansu mortuary urns. Pl. XX.

Fig. 8. Vessel with a fairly low neck. A large handle has been attached partly to the neck and partly to the body.

The ware is black to dark brown. The whole of the outside and part of the mouth are sooty. The surface is granulated.

Décor in relief.

Fig. 9. Vessel with a low neck and four small annular handles.

The ware is light grey with a brownish grey surface, which is rough.

Décor in relief.

Fig. 10. Vessel with a very low neck and two large annular handles.

The ware is rough, of a dirty grey colour with darker spots. The surface is uneven.

Décor in relief.

Fig. 11. Vessel with a low neck.

The ware is greyish, sometimes with a lighter grey and sometimes with brownish spots. The surface rough and irregular.

The décor, in relief, is very weak and irregular and represents a highly rudimentary and degenerate style.

Fig. 12. Vessel with a low neck.

The ware is grey—greyish brown, with darkish spots on it. The surface is uneven.

Décor in relief.

PLATE. XXI

PLATE XXI.

Painted vessels of the Pan Shan style, Yang Shao period, bought or excavated in Kansu.
(Figs. 1, 3—1, 8, 10, 11 = ¹/₃, figs. 2, 9 = ³/₈, fig. 7 = ¹/₄ of natural size.)

Fig.	No.	Preserved in	Provenience	Height cm.	Diam. of Body cm.	Diam. of Mouth cm.	Diam. of Bottom cm.	Thickness of the ware at the neck. cm.	Form type	Décor Fam.	Style
1	K. 5460	S	Yü Chung Hsien	7.0	9.8	6.0	5.0	0.6	P. S:r : I	Relief 3	—
2	K. 5456	P	,, ,, ,,	9.7	11.5	7.0	6.3	0.4	P. S:r : I	Relief 3	—
3	K. 5607	S	Kao Lan Hsien, Kao Ying	11.0	12.7	6.2	6.0	0.4	P. S:r : VII	Relief 4	—
4	K. 5808	S	Ning Ting Hsien, P'ai Tzu P'ing, Sk. 2, Pot 1	11.2	11.2	7.5	6.0	0.5	P. S:r : IV	Relief 1	—
5—6	K. 5459	S	Lanchow	8.5	9.7	4.0	4.7	0.5	P. S:r : VII	Relief 4	—
7	K. 5448	S	,,	12.2	14.0	8.5	7.0	0.5	P. S:r : IV	Relief 3	—
8	K. 5457	P	Ning Ting Hsien, Wa Kuan Tsui	9.3	11.0	6.7	6.7	0.5	P. S:r : IV	Relief 1	—
9	K. 5455	S	,, ,, ,, Pan Shan	10.7	12.2	7.5	7.0	0.5	P. S:r : IV	Relief 2	—
10	K. 5790	S	,, ,, ,, Pien Chia Kou, The large tomb, Pot 9	10.8	12.2	8.5	6.0	0.6	P. S:r : IV	Relief 3	—
11	K. 5788	S	Ning Ting Hsien, Pien Chia Kou, The large tomb, Pot 10	10.5	10.5	9.8	6.0	0.4	P. S:r : IV	Relief 2	—

Fig. 1. Vessel with a low neck and two ears pierced with holes.
The ware is a light reddish grey.
Décor in relief.

Fig. 2. Vessel with a low neck and two horizontally attached ears, which have notched edges but are without holes.
The ware varies between reddish brown and brownish grey. The surface is rough and coarse-grained, and a great deal of it is black with soot.
Décor in relief.

Fig. 3. Vessel with one handle and a spout, quite similar to figs. 5, 6.
The ware is somewhat coarse, grains of mica and quartz being clearly visible. The surface is rough. The ware is red brick-colour toning into grey.
Décor in relief.

Fig. 4. Vessel with a low neck and a large handle.
The ware is grey to greyish brown. The surface is rough and contains large mineral grains. On the inside it is possible to see very distinctly the method of construction in rings.
Décor in relief.

Figs. 5, 6. Vessel with a spout and one handle.
The ware is somewhat coarse, grains of mica and quartz being clearly visible. The surface is rough. The ware is red brick-colour toning into grey.
Décor in relief.

Fig. 7. Vessel with a low neck and a large handle, now broken off.
The ware is coarse, of a dirty brownish grey. The surface is porous, with weak textile impressions.
Décor in relief.

Fig. 8. Vessel with a low neck and a large handle.
The ware is a somewhat dark greyish brown. The surface of the mantle between the two horizontal bands is rough and has weak textile impressions running in a vertical direction. The bottom surface is also rough and shows the impressions of a plaited mat.
Décor in relief.

Fig. 9. Vessel with a low neck and a large handle divided into two lobes.
The ware is rough, grey in colour and almost entirely crackled, that is to say, having a network of cracks (particularly on the basal surface). The surface is uneven.
Décor in relief.

PALÆONTOLOGIA SINICA. SER. D. VOL. III. FASC. 1.

PALMGREN: Kansu mortuary urns. Pl. XXI.

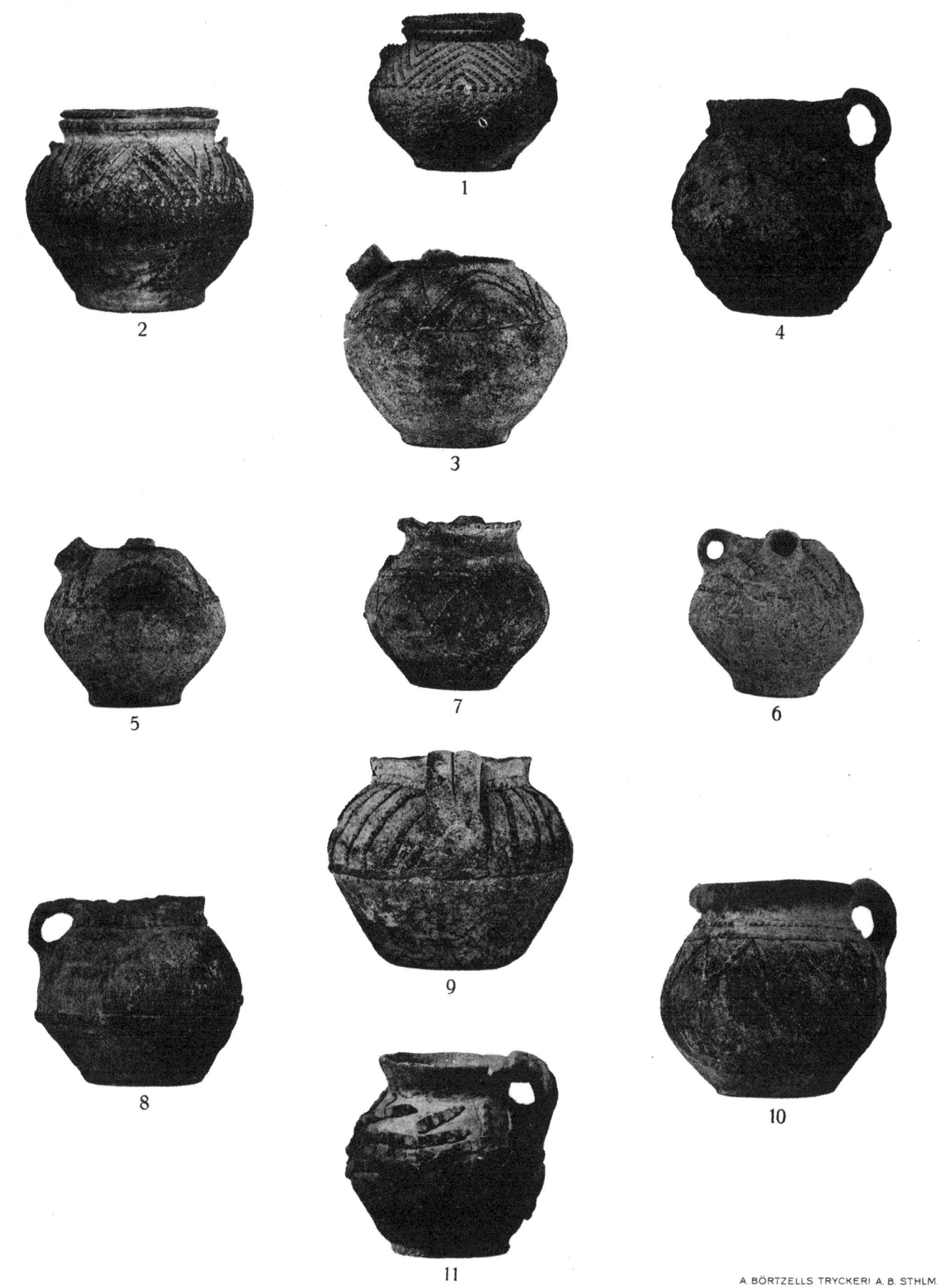

Fig. 10. Vessel with a low neck, a large handle and a rudimentary ear.

The ware is a rough, greyish brown, with spots of a warmer shade here and there. It is much blackened with soot.

Décor in relief.

Fig. 11. Vessel with a low neck and a large handle, consisting of three circular strips of clay twisted round one another.

The ware is greyish brown with spots of a warmer colour. The surface is uneven and somewhat rough.

Décor in relief. The cup is decorated with thick wavy bands somewhat irregularly placed, partly in a horizontal and partly in a vertical direction. They can hardly be said to form a definite pattern. The ornamentation is obviously quite degenerate.

PLATE. XXII

PLATE XXII.

Painted vessels of the Ma Chang style, bought in Kansu.
(¹/₆ of natural size.)

Fig.	No.	Preserved in	Provenience	Height cm.	Diam. of Body cm.	Diam. of Mouth cm.	Diam. of Bottom cm.	Thickness of the ware at the neck. cm.	Form type	Décor Fam.	Style
1	K. 5285	P	Lanchow	33.5	30.5	7.7	9.2	—	M. C. IX	IM. Subfam. I	Early
2	K. 5295	P	„	29.6	23.2	9.0	10.0	—	M. C. IX	IM. Subfam. I	„
3	K. 5297	S	„	25.3	24.4	9.0	10.5	0.5	M. C. IX	IM. Subfam. I	Early or middle
4	K. 5307	S	„	30.0	26.5	11.7	7.5	—	M. C. IX	IM. Subfam. II	Middle
5	K. 5303	S	Chin Hsien	30.5	30.0	7.0	10.0	—	M. C. VIII	IM. Subfam. III	„
6	K. 5289	P	Lanchow	39.4	34.8	6.7	11.6	—	M. C. IX	IM. Subfam. I	Late
7	K. 5300	P	„	38.0	33.8	11.5	10.3	—	M. C. IX	IM. Subfam. IV	„
8	K. 5466	S	„	39.0	40.0	12.0	12.5	—	M. C. VIII	IM. Subfam. IV	„

Fig. 1. Vessel the neck of which is broken off. Two handles.
The ware is hard-baked, of a reddish brown colour. The surface not very smooth, unpolished.
The décor is in dull greyish black and dark reddish violet. The band at the boundary of the neck and the inner half of the circular contours are violet, the rest of the décor is in black. The interior of the neck has also been decorated, but it is impossible to ascertain the nature of the décor from the small traces that have been preserved.
At least a couple of features in the ornamentation of this pot are reminiscent of the Pan Shan ornamentation, such as, for instance, the dentated edge on the black bands forming the upper border, and the rapid rhythm of the wavy band that forms part of the lower border.

Fig. 2. Vessel with a high neck and two handles.
The ware is a warm greyish brown. The surface is granulated and very uneven on the base.
The décor, in black with a brown tone and dirty reddish violet, starts at the lower end with a black band. Above, the décor on the mantle ends in a broad band, the lower half of which is black and the upper half red. The circles consist of an outer red and an inner black band. In the centre of the circles are small violet squares with black contours. The chessboard pattern is in black. The triangles on the neck are black, the band violet. On the interior of the neck a band of tooth-shaped spots encircles the rim.

Fig. 3. Vessel with a high neck and a hole in the middle of the bottom. Two handles.
The ware is rough, its colour brown. The surface is dull.
The décor, in two colours, black and dark red, starts at the lower end with a red horizontal band. Close to the border-line of the neck is a horizontal band, red above and black beneath. The four large circles consist of two concentric bands, the outer red, the inner black. The interior surfaces of two diametrically opposite circles have a similar decor, while the two adjacent circles are decorated quite differently. On the inner surfaces of the one pair there are short, broad crosses, consisting of five rhombic surfaces. The middle one of these rhombi is filled with zigzag bands, four in number, running obliquely from above downwards. The rest of the rhombi are filled with trelliswork. All the contours are thick and the pattern is executed entirely in black. The other pair of circles likewise contains a cross décor (see fig. 3). The cross has black contours and a red strip down the middle. From the arms of the cross extend, at right angles, rectangular surfaces, which are arranged along adjacent arms somewhat resembling dominoes. The rest of the décor in the circle is black. The bands around the circles are black. The network on the neck is black. The rim of the neck is painted black, with a dentated edge pointing inwards. Below this on the interior of the neck is a broad, red horizontal band, from which hangs a slender garland-band with small festoons. Each festoon consists of two black bows.

Fig. 4. Vessel with a neck of medium height and two handles.
The ware is greyish brown. The surface is smooth, though much scratched, and unpolished.
The décor is in two dull colours, black and blue. On the interior of the neck is a garland décor.

PALMGREN: Kansu mortuary urns.

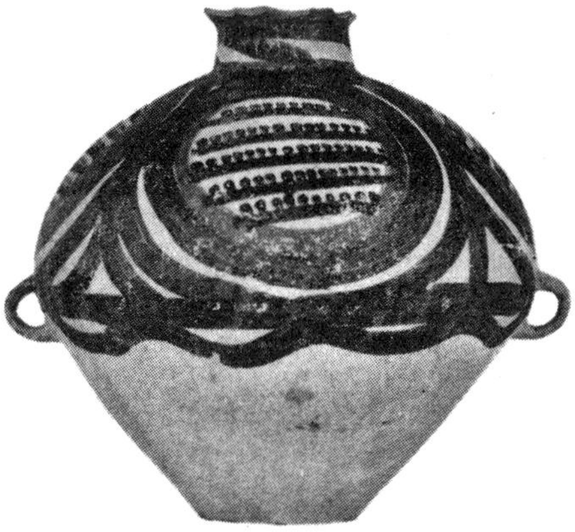

PALÆONTOLOGIA SINICA. SER. D. VOL. III. FASC. 1.

Pl. XXII.

Fig. 5. Vessel with a low neck and two handles.

The ware is a light, warm brown, the surface smooth.

The décor is in black and dark reddish violet. The black paint has a grainy surface, and is dull and greyish.

On the brim and the interior of the neck a red and black band, from the lower red part of which there hangs a garland-décor.

Fig. 6. Vessel with a high neck and two handles.

The ware is a warm brown. The surface polished but not very smooth, having a number of scratches and pits in it.

The décor is in black and very dark red. The interior of the neck is ornamented with three bands, the middle one black and the two others red. Below that décor are three cowrie patterns.

Fig. 7. Vessel with a high neck and two handles.

The ware is reddish brown, the surface much pitted.

The inside of the neck has a black dentated band round the rim, below that a red band, and beneath that again a row of black angles pointing left.

The décor is in two colours, black and dark reddish violet.

Fig. 8. Vessel with low neck and two handles.

The ware is a light reddish brown. The surface is slightly striated in different directions.

The décor is in brownish black and red, both dull. On the unpainted basal surface there are three slanting black lines on one side. The wavy and straight bands below are red and the contours of the circles consist of a red band surrounded by two black bands. The rest of the décor is black. The interior of the neck has a row of narrow black dots at the rim and below these a narrow black horizontal band, from which is suspended a band of garlands. The actual rim of the neck is decorated with a narrow red band.

PLATE. XXIII

PLATE XXIII.

Painted vessels of the Ma Chang style, bought in Kansu.
(¹/₄ of natural size.)

Fig.	No.	Preserved in	Provenience	Height cm.	Diam. of Body cm.	Diam. of Mouth cm.	Diam. of Bottom cm.	Thickness of the ware at the neck. cm.	Form type	Décor Fam.	Style
1	K. 5755	S	Lanchow	27.9	26.0	9.0	9.0	—	M. C. IX	1 M. Subfam. I	Early
2	K. 5777	S	,,	20.0	19.0	8.3	9.3	0.5	M. C. XX	1 M. Subfam. I	—
3	K. 5311	P	,,	22.0	21.0	7.0	8.5	—	M. C. IX	1 M. Subfam. II	Middle
4	K. 5504	P	Yü Chung Hsien	23.0	22.5	8.0	6.4	—	M. C. IX	1 M. Subfam. II	,,
5	K. 5981	P	Nien Po Hsien, Mi La Kou, Hei T'ou Chuan	22.7	23.0	6.2	8.5	—	M. C. VIII	1 M. Subfam. IV	,,
6	K. 5979	S	Nien Po Hsien, Ma P'ai Tzu	35.3	27.8	6.5	11.0	—	M. C. IX	1 M.	—
7	K. 5976	S	Chin Hsien, Yeh Chi Kou, Pei P'o	24.8	22.0	10.5	9.4	—	M. C. IX	1 M. Subfam. IV	Middle
8	K. 5980	S	Nien Po Hsien, Ma P'ai Tzu	27.5	22.0	10.0	11.0	—	M. C. IX	1 M.	—

Fig. 1. Vessel with a high neck and two handles.
The ware is a hard-baked greyish brown. The surface of the vessel is smooth and polished.
The décor is in black and dark red, both colours covering the surface well. On the interior of the neck a garland décor consisting of 3—4 narrow black lines.

Fig 2. Vessel with a high neck, one annular handle and one rudimentary ridge handle.
The ware is brown, coarse but hard. The surface not very smooth.
The décor is in two thin colours, black and brownish red. The interior edge of the neck is ornamented with a narrow band of points facing downwards.

Fig. 3. Vessel with a high neck and two handles.
The ware is brownish grey, hard-baked. The surface is considerably scratched, on the mantle usually in a vertical direction, on the base in an oblique horizontal direction.
The décor is in black and dark rose. The black colour has a greyish tone. The interior of the neck has a garland décor in black, each garland consisting of two narrow lines.

Fig. 4. Vessel with a high neck and two handles.
The ware is a fairly light reddish brown colour. The surface not very smooth, unpolished.
The décor is in black and brownish red. The colours are indistinct. The interior of the neck has at the top a garland-like décor in a square setting round the mouth. Each garland is formed of two bands.

Fig. 5. Vessel with a low neck and two handles.
The ware is light reddish brown, the surface not very smooth and unpolished.
The décor is in black and a somewhat thin, brownish red tone. The interior of the neck is decorated at the top round the rim with vertical black lines, below them a black horizontal band, quite narrow, and below that again a broader, red vertical band.

Fig. 6. Vessel with a narrow mouth and two large handles.
The ware is a reddish brown brick-colour, the surface smooth and polished. Slight striation is visible on the inside of the neck.
The décor is in three colours, viz. a white paint covering the whole of the bottom and the base, as well as the lowest part of the mantle, a dark whortleberry-red paint covering the entire neck and the mantle surface, and finally a black paint for the decorative patterns. The red paint covers the white paint on the lower part of the mantle. The interior of the neck has been painted, the décor consisting of a black band with round spots in ground colour.

Fig. 7. Vessel with a high neck and two handles.
The ware is reddish brown, the surface smooth and unpolished. The collar round the neck is striated at the top.

PALÆONTOLOGIA SINICA. SER. D. VOL. III. FASC. 1.

PALMGREN: Kansu mortuary urns.

Pl. XXIII.

The décor in black and dark red. The black paint is somewhat granulated and therefore looks dull and greyish. The interior of the neck is decorated round the rim with a black band containing a row of small round surfaces in ground colour. Beneath this band is a red band, which merges into the black one. Below the red band is a simplified décor of garlands consisting of a single line (black).

Fig. 8. Vessel with a high neck and two handles.

The ware is light brown, with a warm red tone. The surface is very irregular, uneven and scratched. On the handles are curious oblong and rectangular impressions. The vessel seems on the whole to be primitive.

The décor is in a blue-black tone. The paint is rough and dull. The décor is very primitive, indeed it is unskillfully done; in one place, for instance, the paint has run down on to the base, where a long narrow splash has formed. The interior of the neck is decorated with a very poorly executed décor consisting of a single band of garlands.

PLATE. XXIV

PLATE XXIV.

Painted vessels of the Ma Chang style, bought or excavated in Kansu.
(Figs. 1, 2, 4—9 = ¹/₆, fig. 3 = ²/₉ of natural size.)

Fig.	No.	Preserved in	Provenience	Height cm.	Diam. of Body cm.	Diam. of Mouth cm.	Diam. of Bottom cm.	Thickness of the ware at the neck. cm.	Form type	Décor Fam.	Style
1	K. 5304	P	Lanchow	40.5	39.0	13.7	11.5	—	M. C. VIII	1M.Subfam.V	Late
2	K. 5288	S	„	41.0	39.5	14.2	11.4	—	M. C. VIII	1M.Subfam.V	„
3	K. 5294	S	„	20.5	20.0	5.3	9.2	—	M. C. VII	2 M.	„
4	K. 5990	S	Nien Po Hsien, Ma Chang Yen	32.5	29.5	14.0	10.0	—	M. C. IX	2 M.	Early or Middle
5	K. 5308	P	Lanchow	32.9	23.5	8.7	9.2	—	M. C. IX	2 M.	Middle
6	K. 5786	S	„	33.8	32.0	12.0	10.0	—	M. C. VIII	2 M.	Late
7	K. 5787	S	„	38.0	35.0	13.0	10.5	—	M. C. VIII	2 M.	„
8	K. 5301	P	Nien Po Hsien, Ma Chang Yen	39.0	36.5	13.3	11.5	—	M. C. VIII	2 M.	„
9	K. 5309	S	Lanchow	25.0	26.5	15.0	9.5	—	M. C. VIII	2 M. (4 M.)	„

Fig. 1. Vessel with a low neck and two handles.

The ware is reddish brown, the surface fairly smooth, unpolished. On one side is a dent. The collar is striated both on the inside and on the outside.

The décor is in black and reddish violet. The interior of the neck is decorated with a row of black radial lines round the edge of the brim, and beneath them a red horizontal line. From this is suspended a garland décor consisting of three black bands in each bow.

Fig. 2. Vessel with a low neck and two handles.

The ware is reddish brown. In spite of the stiff shape the surface is not very smooth, being much pitted and in places having corrugations. The collar is distinctly striated both on the inside and on the outside. On the basal surface there are a few indistinct and small brand-marks.

The décor, in black and a very dark reddish violet colour, starts with two black bands, the lower one wavy, the upper one straight. The band at the top, which also covers the lowest portion of the neck, is composed of two strips, the lower one black and the upper one red. The four circles have a circumference of two strips, the outer black and the inner red. The patterns on the circular surface are black. Round the inside rim of the neck are narrow, black, radial dabs. Below these is a red band, from which is suspended a garland pattern. Each garland consists of two black bands.

Fig. 3. Vessel with a high neck, partly broken off, and one handle.

The ware is a light reddish brown. The surface polished.

The décor is in red, which covers the whole surface of the mantle and the outside of the neck, and black for the decorative patterns.

Fig. 4. Vessel with a fairly high neck, partly broken off, and two handles.

The ware is reddish brown. The surface not very even.

The décor is in one colour, varying between black and dark brown. On the mantle and on the collar there is, besides, a brown venation.

Fig. 5. Vessel with a fairly high neck and two handles (Cf. Plate XXV: 1).

The ware is a light reddish brown. The surface is not very smooth and is dented.

The décor is in two colours, a brownish red slip over the entire surface of the mantle, and black for the decorative pattern. The interior of the neck has a décor now partially worn away, but originally consisting of a horizontal band, from which is suspended a simple garland décor.

Fig. 6. Vessel with a fairly low neck and two handles.

The ware is greyish brown with fair-sized red patches. The surface is polished, thought somewhat uneven.

The décor is in dark violet brown. On the middle of the bottom is a black cross. The interior of the neck is decorated with a broad horizontal band at the top round the brim.

PALÆONTOLOGIA SINICA. SER. D. VOL. III. FASC. 1.

PALMGREN: Kansu mortuary urns.
Pl. XXIV.

Fig. 7. Vessel with a low neck and two handles.

The ware is reddish brown, of a quite light colour. The surface smooth, the collar of the neck striated.

The décor is in black and dark violet red. The colours are dull, the black paint being somewhat greyish. The interior of the neck is decorated with a row of radially drawn black dashes. Round the edge, beneath them, is a red horizontal band, and suspended from it a black garland décor consisting of three black lines.

Fig. 8. Vessel with a low neck and two handles.

The ware is brown, the surface smooth, unpolished.

The décor is in black and greyish violet, both colours dull. The interior of the neck was originally decorated with narrow, black vertical dashes round the rim, and beneath them a violet horizontal band, from which was suspended a décor of garlands consisting of single black lines.

Fig. 9. Vessel with a low neck and two handles.

The ware is reddish brown, the surface smooth and unpolished.

The décor is in very dark red and black. The surface of the black paint is granulated and greyish. The interior of the neck is decorated with a narrow row of dentations round the edge of the rim (in black). Below this is a broad red horizontal band and below that, on the lower part of the inside of the mouth, a black horizontal band. From this project oblique black bands, which slope to the right and eventually meet the red horizontal band above them.

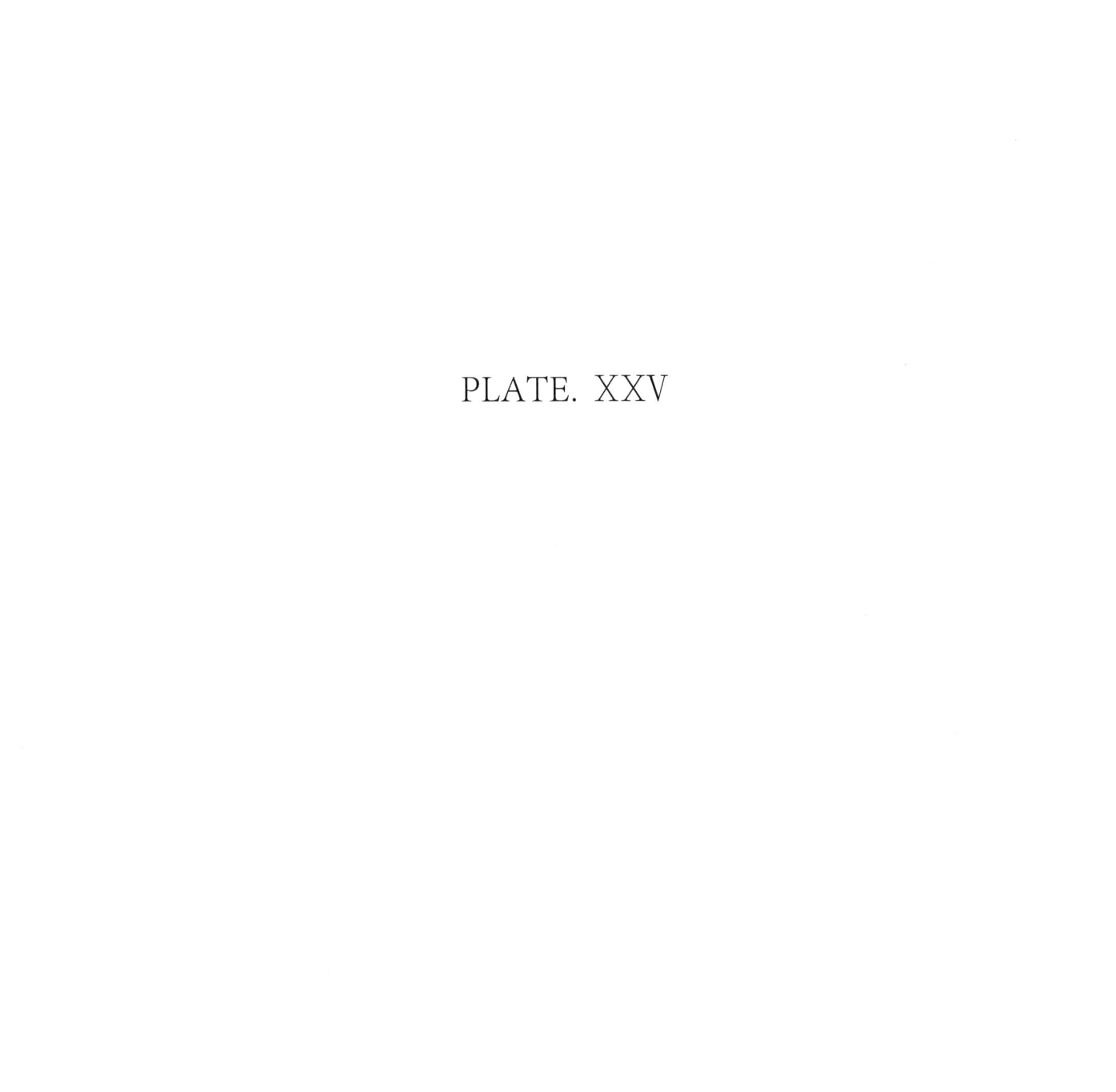

PLATE. XXV

PLATE XXV.

Painted vessels of the Ma Chang style, bought in Kansu.
(Figs. 1, 3, 4, 6—8, 10 = $^1/_4$, figs. 2, 5 = $^2/_9$, fig. 9 = $^3/_8$ of natural size.)

Fig.	No.	Pre-served in	Provenience	Height cm.	Diam. of Body cm.	Diam. of Mouth cm.	Diam. of Bottom cm.	Thickness of the ware at the neck. cm.	Form type	Décor Fam.	Style
1	K. 5308	P	Lanchow	32.9	23.5	8.7	9.2	—	M. C. IX	2 M.	Middle
2	K. 5298	P	"	30.0	26.0	10.7	9.0	—	M. C. IX	2 M.	Middle or late
3	K. 5333	S	"	11.0	13.0	9.0	6.3	0.4	M. C. XIV	5 M.	Early
4	K. 5946	S	Chin Hsien, Hsia K'o, Ya Tzu Tsui	13.5	14.5	10.5	6.5	0.5	M. C. XIV	5 M.	Early or middle
5	K. 5362	P	Lanchow	13.4	13.9	11.0	5.5	0.5	M. C. XIV	5 M. — 3 M.	Early
6	K. 5330	P	"	17.8	18.5	10.7	8.0	0.4	M. C. XIV	15 M.	Late
7	K. 5342	S	"	12.4	14.0	11.6	6.5	0.5	M. C. XIV	3 M.	Early
8	K. 5377	P	Ti Tao Hsien, Chan Chuang	8.0	9.3	8.0	4.8	0.3	M. C. XIV	3 M.	—
9	K. 5360	S	Lanchow	8.3	9.1	7.8	6.3	0.6	M. C. IV	3 M.	—
10	K. 5363	P	Ti Tao Hsien, Shih Chia Wan	9.9	11.4	9.2	5.5	0.5	M. C. XIV	3 M.	—

Fig. 1. See plate XXIV fig. 5.

Fig. 2. Vessel with a high neck and two handles.
The ware is greyish brown, the surface fairly smooth.
The décor is in black with a greyish tone, here and there shifting to brown. The interior of the neck has a band round the rim and suspended from it a plain garland décor.

Fig. 3. Vessel with a low neck and two handles.
The ware is a dirty greyish brown. The surface somewhat uneven and dull. The neck is concentrically striated at the top.
The décor is in black and dark reddish violet. The inner rim of the neck is ornamented with a row of dentations close together. Below them on the inner surface of the neck is a broad violet horizontal band, from which is suspended a black garland décor of four festoons, each festoon consisting of two narrow arcs.

Fig. 4. Vessel with two handles (one of which is broken off) and a low neck.
The ware is reddish brown, spotty, rather dark. The surface is smooth and slightly polished. There is concentric striation on the neck.
The décor is in black and dark brownish red. The interior of the neck has three black horizontal bands at the top. There is a black cross in the middle of the handle.

Fig. 5. Vessel with two handles and a rather high neck.
The ware is grey to reddish brown. The surface is smooth, not polished. There is concentric striation on the neck.
The décor is in black and dark reddish violet. The handles are ornamented with black horizontal bands. On the interior of the neck is a broad horizontal band composed of a violet strip above and a black strip below. From this lower band is suspended a row of garlands in black.

Fig. 6. Vessel with two handles and a low neck.
The ware is reddish brown, hard and rather light in colour. The surface not very smooth, dull. Concentric striations at the top of the neck. The rings out of which the surface is welded together are distinctly visible on the base (Cf. Plate XXXIII: 6). Even the points of attachment of the handles at top and bottom are quite easily discernible.
The décor is a dull blue-black colour.

Fig. 7. Vessel with a rather high neck and two curved handles ornamented down their centres with imposed strips of clay showing a wavy surface.

PALÆONTOLOGIA SINICA. SER. D. VOL. III. FASC. 1.

PALMGREN: Kansu mortuary urns.

Pl. XXV.

The ware is a light greyish brown with spots of a warmer colour (a complete coating of slip): a reddish tone in the break. The surface is dull and fairly rough. There are concentric striations at the top of the neck.

The décor is in two dull colours, black and brownish red.

Fig. 8. Vessel with two handles and a high neck.

The ware is light greyish brown with a slip applied over a warmer-coloured inner surface. There is no such slip inside the vessel, which is a warm brownish red. The surface is smooth and dull. Concentric striations round the neck.

The décor is in black and dark reddish violet.

Fig. 9. Vessel with a large handle.

The ware is reddish brown. The surface smooth, not polished.

The décor is carried out in a dull black colour, with a brownish violet tone here and there. On the handle is a cross.

Fig. 10. Vessel with two handles and a high neck.

The ware is reddish brown, with greyer patches. The surface fairly smooth, not polished. On the neck are concentric striations.

The décor is in a brownish violet colour.

PLATE. XXVI

PLATE XXVI.

Painted vessels of the Ma Chang style, bought in Kansu.
(Figs. 1—3 = ¹/₃, figs. 4—9 = ¹/₆, fig. 10 = ²/₉ of natural size.)

Fig.	No.	Preserved in	Provenience	Height cm.	Diam. of Body cm.	Diam. of Mouth cm.	Diam. of Bottom cm.	Thickness of the ware at the neck. cm.	Form type	Décor Fam.	Style
1	K. 5359	S	Lanchow	8.1	8.7	7.5	4.5	0.5	M. C. XIV	3 M.	Late
2	K. 5354	S	Ti Tao Hsien, Shan Chuang	7.8	9.7	9.7	5.0	0.3	M. C. XIV	3 M.	Early
3	K. 5358	S	Lanchow	9.6	9.4	8.0	4.5	0.5	M. C. XIV	3 M.	Late
4	K. 5302	S	„	31.8	28.0	12.0	10.0	0.5	M. C. IX	3 M.	„
5	K. 5290	P	„	38.2	28.5	11.5	9.0	—	M. C. IX	4 M. (Indiv. déc.)	„
6	K. 5611	P	Yü Chung Hsien, Ting Yuan Chen	22.5	20.6	10.5	7.5	0.5	M. C. VI	4 M.	Middle or late
7	K. 5299	P	Lanchow	35.8	32.4	11.0	11.0	0.6	M. C. IX	4 M.	Late
8	K. 5754	P	„	25.2	24.2	10.5	8.2	0.6	M. C. IX	5 M.	Middle
9	K. 5293	P	„	32.5	24.0	11.8	10.8	0.7	M. C. IX	4 M.	Late
10	K. 5268	P	„	14.3	16.5	10.2	6.5	0.5	M. C. XIV	6 M. Subfam. II	„

Fig. 1. Vessel with two handles.
The ware is reddish brown, fairly light in colour. The surface not very smooth and not polished. The décor is in dull dark brown.

Fig. 2. Vessel with two handles.
The ware is a dirty yellowish brown colour. The surface smooth, dull. There are concentric striations on the upper part of the neck.
The décor is in black, but on the boundary of the neck is a violet band. On the rim of the neck are radially drawn black lines, and beneath them, on the interior surface of the neck, a violet horizontal band. Below this band is a row of small black angular spots pointing left.

Fig. 3. Vessel with two handles.
The ware is brown, rather dark in tone. The surface is smooth and slightly polished. There are concentric striations on the upper part of the neck.
The décor is in dark brown slip with violet-black ornamentation.

Fig. 4. Vessel with a high neck and two handles.
The ware is of a light brown colour. The surface fairly smooth and dull. The brim of the neck has concentric striations.
The décor is in black and very dark violet blue. The colours are very difficult to distinguish from one another.

Fig. 5. Vessel with a high neck and two handles.
The ware is greyish brown, in some places more the colour of red brick. The surface is smooth but not polished. There are striations on the edge of the neck.
The décor is in black, with a grainy, dull surface. The edge of the neck is ornamented with a row of unpainted halfmoon-shaped spots on a black band, and below that a simple garland decoration.

Fig. 6. Vessel with a high neck and one handle.
The ware is a light reddish brown. The surface uneven and dull.
There are concentric striations on the neck.
The décor is in black and violet. The inside of the neck has a black band, with spots in ground colour, and below that a violet band with a hanging garland décor.

Fig. 7. Vessel with a fairly low neck and two handles.
The ware is brown with redder patches. The surface smooth and somewhat dull.
The décor is in two dull colours, greyish black and violet. Round the inside of the mouth a garland décor. Each festoon consists of two black lines.

PALÆONTOLOGIA SINICA. SER. D. VOL. III. FASC. 1.

PALMGREN: Kansu mortuary urns.   Pl. XXVI.

Fig. 8. Vessel with a high neck and two handles.

The ware is of a fairly light brown colour. The surface smooth and dull. There are concentric striations on the neck.

The décor is in black and greyish violet. The décor on the inside of the neck is no longer decipherable.

Fig. 9. Vessel with a neck of medium height, and two handles.

The ware is brown, the surface fairly uneven, dull.

The décor is in black-blue on an orange-brown slip. On the base, between the two handles, is an ornament like the figure "4" turned upside down, painted in brown. On the upper surface of the brim is a broad band.

Fig. 10. Vessel with two handles.

The ware is brown, with paler and warmer patches. The surface smooth and slightly polished. Concentric striations on the neck.

The décor is in black and dark reddish brown. On the inside of the neck is a décor consisting of a black band with a zigzag line in ground colour and three series of black dots in a row.

PLATE. XXVII

PLATE XXVII.

Painted vessels of the Ma Chang style, bought in Kansu.
(¹/₄ of natural size.)

Fig.	No.	Preserved in	Provenience	Height cm.	Diam. of Body cm.	Diam. of Mouth cm.	Diam. of Bottom cm.	Thickness of the ware at the neck. cm.	Form type	Décor Fam.	Style
1	K. 5978	P	Nien Po Hsien, Mi La Kou, Hei T'ou Chuang	12.3	14.4	10.8	6.3	0.5	M. C. XIV	6 M. Subfam. I	Early
2	K. 5343	P	Lanchow	12.9	15.2	10.0	6.0	0.4	M. C. XIV	6 M. Subfam. I	,,
3	K. 5337	P	,,	13.5	15.3	10.3	7.5	0.5	M. C. XIV	6 M.	Late
4	K. 5369	P	,,	15.0	17.3	10.0	7.5	0.5	M. C. XIV	6 M. Subfam. III	—
5	K. 5340	P	,,	10.0	12.3	9.3	5.5	0.4	M. C. XIV	6 M. Subfam. IV	Late
6	K. 5483	S	,,	11.0	19.0	—	10.0	0.7	M. C. XII	6 M. Subfam. II	Middle
7	K. 5322	S	,,	13.3	15.4	10.5	6.0	0.5	M. C. XIV	6 M. Subfam. IV	Late
8	K. 5349	P	,,	12.5	13.0	7.3	6.8	0.4	M. C. XIV	7 M.	Middle
9	K. 5324	P	,,	13.7	16.2	9.6	6.5	0.4	M. C. XIV	7 M.	Early
10	K. 5323	P	,,	10.8	13.7	11.0	7.5	0.5	M. C. XIV	7 M.	,,
11	K. 5314	S	,,	17.4	20.2	9.3	8.5	0.6	M. C. XIV	7 M.	Late
12	K. 5316	S	,,	19.5	19.5	10.5	8.5	—	M. C. XV	7 M.	—

Fig. 1. Vessel having had two handles attached to the low neck, but they are now broken off.
The ware is brown with greyish and reddish patches. The surface is not very smooth and not polished. There are concentric striations on the neck, particularly in a couple of places where the handles have been attached.
The décor is in black and red. The décor with its rudimentary death-system represents an intermediary type between the Pan Shan and the Ma Chang styles.

Fig. 2. Vessel with a low neck and two handles ornamented down their centres with imposed strips of clay showing a wavy surface.
The ware is entirely covered with a light brown slip, but is redder beneath the surface. The surface is smooth but not polished. There are concentric striations at the top of the neck.
The décor is in black and red.

Fig. 3. Vessel with two handles and a low neck.
The ware is greyish brown. The surface smooth but not very highly polished. Concentric striations at the top of the neck.
The décor is in dull black against a dirty brown and somewhat shiny slip.

Fig. 4. Vessel with two handles and a low neck.
The ware is a dirty greyish brown. The surface is not very smooth and not polished. Concentric striations on the neck.
The décor is in black with a brown tone and violet. The violet paint covers the surface better than the black.

Fig. 5. Vessel with two handles and a low neck.
The ware is brown, fairly light in colour but with darker and warmer patches. The surface is fairly uneven and dull.
The décor is in a dull paint — black with a brownish-violet tone.

Fig. 6. Vessel with a wide mouth and two handles.
The ware is coarse and reddish brown. The surface is uneven, dull and granulated.
The décor is in black and dark brownish violet.

Fig. 7. Vessel with two handles and a high neck.
The ware is brownish red, fairly light in colour and clear. The surface smooth and dull.
The décor is in a dull black colour with a bluish grey tone on a reddish-brown slip.

PALÆONTOLOGIA SINICA. SER. D. VOL. III. FASC. 1.

PALMGREN: Kansu mortuary urns.

Pl. XXVII.

A. BÖRTZELLS TRYCKERI A. B. STHLM

Fig. 8. Vessel with a high neck and two handles on the centre of which are strongly marked wavy vertical bands.

The ware is coarse and now dark brown. The surface is not smooth and is dull.

The décor is in a dark colour, which is sometimes quite black and, where it is more thinly laid on, tones off into brown and violet. In the middle of the bottom is a scutiform mark.

Fig. 9. Vessel with two handles and a low neck.

The surface smooth and not polished. Concentric striations on the neck.

The décor is in black with a brown tone and dark brownish violet.

Fig. 10. Vessel with two handles and a medium-sized neck.

The ware is brown and coarse. The surface not very smooth but somewhat polished.

The décor is in dull black and dull reddish violet. On the bottom is a large x-shaped cross in violet.

Fig. 11. Vessel with two handles and a low neck.

The ware is greyish brown of a fairly dark tone. The surface smooth, slightly polished. Concentric striations on the neck.

As regards the décor see Plate XL:6.

Fig. 12. Vessel with a low neck and having had two large handles (one is broken off).

The ware is light brown. The surface is smooth and unpolished.

The décor is in dull black and a streaky brownish red, in parts quite brown and in parts more red.

PLATE. XXVIII

PLATE XXVIII.

Painted vessels of the Ma Chang style, bought in Kansu.
(¹/₄ of natural size.)

Fig.	No.	Preserved in	Provenience	Height cm.	Diam. of Body cm.	Diam. of Mouth cm.	Diam. of Bottom cm.	Thickness of the ware at the neck. cm.	Form type	Décor Fam.	Style
1	K. 5350	P	Lanchow	10.2	12.2	9.3	5.5	0.5	M. C. XIV	9 M.	Early or middle
2	K. 5376	S	„	9.3	11.9	8.7	5.7	0.3	M. C. XIV	9 M.	Early or middle
3	K. 5989	S	Mien Po Hsien. Ma P'ai Tzu	13.5	16.4	9.0	4.5	0.5	M. C. XIV	9 M.	Late
4	K. 5229	P	Lanchow	12.2	15.2	9.0	6.3	0.3	M. C. XIV	9 M.	„
5	K. 5262	S	„	19.2	19.4	11.5	7.0	0.5	M. C. XIV	9 M.	„
6	K. 5243	S	„	14.2	16.5	11.2	6.5	0.4	M. C. XIV	9 M.	„
7	K. 5372	P	„	13.6	15.2	9.0	5.6	0.4	M. C. XIV	9 M.	Middle
8	K. 5237	S	„	15.0	15.0	9.5	8.0	0.5	M. C. XIV	11 M.	Late
9	K. 5238	P	„	13.0	13.7	10.3	7.0	0.5	M. C. XIV	11 M.	„

Fig. 1. Vessel with two handles and a low neck.
The ware is a dirty greyish brown. The surface fairly smooth and dull. Concentric striations on the neck.
The décor is in dull black and dull dark violet.

Fig. 2. Vessel with two handles and a low neck.
The ware is dark reddish brown. The surface not very smooth and not polished. Concentric striations round the neck.
The décor is in a black-brown colour, often with a blue tone.

Fig. 3. Vessel with two handles and a low neck.
The ware is light brown with reddish patches. The surface is smooth and slightly polished.
The décor is in black and violet; the latter has now practically disappeared.

Fig. 4. Vessel with two handles and a low neck (Cf. Plate XXXIII : 4).
The ware is brown with patches of a sometimes reddish, sometimes yellowish brick-colour. The surface is smooth and slightly polished.
The décor is in dull black-blue and dull violet.

Fig. 5. Vessel with two handles and a low neck.
The ware is a light reddish brown with a paler-coloured slip. The surface smooth, dull.
The décor is in black with a brown tone. One or two drops of paint have dried on the unpainted base.

Fig. 6. Vessel with two handles and a low neck.
The ware is dark greyish brown, somewhat spotty. The surface fairly smooth and slightly polished. There are concentric striations on the top of the neck.
The décor is in blue-black on a dark reddish brown slip. On the bottom is an x-shaped cross, the one arm straight and short and the other arm s-shaped and longer.

Fig. 7. Vessel with two handles and a low neck.
The ware is dark brown. The surface smooth and dull.
The décor is in black and dark violet.

Fig. 8. Vessel with two handles and a low neck.
The ware is of a brownish colour. The surface not very smooth but slightly polished.

PALÆONTOLOGIA SINICA. SER. D. VOL. III. FASC. 1.

PALMGREN: Kansu mortuary urns.

Pl. XXVIII.

A. BÖRTZELLS TRYCKERI A. B. STHLM

The décor is in black and brown with a reddish tone. The brown colour serves a slip on the decorated portions of the vessel. On the handles is a vertical zigzag décor. The décor on the inside of the neck is very indistinct. One can just discern a horizontal band with triangular points along the top.

Fig. 9. Vessel with two handles and a low neck.

The ware is reddish brown and fairly coarse. The surface not very smooth and not polished.

The décor is in black and reddish brown, the latter colour being used as a slip on the decorated portions.

PLATE. XXIX

PLATE XXIX.

Painted vessels of the Ma Chang style, bought or excavated in Kansu.
(Figs. 1, 6, 7 = $1/3$, figs. 2—5, 8, 9, 12, 13 = $1/4$ and figs. 10—11 = $2/5$ of natural size.)

Fig.	No.	Preserved in	Provenience	Height cm.	Diam. of Body cm.	Diam. of Mouth cm.	Diam. of Bottom cm.	Thickness of the ware at the neck. cm.	Form type	Décor Fam.	Style
1	K. 5693	S	Nien Po Hsien, Ma Chang Yen. Loc. 4. Sk. 1. Pot 2	11.3	11.0	9.4	5.3	0.4	M. C. XIV	13 M.	Late
2	K. 5375	P	Lanchow	10.2	10.6	9.5	5.5	0.5	M. C. XIV	13 M.	”
3	K. 5137	S	”	11.0	14.4	8.5	6.5	0.6	M. C. XIV	12 M.	”
4	K. 5319	P	”	12.2	15.5	9.2	6.5	0.3	M. C. XIV	12 M.	Middle
5	K. 5326	P	”	13.8	16.0	9.5	6.6	0.5	M. C. XIV	15 M.	Late
6	K. 5776	S	Kao Lan Hsien, 80 li S. Chi Tao Liang	11.0	13.0	7.2	8.0	0.4	M. C. X	Indiv. déc. M.	”
7	K. 5381	S	Lanchow	9.0	—	11.0	6.7	0.4	M. C. XVI	16 M.	—
8	K. 5379	P	”	8.6	—	15.7	11.0	0.5	M. C. XVI	16 M.	—
9	K. 5382	S	”	5.0	—	17.0	9.5	0.6	M. C. I	16 M.	Late
10—11	K. 5380	P	”	10.0	—	12.0	7.0	0.5	M. C. XVI	16 M.	”
12—13	K. 5616	P	Nien Po Hsien, Ma Chang Yen. Loc. 4. Sk. 2. Pot. 2	7.0	—	18.7	7.0	0.5	M. C. II	16 M.	”

Fig. 1. Vessel with two large handles and a high neck.
The ware is a brownish red brick-colour, coarse and grainy. The surface is smooth but not polished.
The décor is in black violet on a thin brown slip. The black violet colour is dull, the slip shiny.

Fig. 2. Vessel with two large handles and a medium-sized neck.
The ware is coarse and reddish brown. The surface rather uneven and dull. On the inside the joints between the rings of which the pot has been built up are very clearly discernible. (Cf. Plate XXXIII: 5.)
The décor is in blue black and dark yellowish brown.

Fig. 3. Vessel with two handles and a high neck.
The ware is a light brownish red brick-colour. The surface is smooth and slightly polished.
The décor consists of a black-blue design against a slightly reddish brown slip, which covers only the upper part of the vessel above the basal surface.

Fig. 4. Vessel with two handles and a low neck.
The ware is reddish brown. The surface smooth but not polished. Concentric striations on the neck.
The décor is in two dull colours, black and dark reddish violet.

Fig. 5. Vessel with two handles and a low neck.
The ware is brick-red with paler patches. The surface not very smooth, dull. Concentric striations on the neck.
The décor is in black violet.

Fig. 6. Vessel with one handle and a low neck.
The ware is light greyish brown, hard-baked and composed of fairly coarse grains. The surface not very smooth, dull and covered with a light-coloured slip.
The décor is in black and brownish violet.

Fig. 7. Dish on a ring-shaped foot having two holes diametrically opposite to one another.
The ware is a fairly light greyish brown. The surface not very smooth.
The décor is in two dull colours, black and brownish red, the latter colour for the most part having the tone of a somewhat thin transparent coating. Only the upper surface of the dish is decorated. The border is black, the swastika is red with black contours.

PALÆONTOLOGIA SINICA. SER. D. VOL. III. FASC. 1.

PALMGREN: Kansu mortuary urns. Pl. XXIX.

Fig. 8. Dish on a foot.
The ware is dark brown. The surface not very smooth. Concentric striations on the dish.
The trellis pattern on the upper surface of the dish is black. Otherwise the vessel is unpainted.

Fig. 9. Dish with a fairly large bottom, the sides sloping upwards and outwards, and a narrow horizontal edge at the top.
The ware is greyish brown. The surface somewhat uneven, dull and rough.
The décor is in dark reddish brown and black, the latter colour somewhat thin.

Figs. 10—11. Dish on a foot having two holes diametrically opposite to one another.
The ware is a fairly light greyish brown. The surface not very smooth.
The décor is in two dull colours, black and brownish red, the latter colour for the most part being a somewhat thin transparent coating.

Figs. 12—13. Dish.
The ware is brownish red. The surface uneven, rough and dull.
The décor is in black with a blue tone and a reddish brown colour with a thin transparent coating serving as a slip. This coating covers an irregular band on the upper part of the exterior and on the whole of the interior. For the rest, only the inside is decorated.

PLATE. XXX

PLATE XXX.

Painted vessels of the Ma Chang style, bought in Kansu.
(¹/₄ of natural size.)

Fig.	No.	Pre-served in	Provenience	Height cm.	Diam. of Body cm.	Diam. of Mouth cm.	Diam. of Bottom cm.	Thickness of the ware at the neck. cm	Form type	Décor Fam.	Style
1	K. 5339	S	Tao Sha Hsien, Ka Tu Ma Kou	10.5	13.0	9.5	5.5	0.3	M. C. XIV	Indiv. déc. M.	—
2	K. 5355	P	Lanchow	11.0	13.7	9.3	6.0	0.3	M. C. XIV	Indiv. déc. M.	—
3	K. 5313	S	„	18.4	18.3	10.0	7.0	0.4	M. C. XIX	Indiv. déc. M.	Middle
4	K. 5346	S	Ti Tao Hsien, Su Chia Yang	8.8	9.8	8.3	5.5	0.3	M. C. XIV	Indiv. déc. M.	—
5	K. 5737	P	Lanchow	11.2	13.5	12.3	5.5	0.4	M. C. XIV	Indiv. déc. M.	—
6	K. 5490	S	„	14.4	19.0	11.6	7.7	0.4	M. C. XIV	Indiv. déc. M.	Late
7	K. 5317	S	„	20.5	22.7	14.0	9.0	0.5	M. C. XIV	Indiv. déc. M.	„
8	K. 5321	S	„	16.6	16.6	11.3	6.0	0.5	M. C. XIV	Indiv. déc. M.	„
9	K. 5949	S	Chin Hsien, Feng Huo Cha, Chien Yang Tsui	14.0	16.0	11.0	6.5	0.5	M. C. V	Indiv. déc. M.	—
10	K. 5244	S	Lanchow	10.8	13.0	9.8	5.5	0.4	M. C. XIV	Indiv. déc. M.	Late
11	K. 5370	S	„	13.5	17.5	18.7	8.3	—	M. C. XVIII	Indiv. déc. M.	—

Fig. 1. Vessel with two large handles.
The ware is grey to brown. The surface smooth but somewhat dull. Concentric striations on the neck.
The décor is in two colours, black and dark reddish violet.

Fig. 2. Vessel with two large handles and a rather high neck.
The ware is greyish brown, with darker grey patches. The surface is smooth and polished. Concentric striations at the top of the neck.
The décor is in two colours, both shiny, black and brownish red.

Fig. 3. Vessel with a high neck and two handles on the neck.
The ware is somewhat rough, brown, in some parts paler, in others reddish. The surface is smooth and dull. Concentric striations on the top of the neck.
The décor is in two dull colours, black and dark violet. The lower arms of the swastika-like patterns have in one case a true hand with distinct fingers. The hand in this case has a menacing aspect. In other cases the arms of the swastika have "fingers". This pattern is to a certain extent related to the anthropomorphic pattern that frequently occurs in this style.

Fig. 4. Vessel with two large handles a rather high neck.
The ware is reddish brown, a fairly light colour. The surface smooth and somewhat dull.
The décor is in two dull colours, black and dark red.

Fig. 5. Vessel with two large handles and rather high neck.
The ware is brown. The surface fairly smooth and dull. Concentric striations on the neck.
The décor is in black and dark red.

Fig. 6. Vessel with two handles and a low neck.
The ware is brownish red. The surface smooth and slightly polished. Concentric striations on the neck.
The décor is in a somewhat shiny black colour.

Fig. 7. Vessel with two handles and a low neck.
The ware is reddish brown with warmer-coloured spots. The surface is smooth and slightly polished.
The décor is in a dark brownish violet colour, which is dull and often changes to a dewy blue tone. A thin, spotty and streaky transparent coating, probably made of the same paint, forms a kind of slip on the decorated surfaces. In the middle of the base, beneath one of the handles, is a mark consisting of a somewhat slanting horizontal band and, projecting vertically downwards from the middle

PALÆONTOLOGIA SINICA. SER. D. VOL. III. FASC. 1.

PALMGREN: Kansu mortuary urns. Pl. XXX.

A. BÖRTZELLS TRYCKERI A. B. STHLM

of this band is a line, pointed at the lower end. The décor on this pot is very peculiar and extremely important, for here we find the earliest known quite definite meander décor from the Far East. This meander décor is highly original and, moreover, is in complete harmony with the rest of the highly geometrized and complicated décor dating from this epoch. It is probable therefore that the décor on this pot is a new creation in the Far East and was not borrowed from Western prototypes. The meander furthest to the left starts vertically downwards from the upper belt, coiling in an anti-clockwise direction. The middle meander starts from the former one at the right-hand top corner and coils to the right, while the third meander, furthest to the right, starts from the bottom right-hand corner of the middle meander and coils to the left.

Fig. 8. Vessel with two handles and a low neck.

The ware is greyish brown. The surface smooth but not polished. Concentric striations at the top of the neck.

The décor is in two fairly dull colours, black and dark violet red.

Fig. 9. Vessel with a large handle and a low neck.

The ware is greyish brown. The surface very uneven, slightly polished.

The décor is in black and dark violet.

Fig. 10. Vessel with two handles and a low neck.

The ware is brown with greyer and warmer-coloured spots. Concentric striations on the outside of the neck at the top. The surface is fairly smooth. The method of building up the vessel in rings is fairly distinctly visible on the inside.

The décor is in black on a dark reddish brown slip.

Fig 11. Vessel with two large handles.

The surface is smooth and unpolished. The ware is greyish brown.

For the décor see Plate XLI:5.

The inner surface of the bowl is decorated with four horizontal, s-shaped spiral lines.

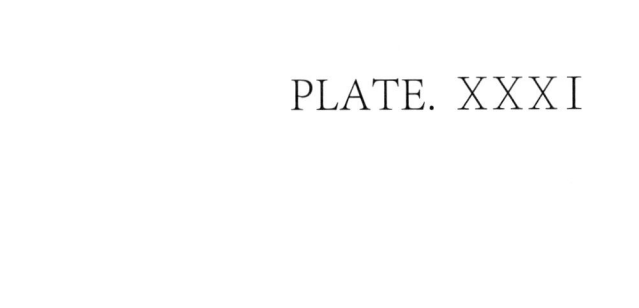

PLATE. XXXI

PLATE XXXI.

Details of vessels of the Pan Shan style, Yang Shao period, bought or excavated in Kansu.
(Fig. 1 = ²/₃, figs. 2, 5 = about ½, figs. 3, 4, 7 = about ⅙, fig. 6 = ²/₅ of natural size.)

Fig.	No.	Pre-served in	Provenience	Height cm.	Diam. of Body cm.	Diam. of Mouth cm.	Diam. of Bottom cm.	Thickness of the ware at the neck. cm.	Form type	Décor Fam.	Style
1	K. 5496	S	Ning Ting Hsien, Wa Kuan Tsui	17.0	12.2	4.5	6.0	0.6	P. S. XVIII	1 P.	Early
2	K. 5021	S	” ” ” ” ” ”	45.8	40.4	13.3	16.0	0.8	P. S. XXIV	1 P.	”
3	K. 5025	S	” ” ” Pan Shan	23.0	29.0	23.0	11.2	0.8	P. S. IV	1 P.	”
4, 7	K. 5797	S	” ” ” Pien Chia Kou, Pot. 7	37.3	49.0	13.0	16.0	0.6	P. S. XXIV	11 P.	—
5—6	K. 5962	S	Kao Lan Hsien, 50 li S. E. Kao Ying	39.0	38.0	11.0	—	0.6	—	—	—

Fig. 1. Neck of a Pan Shan vessel built up of 3 bands. (Cf. Plate I: 4.)

Fig. 2. Neck of a Pan Shan vessel built up of 6—7 bands. (Cf. Plate II: 4.)

Fig. 3. The method of construction with bands can be observed on the inside. (Cf. Plate I: 9.)

Figs. 4, 7. Bottom and upper part (inside) showing the marks left by the potter's fingers while »throwing» the vessel.

Fig. 5. Detail (inside) showing the marks left by the potter's fingers and the method of construction with bands.

Fig. 6. Inside of a vessel round the mouth, showing how the bands were joined.

Pl. XXXI.

PLATE. XXXII

PLATE XXXII.

Details of vessels of the Pan Shan style, Yang Shao period, bought in Kansu.
(Fig. 1 = ¹/₈, figs. 2—4, 8 = ¹/₆, figs. 5, 7 = ²/₃, fig. 6 = ²/₉, fig. 9 = ⁴/₉ of natural size.)

Fig.	No.	Preserved in	Provenience	Height cm.	Diam. of Body cm.	Diam. of Mouth cm.	Diam. of Bottom cm.	Thickness of the ware cm.	Form type	Decor Fam.	Style
1	K. 5041	S	Ning Ting Hsien, Wa Kuan Tsui	33.0	30.0	8.3	13.5	0.7	P. S. XXIV	10 P.	Early or middle
2	K. 5053	S	" " " Pan Shan	37.0	38.2	13.8	14.5	0.6	P. S. XXIV	8 P.	Middle
3	K. 5213	S	Lanchow	13.5	26.5	7.5	11.0	0.5	P. S. XXVII	15 P.	—
4	K. 5781	S	"	36.8	37.0	12.5	12.5	0.7	P. S. XXIV	16 P.	Late
5	K. 5472	S	Ning Ting Hsien, Pan Shan area	14.8	—	—	—	0.5	P. S. XL	Indiv. déc. P.	Middle
6	K. 5492	S	" " " Pan Shan	13.4	12.6	5.0	6.5	0.5	P. S. XVIII	1 P.	Early
7	K. 5165	S	" " " P'ai Tzu P'ing	32.4	35.3	8.5	15.6	0.7	—	—	—
8	K. 5155	S	" " " Pan Shan	42.5	43.6	17.5	14.0	0.8	P. S. XXIV	11 P.	Early or middle
9	K. 5078	S	Lanchow	23.0	26.0	8.5	9.0	0.5	P. S. XXIV	10 P.	Late

Fig. 1. The method of constructing a vessel with bands is visible on the surface.

Fig. 2. The method of constructing a vessel with bands is visible on the base (Cf. Plate V: 7, 8).

Fig. 3. The method of constructing the bottom is visible.

Fig. 4. The method of constructing the bottom and a brand-mark on the unpainted base are visible (Cf. Plate XXXVIII: 3).

Fig. 5. The head in Plate XIX: 7 seen from above, showing how the horns were fixed on to the surface of the head.

Fig. 6. Shows how a handle was attached (Cf. Plate I: 8).

Fig. 7. Detail showing the two scores made in the surface for the purpose of attaching a handle.

Fig. 8. There are brand-marks in four places on the pot, two on the mantle and two on the base. The two former are accompanied by slight dents in the convex surface of the mantle, also by variations in the colour of the ware and in that of the fired paints. On the deeper indentation to the right the marks or impressions of black bands are clearly visible. The two patches on the basal surface lie, the one just below the border and the other just above the bottom, a quarter turn from one another and almost immediately below the two brand-marks on the mantle. The marks, which have manifestly arisen in the course of the firing, were made by four vessels leaning against this large pot. This is clearly indicated by the combination of brand-marks on the ware, changes in the tone of the fired paints, impressions of coloured bands from other vessels, and, finally, indentations in the surface of the vessels. (Cf. Plates X: 4 and XXXVII: 1.)

Fig. 9. A circular piece is missing from the bottom of the vessel on Plate IX: 6. Round one side of it is a ring of six drilled holes, which have clearly served as a means of keeping in place the piece that had been knocked out. These holes pierced in neck and bottom clearly show that the vessel had been broken and had consequently been in use before being deposited in the grave. This indicates that only solids could have been preserved in the vessel, as it is hardly likely that a vessel with a bottom repaired in this way could have held anything liquid. On the other hand, it is now of course impossible to determine whether the vessel was in daily use at the dwelling-site or had been broken and repaired only in the course of the burial ceremonies that no doubt took place in the village prior to the departure of the lengthy funeral procession. The latter theory seems, however, to be the more likely. It is manifest that the pot was mended before it left the village, as in this case the method of repairing the vessel seems to have been somewhat complicated.

PALÆONTOLOGIA SINICA. SER. D. VOL. III. FASC. 1.

PALMGREN: Kansu mortuary urns.

Pl. XXXII.

A. BÖRTZELLS TRYCKERI A. B. STHLM.

PLATE. XXXIII

PLATE XXXIII.

Details of vessels of the Pan Shan and Ma Chang styles, bought in Kansu.
(Fig. 1 = about ¹/₂, fig. 2 = about ⁵/₇, fig. 3 = ²/₈, fig. 4 = ¹/₈, fig. 5 = ⁸/₅, fig. 6 = ⁷/₁₂, fig. 7 = ¹/₁ of natural size.)

Fig.	No.	Preserved in	Provenience	Height cm.	Diam. of Body cm.	Diam. of Mouth cm.	Diam. of Bottom cm.	Thickness of the ware at the neck. cm.	Form type	Décor Fam.	Style
1	K. 5457	P	Ning Ting Hsien. Wa Kuan Tsui	9.3	11.0	6.7	6.7	0.5	P. S:r IV	Relief 3 P.	—
2	K. 5442	S	" " " Pien Chia Kou	17.6	26.0	22.5	11.0	0.7	P. S:r VI	Relief 2 P.	—
3	K. 5460	S	Yü Chung Hsien	7.0	9.8	6.0	.5.0	0.6	P. S:r I	Relief 3 P.	—
4	K. 5229	P	Lanchow	12.2	15.2	9.0	6.3	0.3	M. C. XIV	9 M.	Late
5	K. 5375	P	"	10.2	10.6	9.5	5.5	0.5	M. C. XIV	13 M.	"
6	K. 5330	P	"	17.8	18.5	10.7	8.0	0.4	M. C. XIV	15 M.	Early
7	K. 5452	S	Ning Ting Hsien, Pien Chia Kou	12.0	12.0	8.0	5.5	0.5	—	—	—

Fig. 1. Cast from the bottom of the Pan Shan vessel in Plate XXI: 8 showing impressions of a bast-mat.

Fig. 2. The bottom of the Pan Shan vessel in Plate XXXVIII: 6 showing impressions of a bast-mat.

Fig. 3. The surface of the Pan Shan vessel in Plate XXI: 1.

Fig. 4. The surface of the Ma Chang vessel in Plate XXVIII: 4 showing flakes falling away.

Fig. 5. The inside of the Ma Chang vessel in Plate XXIX: 2 showing how it is built up of bands.

Fig. 6. The base of the Ma Chang vessel in Plate XXV: 6 showing how it is built up of bands.

Fig. 7. The bottom of a Ma Chang vessel showing impressions of a bast-mat.

PALÆONTOLOGIA SINICA. SER. D. VOL. III. FASC. 1.

PALMGREN: Kansu mortuary urns.

Pl. XXXIII.

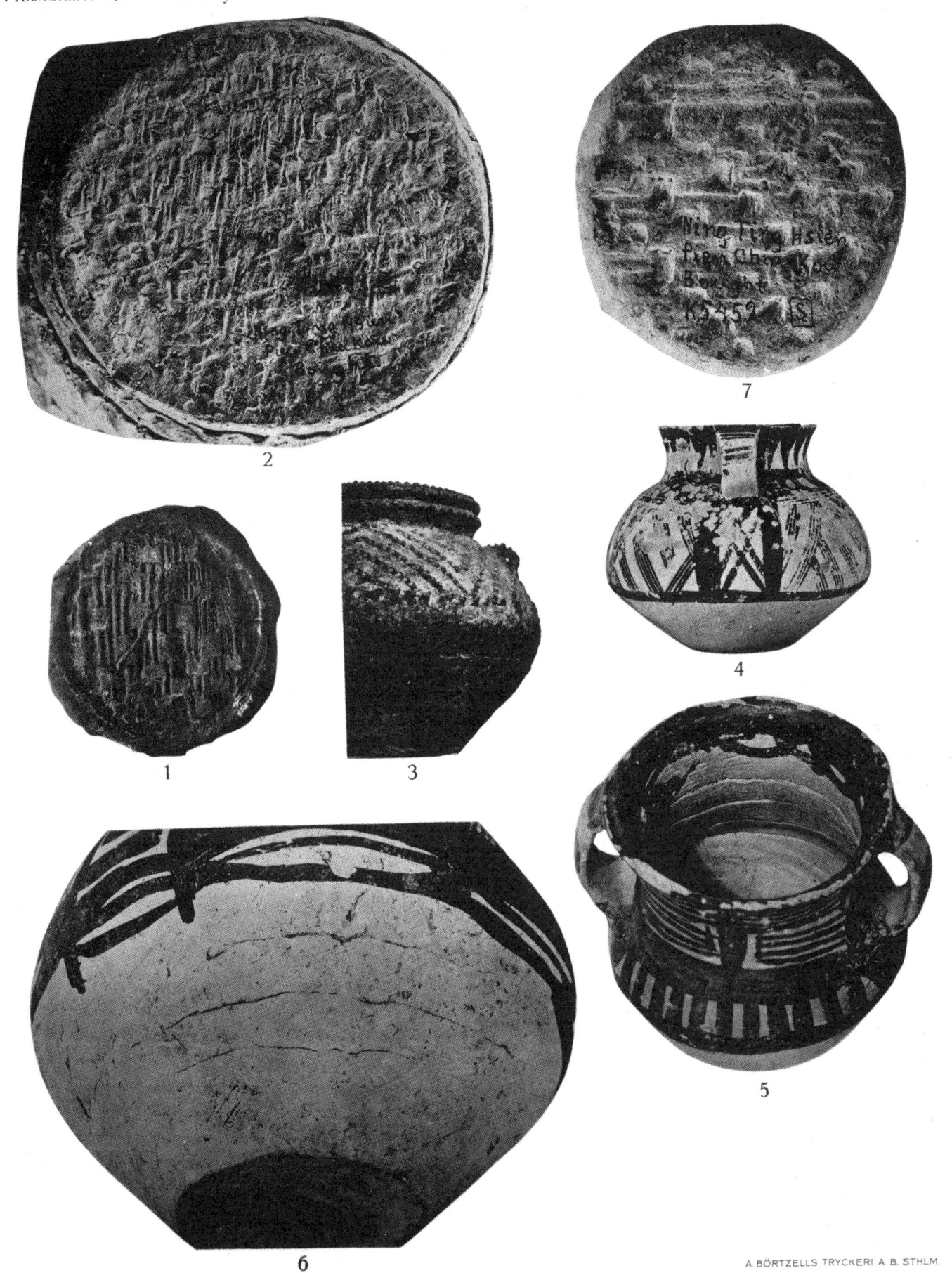

PLATE. XXXIV

PLATE XXXIV.

Painted vessels of the Pan Shan style, Yang Shao period, bought in Kansu.
($2/11$ of natural size.)

Fig.	No.	Pre-served in	Provenience	Height cm.	Diam. of Body cm.	Diam. of Mouth cm.	Diam. of Bottom cm.	Thickness of the ware at the neck. cm	Form type	Décor Fam.	Style
1	K. 5003	S	Ning Ting Hsien, Pien Chia Kou	23.5	20.2	8.0	8.8	0.4	P. S. XVIII	1 P.	Early
2	K. 5001	S	,, ,, ,, Pan Shan	30.4	35.9	15.8	12.4	—	P. S. XXIII	1 P.	,,
3	K. 5024	S	Lanchow	20.2	25.3	8.6	8.5	—	P. S. XXIII	1 P.	Middle or late
4	K. 5006	S	Ning Ting Hsien, Wa Kuan Tsui	35.3	37.0	15.5	14.2	0.7	P. S. XXIII	3 P.	Early or middle
5	K. 5752	S	,, ,, ,, ,, ,, ,,	30.5	35.7	18.5	11.5	—	P. S. XXIII	4 P.	Early
6	K. 5116	S	Yü Chung Hsien	23.0	21.3	8.0	8.0	0.5	P. S. XXVII	1 P. — 11 P.	,,
7	K. 5214	S	Ning Ting Hsien, Wa Kuan Tsui	26.6	20.0	7.5	7.5	0.5	P. S. XVIII	11 P.	,,

Fig. 1. Jug with a high neck and one handle.

Fig. 2. Vessel with a low neck and two handles.

Fig. 3. Vessel with a rather low neck and two handles.
The ware is extremely fine and hard in texture. The surface is smooth and polished. There are concentric striations on the neck, particularly on the outside.

Fig. 4. Vessel with a low neck and two handles.
The surface is polished and the ware moderately porous. No concentric striations are discernible.

Fig. 5. Vessel with a low neck and two handles.
The surface of the mantle is smooth and polished.

Fig. 6. Vessel with a high neck and two handles. On the neck are two ears notched and with a hole pierced in the lower part. One of the handles was apparently broken off and filed down before the vessel was placed in the grave. The upper portion of the handle is still attached to the vessel, but it is obvious that already in ancient times a large hole was pierced in it, apparently for the purpose of fastening a sinew or cord to it, the loop thus formed having had to serve as the handle. The observations made on Plate XXXII: 9 apply equally to this vessel. The surface is smooth and polished.

Fig. 7. Jug with a high neck and a large handle.
The surface is smooth but not very highly polished. The rings of which it is constructed are visible on the inside of the neck.
The décor on the exterior of the neck represents a decorative system that is more primitive than the spiral system forming the mantle design; in other words, the spiral pattern on the body has supplanted a pattern that is retained on the neck as a survival.

PALÆONTOLOGIA SINICA. SER. D. VOL. III. FASC. 1.

PALMGREN: Kansu mortuary urns.   Pl. XXXIV.

PLATE. XXXV

PLATE XXXV.

Painted vessels of the Pan Shan style, Yang Shao period, bought in Kansu.
($^1/_6$ of natural size.)

Fig.	No.	Preserved in	Provenience	Height cm.	Diam. of Body cm.	Diam. of Mouth cm.	Diam. of Bottom cm.	Thickness of the ware at the neck. cm.	Form type	Décor Fam.	Style
1	K. 5040	S	Ning Ting Hsien, Pan Shan	31.2	37.2	17.8	13.0	—	P. S. XXIII	6 P.	Early
2	K. 5017	S	„ „ „ Wa Kuan Tsui	30.0	36.6	17.0	12.3	0.7	P. S. XXIII	9 P.	„
3	K. 5082	S	„ „ „ „ „	40.6	37.0	9.2	14.0	0.5	P. S. XXIV	18 P.	Early or middle
4	K. 5027	S	Lanchow	30.5	33.5	16.0	11.0	0.7	P. S. XXIII	12 P.	Early

Fig. 1. Vessel with a low neck and two handles.
The surface of the mantle is smooth and polished. The collar is striated.
Below, on the unpainted base, is a brand-mark consisting of an impression from another vessel.

Fig. 2. Vessel with a low neck and two handles.
The surface of the mantle is even and slightly polished. There are concentric striations on both sides of the neck.

Fig. 3. Vessel with a high neck having two notched ears pierced with extremely fine holes. Two handles.
The surface is smooth and polished. On the outside of the neck, at the top, is a slight concentric striation. On the inside of the neck one can distinctly see the eight or nine bands of which it is constructed. At the bottom of the basal surface is a brand-mark with two very distinct bands of black points.

Fig. 4. Vessel with a low neck and two handles.
The ware is hard. The surface smooth; it has been varnished in recent times.

PALÆONTOLOGIA SINICA. SER. D. VOL. III. FASC. 1.

Palmgren: Kansu mortuary urns.

Pl. XXXV.

1

2

3

4

PLATE. XXXVI

PLATE XXXVI.

Painted vessels of the Pan Shan style, Yang Shao period, bought in Kansu.
(¹/₆ of natural size.)

Fig.	No.	Preserved in	Provenience	Height cm.	Diam. of Body cm.	Diam. of Mouth cm.	Diam. of Bottom cm.	Thickness of the ware at the neck. cm.	Form type	Décor Fam.	Style
1	K. 5031	S	Ning Ting Hsien, Pan Shan	41.3	39.4	11.6	15.4	0.5	P. S. XXIV	10 P.	Early
2	K. 5085	S	Lanchow	38.8	39.0	12.0	14.5	0.6	P. S. XXIV	10 P.	Middle
3	K. 5030	S	Ning Ting Hsien, Pan Shan	29.0	34.0	16.7	13.5	0.7	P. S. XXIII	10 P.	”
4	K. 5831	P	” ” ” ” ”	33.7	40.2	19.5	15.5	—	P. S. XXIII	10 P.	”

Fig. 1. Vessel with two handles and a high neck with two ears having clumsily notched edges and holes in the middle.

The surface is smooth and slightly polished. The rings, or rather ring-shaped bands, of which the neck is constructed are very clearly discernible on the inside. The neck is built up of six bands, one above the other, and over these bands is smeared an outer coating of clay, which in places, however, has not been applied in sufficient quantity. One can easily see on this layer of clay a concentric striation, which is not found on the bands themselves.

Fig. 2. Vessel with two handles and a high neck, which has had two small ears having neither notched edges nor holes. One of them is broken off.

The surface is smooth and slightly polished. There are concentric striations at the top of the neck.

Fig. 3. Vessel described in Plate VII: 6.

Fig. 4. Vessel with two handles and a low neck.

The surface is smooth and polished. On the unpainted base is a dark brand-mark consisting of two angular bands (from another pot) pointing obliquely upwards and having arc-shaped contours.

PALÆONTOLOGIA SINICA. SER. D. VOL. III. FASC. 1.

PALMGREN: Kansu mortuary urns.   Pl. XXXVI.

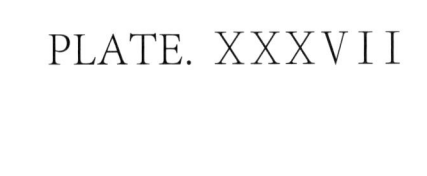

PLATE. XXXVII

PLATE XXXVII.

Painted vessels of the Pan Shan style, Yang Shao period, bought in Kansu.
(¹/₆ of natural size.)

Fig.	No.	Preserved in	Provenience	Height cm.	Diam. of Body cm.	Diam. of Mouth cm.	Diam. of Bottom cm.	Thickness of the ware at the neck. cm.	Form type	Décor Fam.	Style
1	K. 5155	S	Ning Ting Hsien, Pan Shan	42.5	43.0	17.5	14.0	0.8	P. S. XXIV	11 P.	Early or middle
2	K. 5464	S	,, ,, ,, Wa Kuan Tsui	34.1	40.0	17.0	13.5	0.6	P. S. XXIII	11 P.	Middle
3	K. 5169	S	,, ,, ,, Wang Chia Kou	37.0	38.0	13.0	13.0	0.7	P. S. XXIV	11 P.	Late
4	K. 5465	S	,, ,, ,, ,, ,, ,,	39.4	36.8	12.8	13.5	0.6	P. S. XXIV	11 P.	,,

Fig. 1. Vessel described in Plates X : 4 and XXXII : 8.

Fig. 2. Vessel with a low neck and two handles.
The surface is smooth.
On the base there is a large black mark, obviously made with a brush. It slightly resembles a a running animal with short legs, short tail and open mouth. The contours however are very indistinct, and it is impossible to say whether this shape was given deliberately or was purely accidental.

Fig. 3. Vessel with a neck of medium height, and two handles. The neck is of an advanced form and has two rudimentary ears.
The surface is smooth and polished. There are concentric striations on the exterior of the neck. Inside, near the top, about 1.5 cm. below the rim, is a fairly deep horizontal furrow. From this there extends at one place a clear-cut vertical furrow.
On the base, two brand-marks occur on opposite sides between the handles, the one in the middle of the basal surface and the other further down just above the bottom. On one of them are discernible impressions of a black dentated area and close to it a red band shaped like an arc, possibly belonging to a décor of the same kind as that on the pot's own mantle. The other mark is of a more uniform black colour. Around both of the marks the ware is of a fairly bright red, flamey colour surrounding a greyer centre.

Fig. 4. Vessel with an undoubtedly advanced form of neck such as is not found in any other of the Pan Shan vessels at my disposal. It would appear, then, that this form of neck is a new acquisition. At the rim of the neck two rudimentary ears, with smooth edges and without holes. Two handles.
On the surface of the mantle, just below two adjacent spiral nuclei, are two fairly large, grey brand-marks. At these places both the black and the violet colours lose much of their strength and in some spots are almost entirely obliterated. No impression of any other pattern is however discernible on these patches. It is rather to be presumed that the paint that once covered these spots must have adhered to those surfaces of other vessels which came into contact with these spots in the kiln.
The décor is advanced.

PALÆONTOLOGIA SINICA. SER. D. VOL. III. FASC. 1.

PALMGREN: Kansu mortuary urns.

Pl. XXXVII.

1

2

3

4

PLATE. XXXVIII

PLATE XXXVIII.

Painted vessels of the Pan Shan style, Yang Shao period, bought in Kansu.
(¹/₅ of natural size.)

Fig.	No.	Preserved in	Provenience	Height cm.	Diam. of Body cm.	Diam. of Mouth cm.	Diam. of Bottom cm.	Thickness of the ware at the neck. cm.	Form type	Décor Fam.	Style
1	K. 5060	S	Ning Ting Hsien, Wang Chia Kou	39.7	38.8	13.0	13.8	0.6	P. S. XXIV	14 P.	Late
2	K. 5282	S	Lanchow	34.0	34.5	10.2	10.6	0.5	P. S. XXIV	19 P.	”
3	K. 5781	S	”	36.8	37.0	12.5	12.5	0.7	P. S. XXIV	16 P.	”
4	K. 5046	S	Ning Ting Hsien, Pan Shan	16.0	18.8	12.5	7.0	—	P. S. XXXIII	17 P.	”
5	K. 5074	S	Lanchow	16.8	15.0	7.3	6.5	0.4	P. S. XIX	15 P.	”
6	K. 5442	S	Ning Ting Hsien, Pien Chia Kou	17.6	26.0	22.5	11.0	0.7	S. S:r : VI	Relief 2 P.	—

Fig. 1. Vessel with two handles and a high neck having two rudimentary ears without holes. The one is in the shape of a true ear, the other is compressed and forms merely a flattened disc on the surface of the neck.

The surface is smooth and unpolished. There is a concentric striation on the top of the neck.

Fig. 2. Vessel with a shape closely related to that of the Ma Chang urns. No ears. Two handles. The surface is smooth and polished. On the upper part of the neck is a sharply defined concentric striation.

On the surface of the mantle and on almost diametrically opposite sides, in the neighbourhood of the handles, are two brand-marks, both on the lower half of the central belt. Moreover, it can be observed in both cases that they occur in slightly deepened places on the mantle surface. On the interior of the neck, at the top, is a delicate garland décor of an advanced type. There are a large number of festoons, each consisting of a plain, black, narrow arc.

Fig. 3. Vessel with two handles and a neck of medium height. Just below the rim of the neck are two very small rudimentary ears, without notches and without holes.

There are marked concentric striations on the top of the neck. The surface is smooth and polished.

On the surface of the mantle and on two adjacent bottle-shaped ornaments are two discoloured brand-marks on places that are slightly buckled. Further, there are two coloured brand-marks on the basal surface. (Cf. Plate XXXII : 4.) These lie on either side of the larger and higher brand-marks on the mantle. In this case it is evident that the pot in question lost its colour at the places where the upper brand-marks occur, the paint adhering to the vessels standing next to it in the kiln, while on its base it simply took the colour impressions from adjacent parts of vessels placed in the kiln with it.

Fig. 4. Vessel described in Plate XVII : 9.

Fig. 5. Jug with a high neck and a large handle.
The surface even and polished.

Fig. 6. Vessel with a spout.

The grey tones of the ware predominate on the outside, the red and brown tones on the inside. The surface is rough and contains furrows running obliquely from the bottom upwards, some of them distinctly marked, others more worn down. These furrows have arisen as a result of the vessel's being turned in an anti-clockwise direction. The interior of the vessel is decorated with five series of incised vertical furrows, there being four to six furrows in each series. On the outer bottom surface of the vessel there are clear impressions of a bast-mat.

PALÆONTOLOGIA SINICA. SER. D. VOL. III. FASC. 1.

PALMGREN: Kansu mortuary urns.   Pl. XXXVIII.

PLATE. XXXIX

PLATE XXXIX.

Painted vessels of the Ma Chang style, bought or excavated in Kansu.
(¹/₆ of natural size.)

Fig.	No.	Preserved in	Provenience	Height cm.	Diam. of Body cm.	Diam. of Mouth cm.	Diam. of Bottom cm.	Thickness of the ware at the neck, cm.	Form type	Décor Fam.	Style
1	K. 5286	S	Lanchow	34.3	34.5	11.2	11.5	0.6	M. C. IX	1 M. Subfam. I	Early
2	K. 5617	S	Nien Po Hsien, Ma Chang Yen, Loc. 4, Sk. 1	34.5	29.2	11.5	9.2	0.5	M. C. IX	1 M. Subfam. IV	Middle
3	K. 5991	P	Nien Po Hsien, Ma Chang Yen	35.5	34.0	13.8	13.0	—	M. C. VIII	1 M. Subfam. IV	Late
4	K. 5828	S	Lanchow	41.5	39.0	15.7	11.0	—	M. C. VIII	1 M. Subfam. IV	”
5	K. 5291	S	”	34.5	32.5	13.0	11.0	—	M. C. IX	Indiv. déc. M.	Middle or late
6	K. 5312	S	”	21.0	21.2	8.0	9.0	—	M. C. IX	2 M.	Middle

Fig. 1. Vessel with a neck of medium height and two handles.
The surface is smooth and dull. Concentric striations on the brim of the neck.
The décor is in many respects closely related to the advanced Pan Shan style.

Fig. 2. Vessel with a high neck and two handles.
The surface unpolished.

Fig. 3. Vessel with a fairly low neck and two handles.
The surface is not very smooth and is unpolished; in many places it is much scratched in a vertical direction.

Fig. 4. Vessel with a low neck and two handles.
The surface is smooth.
The mantle is covered, in part at least, with a thin white slip.

Fig. 5. Vessel with a high neck and two handles.
The surface is pitted and corrugated, particularly in a vertical direction on the mantle and in a horizontal direction on the base.

Fig. 6. Vessel with a high neck and two handles.
The surface is smooth, the collar of the neck striated at the top.
There are two figures, roughly resembling human beings, separated on either side by a circle containing concentric elements. Each of the circles consists of a band of two circular elements, the outer one black and the inner one red. Inside the circles, again, are concentric elements, two black rings, or else a single one, and a large round spot in the centre. The interior of the neck is ornamented with a row of small black dentations running round the rim, and below them a red horizontal band, suspended from which is a décor of garlands, each festoon consisting of two black lines.

PALÆONTOLOGIA SINICA. SER. D. VOL. III. FASC. 1.

PALMGREN: Kansu mortuary urns.

Pl. XXXIX.

1

2

3

4

5

6

PLATE. XL

PLATE XL.

Painted vessels of the Ma Chang style, bought in Kansu.
(¹/₃ of natural size.)

Fig.	No.	Preserved in	Provenience	Height cm.	Diam. of Body cm.	Diam. of Mouth cm.	Diam. of Bottom cm.	Thickness of the ware at the neck. cm.	Form type	Décor Fam.	Style
1	K. 5331	S	Yü Chung Hsien	12.7	15.7	10.5	5.0	0.4	M. C. XIV	6 M.	Early
2	K. 5315	S	Lanchow	11.2	15.2	6.6	6.5	0.3	M. C. XIV	6 M. Subfam. II	Middle
3	K. 5292	S	„	30.6	23.0	11.0	9.8	0.7	M. C. IX	4 M.	Late
4	K. 5139	S	Yü Chung Hsien	10.2	12.4	8.5	6.0	0.5	M. C. XIV	3 M.	Middle
5	K. 5327	S	Lanchow	13.7	17.0	10.3	7.5	0.5	M. C. XIV	10 M.	„
6	K. 5314	S	„	17.4	20.2	9.3	8.5	0.6	M. C. XIV	7 M.	Late

Fig. 1. Vessel with a low neck and two handles.
The ware is hard. The surface smooth and polished. There are concentric striations on the neck.
On the interior of the neck is a violet horizontal band, from which is suspended a garland-décor made up of four festoons, each of which has two arcs.
Both the ware and the colour are Pan Shan in character. The dentated edge on the upper border and the triads placed beneath the handles are likewise indicative of the Pan Shan style. The décor on the mantle belongs to both typical Pan Shan and Ma Chang pots. The décor on both the exterior and the interior of the neck is more reminiscent of the Ma Chang style.

Fig. 2. Vessel with a low neck and two handles.
The surface is smooth and slightly polished.

Fig. 3. Vessel with a high neck and two handles.
The surface is smooth and dull.

Fig. 4. Vessel with a low neck and two handles.
The surface is somewhat rough.

Fig. 5. Vessel with a low neck and two handles (one of them, however, is broken off).
The surface is not very smooth and dull.

Fig. 6. Vessel described in Plate XXVII:11.

PALÆONTOLOGIA SINICA. SER. D. VOL. III. FASC. 1.

PALMGREN: Kansu mortuary urns.

Pl. XL

PLATE. XLI

PLATE XLI.

Painted vessels of the Pan Shan style, Yang Shao period, bought in Kansu.
(⅓ of natural size.)

Fig.	No.	Preserved in	Provenience	Height cm.	Diam. of Body cm.	Mouth cm.	Bottom cm.	Thickness of the ware at the neck. cm.	Form type	Décor Fam.	Style
1	K. 5320	S	Lanchow	17.0	20.3	9.0	8.5	0.5	M. C. III	Indiv. déc. M.	Middle
2	K. 5296	S	„	19.0	21.5	19.0	7.8	—	M. C. XIV	8 M.	„
3	K. 5241	S	„	9.5	9.7	8.5	5.5	0.5	M. C. XIV	11 M.	Late
4	K. 5336	S	„	11.8	13.8	10.0	7.0	0.4	M. C. XIV	14 M.	„
5	K. 5370	S	„	13.5	17.5	18.7	8.3	—	M. C. XVIII	Indiv. déc. M.	—
6	K. 5486	S	„	14.8	18.7	17.5	11.5	—	M. C. XVII	Indiv. déc. M.	Late

Fig. 1. Vessel with two handles but without a neck. A couple of centimetres below the mouth are four pairs of holes set in a circle round it — probably for the purpose of suspending the vessel. The surface is smooth and dull.

Fig. 2. Vessel with a high neck and two handles.
The surface is smooth.

Fig. 3. Vessel with originally two handles (one is now broken off).
The surface is pitted and slightly polished. The broad rings of which the vessel is constructed can be clearly seen on the inside.

Fig. 4. Vessel with a very high neck and two large handles.
The ware is somewhat coarse. The surface is smooth and dull. There are concentric striations on the outside of the brim.

Fig. 5. Vessel described in Plate XXX: 11.

Fig. 6. Vessel on a foot. Two handles.
The surface is uneven and dull, covered with a greyish brown slip.
The ware is brick-red.
The interior of the bowl is decorated at the top with a broad black horizontal band, and below that an equally broad violet band. Beneath that again is a broad black belt containing a row of circular areas in ground-colour, and under it a broad violet band. Finally, there was an interior décor in black, but the details of the pattern are now no longer distinguishable.

PALÆONTOLOGIA SINICA. SER. D. VOL. III. FASC. 1.

PALMGREN: Kansu mortuary urns. Pl. XLI.

半山及馬廠隨葬陶器

巴爾姆格倫

甘肅省內所得之石銅器時代過渡期之陶器，安特生先生已於其所著甘肅考古記（地質專報甲種第五號）略有記述，此著特就前所未記者，更爲加詳研究。先述關於寧定縣洮河谷旁半山區所得之陶器，次述碾伯（今稱樂都）縣馬廠沿之陶器，並各詳研其形式花紋及製造方法。從陶器之形式及其耳環之位置，可將半山陶器分爲數類，更以此與馬廠陶器互相比較，即可見後者大部脫胎於前者而更加以逐漸演化。因此可知馬廠時期略晚於半山。由馬廠期而至辛店期則其遞嬗關係稍欠明晰，其間或尙有若干時期之缺失。從陶器之花紋上研究，亦可見由半山而馬廠逐漸演化。半山陶器上幾何圖案尙不發達，馬廠陶器上則已漸顯著，卍字形之漸次發展尤可注意。馬廠陶器上又有貝幣形之花紋。由馬廠而辛店陶器花紋亦略有遞嬗之蹟，但其中間亦非盡無意之作，或係一器實有許多新花樣也。陶器之底面有時顯刻畫之形跡，大致頗爲粗簡，然非盡無意之作，或係一種簡單文字之草創試驗。此文注重於半山及馬廠陶器本身之研究及比較，但對於此項陶器之形狀及其花紋，對於東方或西方文化之關係則未經論及。

中國古生物誌丁種第三號

第一册

巴爾姆格倫著

半山及馬廠隨葬陶器

中華民國二十三年二月

實業部地質調查所
國立北平研究院地質學研究所印行
(學術研究與國立中央研究院國立北京大學兩廣地質調查所湖南地質調查所合作)

Stockholm 1934.
A.-B. Hasse W. Tullbergs Boktryckeri.